MONROE COLLEGE LIBRARY

3 7340 01052433 5

Conversations with Ralph Ellison

Literary Conversations Series

Peggy Whitman Prenshaw
General Editor

D1113971

MONROE COLLEGE LIBRARY
2468 JEROME AVENUE
BRONX, NY 10468

© Nancy Crampton

MONROE COLLEGE LIBRARY
2468 JEROME AVENUE
BRONX, NY 10468

Conversations with Ralph Ellison

Edited by
Maryemma Graham and Amritjit Singh

University Press of Mississippi
Jackson

PS
3555
.L625
Z464
1995

Books by Ralph Ellison

Invisible Man. New York: Random House, 1952.
Shadow and Act. New York: Random House, 1964.
Going to the Territory. New York: Random House, 1986.

Introduction copyright © 1995 by Amritjit Singh and Maryemma Graham
Copyright © 1995 by the University Press of Mississippi
All rights reserved
Manufactured in the United States of America

98 97 96 95   4 3 2 1

The paper in this book meets the guidelines for permanence and durability of the
Committee on Production Guidelines for Book Longevity of the Council on Library
Resources.

Library of Congress Cataloging-in-Publication Data

Ellison, Ralph.
    Conversations with Ralph Ellison / edited by Maryemma Graham and
    Amritjit Singh.
        p.   cm. — (Literary conversations series)
        Includes index.
        ISBN 0-87805-780-3 (cloth : alk. paper). — ISBN 0-87805-781-1
    (paper : alk. paper)
        1. Ellison, Ralph—Interviews.   2. Afro-American novelists—20th
    century—Interviews.   I. Graham, Maryemma.   II. Singh, Amritjit.
    III. Series.
    PS3555.L625Z464   1995
    818'.5409—dc20   95-13829
                                                                  CIP

British Library Cataloging-in-Publication data available

Contents

Introduction

"I'll be my kind of militant."
—Ralph Ellison to Hollie West, August 1973

There have been a few figures in American cultural history who
have engaged their sense of Americanness in the fullest possible
measure. Ralph Waldo Ellison, like the nineteenth-century figure
after whom he was named by his father, embodied such an
engagement in his life and writings. For over fifty years, from the
publication of his first book review in 1937 to his death in 1994,
Ellison spoke and wrote out of his sense of his complex fate as an
American. And while during his long and distinguished career,
Ellison might have been more visible in the public eye at one point
than another, his perspectives on artistic and cultural issues of
importance always commanded attention and often provoked controversy. Refusing to bend easily with fads and fashions, Ellison
maintained a consistent and always independent view of matters
close to the heart of the American experience. Claiming all
American culture as a legitimate domain for his voracious intellectual curiosity, he refused to accept or dignify the reduced and
"racialist" role often assigned to African American artists. He
insisted upon functioning out of his unflinching "responsibility"
to the broader culture, reminding his readers and listeners time and
again that "imagination is integrative. That is how you make the
new—by putting something else with what you've got." As James
Alan McPherson has noted, in resisting the seductive lure of
racial and ideological purity and in affirming the complexity of "his
ethnic and cultural background" throughout his career, Ellison
risked alienating "his own group, often on the merest chance that
someone, sometime in the future, will understand the implications" of his thought. The interviews and conversations collected
here surely demonstrate that the risks Ellison took were well
worth his effort as well as ours.

Maybe this same Melville-like capacity to defy the expectations

of a reading public explains the uncertainty that still surrounds
the possible publication of Ellison's second novel, even forty years
after he published his famous first novel, *Invisible Man* (1952).
Perhaps no other American writer has achieved a reputation for
greatness on the basis of a single book quite the same way as
Ellison. Chosen by several polls in the 1960s and 1970s as the most
"enduring" and most "distinguished" of all American novels published since 1945, *Invisible Man* has achieved the stature of a
modern classic. While steeped in richly African American materials, the novel brings an epic sense to what is peculiarly American
through its representation of the painful mistakes made by its
young protagonist in his search for meaning and identity.

With the publication of the novel, Ellison quickly became identified with an artistic virtuosity which seemed distinct from the speci-
ficity of protest tradition in African American writing and endeared
him to a certain segment of mainstream American critics, including southern conservatives. Perhaps his discomfort with such polari-
ties of race and art—it is helpful here to remember his famous
distinction between "relatives" and "ancestors"—explains why
Ellison felt compelled so often to demonstrate how well he understood
the hybrid nature of his own gifts, gifts that brought him both
pleasure and pain. His anguish and excitement about the challenges of craft in American culture are evident in his long interview
with writer John Hersey, where Ellison explores the paradoxical
nature of the writer's world: "Part of the pleasure of writing, as
well as the pain, is involved in pouring into that thing which is
being created all of what he cannot understand and cannot say and
cannot deal with, or cannot even admit, in any other way. That
artifact is a completion of personality."

Ellison pursued this ideal of "a completion of personality" not
only in his fiction, but also in his essays and interviews, which
surely bear the imprint of his artistic genius. Most readers familiar
with Ellison's essays in *Shadow and Act* (1964) and *Going to the
Territory* (1986), as well as his uncollected short stories, would
corroborate the verbal felicity, intellectual rigor and incisive eloquence with which all of his writings explore the same issues that
challenge us in *Invisible Man*. The interviews gathered in this
volume—only a few of which have been easily accessible so far—are

sure to reinforce Ellison's lasting place in American letters and allow us to hear his sprightly voice as he addresses a vast range of topics on race and art, writing and culture, politics and responsibility.

In the 1960s and later, despite his reluctance to acknowledge a more public role for himself, Ellison made periodic, even frequent, appearances in the media and maintained active memberships in major organizations, such as his work for nine years with the Carnegie Commission which grandfathered the era of public television. Thus, if Ellison eschewed a more public role, he never abdicated his sense of responsibility. His appearances—campus lectures, as well as interviews with TV, newspapers and magazines—accustomed his readers and admirers to memorable bits of conversation and pithy phrasing of cultural paradigms and each such appearance advanced his reputation as a cultural critic.

And yet, until the publication of *Going to the Territory* and *Speaking for You* (1987)—a collection of essays and interviews edited by Kimberly W. Benston which made a bold attempt to change the terminology by which we might understand Ellison's role in culture—popular academic images of Ellison in conversation were based primarily on the three interviews chosen for inclusion in *Shadow and Act*. For the most part, these three pieces provide commentary on what we might call "the politics of literature." Given the radical tenor of the 1960s and the highly politicized nature of African American writing during the period, Ellison's views on race and culture were easily appropriated. During these years, it became common to pit one writer against another and offer breezy readings by which major writers were turned into icons of one ideology or another. In such a fractious atmosphere, Ellison's well-known statement, "I have no desire to manipulate power. I want to write imaginative books," came to be seen as the motto for the apolitical writer. At this time, despite their longstanding friendship and the high regard in which they held each other's work, Richard Wright and Ellison were represented by many as polar opposites—one as a race-centered radical committed to social and political change, the other as a conservative celebrant of art and imagination. It was during these years that Ellison seemed to claim more privacy for himself. He resisted what he described as the "Booker T. Washington's 'crabs-in-a-basket' syndrome" and refused to be drawn into unproductive confrontations with his detractors. In a 1977 interview published originally in the *Y'Bird Magazine,* Ellison told Ishmael Reed, Quincy Troupe, and Steve Cannon: "My attitude toward this complex Negro American situation leads me to feel that there's little to be gained from our fighting with one another that I can afford to ignore such attacks. I learned long before I became a writer that there were Blacks who preferred to put you down rather than try to understand your point of view." In retrospect, Ellison's response appears both sensible and prescient. For example, as Kimberly Benston has observed, despite their many apparent oppositions, Amiri Baraka and Ellison have much more in common than is usually noticed: both view the American scene as imbued with contradiction and ambiguity in their search for strategies to save and improve "the best aspects of the black self" and both are interested in exploring those intersecting lines of tradition that represent specifically African American "responses of life."

This volume is sure to inspire many revisionist readings of Ellison and a renewed opportunity to think about the public and private worlds that Ellison preferred to keep separate. A collection of the best and most representative Ellison interviews and conversations, we hope it provides a more rounded profile of a man who remained a major player on our cultural scene for half a century. Our choice of interviews, arranged chronologically by when they were conducted rather than published, has been informed by our sense that we need to view in unison all of Ellison's writings—the novel, short fiction, essays, reviews and interviews. From this perspective then, these interviews become yet another discursive strategy toward "a completion of personality."

The range of interviewers is broad—journalists; fellow writers, both black and white; academic and independent scholars. Some of the interviews were conducted in the wake of Ellison's initial success with *Invisible Man;* others offered reflections upon the "age-ing" of the novel; many drew out the author concerning his views on a vast range of subjects, especially the relationship among various forms of African American expressive culture and their impact on American life. While some interviewers were able

to persuade Ellison to talk about contemporary politics or his
personal feelings about his attackers, most of them are concerned
with his thoughtful perspectives on matters of art and culture—
about what a writer must "render" and what he might "imply"
as he faces the challenge of giving shape to the chaos and confusion
of reality.

Most of us tend to think of Ellison as aloof in style and manner,
the embodiment of his own metaphor, a kind of "invisible man"
of recent American literature. This may indeed have been the public
Ellison, a man overshadowed by his own reputation, chuckling
with friends to deflect their questions about his second novel, and
reluctant to claim most of what we have often wanted to attribute to
him. But the interviews in this volume evoke a very different Ellison
indeed. We find in them a man of tremendous vitality, alert and
sensitive, well-read and argumentative, a man determined to fight
for his point of view, as he offers his witty and engaging approaches to the complexity of American life and culture, a complexity shaped—he always reminded us—by the rich and diverse
contributions of African Americans throughout history.

As we read through Ellison's conversations, we are provided with
several warnings. The first and perhaps most striking is Ellison's
insistence that *Invisible Man* not be read as a description of an
objective and historical reality, but only as *one* specific construction of reality. Ellison is sure to remind us again and again of the
autonomy of the artistic imagination, maintaining that political
implications of a work are never a given. *Invisible Man* was nevertheless a very political book at the time of its publication and
remains so today. While the African American experience was (and
is) open to essentialist constructions, Ellison has sought in it a
demonstration of American plurality and difference. Ellison's contribution, one might say, is to capture that paradox: the passionately
individual response to the uniformity of oppression and exclusion.
Whenever he talked about his novel or made his other observations about the hybridity of American culture, Ellison managed also
to remind us about how region (in his case Oklahoma and the
Southwest), childhood experiences and class background are as
much shaping factors in the visions and styles of individual black
writers as they are in the case of Euro-American artists, something

many of our students and colleagues continue to have a hard time
coming to terms with.

The subtlety and richness of *Invisible Man* as an artifact work
effectively to unsettle such deepseated attitudes about race and
culture at many levels. If Ellison's Ras the Destroyer came to
signify against many who would define "blackness" in essentialist
terms in the 1960s and later, so Rinehart's trickster-man, both hero
and villain, calls into question contemporary postmodern plati-
tudes about how *all* is performance. Rinehart both prefigures and
critiques postmodernism. Constantly moving in and around the main
events of the novel, Rinehart signatures so silkily that it often seems
he has arrived at the future before we have, beckoning us on—
signalling the need, as it were, for an ideal reader. For Ellison, the
ideal reader of *Invisible Man*—his "attempt to reveal personality
living within certain conditions," specifically African American
conditions—would be "the person who has the imagination, regardless of what color he is." Such a reader, as Ellison had noted
in *Shadow and Act,* must remember that "while objectively a
social reality, the work of art is, in its genesis, a projection of a
deeply personal process" and involves the "deepest psychological motives of the writer." So the full import of Ellison's book is
likely to emerge only through the confluence of the reality as
constructed by the author and the imaginative response of each
reading.

In these interviews, Ellison alerts us also to the need for individuals to take "broad responsibility" for what they say and what
they do. When asked why he did not choose exile like many of his
black contemporaries, Ellison responded that he lived in the US
because "for all of its difficulties, I had to face the challenge of the
US." He told Richard Kostelanetz that he lived near Harlem,
because he had to "hear the language . . . that sounding in my ears.
. . . Things are revealed in speech in the street. There is a lot of humor
and the language is always feeding back to the past; it's throwing
up wisdom, it's throwing up patterns. . . ." In these interviews—
as in his essays and in his fiction—Ellison seems sharply aware of
the unseen ways in which blacks and whites interact to teach each
other American cultural forms, learn elegance and style from one
another. Culture, according to Ellison, "results from the exchange

of different lifestyles and beliefs.'' While Ellison would understand the anxieties expressed by commentators such as Allan Bloom and Dinesh D'Souza about the probable balkanization of America under the pressures of multiculturalism, he sees diversity as an essential characteristic of American life. For Ellison, while diversity might sometimes be ''burdensome'' and a source of conflict, ''in it lies our faith and our hope—I believe in diversity and I think that the real death of the United States will come when everyone is just alike.'' To characterize the culture shared by blacks and whites despite issues of economics or race, Ellison prefers to use the word ''slum'' over ''ghetto'' to describe poor black neighborhoods. ''It's economic, not cultural,'' he asserts. In 1973, he told an audience at Harvard, ''All of us are part white, and all of y'all are part colored.'' In another conversation—in keeping with the many pronouncements of his co-conspirator, Albert Murray—Ellison declares that he does not recognize ''any white culture. I recognize no American culture which is not a partial creation of black people. I recognize no American style in literature, dance, in music, even in assemblyline processes which does not bear the mark of the American Negro.'' In fact, Ellison proposes that ''we view the whole of American life as a drama acted out upon the body of a Negro giant, who, lying trussed up like Gulliver, forms the stage and the scene upon which and within which the action unfolds.''

Since Ellison saw the role of the novelist as inextricably tied to the American experiment in democracy, he considered the African American situation as a quintessentially American challenge. His term, the ''morality of fiction,'' captures in a way his own sense of the terrible difficulty of giving voice to the expressive and chaotic situation of being a ''Negro American,'' the term Ellison almost always preferred. He told novelist John Hersey that the ''problem of communicating across . . . various social divisions, whether of race, class, education, region, or religion,'' would suggest that it is ''dangerous to take things for granted.'' For Ellison, it was important that the writer ''be aware that the reality of race conceals a complex of manners and culture.'' An African American writer's choice to present the experience which is, ''in its immediate sense, that of blacks, . . . [must] influence the shaping of fictional form and govern, to a large extent, the writer's sense of proportion, and determine what he feels obligated to render as well as what he feels he can simply imply."

Ellison viewed the "fictional form" as a preferred way of "dealing with the complexities of a democratic equalitarian society wherein there are so many things that you can't say." For him, the novel is an enduring form in a democratic culture, even in a world dominated increasingly by TV. He told David L. Carson that he found the novel particularly well-equipped to deal with our "many ambivalences toward values, toward the concept of equality itself, toward class." Echoing his friend Kenneth Burke, he declared that his ultimate purpose as a novelist is "to seize upon the abiding patterns of the American experience as they come up within my own part of the American nation, and project those patterns, those personality types, those versions of man's dilemmas, in terms of symbolic actions." In the process, he hopes the reader "is able to recognize the meaning and value of the presented experience and the essential unity of human experience as a whole. This may, or may not, lead to social change or bring the novelist recognition as spokesman. But it is, nevertheless, a form of social action, and an important task."

As biographers and critics pursue the public and private Ellison in new ways to determine the meanings and possibilities of the novel as a form of social action, they will surely find in these interviews a vibrant and persistent voice reminding us of Ellison's superb ability to both persuade and challenge us in unexpected ways. There is increasing recognition today of his already formidable influence on younger writers and scholars engaged in current debates on language and culture in a variety of contexts. Just as *Invisible Man* opened up spaces for African American writers who are experimentalists or whose work exceeds the boundaries of realism, these interviews bolster the emergent theoretical and historical perspectives on culture that reject absolutist definitions of race, ethnicity, gender, and nation. The interviews gathered in this volume serve not only as windows on Ellison's own art and imagination but also permit a fresh understanding of a writer's formative if undervalued role in the shaping of American culture and thought. In the rich texture and anecdotal charm of these interviews, Ellison reaf-

firms the layered, palimpsest quality of American life and expresses his hope that America will redeem itself through every
young American's responsible reclamation of its living past.

These interviews have been reprinted uncut as they originally
appeared and minor errors of fact and spelling have been silently
corrected. Although it would be normal to expect some repetitive-
ness in such a volume of conversations with the same writer over
a period of time, it is a sign of Ellison's originality and intellectual
agility that most readers are likely to find almost none in the
pages that follow. Ellison demonstrates a wonderful gift for placing
old subjects in new contexts every time he has an opportunity to
talk about them.

It is our great pleasure to acknowledge the help we have received
from many sources toward the completion of this project. First of
all, we want to thank the library staffs at Rhode Island College and
Northeastern University for the unfailing courtesy extended to us
in our search for the many interviews included in this volume. We
owe an enormous debt of gratitude to Cheryl Ann Petrarca, Kurt
Hemmer and Brian Pattison (Rhode Island College) as well as to
Ted Williams, Patricia O'Neil and Kelley Norman (Northeastern
University) who served most ably as research assistants at various
stages of the project. Among the many friends and colleagues
who have been supportive in one way or another are Wendy Barker,
Kimberly Benston, J. Birje-Patil, Mark Busby, Peter Schmidt,
and Jerry Ward. We also want to express our appreciation for our
editor, Seetha Srinivasan, for her skills and patience as also for her
faith in us.

The volume is dedicated to the memory of Ralph Ellison who
taught us both in life and literature. We acknowledge with appreciation
the gracious support we have received for this project from Mrs.
Fanny Ellison.

AS/MG
December 1994

Chronology

1914   Ralph Waldo Ellison born 1 March in Oklahoma City to Lewis Alfred Ellison, a construction foreman, and the former Ida Milsap, a church stewardess

1917   Father dies.

1920   Attends Frederick Douglass School in Oklahoma City, where Dr. Inman Page was the principal; receives lessons in symphonic composition from Ludwig Hebestreit, conductor of the Oklahoma City Orchestra.

1922   Begins playing the trumpet

1933   Goes to the Tuskegee Institute to study music

1936   Moves to New York City with plans to study sculpture with Augusta Savage and raise money to return to school; studies instead with Richmond Barthe.

1937   Mother dies; attends mother's funeral in Dayton, Ohio; stays seven months hunting before returning to New York; meets Richard Wright and publishes first book review in *New Challenge.*

1938   Joins the Federal Writers' Project

1939   Publishes first short story, "Slick Gonna Learn"

1940   Publishes short story "Afternoon"

1941   Publishes short story "Mister Toussan"

1942   Edits *Negro Quarterly*

1943   Publishes short story "In a Strange Country"; serves as second cook and baker in Merchant Marine until 1945.

1944   Publishes short stories "King of the Bingo Game" and "Flying Home"

1945   Receives a Rosenwald Grant; begins *Invisible Man* at the

Vermont farm of friends John and Amelia Bates; publishes review of *Black Boy,* "Richard Wright's Blues."

1946   Marries Fanny McConnell, who worked then for the
        Urban League and served in the 1960s as director of
        the American Medical Center for Burma

1947   Publishes short story "Invisible Man," which later be-
        came the "Battle Royal" chapter of *Invisible Man*

1952   Publishes "Invisible Man: Prologue to a Novel"; *Invisible
        Man* published by Random House in April.

1953   Receives the National Book Award for *Invisible Man;*
        publishes essay "Twentieth-Century Fiction and the
        Black Mask of Humanity."

1954   Publishes short story "Did You Ever Dream Lucky?";
        lectures in Germany and at the Salzburg Seminar in Austria.

1955   Awarded Prix de Rome Fellowship by the American Acad-
        emy of Arts and Letters; wins a Rockefeller Foundation
        Award and stays in Rome until 1957.

1956   Publishes short story "A Coupla Scalped Indians"

1957   Publishes essay "Society, Morality and the Novel"

1958   Begins Hickman stories; lectures on Russian and Ameri-
        can Literature at Bard College till 1961 and shares a house
        in Dutchess County with Saul Bellow; publishes essay
        "Change the Joke and Slip the Yoke."

1960   Publishes first Hickman story; "And Hickman Arrives"*
        and "The Roof, the Steeple and the People"*; pub-
        lishes essay "Stephen Crane and the Mainstream of
        American Fiction."

1961   Alexander White Visiting Professor, University of
        Chicago

1962   Visiting Professor of Writing at Rutgers University until
        1969; Visiting Fellow, American Studies, Yale Univer-
        sity, 1962–64.

1963   Publishes short story "Out of the Hospital and Under the
        Bar" (originally written as part of *Invisible Man*); pub-
        lishes short story, "It Always Breaks Out," and essay,

"The World and the Jug" (a response to Irving Howe's "Black Boys and Native Sons"); receives the Russwurm National Newspaper Publishers Award and an Honorary Doctorate from the Tuskegee Institute.

1964   Vice President of the American P.E.N.; publishes essay "Hidden Name and Complex Fate"; publishes *Shadow and Act,* and delivers Ewing Lectures at the University of California, Los Angeles, in January and April.

1965   Member, National Council of the Arts; publishes short story "Juneteenth"*; *Invisible Man* selected as the Best American Novel in the post-World War II era in a *Book Week* poll of leading American critics.

1966   Is named to the Carnegie Commission on Educational Television and serves on the commission for nine years; witness at a senate subcommittee hearing on urban issues; receives Honorary Doctorate from Rutgers University; lectures at Yale University and the Library of Congress.

1967   Vice President, National Institute of Arts and Letters; fire in Massachusetts summer home destroys 368 pages of Hickman manuscript; receives Honorary Doctorates from the University of Michigan and Grinnell College.

1968   Supports President Lyndon Johnson's domestic agenda and Vietnam War policy

1969   Publishes "Night-Talk"*; receives the Medal of Freedom from President Johnson.

1970   Receives Honorary Doctorate from Williams College; publishes "A Song of Innocence" in *Iowa Review* (a revised version of this story was read by Ellison at the Library of Congress, March 28, 1983, and a recording is available through the Library); becomes Albert Schweitzer Professor of the Humanities at New York University and serves there until 1980; named Professor Emeritus at NYU in 1982; awarded the Chevalier de L'Ordre des Artes et Lettres by André Malraux, Minister of Cultural Affairs in France.

1971   Receives Honorary Doctorates from Adelphi University and Long Island University

1972   *Invisible Man* named as the "most likely to endure" among two dozen novels published between 1945 and 1972, in a survey of leading American critics conducted by John K. Crane and Daniel Walden of Pennsylvania State University

1973   Publishes "Cadillac Flambe"*

1974   Receives Honorary Doctorates from The College of William and Mary, Harvard University and Wake Forest College

1975   Elected to American Academy of Arts and Letters

1977   Publishes "Backwacking: A Plea to the Senator"*

1978   Receives Honorary Doctorate from Bard College

1980   Receives Honorary Doctorate from Wesleyan University

1986   Publishes *Going to the Territory*

1994   Dies in New York City, 16 April

*Believed to be part of the still unpublished Hickman manuscript

Conversations with Ralph Ellison

Talk with Ralph Ellison

Harvey Breit / 1952

From the *New York Times*, 4 May 1952, sec. 7: 26. Copyright
1942 by the New York Times Company. Reprinted by permission.

Just over medium height and strong and substantial of physique, the
author of *Invisible Man* is visible indeed. His face is firm and
sensitive and remarkably handsome, a scar and a thin mustache
failing to mar it. He's a standout in any company. The name is Ralph
Ellison, heard here and there and one hopes everywhere these days
because of his first distinguished novel. And to be heard of in the
future, if any predictions are worth anything at all.

Though up until this relatively triumphant event Mr. Ellison has
been, it must be admitted, obscure. Before putting him on record
as a thinking, talking chap, it seemed a good idea, therefore, to root
around in Mr. Ellison's biography. It turned out he was born in
Oklahoma City, in 1914. He lived there most of his life. Mr. Ellison
spent three years at Tuskegee Institute, where he studied music
and composition. Then he stumbled on sculpture.

That got him to New York, bent on exploring stone with a hammer
and clay with a wire gimmick. Just about that time, though, along
came *The Waste Land*—T. S. Eliot's, of course, and that turned out
to be the most influential book in his life. "It got me interested in
literature," Mr. Ellison said. "I tried to understand it better and
that led me to reading criticism. I then started looking for Eliot's
kind of sensibility in Negro poetry and I didn't find it until I ran into
Richard Wright."

The work or the man? "Both," Mr. Ellison said. "We became
friends, and still are. I began to write soon after. Meeting Wright
at that time, when he hadn't yet begun to be famous, was most
fortunate for me. He was passionately interested in the problems
of technique and craft and it was an education. Later the Communists took credit for teaching him to write, but that's a lot of stuff. I

3

published a short story in *American Writing,* I think, in 1940. I was in *Cross-Section.* That was, I believe, 1944, in which some of the first work of Norman Mailer, Arthur Miller and Shirley Jackson appeared."

Was *Invisible Man* Mr. Ellison's only novel? "I wrote a short novel in the process of writing this one," Mr. Ellison replied, "just to get a kindred theme out of the way."

Now, Mr. Ellison couldn't just slough off that one. How could he have been that clear? Why hadn't he been just enough confused—as most of us would be—to try to assimilate the kindred theme into the big novel. Mr. Ellison laughed a little. "I could see," he said, "it was not part of the novel because it had to do with a more mature character. While thematically it was part of the book, it nevertheless would have required different treatment; its reality wasn't as intense, as surreal, as the reality of the novel."

That was pretty much that then. Mr. Ellison continued, "Several reviews pointed out parts of the book they considered surrealistic. I'll agree with that; however I didn't select the surrealism, the distortion, the intensity, as an experimental technique but because reality is surreal. I used to get this same sense of a distorted reality years ago when I'd come every once in a while on a shell-shocked veteran of World War I. It was up in Harlem and he used to stop traffic on a street crossing by throwing imaginary bombs at the cars. Of course, the traffic flowed on quite normally. This fellow was reliving a trauma. But people were used to it and they went normally about their business."

What about the business (wasn't it nonsense?) of being a Negro writer? Wasn't one a writer who happened to be a Negro? Mr. Ellison tackled the question with what could only be called a beautiful honesty. "The thing that's forgotten is that everyone has to master his craft or profession. Without the mastery no one is free, Negro or white. You remember Hemingway saying he'd fought a draw with Balzac or whoever? Well, it's right. You enter into mortal combat with the best in your field. It at least keeps your feet on the ground," Mr. Ellison said laughingly. Hands clasped on the table, he went on:

"It is felt that there is something in the Negro experience that makes it not quite right for the novel. That's not true. It becomes important to the novelist because it is in this problem, as Faulkner makes us aware that the American human conflict is at its most intense and dramatic. That's a rough way of putting it. What is exciting about it is that it hasn't really been written about except in a sociological way. That which for the sociologist presents itself as racial conflict becomes for the novelist the American form of the human drama. In Faulkner, Negro and white are catalyst for each other. If Faulkner could have found a more intense catalyst, he would have used it.''

The Art of Fiction: An Interview

Alfred Chester and Vilma Howard / 1954

From the *Paris Review* (Spring 1955), 53–55. Copyright 1955 by
Paris Review. Reprinted by permission.

When *Invisible Man,* Ralph Ellison's first novel, received the National Book Award for 1952, the author in his acceptance speech
noted with dismay and gratification the conferring of the award to
what he called "an attempt at a major novel." His gratification
was understandable, so too his dismay when one considers the
amount of objectivity Mr. Ellison can display toward his own
work. He felt the state of U.S. fiction to be so unhappy that it was
an "attempt" rather than an achievement which received the
important award.

Many of us will disagree with Mr. Ellison's evaluation of his own
work. Its crackling, brilliant, sometimes wild, but always controlled prose warrants this; so does the care and logic with which
its form is revealed, and not least its theme: that of a young Negro
who emerges from the South and—in the tradition of James' Hya-
cinth Robinson and Stendhal's Julien Sorel—moves into the adventure of life at large.

In the summer of 1954, Mr. Ellison came abroad to travel and
lecture. His visit ended with Paris where for a very few weeks he
mingled with the American expatriate group to whom his work was
known and of much interest. The day before he left he talked to us in
the Café de la Mairie du VI about art and the novel.

Ralph Ellison takes both art and the novel seriously. And the
Café de la Mairie has a tradition of seriousness behind it, for here
was written Djuna Barnes' spectacular novel, *Nightwood.* There is
a tradition, too, of speech and eloquence, for Miss Barnes' hero,
Dr. O'Connor, often drew a crowd of listeners to his mighty
rhetoric. So here gravity is in the air and rhetoric too. While Mr.
Ellison speaks, he rarely pauses, and although the strain of organiz-

ing his thought is sometimes evident, his phraseology and the quiet steady flow and development of ideas are overwhelming. To listen to him is rather like sitting in the back of a huge hall and feeling the lecturer's faraway eyes staring directly into your own. The highly emphatic, almost professorial intonations, started with their distance, self-confidence, and warm undertones of humor.

Ellison: Let me say right now that my book is not an autobiographical work.

Interviewers: You weren't thrown out of school like the boy in your novel?

Ellison: No. Though, like him, I went from one job to another.

Interviewers: Why did you give up music and begin writing?

Ellison: I didn't give up music, but I became interested in writing through incessant reading. In 1935 I discovered Eliot's *The Waste Land* which moved and intrigued me but defied my powers of analysis—such as they were—and I wondered why I had never read anything of equal intensity and sensibility by an American Negro writer. Later on, in New York, I read a poem by Richard Wright, who, as luck would have it, came to town the next week. He was editing a magazine called *New Challenge* and asked me to try a book review of E. Waters Turpin's *These Low Grounds*. On the basis of this review Wright suggested that I try a short story, which I did. I tried to use my knowledge of riding freight trains. He liked the story well enough to accept it and it got as far as the galley proofs when it was bumped from the issue because there was too much material. Just after that the magazine failed.

Interviewers: But you went on writing—

Ellison: With difficulty, because this was the Recession of 1937. I went to Dayton, Ohio, where my brother and I hunted and sold game to earn a living. At night I practiced writing and studied Joyce, Dostoievski, Stein and Hemingway. Especially Hemingway; I read him to learn his sentence structure and how to organize a story. I guess many young writers were doing this, but I also used his description of hunting when I went into the fields the next day. I had been hunting since I was eleven but no one had broken down the process of wing-shooting for me and it was from reading Hemingway that I learned to lead a bird. When he describes something in print, believe him; believe him even when he describes the process of art in terms of baseball or boxing; he's been there.

Interviewers: Were you affected by the Social Realism of the period?

Ellison: I was seeking to learn and Social Realism was a highly regarded theory, though I didn't think too much of the so-called proletarian fiction even when I was most impressed by Marxism. I was intrigued by Malraux, who at that time was being claimed by the Communists. I noticed, however, that whenever the heroes of *Man's Fate*[1] regarded their condition during moments of heightened self-consciousness, their thinking was something other than Marxist. Actually they were more profoundly intellectual than their real-life counterparts. Of course, Malraux was more of a humanist than most of the Marxist writers of that period—and also much more of an artist. He was the artist-revolutionary rather than a politician when he wrote *Man's Fate,* and the book lives not because of a political position embraced at the time, but because of its larger concern with the tragic struggle of humanity. Most of the social realists of the period were concerned more with tragedy than with injustice. I wasn't, and am not, concerned with injustice, but with art.

Interviewers: Then you consider your novel a purely literary work as opposed to one in the tradition of social protest.

Ellison: Now mind! I recognize no dichotomy between art and protest. Dostoyevsky's *Notes from the Underground* is, among other things, a protest against the limitations of 19th century rationalism; *Don Quixote, Man's Fate, Oedipus Rex, The Trial*—all these embody protest, even against the limitation of human life itself. If social protest is antithetical to art, what then shall we make of Goya, Dickens and Twain? One hears a lot of complaints about the so-called "protest novel," especially when written by Negroes; but it seems to me that the critics could more accurately complain about their lack of craftsmanship and their provincialism.

Interviewers: But isn't it going to be difficult for the Negro writer to escape provincialism when his literature is concerned with a minority?

---

[1]*La Condition Humaine.*

Ellison: All novels are about certain minorities: the individual is a minority. The universal in the novel—and isn't that what we're all clamoring for these days?—is reached only through the depiction of the specific man in a specific circumstance.

Interviewers: But still, how is the Negro writer, in terms of what is expected of him by critics and readers, going to escape his particular need for social protest and reach the "universal" you speak of?

Ellison: If the Negro, or any other writer, is going to do what is expected of him, he's lost the battle before he takes the field. I suspect that all the agony that goes into writing is borne precisely because the writer longs for acceptance—but it must be acceptance on his own terms. Perhaps, though, this thing cuts both ways: the Negro novelist draws his blackness too tightly around him when he sits down to write—that's what the anti-protest critics believe—but perhaps the white reader draws his whiteness around himself when he sits down to read. He doesn't want to identify himself with Negro characters in terms of our immediate racial and social situation, though on the deeper human level identification can become compelling when the situation is revealed artistically. The white reader doesn't want to get too close, not even in an imaginary recreation of society. Negro writers have felt this and it has led to much of our failure.

Too many books by Negro writers are addressed to a white audience. By doing this the authors run the risk of limiting themselves to the audience's presumptions of what a Negro is or should be; the tendency is to become involved in polemics, to plead the Negro's humanity. You know, many white people question that humanity but I don't think that Negroes can afford to indulge in such a false issue. For us the question should be, what are the specific *forms* of that humanity, and what in our background is worth preserving or abandoning. The clue to this can be found in folklore which offers the first drawings of any group's character. It preserves mainly those situations which have repeated themselves again and again in the history of any given group. It describes those rites, manners, customs, and so forth, which insure the good life, or destroy it; and it describes those boundaries of feeling, thought and action which that particular group has found to be the limitation of the human condition. It projects this wisdom in symbols which express the group's will to survive; it embodies those values by which the group lives and dies. These drawings may be crude but they are nonetheless profound in that they represent the group's attempt to humanize the world. It's no accident that great literature, the products of individual artists, is erected upon this humble base. The hero of Dostoyevsky's *Notes from the Underground* and the hero of Gogol's *The Overcoat* appear in their rudimentary forms far back in Russian folklore. French literature has never ceased exploring the nature of the Frenchman . . . Or take Picasso—

Interviewers: How does Picasso fit into all this?

Ellison: Why, he's the greatest wrestler with forms and techniques of them all. Just the same he's never abandoned the old symbolic forms of Spanish art: the guitar, the bull, daggers, women, shawls, veils, mirrors. Such symbols serve a dual function: they allow the artist to speak of complex experiences and to annihilate time with simple lines and curves; and they allow the viewer an orientation, both emotional and associative, which goes so deep that a total culture may resound in a simple rhythm, an image. It has been said that Escudero could recapitulate the history and spirit of the Spanish dance with a simple arabesque of his fingers.

Interviewers: But these are examples from homogeneous cultures. How representative of the American nation would you say Negro folklore is?

Ellison: The history of the American Negro is a most intimate part of American history. Through the very process of slavery came the building of the United States. Negro folklore, evolving within a larger culture which regarded it as inferior, was an especially courageous expression. It announced the Negro's willingness to trust his own experience, his own sensibilities as to the definition of reality, rather than allow his masters to define these crucial matters for him. His experience is that of America and the West, and is as rich a body of experience as one would find anywhere. We can view it narrowly as something exotic, folksy, or "low-down," or we may identify ourselves with it and recognize it as an important segment of the larger American experience—not lying at the bottom of it, but intertwined, diffused in its very texture. I can't take this lightly or be impressed by those who

cannot see its importance; it is important to *me*. One ironic witness
to the beauty and the universality of this art is the fact that the
descendants of the very men who enslaved us can now sing the
spirituals and find in the singing an exaltation of their own
humanity. Just take a look at some of the slave songs, blues, folk
ballads; their possibilities for the writer are infinitely suggestive.
Some of them have named human situations so well that a whole
corps of writers could not exhaust their universality. For instance,
here's an old slave verse:

> *Ole Aunt Dinah, she's just like me*
> *She work so hard she want to be free*
> *But ole Aunt Dinah's gittin' kinda ole*
> *She's afraid to go to Canada on account of the cold.*
>
> *Ole Uncle Jack, now he's a mighty "good nigger"*
> *You tell him that you want to be free for a fac'*
> *Next thing you know they done stripped the skin off your back.*
>
> *Now ole Uncle Ned, he want to be free*
> *He found his way north by the moss on the tree*
> *He cross that river floating in a tub*
> *The pataleroller² give him a mighty close rub.*

It's crude, but in it you have three universal attitudes toward the
problem of freedom. You can refine it and sketch in the psychological subtleties and historical and philosophical allusions, action and
what not, but I don't think its basic definition can be exhausted.
Perhaps some genius could do as much with it as Mann has done
with the Joseph story.

Interviewers: Can you give us an example of the use of folklore in
your own novel?

Ellison: Well, there are certain themes, symbols and images which
are based on folk material. For example, there is the old saying
amongst Negroes: If you're black, stay back; if you're brown, stick
around; if you're white, you're right. And there is the joke
Negroes tell on themselves about their being so black they can't be
seen in the dark. In my book this sort of thing was merged with
the meanings which blackness and light have long had in Western
mythology: evil and goodness, ignorance and knowledge, and so

---

²*Patroller.*

on. In my novel the narrator's development is one through blackness to light; that is, from ignorance to enlightenment: invisibility
to visibility. He leaves the South and goes North; this, as you will
notice in reading Negro folktales, is always the road to freedom—the
movement upward. You have the same thing again when he leaves
his underground cave for the open.

It took me a long time to learn how to adapt such examples of
myth into my work—also ritual. The use of ritual is equally a vital
part of the creative process. I learned a few things from Eliot, Joyce
and Hemingway, but not how to adapt them. When I started writing,
I knew that in both *The Waste Land* and *Ulysses* ancient myth and
ritual were used to give form and significance to the material; but
it took me a few years to realize that the myths and rites which we
find functioning in our everyday lives could be used in the same
way. In my first attempt at a novel—which I was unable to complete—I began by trying to manipulate the simple structural
unities of *beginning, middle* and *end,* but when I attempted to deal
with the psychological strata—the images, symbols and emotional
configurations—of the experience at hand, I discovered that the
unities were simply cool points of stability on which one could
suspend the narrative line—but beneath the surface of apparently
rational human relationships there seethed a chaos before which
I was helpless. People rationalize what they shun or are incapable
of dealing with; these superstitions and their rationalizations
become ritual as they govern behavior. The rituals become social
forms, and it is one of the functions of the artist to recognize
them and raise them to the level of art.

I don't know whether I'm getting this over or not. Let's put it
this way: Take the "Battle Royal" passage in my novel, where
the boys are blindfolded and forced to fight each other for the
amusement of the white observers. This is a vital part of behavior
patterns in the South, which both Negroes and whites thoughtlessly
accept. It is a ritual in preservation of caste lines, a keeping of taboo
to appease the gods and ward off bad luck. It is also the initiation
ritual to which all greenhorns are subjected. This passage states
what Negroes will see I did not have to invent; the patterns were
already there in society so that all I had to do was present them
in a broader context of meaning. In any society there are many

rituals of situation which, for the most part, go unquestioned.
They can be simple or elaborate, but they are the connective tissue
between the work of art and the audience.

Interviewers: Do you think a reader unacquainted with this folklore can properly understand your work?

Ellison: Yes, I think so. It's like jazz; there's no inherent problem
which prohibits understanding but the assumptions brought to it.
We don't all dig Shakespeare uniformly, or even *Little Red Riding
Hood*. The understanding of art depends finally upon one's willingness
to extend one's humanity and one's knowledge of human life. I
noticed, incidentally, that the Germans, having no special caste assumptions concerning American Negroes, dealt with my work simply as a novel. I think the Americans will come to view it that
way in twenty years—if it's around that long.

Interviewers: Don't you think it will be?

Ellison: I doubt it. It's not an important novel. I failed of eloquence and many of the immediate issues are rapidly fading away. If
it does last, it will be simply because there are things going on in its
depth that are of more permanent interest than on its surface. I
hope so, anyway.

Interviewers: Have the critics given you any constructive help in
your writing, or changed in any way your aims in fiction?

Ellison: No, except that I have a better idea of how the critics
react, of what they see and fail to see, of how their sense of life
differs with mine and mine with theirs. In some instances they were
nice for the wrong reasons. In the U.S.—and I don't want this to
sound like an apology for my own failures—some reviewers did not
see what was before them because of this nonsense about protest.

Interviewers: Did the critics change your view of yourself as
a writer?

Ellison: I can't say that they did. I've been seeing by my own
candle too long for that. The critics did give me a sharper sense
of a larger audience, yes; and some convinced me that they were
willing to judge me in terms of my writing rather than in terms of my
racial identity. But there is one widely syndicated critical bankrupt
who made liberal noises during the Thirties and has been frightened
ever since. He attacked my book as a "literary race riot." By and
large, the critics and readers gave me an affirmed sense of my

identity as a writer. You might know this within yourself, but to have it affirmed by others is of utmost importance. Writing is, after all, a form of communication.

Interviewers: When did you begin *Invisible Man*?

Ellison: In the summer of 1945. I had returned from the sea, ill, with advice to get some rest. Part of my illness was due, no doubt, to the fact that I had not been able to write a novel for which I'd received a Rosenwald fellowship the previous winter. So on a farm in Vermont where I was reading *The Hero* by Lord Ragland and speculating on the nature of Negro leadership in the U.S., I wrote the first paragraph of *Invisible Man,* and was soon involved in the struggle of creating the novel.

Interviewers: How long did it take you to write it?

Ellison: Five years with one year out for a short novel which was unsatisfactory, ill-conceived and never submitted for publication.

Interviewers: Did you have everything thought out before you began to write *Invisible Man*?

Ellison: The symbols and their connections were known to me. I began it with a chart of the three-part division. It was a conceptual frame with most of the ideas and some incidents indicated. The three parts represent the narrator's movement from, using Kenneth Burke's terms, purpose to passion to perception. These three major sections are built up of smaller units of three which mark the course of the action and which depend for their development upon what I hoped was a consistent and developing motivation. However, you'll note that the maximum insight on the hero's part isn't reached until the final section. After all, it's a novel about innocence and human error, a struggle through illusion to reality. Each section begins with a sheet of paper; each piece of paper is exchanged for another and contains a definition of his identity, or the social role he is to play as defined for him by others. But all say essentially the same thing, "Keep this nigger boy running." Before he could have some voice in his own destiny he had to discard these old identities and illusions; his enlightenment couldn't come until then. Once he recognizes the hole of darkness into which these papers put him, he has to burn them. That's the plan and the intention; whether I achieved this is something else.

Interviewers: Would you say that the search for identity is primarily an American theme?

Ellison: It is *the* American theme. The nature of our society is such that we are prevented from knowing who we are. It is still a young society, and this is an integral part of its development.

Interviewers: A common criticism of "first novels" is that the central incident is either omitted or weak. *Invisible Man* seems to suffer here; shouldn't we have been present at the scenes which are the dividing lines in the book—namely, when the Brotherhood organization moves the narrator downtown, then back uptown?

Ellison: I think you missed the point. The major flaw in the hero's character is his unquestioning willingness to do what is required of him by others as a way to success, and this was the specific form of his "innocence." He goes where he is told to go; he does what he is told to do; he does not even choose his Brotherhood name. It is chosen for him and he accepts it. He has accepted party discipline and thus cannot be present at the scene since it is not the will of the Brotherhood leaders. What is important is not the scene but his failure to question their decision. There is also the fact that no single person can be everywhere at once, nor can a single consciousness be aware of all the nuances of a large social action. What happens uptown while he is downtown is part of his darkness, both symbolic and actual. No; I don't feel that any vital scenes have been left out.

Interviewers: Why did you find it necessary to shift styles throughout the book; particularly in the Prologue and Epilogue?

Ellison: The Prologue was written afterwards, really—in terms of a shift in the hero's point of view. I wanted to throw the reader off balance—make him accept certain non-naturalistic effects. It was really a memoir written underground, and I wanted a foreshadowing through which I hoped the reader would view the actions which took place in the main body of the book. For another thing, the styles of life presented are different. In the South where he was trying to fit into a traditional pattern and where his sense of certainty had not yet been challenged, I felt a more naturalistic treatment was adequate. The college of Trustee's speech to the students is really an echo of a certain kind of southern rhetoric and I enjoyed trying to recreate it. As the hero passes from the South to

the North, from the relatively stable to the swiftly changing, his
sense of certainty is lost and the style becomes expressionistic.
Later on during his fall from grace in the Brotherhood it becomes
somewhat surrealistic. The styles try to express both his state of
consciousness and the state of society. The Epilogue was necessary
to complete the action begun when he set out to write his
memoirs.

Interviewers: After four hundred pages you still felt the Epilogue
was necessary?

Ellison: Yes. Look at it this way. The book is a series of reversals.
It is the portrait of the artist as a rabble-rouser, thus the various
mediums of expression. In the Epilogue the hero discovers what he
had not discovered throughout the book: you have to make your own
decisions; you have to think for yourself. The hero comes up from
underground because the act of writing and thinking necessitated
it. He could not stay down there.

Interviewers: You say that the book is "a series of reversals." It
seemed to us that this was a weakness, that it was built on a series
of provocative situations which were cancelled by the calling up of
conventional emotions—.

Ellison: I don't quite see what you mean.

Interviewers: Well, for one thing, you begin with a provocative
situation of the American Negro's status in society. The responsibility for this is that of the white American citizen; that's where the
guilt lies. Then you cancel it by introducing the Communist Party, or
the Brotherhood, so that the reader tends to say to himself: "Ah,
they're the guilty ones. They're the ones who mistreat him;
not us."

Ellison: I think that's a case of misreading. And I didn't identify
the Brotherhood as the C.P., but since you do I'll remind you that
they too are white. The hero's invisibility is not a matter of being
seen, but a refusal to run the risk of his own humanity, which
involves guilt. This is not an attack upon white society! It is what
the hero refuses to do in each section which leads to further
action. He must assert and achieve his own humanity; he cannot
run with the pack and do this—this is the reason for all the
reversals. The Epilogue is the most final reversal of all; therefore it
is a necessary statement.

Interviewers: And the love affairs—or almost-love-affairs—.

Ellison: *(Laughing)* I'm glad you put it that way. The point is that when thrown into a situation which he thinks he wants, the hero is sometimes thrown at a loss; he doesn't know how to act. After he had made this speech about The Place of the Woman in Our Society, for example, and was approached by one of the women in the audience, he thought she wanted to talk about the Brotherhood and found that she wanted to talk about brother-*and-sister-hood*. Look, didn't you find the book at all *funny*? I felt that such a man as this character would have been incapable of a love affair; it would have been inconsistent with his personality.

Interviewers: Do you have any difficulty controlling your characters? E. M. Forster says that he sometimes finds a character running away with him.

Ellison: No, because I find that a sense of the ritual understructure of the fiction helps to guide the creation of characters. Action is the thing. We are what we do and do not do. The problem for me is to get from A to B to C. My anxiety about transitions greatly prolonged the writing of my book. The naturalists stick to case histories and sociology and are willing to compete with the camera and the tape recorder. I despise concreteness in writing, but when reality is deranged in fiction, one must worry about the seams.

Interviewers: Do you have difficulty turning real characters into fiction?

Ellison: Real characters are just a limitation. It's like turning your own life into fiction: you have to be hindered by chronology and fact. A number of the characters just jumped out, like Rinehart and Ras.

Interviewers: Isn't Ras based on Marcus Garvey[3]?

Ellison: No. In 1950 my wife and I were staying at a vacation spot where we met some white liberals who thought the best way to be friendly was to tell us what it was like to be Negro. I got mad at hearing this from people who otherwise seemed very intelligent. I had already sketched Ras but the passion of his statement came out after I went upstairs that night feeling that we needed to have

---

[3]*Marcus Garvey - Negro nationalist and founder of a "Back to Africa" movement in the U.S. during the early 1900s.*

this thing out once and for all and get it done with; then we could
go on living like people and individuals. No conscious reference to
Garvey is intended.

Interviewers: What about Rinehart? Is he related to Rinehart in
the blues tradition, or Django Rheinhardt, the jazz musician?

Ellison: There is a peculiar set of circumstances connected with
my choice of that name. My old Oklahoma friend, Jimmy Rushing, the blues singer, used to sing one with a refrain that went:

> *Rinehart, Rinehart,*
> *It's so lonesome up here*
> *On Beacon Hill,*

which haunted me, and as I was thinking of a character who was a
master of disguise, of coincidence, this name with its suggestion
of inner and outer came to my mind. Later I learned that it was a
call used by Harvard students when they prepared to riot, a call to
chaos. Which is very interesting because it is not long after Rinehart
appears in my novel that the riot breaks out in Harlem. Rinehart
is my name for the personification of chaos. He is also intended to
represent America and change. He has lived so long with chaos
that he knows how to manipulate it. It is the old theme of *The
Confidence Man.* He is a figure in a country with no solid past or
stable class lines; therefore he is able to move about easily from
one to the other. *(He pauses, thoughtfully.)*

You know, I'm still thinking of your question about the use of
Negro experience as material for fiction. One function of serious
literature is to deal with the moral core of a given society. Well, in
the United States the Negro and his status have always stood for
that moral concern. He symbolizes among other things the human
and social possibility of equality. This is the moral question raised
in our two great 19th century novels, *Moby Dick* and *Huckleberry
Finn.* The very center of Twain's book revolves finally around the
boy's relations with Nigger Jim and the question of what Huck
should do about getting Jim free after the two scoundrels had sold
him. There is a magic here worth conjuring, and that reaches to the
very nerve of the American consciousness—so why should I
abandon it? Our so-called race problem has now lined up with the
world problems of colonialism and the struggle of the West to gain

the allegiance of the remaining non-white people who have thus far remained outside the Communist sphere; thus its possibilities for art have increased rather than lessened. Looking at the novelist as manipulator and depictor of moral problems, I ask myself how much of the achievement of democratic ideals in the U.S. has been affected by the steady pressure of Negroes and those whites who were sensitive to the implications of our condition; and I know that without that pressure the position of our country before the world would be much more serious than it is even now. Here is part of the social dynamics of a great society. Perhaps the discomfort about protest in books by Negro authors comes because since the 19th century American literature has avoided profound moral searching. It was too painful and besides there were specific problems of language and form to which the writers could address themselves. They did wonderful things, but perhaps they left the real problems untouched. There are exceptions, of course, like Faulkner who has been working the great moral theme all along, taking it up where Mark Twain put it down.

I feel that with my decision to devote myself to the novel I took on one of the responsibilities inherited by those who practice the craft in the U.S.: that of describing for all that fragment of the huge diverse American experience which I know best, and which offers me the possibility of contributing not only to the growth of the literature but to the shaping of the culture as I should like it to be. The American novel is in this sense a conquest of the frontier; as it describes our experience, it creates it.

What's Wrong with the American Novel

American Scholar / 1955

From the *American Scholar* (Autumn 1955), 464–503. Copyright 1955 by the *American Scholar*. Reprinted by permission.

This is the stenographic record of a discussion held at a private residence in Manhattan on Tuesday evening, July 16, 1955. Present were the following persons: **Stephen Becker,** author of *The Season of the Stranger;* **Simon Michael Bessie,** general editor of Harper & Brothers; **Ralph Ellison,** author of *Invisible Man;* **Albert Erskine,** managing editor of Random House; **Jean Stafford,** author of *Boston Adventure* and *Children Are Bored on Sunday;* **William Styron,** author of *Lie Down in Darkness;* and **Hiram Haydn,** editor of the *American Scholar.*

Mr. Haydn: We are gathered here, as you know, ladies and gentlemen, to discuss the question "What's wrong with the American novel?"

I think when I invited each of you I told you at the time that it was quite possible that this discussion might be printed under the title, "What's right with the American novel?" but there is a reason for beginning with the negative proposition, and that is that I particularly wanted to have in the group tonight some of the outstanding younger American novelists, and at least several of the younger outstanding editors in the book publishing field, because the elder statesmen have been heard a great deal, whether as practitioners or as critics or in whatever relation to the subject.

Some of you, to be sure, have been heard and heard extensively, but not, to the best of my knowledge, in an expository fashion.

One little footnote first: We say the question concerns the American novel. I see no reason why the discussion shouldn't include the contemporary novel in other countries as well, but I do hope that we can keep it primarily concerned with the American novel.

I said a moment ago that I started this with the negative question for a real reason.

I have read or heard or overheard a great many times during the last few years the statement, with varying degrees of intensity and heat, that the American novel at present is not very distinguished.

I have heard it said that the American novel reached its most recent peak in the twenties, and that when the generation of Dreiser and Anderson had had its day, we had seen the end of our "golden period," so to speak.

I have heard that statement extended another generation, with the opinion that after Hemingway, Faulkner, Thomas Wolfe, Fitzgerald and Dos Passos, we have had nothing to equal them.

I have heard animadversions of this sort against the contemporary novel: that we have now really only two general kinds of American novels. One is a popular kind, read by a great many people, which is essentially reportorial. Frequently the word "reportorial" is used with derogatory intent; it is said scornfully that our novelists come out of journalistic or correspondent backgrounds; that many of them are graduates from *Time* magazine and *Life* magazine, and that this is reflected in their work which is highly competent, but somewhat—if not wooden—at least slick and highly polished; that they lack substance, density, texture, thought, vitality. The other group of our novelists, it is said, are those who are in perhaps a more traditional sense interpreters or critics of life, of the main arteries of human experience. It is claimed that they have come to be mandarins; that they write only for themselves and a few others; that they largely coexist in academic circles; that they have lost touch with the main currents of our times and have little or nothing to say to more than a small audience.

Now, as a matter of fact, I have heard many others, and some even worse things said. So it seems to me there have been enough charges of this sort to warrant putting our question, if not "What's Wrong with the American Novel?" then "Is There Anything Wrong with the American Novel?"

Would someone like to speak to one of these points?

Mr. Becker: I will speak to two of them at once. Mike and I have already had fifteen minutes on them at dinner. I started to think about this a couple of days ago.

It seems to me that part of the problem is not the fact that the American novel itself has declined, but that the novel has ceased to be what its public used to expect.

The point I make is that in the old days—before Dickens, let's say—there was a class of people who could write and could read within a kind of common frame of reference, so that the artist's excellence was understood as excellence, what he said was understood, and everyone who read books at all knew enough to interpret them and to apply them to his own life.

Nowadays, we have fewer and fewer people interested in what is done in a literary sense, and more and more people interested in what can help them practically or what will ameliorate their everyday life.

Mr. Haydn: Do you mind if I interrupt before the second point, just for a moment, on this one?

You speak of an audience that was there, a knowledgeable audience which read and wrote, and you suggest the period before Dickens. I suddenly wondered how old the novel is. As we know it, it began perhaps a hundred years before Dickens in England.

Mr. Becker: About that, yes.

Mr. Haydn: And this goes back to Defoe, is that right? And then you have Fielding, Richardson, Smollett and Sterne and a host of minor novelists up to Scott, Jane Austen, and so on.

I'm not really challenging what you say. I am just wondering whether we should take this for granted, whether this audience matter applies specifically to the novel at that time, or rather to other literary circles.

Of course we know that statistical, quantitative literacy has increased enormously. Now the question is, is there really no longer a qualitatively literary audience in your sense?

Mr. Becker: No, I won't say that at all, but I will say that of the people who read nowadays a smaller percentage cares for the serious novel than the percentage of people in 1790 or 1820.

Mr. Haydn: I'm sure a smaller percentage, but you mean more than that, don't you? You mean a smaller number?

Mr. Becker: No, I don't mean a smaller number. There were fewer people reading in those days than read now.

But my second point may throw a little light on this. I think when you talk about the reportorial writers you get close to what people want to read nowadays, what people do read.

There is a whole slew of badly thought out novels, of witness books, of good or bad nonfiction, which seems to mean more to people, possibly because back in the old days there was a certain series of factors that the novel had to reflect or explain that we don't have now.

I am borrowing from Malraux's thesis about art when he says that in medieval times there was a common knowledge that was so restricted that any symbol in any painting was understood by anyone who looked at that painting, and nowadays in modern art you don't have that. There are hundreds of splinters; and the same thing may be true in literature where people read what concerns them most immediately, but are not concerned with broad generalizations, with the basic facets of life that the novelist concerns himself with. Nonfiction largely has become of greater importance to people who read. The novel has become more and more entertainment and less and less guidance or art.

Mr. Haydn: Now there are two or three things from what you said there that I'd like to follow up.

Mr. Becker: By the way, I would like to be challenged successfully on this thing. I don't like to be pessimistic.

Mr. Bessie: The implication is that I didn't challenge it before at dinner, but that isn't so.

Miss Stafford: I wonder if you were talking about the novel or the decline of the audience.

Mr. Becker: For the novelist to be alive, you have to have some sort of an audience to keep him alive. Let me say right now that I think the people Hiram referred to are dead wrong when they say that the novel is not now what it used to be. For every one man who could write English well with some grace and some style fifty years ago, there are ten now.

Mr. Haydn: When you say that the novel has never been anywhere near as good as it is now, are we limiting it to the American and maybe the English novel?

Mr. Becker: For simplicity's sake, yes.

Mr. Haydn: I think of about seven or eight giants in the nineteenth century that we have to go a way to match yet, but most of them are not American or English.

Mr. Bessie: Can I pick up from that for a minute, because I think, before we get into that too far, we ought to discuss or agree or disagree on whether or not the novel is in that shape. We ought to go back to the subject of whether it's wrong or right.

We have had a lot of writing and opinion on the decline of the novel in America and elsewhere, and it struck me that the thing that is most impressive about this is that there are two things thought of when people say this:

That novels, for some reason or other, don't seem to be selling as well as they used to. That's the audience that you want to get at.

I think there's another thing that enters into this judgment when it is voiced. This goes back to what Hiram said, that there isn't any general agreement on a commanding figure to succeed the generation in America of, let's say, Hemingway, Faulkner, Dos Passos, Fitzgerald.

You get a group of people in a room talking about the novel and they are likely not to find anybody after that generation on whom they agree as a "naturally" first-rank figure in the American novel.

I think you have to agree on that before you can get into what's wrong with it. You have to agree on whether or not you think the novel has declined.

I happen not to. I happen not to believe that, for example, the sale of the novel in the large, which really means the reading of the novel, is off. I don't believe that, and I haven't seen figures that could show it.

Mr. Erskine: I could prove the opposite very quickly.

Mr. Bessie: That more people are reading novels? That's right, I think you could. So the audience—I think at least quantitatively, which doesn't get at what you were saying directly, but it begins there—quantitatively has increased. I think maybe you disagree with me, but I don't think novel reading can be shown statistically to be off.

Mr. Haydn: Isn't there something that ought to be said right here? Probably Steve Becker was not saying that not so many people were reading novels, but that he didn't believe there was as much of an audience now for what will again require a definition—the serious novelist.

Mr. Becker: That's right.

Mr. Ellison: That's so.

Mr. Erskine: Steve said so many things, but in talking about the pre-Dickens era and mentioning the time around 1790 and following, he said that there was a group of people of considerable size who had the equipment to appreciate the artistic virtues of a good novel. This is something that I would question a great deal.

Mr. Haydn: So would I.

Mr. Becker: I didn't say "of a considerable size."

Mr. Erskine: I don't think they ever thought in terms of good and bad novels, because as I remember the record, there was not much discussion at that time of what is a "good" novel—the sort of high-powered analysis that we are accustomed to.

Mr. Becker: I didn't mean to say that there was a large audience, but the audience was homogeneous intellectually, in the sense that if you read books at all—I am floundering now a little bit.

Mr. Bessie: Do you think the novel has declined?

Mr. Becker: No, I don't think so. You are being terribly blunt in cutting the whole conversation short. No, I don't think so.

Mr. Bessie: I think we ought to try to get that one, because this is the basic thing, isn't it?

Mr. Haydn: Gentlemen, one thing at a time. This is the basic thing, but one way is to creep around it and surround it, and the other way is to give it a frontal attack.

Mr. Bessie: It will repel it so fast that we will be routed in no time if we give it a frontal attack.

Mr. Ellison: Isn't it possible that the novels of the Dickens period and of the nineteenth century and even of the early twentieth century—isn't it possible that these books, aside from their high artistic qualities (most of which we have assumed, though Dostoyevsky and some of the other giants never did succeed in writing what we call a perfect novel) expressed a sense of wonder which gave the audience, a great part of it being the ordinary newspaper reader, a grasp of contemporary change; a sense of wonder arising out of the multiplicity of events being reduced to form; a sense of discovery?

Mr. Haydn: Well, at the same time, certainly some of those same generations gave the opposite effect, gave with great intensity the sense of what was familiar—say, *Madame Bovary* and *Fathers and Sons*.

Mr. Ellison: But the *newness* within the familiar, it was discovery in that sense, a leap from the known to the unknown. Otherwise the reader would not have had a connection with the newly revealed aspect of reality. *Madame Bovary* became *bovarysme*. It named a situation which, although familiar, had never been so well defined before.

We don't manage to do that so often.

Mr. Haydn: I wish you would elaborate that. I don't think I fully understand it.

Mr. Ellison: Maybe I don't myself. All right. Any day I may walk down 125th Street, say from 8th Avenue on over to Lenox or Fifth, I can see people gesturing wildly on the street; I can hear wild political statements; I can see dope addicts; I can see people acting out wild fantasies; I can see people clinging to rural ways in a hopped-up, whirlwind industrial environment; I can see youth gangs acting fantasies of violence.

Of course, I can do that on 6th Avenue and 42nd Street, too.

I can see clashes of taste in dress, music, religion, morals—everything.

I see a whole chaotic world existing within the ordered social pattern—with the cops on the corner, the busses running on schedule, the subways on schedule, and so forth—everything that it takes to keep a big city operating—and I can see a million contradictions to that order.

I can see all the details of experience which we pass by daily and never stop to define; or, when we do, we attempt it only in sociological terms which cut the heart out of it. As far as the individual man who is caught up within this experience is concerned, he is living out the chaos within the recognized order and though he might be only vaguely aware of it his sense of reality is affected. He is more apt to get a sense of wonder, a sense of self-awareness and a

sharper reflection of his world from a comic book than from
most novels.

Mr. Haydn: Let me ask you this to see if I understand.

It seems to me that you are saying that we fail to see and
communicate to readers, now, all sorts of new things in your
sense, which have not been examined by most readers. But it seems
to me that the emphasis ought to be rather on the fact that the
first-rate novelist has always had a capacity to convey his own
peculiar vision of what is not necessarily new, but—because it's
his unique vision—which makes new insights for the reader.

Mr. Ellison: But don't do violence to what I am saying.

Mr. Haydn: I don't mean to. I'm just trying to find out. Is that
what you mean?

Mr. Ellison: Not simply the new, but the undefined: those areas
of experience which have not been written about—not that they aren't
familiar; they have been lived over and over and over again.

Mr. Haydn: Excuse me, that is what I thought you meant, and
maybe I haven't made clear what I mean, which is that I don't think
it matters very much whether anyone has ever written about the
particular sequence of chaoses that you were describing earlier;
that what rather matters is that the writer himself has the original
vision to bring his own particular and, therefore, new insights to
material which may have been written about hundreds of times, but
which is always shifting, always changing, always new when a
new intelligence comes to bear upon it.

Mr. Ellison: Well, yes. But now we have a kind of competition
with the novel. That is, as I get it, in the early days when the
novel came into being (and before it became super-conscious of
itself as an art form), society had begun to shift, and the novel
was about these new things which were happening so fast that men
needed to get an idea of what was simply temporary and what
was abiding, what was valuable and what was destructive. Society
was new and the form was new, so the writer could work from
two approaches. He could concentrate on the development of the
novel as a literary form, and he could describe the new processes
of society, the emergence of new personality types.

So Balzac could describe how fortunes were made and how
careers were made, how newspapers operated. A writer could

deal with all of this as process and have people read it with a sense
of discovery. They could say, "Yes, this is how it is!" because by
describing it the novelist had made it real; he had snatched reality
from chaos.

But it moved much more slowly than our reality. I mean when
you jump to the United States, say after the Civil War, things just
go a mile a minute; and it's been possible, after Melville and Twain
and that crowd, to make a fairly great novel without touching
one-tenth of the new experience in this country, or even the day-to-
day experience. Where the earlier novel could deal with the new
fairly easily, could see the emerging pattern and describe it and be
satisfied, our twentieth-century writers were bombarded by
change and they restricted their range. Where Balzac took on a
whole society, they settled for a segment.

That is, when Melville wrote *Moby Dick* whaling was a great
industry. He could start by describing this industrial process and
take off from this into realms of symbolism, metaphor, philosophy
and what not, and give you that tremendous sense of discovery which
lies within the familiar. And he could do it and get in all the racial
and social and cultural types, too; all the diverse peoples which
make the country so exciting.

However, Hemingway wrote for years and years, and wrote well,
I think, and so what? How many of our diverse peoples could
really move into his early work?

Mr. Bessie: You've got to explain that last thing a little bit,
because I got you up through Melville, although I'll argue with you
about it, but where's the Hemingway point?

Mr. Ellison: Well, the Hemingway point is this: that here was a
concentration mainly upon technique. Here was a concentration
upon the revolution of the word, and here was the delineation of a
philosophical attitude which expressed what many people, what
many Americans felt in the aftermath of the First World War. A
statement of disillusionment given style.

This defined reality for them and defined their predicament, but
even while this was being praised, reality was ripping along.
What happens?

The Depression comes. Attitudes change and men who only a
few years before had seen themselves in the image of the Heming-

way hero looked around for other images of themselves. Hemingway had his style and his mastery to keep him going; but when I came here in 1936, I found many literary reputations dead which had been very much alive, say, in 1935, when I was still in the South.

Mr. Haydn: Excuse me, let me just try to summarize here a moment. I see one link between what you've been saying and what Steve was saying.

You both seem to be saying that you feel that there has been a failure of audience.

Mr. Ellison: No. There has been a failure of writers.

Mr. Haydn: Well, then I've discovered one thing. One of you says a failure of audience and one of you says a failure of writers, but both of you are talking in quite different terms and idioms about one generality, if I quote you right, and that generality is this:

The whole complex of life in our time is so much more fragmented, so much more, as Thomas Wolfe would call it, "manyfooted," maybe; so much more manifold, there is so much more obvious diversity, that it is very difficult—says which of you?

Mr. Becker: Possibly both.

Mr. Haydn: It is very difficult for an audience to have the sense of rapport, to take only one example, with the context of symbolism within which a particular artist may work, for one thing; and that, on the other hand, you, Ralph, are saying that you feel that the artist has failed to take advantage—

Mr. Ellison: That's right.

Mr. Haydn: (Continuing)—of what you find to be the manifestly new facets of life in our time, and hence doesn't convey a sense of them to his readers, or doesn't find that audience which is searching for new ideas, new experience, new expression of that experience, within this form.

Mr. Ellison: Yes, we continue to write the books which should have been written ten or twenty years ago.

Mr. Styron: And may I say this: that I think that a large part of what you were talking about concerning the early writers—the Sternes, the Smolletts, and so on—was simply that they were often writing something equivalent to pure entertainment.

It seems to me that we simply have nowadays just too much competition with the novel.

Miss Stafford: What's the competition?

Mr. Styron: We have television.

Mr. Ellison: I don't mean that.

Miss Stafford: Sociologists.

Mr. Ellison: Sociologists and everything; and events themselves are so much more momentous than they were in those relatively placid times.

Mr. Styron: Events are momentous, and one sees these events in moving pictures and on television. I think that fills in a huge gap which novels used to fill, but very rarely do any longer.

Mr. Haydn: This may also relate to the reportorial tradition.

Mr. Styron: Yes.

Mr. Ellison: Yes, isn't this only because novelists want to compete? I mean, after all, we start writing sociology. We went through the phase in which everything had to be psychoanalyzed. And that has really nothing to do with fiction.

Miss Stafford: What happens is that we become so inhibited, we are so afraid that we won't parse medically or sociologically.

Mr. Haydn: Let me put a general proposition to you, just something to knock over, because this will do something that Mike suggested a while back; it will at least bring the focus back on "Is the novel worse or better, or for the most part unchanging in this sense: the same proportion of good, the same proportion of bad?"

The only way we can get at this, perhaps including the point that Steve made when he was talking about the *serious* novel, is to attempt a definition. So let me set myself up as a clay pigeon, and say that a novel is a long story which contains a certain number of characters and various elements of conflict, usually having a beginning, a development, and a climactic culmination.

I'm not ready to be knocked down yet. Now, before I get at the serious novel, let's say that there is a kind of novel which, however expert or competently done in whatever terms, is primarily intended or is almost exclusively intended for entertainment and/ or inspiration on a relatively superficial level—suppose we include the excitement of the mystery, and so on.

Then I offer you this for the serious novel as something just to knock down: that the concern of the serious novelist is always to extract—no, that's a bad word, "extract"—is always to find and express what is peculiarly and continuingly human in whatever experience he chooses to record.

Now, that sounds awfully vague, I guess, but I mean it as against the sociologist who is concerned basically in finding what certain large tendencies among human beings are, against the reporter whose attempt is to present the more or less precise facts of a given event, against the function of a psychologist or clinician who is attempting to discover body, mind, or whatever you want to call it, relationships, which could have been the cause of particular actions, and so on.

The novelist is concerned with the basic and permanent human relationships: to put them in the simplest and perhaps most old-fashioned way, with man's relationship to himself, to other men, to the society in which he lives, to the natural universe in which he finds himself, and perhaps to God.

Now, knock me down.

Mr. Bessie: There's too much in there to knock it down. It sounds fine to me. It's all there. I won't knock that down.

Mr. Styron: Yes.

Mr. Becker: I would add to it something that bears on what Ralph said a minute ago, that he tries to find, in the words you use, what is continuing, and to present it in some fresh way that will make its reader *aware* of the fact that it is continuing.

Mr. Styron: But just following what you started out with at the very beginning is the fact that if there is no audience to speak of, no one who cares any more for the prose expression of these relationships which you described, the novelist, at the very least, is likely to feel kind of daunted from the beginning.

Mr. Bessie: Do you think that is the case, Bill?

Mr. Styron: I think it is the case; at least it's often the way I feel.

Mr. Bessie: Let me play the devil's advocate on this, because if you feel that way, it might be quite complicated as to why you feel that way.

Mr. Styron: Of course.

Mr. Bessie: But Ralph named a book which was a spectacularly unappealing book to large numbers of people, and which failed to find an audience for years.

Mr. Styron: Namely, *Moby Dick.*

Mr. Bessie: Yes. A book which—I don't know if you like it as much as I do or not—but it would seem almost impossible for me, for somebody with any kind of serious pleasure concerned with the novel, not to read it and see that it is a very, very good book.

Well, a large number of people managed not to read that book for a long, long time, and if we are talking about the declining novel, is it declining or isn't it?

Mr. Styron: Well—

Mr. Haydn: Just one more point, and I really hope that all of you will open up on this; that even with the qualifications made, and if you accept my definition, my purpose in giving it is to give us a working basis in getting together on the central question.

Here is some kind of yardstick by which you can answer the question for yourselves.

Do you believe that in the face, to be sure, of all the chaos and confusion and complexity and diversity, and incidentally, the great and terrific speeds with which we can cover great distances in our time, and so on, and hence become familiar with things that were most exotic a hundred years ago—in the face of all this, nevertheless, are a large number of our novelists continuing to deal with these basic human experiences in, what shall I say, in a strong, in an effective, in a stimulating—I don't know what to say—

Mr. Bessie: Satisfactory.

Mr. Styron: I think they are. I start with the end of World War II, just for convenience's sake. We have had quite a few novels, I think, which deal very strenuously with the human condition. Nonetheless, there seems to be, at least I feel, a lack of interest in these statements.

I think that people have ignored these statements.

Mike, I think you were very right about Melville, and *Moby Dick* in particular, but *Moby Dick* was preceded by, I think, two novels, *Typee* for one. And Melville was an extremely well-known entertainer.

Mr. Erskine: It was preceded also by several others.

Mr. Styron: That's true.

Mr. Bessie: Don't let Melville stop you, because you're getting somewhere.

Mr. Haydn: You had just reached the place where you were saying that you felt there had been strong, effective and satisfying novels out of the last war, but that you felt—

Mr. Styron: Or since then. Not necessarily war novels.

Mr. Bessie: You haven't found the proper response, and by response you mean readers, not critics.

Mr. Styron: Yes, readers.

Mr. Haydn: How do you measure that?

Mr. Styron: I don't know.

Mr. Haydn: In numbers?

Miss Stafford: What do you mean by saying that there has been no concern?

Mr. Styron: Well, let me try to go into that.

I think Ralph's book, for instance, is a book which in another century, say the nineteenth, would have reached a much larger audience than, in proportion, it has in our time.

Mr. Ellison: That's when it should have been written. (Laughter)

Mr. Bessie: You are being suppositious, Bill; you just can't know, can you?

Mr. Styron: You really can't know, but it's just intuition.

Mr. Haydn: What I wonder is something that I have heard, really since, literally, I was a little boy, and more from American men than women: the remark, "I like to read facts"—now, I am leaving out the woman's magazine audience; I am talking about the people who might be a serious audience for this serious kind of novel—and I remember what was for me almost the *locus classicus* of this, when I was a young, ardent man sitting next to a famous clergyman at dinner, and I was so embarrassed, anyway, to be talking to him, I didn't know what to do.

Finally, I talked about what I was interested in, and asked him whether he had ever read Thomas Mann's *Magic Mountain,* and he said, "I have no time for light reading." (Laughter)

This is one little, tiny incident that is really symptomatic of a great many conversations that I have had a great many places, that somehow there is, I think, a very large representation of the kind of mentality in our society in our times which feels that the novel is, after all, if not light, at least somehow special, somehow for *other* kinds of people.

Miss Stafford: You can't read it before noon.

Mr. Bessie: That's right. It's not very long ago, if not even more recently, that the proper Edwardian could say, without feeling self-conscious, that somebody who was a novel reader was light-minded.

Mr. Styron: What?

Mr. Bessie: Light-minded. And the thing that fascinates me about this is that in relation to what we are talking about now, I think that if you feel that the novel in American society has declined, either in its own merits or in its audience, you have to explain something which you may not agree with, but which I feel very strongly, that the novel has a higher prestige today than at almost any other time.

That is, I think in the community it's a matter of higher prestige to be a novelist, and I think that a high accomplishment in a novel is probably as high as it's ever been.

I think the very intensity of the conversation about the novel, and the amount of just sheer attention paid to it—

Mr. Styron: What community is this? I don't mean to be facetious.

Mr. Bessie: I hoped we could stay away from present company— but there isn't anyone in this room who hasn't had a reasonably successful response—any writer, I mean.

Mr. Styron: Reasonable standards.

Mr. Bessie: That's right. I don't know what you mean when you say this sense of the audience being so far behind you that you can't feel that they are there, that you feel the absence of an audience.

Mr. Styron: I'm a great television viewer these days, because I have one.

Mr. Bessie: Because *you* have one?

Mr. Styron: Yes, because *I* have one, thank you. And I don't read novels. (Laughter)

Mr. Bessie: Because it's there.

Mr. Styron: I do. It came with the house. Take a quiz program I was watching—a gruesome one (I was looking at it, anyway)—and the M.C. asked the audience, he said (this is a new approach to a quiz program)—he asked the audience three or four simple questions, starting with: "Was Davy Crockett a real or fictitious person?" A terrific "Real!"

"What is the capital of the United States?" "Washington."

And then, finally (it surprised me), "Who wrote *Look Homeward, Angel?*"

Well, the man who wrote the show, I don't know where he got the question, but there was an absolute dead silence, a total dead silence.

Now, admittedly, this was a simpleheaded audience. It's true that they aren't novel readers.

Mr. Bessie: Who admits this?

Mr. Styron: I admit this.

Mr. Bessie: On the basis of the results?

Mr. Styron: You're cutting me too close.

Mr. Bessie: Pardon me. (Laughter)

Mr. Styron: A group of people who do not read novels.

Mr. Haydn: One question, Bill, which really, I think, is relevant to that is: Aren't we confusing something here? Aren't these the rough equivalents of the people who fifty years ago, perhaps one hundred years ago (witness all the people who waited for the new edition of some of Dickens' novels) really were not (in the sense we have defined) readers of serious novelists, but readers of novelists who were entertainers; and that Dickens had this side to him, which was what made him so popular; and that now there are other forms in which they seek that entertainment?

Miss Stafford: And quite possibly a similar audience would not be able to tell you who the author of that was.

Mr. Haydn: That's right.

Mr. Erskine: They just knew what magazine it was appearing in.

Mr. Bessie: That's right.

Mr. Styron: I think in France today—do they have quiz shows in France, Mike?

Mr. Bessie: They haven't got TV yet on our scale, but they have them on radio, I believe.

Mr. Styron: You have simple-minded audiences in France, but if they were asked who wrote *Jean Christophe,* I think there would be at least seven or eight voices from the audience who would answer the name of the author.

Mr. Haydn: It is not peculiar to the immediate situation of the American novel, but to the American people?

Mr. Styron: Yes, which is the way that Steve started: that we face a rather weird 165 million deaf people, in a way.

Mr. Ellison: Let's look at it from this point of view. After all, the novel entertains, it expresses a partial vision, it celebrates a human condition, and it does all this by communicating, and it communicates on the basis of some things known and a hell of a lot that is unknown.

I am just unwilling to turn that audience over to television.

Mr. Bessie: Do you think that audience has been thrown over to television?

Mr. Ellison: I think that we are now getting away from this attitude, but I think that for much too long, American novelists have set up certain aesthetic ideals which they are trying to realize; that these aesthetic ideas and ideals came to us in the guise of certain class values, certain regional values, and certain—well, for want of a better word—national values, which very often have gotten in the way of the novelist's sense of reality. For a long time if you asked someone what an American was, he would usually describe an Anglo-Saxon of New England background—really one of many American types.

Something else has had a lot to do with the lack of communication between the novelist and his larger audience, and that is an over-investment in certain stylistic methods, a kind of snobbery of style.

But if artistic excellence is to be achieved only through a Henry James type of technique (and certainly there is artistic excellence there) to the exclusion of that great mass of experience which will not be hammered into shape by such delicate subtleties, then you are going to lose a great part of that audience.

Mr. Becker: How far would you go in the other direction?

Mr. Ellison: That the audience is without responsibility or that they have responsibility, but this is what we start with. You can't complain really about the audience.

My task is to reach them, doing the least violence to what I think are the great artistic achievements of the craft.

Mr. Haydn: I certainly like the angle you are coming in at, but I just have to say this, by way perhaps of initiating Act II, Scene 2, and it comes directly from what you have been saying.

We have talked a lot about the audience and perhaps we can summarize that later, but as far as the artist goes, isn't it true that those imaginative writers whom we have always thought of as great, to use a word which is currently not popular, at least in this sense, have meant something very real, both to the learned and to the simple; that, applying that test, I look around me and find many brilliant practitioners but relatively few who are of the first rank in having something to convey to all kinds and conditions of people.

That does not mean that I think the American novel is going to the dogs, but it does mean that I miss this kind of major voice, with a few exceptions.

This ties in, too, with something that both Steve and you said earlier, for it is mighty hard, perhaps, to grasp in any comprehensive fashion so highly complex a world as the one we live in, and to communicate your sense of it to all kinds of people. The ones who have done this the most effectively in literature, it seems to me, have come at the end of established orders, like Dante, who gave a great imaginative vision of a world order—the one you were referring to, Steve—that was really in a sense ending already, but which he could encompass, it was there to see in clarity. Only it required a great poetic talent to lift it to the quality that it had.

Similarly, in other periods, as when John Milton wrote an epic poem, the world view that that epic poem contained was familiar to everybody, to the learned and the simple alike.

You see, this gets back to where you started. Each to his own degree had some comprehension of it. I think that is true, adds some interest in it, and it is true even more certainly of Shakespeare's plays; and really epic poetry and poetic tragedies seem to me to be the forerunners of the serious novel, rather than romances and legends and tales in prose.

Mr. Erskine: Well, how many people do you think read *Paradise Lost*?

Mr. Haydn: That was a poor example.

Mr. Bessie: It depends upon what you are trying to show.

Mr. Haydn: But Shakespeare is not a poor example, but, of course, he had the advantage of the stage.

Mr. Ellison: *Crime and Punishment* was published in the newspapers.

Mr. Haydn: Witness 80,000 people in Dostoyevsky's funeral cortege, though probably some for the wrong reason.

Mr. Styron: I think, again, Dostoyevsky was serving the place of an entertainer, as fabulous as he was.

Mr. Haydn: That's true, certainly.

Mr. Ellison: Is this a negative word, Bill?

Mr. Styron: No, because a novel has to entertain of course. I don't mean to deny that.

Mr. Bessie: If you are agreeing with what Hiram is suggesting, that this is a distinction that ought to be made—

Mr. Haydn: Which is that?

Mr. Bessie: Between entertainment and the serious novel.

Mr. Haydn: I would like to check that, because I meant only that there were all these different kinds which were written almost exclusively for entertainment. I didn't mean I didn't think the serious novel was written for entertainment, too.

Mr. Erskine: When you were setting up your definition for us to shoot at, I thought you were introducing a wider range between them.

Mr. Haydn: I didn't mean to, but I neglected to say this other half.

Miss Stafford: It hasn't changed. Its intent is still to teach and to delight.

Mr. Haydn: But there are all kinds of teachings, and that's why I threw in that little side comment about "inspiration" with the entertainment for the lighter kind of novelist—because he, too, feels that he is teaching.

Mr. Becker: You've got hold of a big point here, teaching and delighting. I'm sure a lot of us are delighted by books which are in spots incomprehensible to many people.

I'm thinking of *Ulysses* now, for example. There are great gaps in my literary education. I know practically nothing about the nineteenth century. I have read *Ulysses* five times. Each time I feel more intrigued.

I can't conscientiously recommend it to everybody, but it's edifying, it's entertaining, I laugh like hell, I think it's a wonderful book, and where are you going to draw the line?

Mr. Bessie: Why draw a line?

Mr. Becker: Because if you don't draw a line, then you are putting *War and Peace* which, in the sense of words, is entirely comprehensible to anyone who wants to put in the time necessary to read it, in the same category with *Ulysses* which requires, for example, some knowledge of mythology.

Miss Stafford: *Ulysses* is *sui generis*.

Mr. Becker: That belongs to the discussion, too, somewhat.

Mr. Haydn: It's very special, even as Rabelais was, really. I mean if we don't read Rabelais, we don't know that, but if you do read it, you know that it, too, requires a special sophistication in much the same sense that *Ulysses* does.

Mr. Bessie: With this small distinction, which I would like to make: I would encourage the imitation of Rabelais and I would hope to be given the power to discourage the imitation of *Ulysses*.

Mr. Haydn: In the strict sense, Mike, discourage both imitations. If emulation, that's a different word—

Mr. Bessie: That is another session, I suppose, for another night. But the relationship of the novelist to where he comes from—

Mr. Haydn: I feel vulnerable enough about my definition of novels and great novels, but let me ask you this:

Mr. Erskine: Don't you think that *Ulysses* has complicated the life of editors perhaps as much as anything? (Laughter)

Mr. Becker: Except its counterpart, Dr. Freud. (Laughter)

Mr. Haydn: Out of all this discussion I want to come back to one thing. I'm clear only—and then perhaps only partly—on what Mr. Ellison thinks on this question. With the rest of you I am not.

Do you believe that the serious American novel, as defined and amended, is as strong today, has approximately as many strong individual practitioners as it has had in the preceding hundred years?

Mr. Styron: I would like to answer by seconding what Steve said very early; that, if anything, the quality of the novel, it seems to me, in its depth and perception, and—to use a sort of tenuous word—universality, is greater now than it ever was. Or, at last, it has greater possibilities.

Mr. Haydn: Now, starting there, I'd like to know why.

Mr. Styron: Well, go on. All right, *I'll* go on. (Laughter) I think,

for instance, that Faulkner certainly achieves a kind of greatness
that no one else since Dostoyevsky has achieved.

Now I am not a critic, and so I don't think I can go into analyzing
my feelings, but I think he is a profound novelist. I think that
most anyone who reads novels seriously will agree with that, despite
all of Faulkner's faults.

Mr. Becker: I would like to pick that up, if I may. I think that it's
very good that you put him with Dostoyevsky and not Tolstoy,
because one of the reservations that I was going to make to my
previous statement that I think that novelists today do on the
whole a better job than novelists in any period, is that it's more and
more impossible for them all the time to reflect their entire world.
They have got to do by means of examination in depth of one part
of that—

Mr. Haydn: May I stick another parenthesis in here, because I
know it won't belong anywhere else?

I believe that what you call universality comes from the intensity
with which a particular is represented, and I put alongside these
great comprehensive books—and I'm second to none in my admiration of Tolstoy—a book of the same generation called *Fathers and
Sons,* which is laid in a little provincial setting with only three or
four important characters, and the thing is so intensely and
wonderfully rendered that it just spills over the sides, and I find
meanings—

Well, I first read it in a town called South Euclid, Ohio, and I
found meanings for South Euclid, Ohio, in that book.

Now, it doesn't at all represent all of his known world, yet by
implication, by entension, it has all sorts of overtones that are tremendous.

Mr. Becker: Well, you think hard.

Mr. Haydn: Well, I'm really asking, not stating. Can't you write
today about a little patch, so to speak, and render meanings that
are universal or semi-universal?

Mr. Becker: Yes.

Mr. Ellison: It occurred to me that otherwise I would have to give
up writing novels.

Mr. Erskine: But you can't write about it with the particular limitations that Dickens had, or that someone a hundred years ago had, and satisfy a modern audience.

Mr. Haydn: You mean you cannot help—Well, did you mean something like this, Albert, for instance? I don't see how anyone, any novelist who is concerned with character at any depth or density can ignore the fact that Freud and all the other doctors and disciples and opponents, and whatever of psychology, psychoanalysis and psychiatry, have come along since.

We all know what mistakes some novelists have made, reading with a volume of Kraft-Ebing open on one side and one or another pundit on the other side, and written case histories instead of a novel.

Mr. Erskine: That's one of the things I mean.

Mr. Haydn: And it's terribly important, I think, for the novelist to let whatever he absorbs of that be absorbed, but not to give it back in the terms in which he secured it.

Mr. Erskine: Not in jargon, anyhow.

Miss Stafford: Well, anyhow, all they did was steal language from us.

Mr. Haydn: That's true, and all the good ones admit that.

Miss Stafford: The analysts wouldn't have existed if it hadn't been for the writers.

Mr. Erskine: Let me give an example, not from the distant past, but my own reaction to reading for the first time *Winesburg, Ohio* two years ago. I found this just incredibly dull, but I could understand why at the time it was published, it might not have seemed so.

Mr. Haydn: I quite agree with your judgement.

Mr. Styron: Why do you think it's dull?

Mr. Erskine: I don't know that I can really define that. It just seemed to me to be—

Mr. Bessie: It wasn't interesting?

Mr. Haydn: I reread it. You see, I read it years ago and thought it wonderful. Then I reread it not long ago, and it seemed to me apparent that Anderson, probably unconsciously, but anyway, that he was so aware of a mission, in the sense of breaking open the conventional, and as he thought of it, the hypocritical, and so on, that it had all the crudeness and rawness of some—it's hard to say,

but I'm thinking of somebody breaking ground and his consciousness of breaking ground. It is as though he had not assimilated
this way of dealing with familiar phenomena.

Miss Stafford: That is very true. You can't read *Main Street* now.

Mr. Haydn: And yet you can see what a lot of novelists owe to
him if you read it after reading his predecessors.

Mr. Ellison: And you can see why people read it, too, because I
can remember how kids used to flock into libraries to read anything
he wrote.

Miss Stafford: Certainly.

Mr. Haydn: A few years ago, on this same sideline, I had to
reread for a particular class purpose, about ten novels written in
the twenties, very famous novels, and the only one, as I think I told
you the other day, Mike, that stood up for me at all was *Point
Counter Point.*

It is not the kind of novel that I particularly like, but it is just as
strong and just as good, of its own kind, now, as it was then.

Mr. Styron: And not *A Farewell to Arms?*

Mr. Haydn: No, not to me. But what are we saying with all this?
We are saying, aren't we, that we think that in many ways the
contemporary novelist has a tougher job.

Mr. Erskine: I think that we have been talking about the novelists
of the past a great deal more than we have about the ones of
the present.

Mr. Haydn: That's very true.

Mr. Erskine: But I feel that I have, and many other people have,
a tendency in reading the eighteenth-century novel, say, to dis-
count certain things in advance when we are reading them, which
gives us a more charitable view of their work than we have toward
contemporary novels. We expect more of the contemporary.

What Ralph is talking about, that the contemporary hasn't met
the situation—we don't expect Dickens to have done this.

Mr. Haydn: To have met our situation?

Mr. Erskine: I found in rereading some of Thomas Hardy's novels
not so long ago, and reading some of those that I had never read
before, that I was just cringing with embarrassment, because I
really like this man, but I had to say, "Well, after all, he was
writing *then*."

Mr. Haydn: You are thinking of floridness and of the author intruding and of no concern for preserving the illusion, as most contemporary novelists do, through limiting their point of view to a character, and so on?

Mr. Erskine: I don't think so much that, but I think it was partly the things which seemed naive. It seems to me, I would think—

Miss Stafford: Making mistakes.

Mr. Haydn: Let me ask you this: Maybe this is a comment on those novelists, but does Shakespeare seem naive to anybody?

Miss Stafford: No.

Mr. Bessie: Hiram, Shakespeare wasn't a novelist.

Mr. Haydn: He is to me a predecessor of the serious novelist, the imaginative writer. This is to me the heritage of the best of the nineteenth-century novels rather, as I said before, than the tales in prose narrative, and so on, that preceded them.

Mr. Bessie: I don't see what your point is.

Mr. Ellison: Isn't it—whenever these first great writers, when we reread them and they fail—isn't it a failure of eloquence really, and that's precisely where Shakespeare does not fail?

We know what's going to happen, we have read the plays many times, I'm sure most of us have. I've read most of them myself. I know what's going to happen. I know the situation.

And yet the language, the eloquence itself, is what remains and what abides.

I recently reread *A Farewell to Arms,* because somehow I had a theory about it, and so I went back and reread it. Some of the guys get very, very special—anyway, I reread this book. (Laughter)

Pardon my rhetoric—but going over it again, I was very interested to see how well some of the stuff held up for me, not because I didn't know what was going to happen, and not because it hadn't been redone by Hemingway imitators over and over again, but because of the way he had done it, because of his angle of vision, and because of his own personal statement.

Mr. Styron: I agree, and that's why I cannot see why *Point Counter Point* and the novels of the twenties—

Mr. Haydn: Make some allowance for personal opinion.

Mr. Styron: I do, but I just wanted to express my own admiration of the book.

Mr. Haydn: This will probably go off the record altogether, but may I come back to your asking why did I pick this Shakespeare thing? I think that what Ralph said in a sense applies directly.

I remember the other day having some reason for going back through *Hamlet* and discovering two lines that I had never noticed before—this is the most minor kind of thing, but this had to do with the scene where Osric has come in to tell Hamlet that he must duel with Laertes and has talked all that fancy court language, and Hamlet and Horatio are commenting on him after he goes off-stage again—and I don't even remember which one said it, but one says, "He did comply with his dug before he sucked it." (Laughter)

This is what—250 years ago? Somebody help me on my arithmetic. (Laughter) Maybe 350 years ago. But that's all I mean.

Now, I think a lot of Hardy is naive one way and a lot of Meredith is naive another way, but still *Jude the Obscure*, as a whole, stands up for me very wonderfully.

Mr. Ellison: I can still remember the wrenching that I went through reading the stuff, when the girl has gone so far, and then begins to reject and fall back—oh, Lord, I suffered through this in *Jude the Obscure*.

Mr. Styron: I think the eloquence of a book like *The Naked and the Dead* is immense in its own way, and I certainly believe that just in that way the contemporary novel is alive and jumping.

Mr. Haydn: To me the one thing that is most exciting in a good novel is—well, there are two things really:

One is the sense of life, of vitality, of things coming to life, so that it ceases to be something I am reading and becomes an experience I am having, and I don't think that is being sentimental. I think it really does happen.

The other is the sense of the person behind the book, not intruding, but as I read on, the sense of—gosh, I think—

Mr. Styron: Authority?

Mr. Haydn: Yes, authority; but also originality in the sense of what is unique in one person.

Mr. Bessie: One person?

Mr. Haydn: That's another way of putting it. Do we have our fair proportion of them still?

Mr. Bessie: We can all give testimony on this, I suppose, because this then becomes confession. What you are saying now is, who are there among the living, or who have there been among the living (if it's the living we are talking about), at any rate, the modern American novelists, are there such?

Yes, I think there are.

Mr. Haydn: I suppose so. Well, I am not asking are there such—or perhaps I am asking that. But I'm asking also, is there a marked falling off in numbers among them?

Mr. Bessie: I would abdicate completely from making a numerical comparison.

You can say are there many or few or some; this is really in a sense what we are dealing with.

You see, I go back to what I said at the outset. We agree or we could agree upon almost any previous period as recently as twenty years ago on figures of major novelists, people who we thought were major in the sense in which Bill Styron set forth, but he attaches it to at least a pre-World War II generation.

Of those who came since, could we—of novelists—agree on any number of people who we felt were of comparable stature?

Is that the question that you are now raising?

Mr. Haydn: I think it is, Mike. I got a little lost.

Mr. Becker: Isn't it a little bit early to talk about figures?

Mr. Bessie: You mean in person or in numbers?

Mr. Styron: No, I'm talking about a person, a figure as a literary figure.

Mr. Haydn: I'll put it another way:

As year follows year in the 1950s, do you have this same sense of impact, with a fair degree of regularity—never mind about more or less? And I would like to know what everybody feels about that.

Mr. Styron: Well, what kind of impact was there in the twenties? Was Hemingway instantly conceived of as a figure?

Mr. Bessie: Two books, no; the third book, yes.

Mr. Haydn: Hemingway is alive. I'm talking about the state of the American novel. I asked the younger generation to come here, but I think we're talking about several living generations.

Mr. Bessie: If I were to answer it in general terms, I think what I would say is this: That I personally feel that there are a considerable number of people who are alive, moderately young and in vigor, whose works I have read, and of whom I feel that if they have not yet delivered, have produced what I consider a satisfactory work. They have the equipment and the possibility of doing so, and so I feel a sense of expectancy in that sense.

Mr. Haydn: I agree with that.

Mr. Bessie: There are a number of people of whom I feel this is true, wholly aside from the people in this room.

Mr. Haydn: The people in this room know that we think they're good or they wouldn't be here, but we agree with what you have said.

Mr. Bessie: Also, there are people who have come very, very close, if not there, to doing it, to producing a book or books which I think are as good as novels ever written anywhere.

I personally don't for a moment think that the novel is in a decline, and I don't think it's in a decline as to the figures writing it or as to the audience.

Mr. Styron: May I again address this to Ralph and Steve?

Do you feel hypothetically a sort of lesser excitement about writing than that which you might think you would feel if you were living in the twenties?

Mr. Haydn: Boy, that's a hypothetical feeling!

Mr. Styron: I know it's hypothetical, but all I'm trying to say is that there is, I think, a kind of—there was an excitement in the twenties, from what I gather in reading the literary history of the twenties, which is just not generated now—not that it's necessarily important, but that is a nagging sort of thing.

Mr. Ellison: Aren't we getting a lot about the authors all mixed up with what they were doing?

Mr. Styron: Sure.

Mr. Ellison: Yes, it was the Jazz Age, so-called, and Fitzgerald was burning the candle at both ends sometimes, and a little later on the Hemingway legend started—well, this is all very good. It caught the imagination of a lot of people.

I don't think we can put ourselves in that position, because ours is a different world. Maybe around the colleges and maybe around the *Paris Review* and so forth, you have just the same kind of excitement.

Certainly there was that kind of excitement around *Partisan*

Review during—well, we'll say around 1939, before the Nazi-Soviet Pact.

When I first came here, there was a great deal of excitement. Everyone felt that the world was really spinning along, and you had quite a number of people who were considered culture heroes.

Well, theories wear out and then you have to have something else. It's a little bit more difficult now, I think, to produce a work of art, a worthwhile work of art.

Mr. Becker: This is something I wanted to say before: that my memories of the twenties are understandably vague, but it seems to me a novel which captured you in the twenties could influence you far more than a novel that captures you now.

You may admire a book immensely—

Mr. Styron: I certainly agree.

Mr. Becker: Influencing the way you live.

Mr. Ellison: It depends on who you are, too.

Mr. Becker: Your relations with your fellow man, the kind of thing you decide you want to do.

Mr. Haydn: I'm just immensely moved. I haven't been very much of a chairman. I am immensely moved to state a heresy.

I think that the most overrated novelist in the history of American novelists is Scott Fitzgerald. I think he is a competent second-rater.

Mr. Styron: I disagree.

Miss Stafford: I disagree heartily.

Mr. Haydn: I think if anybody asked me who has outstripped him already at an early age, I would say you have. I could name some others, too, but I certainly say you have.

I only recently read *This Side of Paradise,* and I think it is a most nonsensical, sophomoric novel.

Mr. Styron: But *The Great Gatsby* is a good novel.

Miss Stafford: *The Great Gatsby* is almost a perfect novel.

Mr. Haydn: I disagree. I think it's a good novel, but it has sort of been finessed into a position which it could ill afford to have. But this is really just personal stuff, I didn't mean to throw that out.

Mr. Erskine: I think Hemingway is even more overrated.

Mr. Haydn: He is certainly my second choice.

Mr. Ellison: For me he has had a lot more to say than Fitzgerald—

definitely, *Gatsby*—fine; but Hemingway links up pretty close
to Twain.

You might feel that Twain is overrated and certainly he isn't
as subtle.

Mr. Haydn: Well, Ralph, show me the novel of Hemingway to
stand beside *Huckleberry Finn*.

Mr. Ellison: His short stories don't do so badly.

Mr. Haydn: You know, it is not altogether irrelevant, because one
of the great detractors of contemporary novels said to me just
about a week ago, "One thing I would like to point out to you," he
said, "the older generation has produced some very good novels,
and individuals in it have produced two or three very good novels,
but our new younger novelists"—he took the ones under thirty-
five—"Name one," he said, "who has followed an initial first-rate
book with a strong second or even third or even a fourth one."

Mr. Bessie: That's the mystery. That, I think, is very close to the
mystery of the "under forty" novel.

Mr. Styron: Why is that particularly important?

Mr. Haydn: Whether he has or not?

Mr. Styron: Yes.

Mr. Haydn: Well, I don't know whether it is important, but I
know that one test—I'll go this far with you—that one test of a
really first-rate novelist, I should say, as against the writer of a first-
rate novel, is that he should produce more than one first-rate
novel.

Mr. Erskine: Or even more than one novel.

Mr. Bessie: That's right.

Mr. Haydn: Well, a number of those he referred to have produced
second novels and third novels which were, most people felt,
inferior, and markedly so.

Mr. Bessie: Don't you think that there is a distinction in this
respect, Bill?

Mr. Styron: I do in a sense, but I also think—Well, take for
instance, Fitzgerald, whom I greatly admire. His first novel was a
great success. However, it's not very good. His second novel was
even worse. He had to wait until his third novel before he
produced what I think is not only good but superb.

Mr. Haydn: I think you are right, Bill, that many, many novelists

develop that way, only, also, in almost every generation some
develop the other way, and this was what this man—I'm not saying
he's right—but this is what he offered.

Mr. Becker: I think there's a reason for that, which is that a great
many people these days reach the age of twenty-five or so with a
very good basic equipment for writing and go through fairly serious
experiences which affect them seriously, heavily, at that age,
write a crackerjack novel right out of the heart, and then become
"writers," and cease to consider their art.

Mr. Haydn: Also, there is an economic factor.

Miss Stafford: Certainly.

Mr. Haydn: There must always have been an economic factor,
but I think there's a difference.

Mr. Ellison: Hemingway was writing about this in the thirties in
the *Green Hills of Africa,* and he discusses just what happens.
This is an American phenomenon. That is, not simply a phenomenon of the forties and the fifties.

Mr. Becker: I agree with Ralph that it is an American phenomenon, too.

Mr. Ellison: And one thing is the extreme fluidity of our society.
Reality changes fast, and if you don't keep up with it, you are apt
to fall into writing the same book or writing the book—I mean,
writing the book which is expected of you.

Mr. Becker: Not only that, but the veriest pauper in this country
can sometimes, very often, through education, make of himself a
good writer, and he has none of the family or the money or the
assistance from outside that many European writers get, because
belonging to a certain level of society they are expected to be
writers, professional men.

Mr. Haydn: That certainly is one factor.

Now the other one that you raised just a moment ago, Ralph,
what is expected of the writer who has produced a good first book
is not unlike—I'm tired of people bringing athletic similes into every
context—but, anyway, not unlike the second season of a baseball
player, which is notoriously a bad season.

Somehow there is a sense of pressure. Isn't that true? I don't
know. The greater amount of ballyhoo may have something to do
with it, too.

Mr. Erskine: I think that is a thing which frequently destroys people.

Miss Stafford: The ballyhoo you get. All that preliminary publicity.

Mr. Ellison: Your integrity is destroyed.

Mr. Becker: The greatest professionalism in the whole vocation.

Miss Stafford: We have the kind of thing that belongs to the stage, to the theatre, and to politics.

Mr. Bessie: Doesn't this carry a little bit back to the prestige of the novel—without trying to be too objectionable?

Mr. Styron: That is not an objectionable question at all. I think that a novelist feels that he is very definitely in competition with just what you are talking about.

Mr. Haydn: There seems to be quite a bit of prestige attached to being a novelist.

Mr. Styron: I don't object to that at all.

Mr. Bessie: If the novelist is thought of as a competitor of Jinx Falkenburg—

Mr. Styron: By whom?

Mr. Bessie: By the mass media audiences.

Miss Stafford: This is quite a vulgar note to introduce—you remember when *Forever Amber* came out, there was advance publicity for that book. She was built up the way Marilyn Monroe was, in exactly the same way.

Mr. Bessie: And in exactly the same places.

Mr. Haydn: Did you notice in *Publishers Weekly* the advance notice?

Miss Stafford: Exactly the same reasons.

Mr. Becker: These are the eternal verities.

Mr. Haydn: The advance notice for the second book: "The theme of our advertising will be the author's picture"—that was the quotation. (Laughter)

Mr. Bessie: The solution to a harrowing problem.

Mr. Haydn: Another aspect of it appeared in the paper the other day, not with someone whose reputation needs to be made, but it was on the movie page—an advertisement of *Land of the Pharaohs* saying: "Written by that winner of the Nobel Prize and the Pulitzer Prize."

Mr. Styron: And Harry Kurnitz didn't get a nickel's worth.

Mr. Bessie: But Harry had a great experience working with a great man.

Miss Stafford: I'm sure no one in this room read the sequel—well, not the sequel, but Kathleen Winsor's second book, which is called *Star Money.*

Mr. Bessie: I read the first page of it.

Miss Stafford: I have a great appetite for trash and I read this one. It's a novel about a beautiful "clothes horse" who wrote a novel in the sixteenth century, and oh, the invasion of privacy!

Mr. Bessie: And lost love!

Miss Stafford: Miserable lost love!

Mr. Bessie: But had a good apartment.

Miss Stafford: An awfully good apartment. They drank cointreau as a cocktail.

Mr. Erskine: I wanted to say at some point that this interests me a great deal, and I wasn't aware of this Kathleen Winsor thing, which indicates that even the writer of a most popular sort of fifth-rate novel then becomes aware of himself as a writer, and writes a book about the writer.

I have found in my manuscript reading, mostly of unpublished books—but this is true of many published books in the last twenty years—that writers are writing too much about writing and about writers and about the conflict between the writer and society.

And I think that is one thing that is terribly wrong with the American novel.

Mr. Styron: That sounds like Thomas Wolfe.

Mr. Ellison: How many people really know about that problem and how many people have a way into it?

Mr. Bessie: Unless it applies to everything. Unless it's darn good.

Mr. Styron: Of course.

Mr. Ellison: I would like to carry on for a minute.

Here we are, really teaching writing in colleges, which is very good. I have attended classes, I mean my friends' classes. I have never taken one.

But along with that goes a kind of piety toward standards of excellence, which is not so good; so many of the people who have taken these courses will tell you that so-and-so is good, and if you

say, well, so-and-so is also good, they'll say, oh, no, he couldn't
possibly be that good.

This is bad for this reason—here we are around the East Coast—

Mr. Haydn: Just develop that a little more. I have missed this.
Why can't so-and-so possibly be good?

Mr. Ellison: Because he wasn't called good, first by the teacher,
who very often is a novelist or a famous critic who has his own
theories and his own motives for having theories about what is
excellent, and you get a kind of ingrown thing whereby writers
write for other writers rather than writing for a big audience.

Mr. Haydn: This is one of the initial charges, you may remember,
that I quoted.

Mr. Ellison: Yes, and I agree. Certainly. And this is the great
wrong about it: that the whole tendency in American life, historically,
technologically, statistically, and every other way, is to mix up everything.

The South is becoming industrialized. It's a great industrial
frontier. They build battleships in Oklahoma, planes in Kansas.

I mean, here you have this diversity of function no longer in
stable geographical locations. You have population shifts. Washington State, which had no Negroes before World War II, or had
very few, now has a Negro problem, as such. Great masses of
Negroes went up there during the war.

You have all these great things happening; and on the other hand,
you have writers like me—though I do travel a bit, I have lived
here since 1936, and I haven't made a trip out there, or to many
other parts of the country, to learn exactly what is happening.

So how am I really going to communicate? I can communicate
out of my own personal vision and out of my personal knowledge
of that process of being transplanted and whirled around.

But time passes so fast that I could not, for the life of me,
describe what's happening to my brother who went to California
in 1938.

Mr. Becker: Wasn't one of your original points the fact that you
can take a perfectly commonplace happening and by giving it
your own fresh impetus make out of it a work of art?

Mr. Ellison: Yes, but if you aren't careful, you'll limit yourself
only to people who live pretty much the same pattern that you

live. And you are apt to limit your range of reference, the richness of your symbolism, your eloquence, to that group whose experience most closely matches the curve of your narrative.

One of the great pleasures of publishing a book was to have a fellow who did not read novels, who only read it because I wrote it, talk to me in terms which sounded like those of a "new critic."

The man said, "I read it; it meant this." And I went back—and you know, damn it, it meant that. Well, here was something. This was better than any favorable review that I got, because I felt that I had communicated with him.

Mr. Haydn: And that may not be the learned and the simple, but that's at least the initiated and the uninitiated.

Mr. Ellison: Yes. I just feel that we are called upon to do a big job, not because someone is going to give us a star on the report card, but because this is America and our task is to explore it, create it by describing it.

A Frenchman has been exploring France—each French writer explores the nature of the French personality, French reality, French culture, and the universality of the Frenchman.

He can do that. He's got a small country. We've got a big country. Here it takes more doing, but it'll be new.

Miss Stafford: I don't see that the problem for the novelist today in America is any different from that of a novelist in any point in history.

Mr. Ellison: It is not essentially, in general, Jean, but for instance, up until 1946 you got very few people, and maybe after 1946, who considered Faulkner as a readable novelist; and certainly they did not consider him as an important or a great novelist.

Now he is recognized as such.

Mr. Styron: Even by *Time* magazine. (Laughter)

Mr. Ellison: All right, by *Time* magazine.

Mr. Erskine: But not by the *New Yorker*.

Mr. Styron: Not yet.

Mr. Haydn: Ladies and gentlemen, we can continue this well on, and of course, you are all invited to. Many people have written in after these conversations and said it didn't seem that we stayed on the point. Yet no one has written in and objected to the digressions, because the digressions are often the heart of the thing.

Now, I would like to conclude this by going around the circle
from left to right, and giving each person an opportunity, if he
cares to, to say something on the central point, which is: "What is
wrong with the American novel?" or "What is right with the
American novel?" or both.

Bill?

Mr. Styron: May I do something very ungracious and pass to
Jean? Or are you taken off guard, too?

Miss Stafford: Yes, I am.

Mr. Styron: Let's pass to Mr. Erskine.

Mr. Erskine: I have nothing at this moment.

Mr. Ellison: Oh, come now, you can't do this.

Mr. Haydn: I'll start with you and come around this way.

Mr. Ellison: Well, I think that technically the American novel is
far more conscious (maybe too self-conscious) than ever before.

There is a technical awareness and mastery, which has not existed
so widely before.

I don't think that it has interested itself in communication of the
wonder of the American experience as it might. I think we are
groping toward that, and that in the younger novelists you are
getting, you are *beginning* to get it.

I was quite surprised, encouraged, to talk with writers, publishing
writers, who seemed to know absolutely nothing which occurred
before 1940. I think there is a kind of hope in that, as well as the
obvious danger.

Mr. Haydn: Thank you very much.

Steve?

Mr. Becker: I agree with Ralph that American writers are now
better equipped and, in general, can turn out better books than
they have ever done before.

I think that part of the difficulty lies in the changing functions of
the novel, again in terms of the audience. Certain jobs that the
novel used to do are now being done for far too many people by the
news magazine, by television, by periodical literature in general,
rather than by books which could be expected to last and to supply
some sort of guidance or entertainment for some time.

I think—give me a minute.

Mr. Haydn: Take your time.

Mr. Becker: We are succeeding much more thoroughly in illuminating specific areas of experience, and the only lack that I feel, and it may not be a very serious lack at all, is in the step between specific experience and universal experience, so that too many readers may pass by the total significance of the book.

I don't know whether too few writers can feel life as a whole and write a book which expresses their vision of the whole, although there are a great many who can do a wonderful job on a small part of that thing.

Mr. Haydn: Mike?

Mr. Bessie: Unfortunately, it gets more and more difficult to add to what's been said, because what's been said is so well put.

I think I would try to say these things: In the first place, I think that the very amount of concern with the state of the novel is an indication less of any decline in the novel, or any real problem with the novel, than it is of the sense of expectancy, a sense that the novel and novelists are perhaps about to give us—as we have had now at pretty swift intervals for more than a hundred years—extraordinary achievements in writing.

And they have come, on the whole, I think, fairly close. There have been quite a few of them, until I think that what we are really saying, all of us, is where is it? or where is he? or where is she? where is the novel? where is the novelist? or—although we think less in terms of groups and schools than we did a while ago—where is the group? That is the first thing.

The second thing, I think, is: Difficult as it is to produce a novel which, in the sense that Steve Becker says, encompasses the whole, I find it difficult to believe that this is a more difficult time to encompass than, for example, Stendhal's.

I have a feeling that the time in which Stendhal lived, to him and to the people who read him, was a time that justified that preposterous and wonderfully prophetic statement that so few novelists today would have the courage, in the face of publicity, to make, as Stendhal himself made about his own books.

I would sort of welcome a novelist today who would say of himself, not in the Henry Miller sense, but in the sense in which Stendhal said it: that this will be read in—well, you name the date.

I'm baffled, as an editor, by this sense, which God knows, Bill

Styron is not the only one to have, of the separation from readers. (If I'm rephrasing it badly, you'll have a chance to do it yourself.)

I don't really understand it. I have the feeling that the writer today, that the novelist today, must be as close to his reader as Balzac was, and if Balzac had this sense of alienation from his reader, I fail to find it.

And I would like to know—I don't think it's our purpose now—but I would like to know why the novelist, if he does feel this, feels it. I think that the rewards of success in the novel have become disproportionate with the merits of a novel, as we seriously know it.

A successful book brings more in acclaim and rewards than the writer knows is justified. And I think that the novelist may have a small piece of the Hollywood writer's problem of getting more of something that isn't serious in its values than he knows what to do with.

The last thing I think about the novel now is the thing that I tried to say a while ago, which is that there are so many people—I couldn't begin to name them or number them—who, I think, can write good novels, and quite a number who, I think, can write very good novels, and I think, this is why we talk about the state of the novel. Where is that very, very good one?

Mr. Haydn: Thank you.

Bill, may I come around to you now?

Mr. Erskine: Can I precede him now, because all I want to say is—

Mr. Haydn: I will ask Bill. May he precede you?

Mr. Styron: He certainly may.

Mr. Erskine: This is no summing up.

Mr. Haydn: Is this a way of evading the summing up?

Mr. Erskine: Perhaps. (Laughter)

What Mike was saying about the sense of separation from the audience that a lot of people who write novels today feel—I have encountered so many people through reading their manuscripts and through seeing them, who have written unpublished novels, and some who have written novels which have been published, who are proud of this sense of separation and who would not like to do anything about it at all, but who, if you publish their novel, and the separation continues to exist, are very much distressed about it.

I am distressed by the fact that so many people seem to feel that it is important to be separated from this corrupt world in which we live, and I think that this is a real problem.

Mr. Haydn: This is another echo from the initial impeachment from outside, isn't it? Only this is from the inside.

Ralph, you remember that I said a little while ago—

Miss Stafford: I think that certainly silences me. (Laughter)

Mr. Bessie: If you were going to say it, you've got to say it.

Miss Stafford: I will say this:

Mr. Haydn: Bill—

Mr. Styron: Of course, ladies first. (Laughter)

Miss Stafford: I don't have any sense of separation from the audience. When I'm writing I'm writing for God—

Mr. Haydn: But did Albert mean while you were writing? I don't think that he did.

Mr. Erskine: Well, I didn't mean you.

Miss Stafford: Let's not let this get to be a personal quarrel.

Mr. Haydn: But you didn't mean the writer had this sense of separation while he was in the act of writing, did you?

Mr. Erskine: I think the ones that I'm talking about have it from the very beginning.

Mr. Haydn: Have it perennially?

Mr. Erskine: Yes. They like to think that this is too good for people to read, and then when people don't read it, they are disappointed.

Mr. Haydn: I would then like to ask you a question: How many of these are in your opinion really first-rate writers?

Mr. Erskine: I think that some of them basically are, but they have gotten, out of the air, or somewhere, this notion. I don't know how to explain it.

Mr. Haydn: Because—

Mr. Erskine: They like to think that they are Shelley, that they will be appreciated after they are dead.

Mr. Haydn: I think that the prime examples of this could not possibly uphold this point of view logically and still submit their books to publishers.

Mr. Bessie: Oh, Hiram, if you're going to be a full-time masochist, you're going to get somebody to hurt you.

Mr. Haydn: Well, all right.

Mr. Erskine: Well, don't you know these?

Mr. Bessie: I do, indeed.

Mr. Becker: What is behind it? A great contempt for the American public?

Mr. Erskine: Something like that.

Mr. Bessie: I don't think there is anything—

Mr. Styron: I really would like to know about that.

Mr. Haydn: I do agree with you both. I don't know. I know people who talk like that, but my God!

However, I really don't know how anyone, if you make the most modest effort to track it down, can defend this point of view, and seriously go on and submit his book to you and ask it to be published, holding his nose, and then count—well, you said this, didn't you—and then count how many advance orders you have and how many reorders you get after publication.

So that this simply annihilates the whole argument. I don't mean your argument. I mean theirs.

Mr. Bessie: This is thoroughly out of turn, but I don't think there is any particular relationship between what Bill was talking about and what Albert was talking about at all.

Mr. Haydn: I don't either.

Mr. Bessie: If Bill would say, I would be very interested personally in what he means about this.

Mr. Haydn: In spite of the resemblance that you have begun to bear to either Mr. Sherlock Holmes or to Dr. Watson, I forget which, on the trail of the notorious—well, I would like to say I don't think any of us thought there was any relation.

Mr. Bessie: I'm sure that I just wanted to get to Bill.

Mr. Styron: Will you just briefly say what you're getting at?

Mr. Bessie: The first thing that you said, which you haven't had a chance to get back to, about the feeling that the novelist today— well, you said nobody is interested in the document. Nobody is interested in what it is that he produces, the statement, or something like that.

Mr. Styron: Something like that.

Mr. Haydn: That he misses the feeling of a really interested, concerned audience.

Mr. Styron: Now, you want me to elaborate on that?

Mr. Bessie: Not if you don't want to.

Mr. Styron: I don't know precisely how to, but I'll try.

I think Steve said, at least one of the first hypotheses, was that of a missing public. Isn't that right? Or, at least the suggestion of that.

And I still feel, I mean all glitter aside, all Hollywood aside, all romance aside, that the novelist in America today is a writer who is writing to an audience which is specialized as never before; that Melville, *Moby Dick* aside, was a tremendously—he was read in—I don't know what the population of the U.S.A. was in 1850. But I would imagine that the proportion of his readers was just fantastically greater than it is now.

Mr. Erskine: You would be wrong.

Mr. Styron: All right, then I would be wrong.

Do you mean to tell me—we will have to check on that. Disregard the Melville remarks. Nevertheless, I think the writer, at least I do, I feel a tremendous kind of—I feel I should be like the fellow who was sure to write for television some time. I really do.

Mr. Bessie: Why?

Mr. Styron: I feel that if there is a possibility to be moved by a medium, I think there's a possibility to be moved by the television medium. I don't say that I'm even going to think about being a TV writer, but if there is this possibility, why should I not write for television?

Mr. Bessie: Maybe you like words.

Mr. Styron: I love words, but then, again, there's the economic factor.

Mr. Bessie: This is a really serious point.

Mr. Becker: You always want to reach more people than you do.

Mr. Styron: Of course you do. For instance, if on a one-night program at CBS, something like that, I could reach—oh, I don't know how many, 14 million people—

Mr. Bessie: You can tell me what you mean by reaching.

Mr. Erskine: Yes. (Laughter)

Mr. Styron: Well, look, the movies have done it. Why can't TV do it? I have seen movies which have moved me. Why don't I write for the movies or TV instead of books?

Mr. Ellison: Your books move people. Your works—

Mr. Styron: But if I can write in a medium, without sacrificing my sincerity and my integrity, which will reach more people, why should I not do that?

Mr. Bessie: I'll give you the answer very simply. The answer is because you don't use yourself to the extent and in the way that you want to use yourself.

Mr. Styron: How do you know?

Mr. Bessie: I know by the fact that you haven't done it. That's the only way I can know. I know an awful lot of people who have done it, and this is one of the problems—a lot of people find it not only more rewarding economically and in acclaim, and also get a sense of contact with a larger number of zeroes by talking through TV or the movies to a greater audience than they do in a novel. If this is their satisfaction, I say more power to them.

Mr. Ellison: It is not really a task, is it? I can remember reading things by Faulkner long before he was generally acclaimed, and just wishing that I could have written those things. I mean they are powerful and they are still good, and I think they'll be here forever.

Mr. Styron: I agree.

Mr. Ellison: But to have judged them on the basis of how many people were reading him at that particular time would have been unfair.

Mr. Becker: That is what he means. You are not judging. You are feeling this.

Mr. Styron: Yes, it's a feeling of a steadily declining audience, of an almost minuscule audience.

Mr. Bessie: Gee, I wonder, Bill. I think maybe it's just this other great big thing that's growing up in an area vaguely called communications.

Mr. Haydn: Well, it all depends what you mean by minuscule. There are 165 million people in the United States. I don't know how many of these are totally illiterate.

I do know that when a book sells 100,000 copies, not 100,000,000 copies, but 100,000 copies, all of us who are associated with the publishing firm that published it are jubilant in terms of what's coming into our coffers, because this is a very large sale indeed, and yet it is a very small percentage of the American population.

Now, possibly Bill means something like this; and we know, through Hooper Ratings, or whatever they call them, that the number of those who listen to a particular television show is enormously larger.

Mr. Bessie: That's right.

Mr. Haydn: So that if you care at all about the sense of the size of the audience, there is really an enormous difference.

Mr. Bessie: I agree with that.

Mr. Haydn: Ladies and gentlemen, I have seldom conducted a meeting in which I have felt more impotent to keep the train on the tracks. Begging your pardon, I would like to continue around my circle, for anybody else who would like to state his reply to that question: "What is wrong with the American novel?" or "What is right with the American novel?"

There are three people who may have given their answers, but in the course of the "backing and forthing" I'm not sure.

Bill, do you want to say something?

Mr. Styron: Well, I think Mike has done it and Steve has done it, too. I think I have sounded unduly pessimistic, and as far as I know, I will write novels for a long, long time.

And if I sound pessimistic, it's only because of the fact that television dazzles me, not because I want to write for television, but because I think there is always this very intrinsic thing of reaching people whom you might call zeroes, and maybe they are, a lot of them are, but nonetheless, reaching a lot of people.

Mr. Becker: Thank God this isn't for the *Saturday Evening Post*.

Mr. Bessie: I was going to take the magazines out of the—take the zeroes out of the magazines. That is the most bedeviled statement I have ever heard.

Mr. Haydn: The cynicism of several commentators is going to look equally bad, but I'm going to leave it all in. (Laughter)

Mr. Styron: Anyway, I think that the kind of emotional problem affecting the novelist is this feeling that—oh, that all these tremendous, fantastic, grandiose, marvelous things that he has to say do not reach nearly the number of people that they might.

Mr. Bessie: That's right.

Mr. Styron: I think in America today it has reached a point which it has never reached before, in that sense. I'm going to keep on writing novels and I'm going to write the best kind of novel I know, but this will always be important to me, I think.

Mr. Bessie: I think it will.

Mr. Haydn: Jean?

Miss Stafford: Well, it may be a problem, but you have got to stick to that. I would like to say this: I don't think that the American novel is moribund. I think it's rather morbid for the novelist to discuss its morbidity.

Mr. Haydn: Albert, will you deliver the *coup de grâce?*

Mr. Erskine: No.

Mr. Haydn: In that case I shall simply say thank you very much and Amen!

Five Writers and Their African Ancestors

Harold Isaacs / 1960

From *Phylon* (Winter 1960), 317–36. Copyright 1972 by Clark Atlanta University, Atlanta, Georgia. Reprinted by permission. Only the interview with Ellison is reprinted here; in the original this interview appears with four others.

"Richard Wright," said Ralph Ellison, "has a passion for ideology and he is fascinated by power. I have no desire to manipulate power. I want to write imaginative books." The books Ellison wants to write are books that will come out of the American Negro's own culture and as works of art become part of the culture of man. He has made it his problem to identify that culture and preserve it in literature, while Wright's problem, he said, is that "he has cut his ties to American Negroes" and is more concerned with world politics and world sociology. "People who want to write sociology," Ellison has written, "should not write a novel."

Like Wright, Ellison rejects racial mysticism and he also strongly rejects the idea that there is any significant kinship between American Negroes and Africans. But unlike Wright, Ellison feels this so strongly that he has not even allowed himself any curiosity about the matter. He was offered a trip to Africa in 1955 but turned it down. "I said I had no interest in it," he told me, "no special emotional attachment to the place. I don't read much on Africa nowadays. It is just a part of the bigger world picture to me."

At the time we talked, events in Africa had already begun to make a visible impact among Negroes, but Ellison had remained quite unimpressed by it. In years past, he remarked, "Negroes either repeated all the very negative clichés, or else laughed at Africa, or, in some cases, related to it as a homeland." As an example of the latter type he mentioned the black nationalists, like the character Ras the Exhorter in *Invisible Man,* and he also remembered that he had felt involved in the Ethiopian war. "Back in the 1930s, I was for Ethiopia too, of course, but I did not identify with

the Ethiopians as people. I remember being amused when Haile
Selassie denied any identity with American Negroes." At the present time, Ellison went on, the rise of nationalism in Africa has
made many Negroes feel good. "The man-on-the-street might say
now that Africa is justifying Garvey. He might say: 'They said
Garvey was a boob, but look now, just watch, they'll go right on to
South Africa and kick those crackers out of there.' There is a lot
of this pride, predicting things, putting the bad mouth on the whites,
now that things are finally moving in Africa." Middle-class Negroes might share this pride to some extent, but Ellison said he did
not know much about middle-class Negroes. As for intellectuals,
he was contemptuous. He thought that there was a lot of "fakery"
in some of the new organizations springing up to exploit the new
feeling about Africa and he scornfully referred to a certain well-
known Negro intellectual who "had taken to wearing African
robes at Alabama State."

Ellison himself had been unable to respond in any direct way to
Africans and the experience had been mutual. "The Africans I've
met in Paris and Rome have seen me as an alien. They see most
American Negroes this way. I never really got into contact. I
won't have anything to do with racial approaches to culture." His
only point of contact, he said, was an interest in African art. He had
read Malraux's new interpretations of it, and gone to some exhibi-
tions, but that was all. Not having any political interests like Wright's,
and believing that the African origins had only the most remote
place in the making of a distinctively American Negro culture, Ellison
has not written at all on the subject, alluding to it only in glancing
remarks in some of his essays. Hence what I report here on the
way in which Ellison sees Africa (as well as himself) comes out of a
long day's talk during which he freely and generously and with
cool candor answered a great many questions.

As we spoke of Wright and other Negro writers who have chosen
to live as expatriates in Europe, Ellison showed me a clipping
from *Time* in which he had been included among the exiles because
he had just spent two years in Rome on a fellowship. In a letter
sharply correcting the report, Ellison said that "While I sympathize
with those Negro Americans whose disgust with the racial absurdities
of American life leads them to live elsewhere, my own needs—both

as citizen and as artist, make the gesture of exile seem mere
petulance." He said he thought for a writer the key question was
where he could work well, adding that Faulkner did all right in
Mississippi and Hemingway and Henry James in Europe, while
"Richard Wright wrote better in Chicago and Brooklyn than he
has in Paris." As for himself: "Personally I am too vindictively
American, too full of hate for the hateful aspects of this country, and
too possessed by the things I love here to be too long away."

Ralph Ellison came up just behind Richard Wright—he is five
years younger—and for a few years in the 1930s they travelled
together in the orbit of the Communist movement, with Wright
serving as a help and an inspiration to the younger man. But
Ellison had come up by a different path, from Oklahoma via
Tuskegee, and out of a life that eventually shaped him into
becoming a different kind of writer. Like Wright, Ellison had lost
his father at an early age, but to death, not desertion. His father
had been a construction foreman, served in the army in the Philippines and the Orient, had read widely, and had named his son
after Ralph Waldo Emerson. Ellison's mother was a strong minded
woman who worked as a servant in a white home, but also helped
canvass Negro voters for Eugene Debs' Socialist Party and was in
touch with "liberal whites who tried to keep Oklahoma from becoming like Texas, but failed." His mother bought her two sons a
phonograph and records, electrical sets and chemical sets, and a
toy typewriter, and told them the world would get to be a better
place if they fought to change it. Oklahoma was Jim Crow and
"you knew about the villainies of white people, yet in Oklahoma it
was possible to realize that it was not a blanket thing. . . . We had
some violence, there was fighting between Negro and white boys,
but it was not too deeply fixed in the traditions or psychology of
people." Ellison's mother had encouraged him to read and at
Tuskegee he "blundered onto T. S. Eliot's *Waste Land,* and started
to follow up all the footnotes, reading all those books. . . ." Ellison
came to New York, then, not as Wright had come to Chicago, out
of a seared childhood and with a parched mind. He did not come
escaping, but seeking, and this difference laid its mark on their
preoccupations and their work as writers. Wright became the rest-
less ideologue, pulling away from the near, small things, and

looking for the large solutions, while Ellison, as he began to write
Invisible Man, asked himself: "Could you present the Negro in
his universal aspects and not keep your imagination in the leash of
sociology? How do you do this and have it understood?"

In trying to think his way through to expressing what he believes
to be a distinctive American Negro culture, Ellison has little or
no thought at all of any African influence on this culture, past or
present, or on himself. "I have great difficulty associating myself with
Africa," Ellison said. "I suppose this is because so many people
insist that I have a special tie to it that I could never discover in
any concrete way. I mean the sociologists, Negro friends of mine
who are trying to find some sort of past beyond the previous
condition of servitude. I have always felt very Western. I can't find
that in Africa in any way. I think now of Ghana, new countries, their
problems, their need to bridge the gap between tribal patterns and
the needs of modern government and life."

As we began to talk of his awareness of Africa and began to move
back in time, all the familiar experiences quickly turned up in his
memories. He brought them in and flicked them away: "the usual
crap" in geography class, "the African villain in jungle movies."
By his account, these had simply rolled off his hard surfaces:

"As a small boy, I remember the Garvey movement. We had
some enthusiasts out there in Oklahoma. People wanted to go to
Africa. The people I knew thought this was very amusing, going
back to a place they had never been. The other association I can
remember was in geography class, the usual crap, Africans as lazy
people, living in the sun. I always knew we were partially descended
from African slave stock. I knew that Negroes were black and that
blacks came from Africa. . . . There were expressions, the fist,
for example, was called 'African soupbone.' No"—he dismissed
my question shortly—"I don't think this was an allusion to
cannibalism."

"You ran into the African villain in jungle movies," he went on,
"I suppose that like all other kids I identified with the white
heroes. I have no vivid memories of them or the feelings they
aroused. I don't remember being repelled. You might have related
to the blacks in some way, but you identified with the hero, not
with the villains. I do remember a Negro named Noel Johnson

who always played Indian roles, and all Indians, of course, were
villains. We always went for him, though, and when they would
be coming after him, the kids in the movie would shout: 'Look out,
Noel, here they come after you!' "

In his reading, Ellison came across it quite incidentally, as in
Countee Cullen's poem "Heritage." At the time, 1931, he said,
"I felt it to be artificial and alien. I was reading all these people
very intensely and I felt something missing in them that I ran into in
Eliot, the folk tradition they had and didn't know what to do with."
This was at Tuskegee where "we had African princes walking
around the campus. There was a girl from Sierra Leone and West
Indians—we tended to link them all together. The sense of the
alien was strong. It was not antagonism but a matter of totally
different cultural backgrounds. I didn't share much of the interest in
these people. . . . Usually I thought them quite British. I had no
cultural identification with them. I rejected any notion of a link,
just as I later rejected Herskovits' ideas [about African cultural
survivals]. Lorenzo Turner on African survivals in American
speech interested me. But I did not—and I do not—feel a lack in
my cultural heritage as an American Negro. I think a lot of time is
wasted trying to find a substitute in Africa. Who was it that saw
Americans as 'a people without a history but with a new synthesis?' The thing to do is to exploit the meaning of the life you have."

In *Invisible Man,* the African theme appears only in the person of
Ras the Exhorter, leader of the ultra-racist black nationalists in
Harlem, patterned on one of several successors to Marcus Garvey
in the Harlem of the 1930s. In Ellison's novel, Ras, a West Indian
black man, contests the streets of Harlem with the Communists.
During a fracas caused by Ras' attempt to break up a Communist
street meeting, Ras, knife in hand, makes a passionate appeal to a
black Communist:

> "You *my* brother, mahn. Brothers are the same color; how the hell
> you call these white men *brother?* . . . Brothers the same color. We
> sons of Mama Africa, you done forgot? You black. BLACK! You—
> *Godahm,* mahn!" he said, swinging the knife for emphasis. "You got
> bahd *hair.* You got thick *lips!* They say you stink! They hate you, mahn.
> You African. AFRICAN! Why you with them?"

The two Communists, one of them Ellison's protagonist, listen fascinated despite themselves as Ras tells them the only allies to seek were not white men, but black and yellow and brown allies, and that the white men would only betray and betray and betray them in the end. "This man's full of pus," says Ellison's hero as he pulls his friend away, "black pus." At the novel's end, in the wild and bloody rage of a Harlem riot, Ras the Exhorter appears on a black horse in the midst of his followers, dressed "in the costume of an Abyssinian chieftain, a fur cap upon his head, his arm bearing a shield, a cape made of the skin of some animal around his shoulders." Ras confronts Ellison's hero on the dark street just as he has come to realize the perfidy involved in bringing on the bloodshed. He tries to reason with Ras, he wants to say: "Look, we're all black folks together. . . ." But Ras is blood mad and they fight, and it is in fleeing from Ras the Destroyer that Ellison's hero descends into the deep cellar where he begins to reorder everything he has learned in his life. His principal discovery seems to be that not only the black man but every man shares the common plight: "None of us seems to know who he is or where he's going." He decides ultimately that he must shake off the "old skin," leave it in the hole behind him, and re-emerge into a world of "infinite possibilities"—"a good phrase and a good view of life and a man shouldn't accept any other."

Thus while Richard Wright wandered over the world holding fast to his outsiderness, Ellison, clinging hard to his home ground, began trying to reach for a new sense of Negro insiderness, for a distinctive cultural personality that asserted its legitimacy within the American society and, for that matter, within the total human culture. Ellison, trying to look beyond the threshold of the conquest of civil rights and equality of status for Negroes, asks himself: what does the Negro become when he has shed his second-classness? "What part of Negro life has been foisted on us by Jim Crow and must be gotten rid of; what part of Negro life, expression, culture do we want to keep? We will need more true self-consciousness. I don't know what values, what new tragic sense must emerge. What happens to the values of folk life, of church life? Up to now it has been a matter of throwing things off. But now we have to get conscious of what we do not want to throw off." Ellison believes that the Negro identity of the future will be shaped out of the

unique Negro folk tradition. He believes this can be preserved—
though he is not sure how—and that the Negro is not struggling to
become free simply in order to disappear.

"To the question, *what am I?,*" Ellison said, "I answer that I am
a Negro American. That means far more than something racial. It
does not mean race, it means something cultural, that I am a man
who shares a dual culture. For me, the Negro is a member of an
America-bound cultural group with its own idiom, its own psychology, growing out of its preoccupations with certain problems for
hundreds of years, out of all its history. The American Negro stock
is *here,* a synthesis of various African cultures, then of slavery,
and of all the experience of Negroes since."

Of all these ingredients, the African is the least: "The African
content of American Negro life is more fanciful than actual,"
Ellison said, and this is why he has such a minimum interest in it.
He thinks that it is the novelist's business to translate the unique
Negro experience into literature. "As long as Negroes are confused
as to how they relate to American culture," he said, "they will
be confused about their relationship to places like Africa."

An Interview with Ralph Ellison
Allen Geller / 1963

From the *Tamarack Review* (Summer 1964), 221–27. Copyright
1964 by the *Tamarack Review*. Reprinted by permission.

The interview that follows with the distinguished American
novelist Ralph Ellison took place on October 25th, 1963, in
Montreal, where Mr. Ellison had gone to deliver a lecture
on 'The Novel and the American Experience' at McGill University.

Interviewer: Did you have a difficult time finding a publisher for
Invisible Man?

Ellison: No, not at all. A publisher gave me a contract while I was
serving as a merchant-seaman during the war. He had seen some
of the short stories and essays which I was publishing from time to
time and called me in and wanted to know if I had other things,
and I sent him some of the other things that I had. I had already
published a few things but I showed him a number of unpublished
things. He called me in, finally, and said, 'Look, would you like to
do a novel?' I said, 'Yes, that's my ultimate ambition, to write
novels.' And he said, 'Well, do you have one in mind?' I said, 'No,
I don't have one in mind.' He said, 'Well, we would like to give
you a contract.' So he gave me a contract—$1,500 in advance—and
then waited about five years before he actually got a book. There
was no problem in getting a contract.

Interviewer: You say your book took five years to write. Why so
long? Did you find it a hard book to write, or are you a meticulous worker?

Ellison: Well, I write sometimes with great facility, but I question
it; and I have a certain distrust of the easy flow of words and I
have to put it aside and wait and see if it's really meaningful and if
it holds up. It's an inefficient way of working, but it seems to be
my way.

Interviewer: Were you influenced at all by Nathanael West?

Ellison: No, not at all. But I was influenced by the comic movies, the Marx Brothers, the Negro comedians. You don't have to go to Nathanael West for tradition. You inherit it.

Interviewer: Well, West, I believe, wrote some scripts for the Marx Brothers in collaboration with his friend S. J. Perelman when they were both in Hollywood.

Ellison: Is that right? Well, this is a long tradition in American life. It's one which is apt to get to you long before you start reading for influence. In fact I hadn't read Nathanael West before I wrote *Invisible Man* and people started telling me about *A Cool Million* and that was the first West that I read and then I went on to the others, *Miss Lonelyhearts, Day of the Locust. . . .*

Interviewer: I notice that you're an admirer of Malraux who visited us recently in his role as Minister of Culture of France. In the States you don't have anything like a ministry to promote art, but what effect do you think Kennedy is having on the literary scene?

Ellison: He's certainly paid more attention to writers than any other president in a long time, that is in a social way—except for President Roosevelt, who was the architect of the writers' projects (at least it was during his administration) and that gave me a chance to be a writer. I first started writing under WPA—that is, I was able to give time to writing because I could do work for them and learn to do my own. . . . I think it will be a little while before we can get a clear idea of the effect of the New Frontier upon literature.

Interviewer: You also studied sculpture and painting for a while, I believe?

Ellison: I studied sculpture for about a year, a year and a half, and found out that I had a certain knack of doing naturalistic sculpture, but after a year I gave that up. . . . I thought of myself as a musician in those days.

Interviewer: To get back to *Invisible Man,* you said last night that you do not concentrate on theory or form when writing; you said that 'the content will dictate the form'—

Ellison: No, I meant this last night. When you are influenced by a body of literature or art from an earlier period, it is usually the form of it that is available to you; the content changes so rapidly.

By that I meant that the work of literature is at its best when it has processed the content into the form itself.

Interviewer: There are many scenes in *Invisible Man* which are surrealistic. Does that mean that your vision of some aspects of American life is surrealistic?

Ellison: You see, that's from the outside. I mean, it's looking at what is done in a book and assuming that it comes from a theory and I know the theories. Let's put it this way—I'm a highly conscious writer. I know what has been done and just about who did it because I've read the books, I've studied them. Now having said that, you don't want to confuse the theory of surrealism with the eye that sees the chaos which exists within a given society.

Interviewer: No, I realize that you do not use theory to interpret what you see or mechanically change reportage into a certain style. What I meant is, in a descriptive sense is your vision of life directly surrealistic?

Ellison: I try to see life as it is. I try to see it in terms of its contradictions, in terms of its values, in terms of its pace, in terms of its nervous quality. Now what is called surrealism in one place might be seen as mundane reality in another. In highly formalized sections of society (and this is true of the United States), in the decorous areas of society, you don't always see the individual in his naked state, but if you go to Sixth Avenue in the Broadway section of New York, it takes on a kind of surface atmosphere— people standing on the street talking to themselves, winos walking along. . . .

Interviewer: You said that you are a highly conscious writer aware of what other writers had already done. Doesn't this inhibit you, inhibit your writing in any way once you know this has been done, and this has been done . . . ?

Ellison: No, there's no reason for not doing it again in your own way. You're not going to make a completely new novel. Fiction is by now a traditional form, the techniques are known, but you have the advantage of bending the techniques to your own uses, and the more guns you have in the arsenal the better you can fight the battle. I know that certain very sublime pieces of fiction have been done and there would be no point in trying to imitate them, but you do

have the obligation to know what has been done and how it was
done so as to give your own imagination the freest range.

Interviewer: What problems have you had as a writer?

Ellison: Problems of understanding what's happening around . . .
problems of self-discipline, problems of making my fiction do
what I think it should do, problems of distraction, problems of
wanting to go off and hunt instead of sitting at the typewriter. The
usual problems which writers have.

Interviewer: At the end of *Invisible Man* the hero is waiting in his
cubicle, waiting for the right moment for action. What exactly
does this mean? He is still left in a dilemma. After all his many
experiences, after finding out that the concepts he started out with
were superficial, after getting a more realistic view of the world,
abandoning religion, his academic aims, his cultural background,
the Communist Party, all his political and social theories—

Ellison: It wasn't the Communist Party.

Interviewer: It wasn't the Communist Party?

Ellison: No, it wasn't called the Communist Party. It was like
that, but—

Interviewer: Well, he eventually comes to a personal view of life
which is more realistic and mature. But where does he go from
there? What is the action he waits for? You have your hero say, 'All
sickness is *not* unto death,' a reference to Kierkegaard's work,
implying that he had already freed himself from the 'sickness'
through his experiences. Kierkegaard discusses a similar development in *Stages on Life's Road* and he reaches the conclusion that
you have to have a religious or mystical experience to continue or
complete your life. But your hero seems to have *had* this experience
by the end of the novel—yet he still does nothing.

Ellison: Yes, he had a mystical, prophetic dream of war toward
the end of the book. But you mustn't miss the fact that it's *his*
book, not mine, and the writing and publication of his experience is
an act of self-definition and also an act of some social significance.
The moment had occurred.

Interviewer: Yes. Well, I asked you this question yesterday. If
one is not able to recreate his experience in art, where would that
same hero be? Yesterday you said you wouldn't have the slightest
idea. But a person could have very similar experiences, go through

this process and end up in the state of hibernation that your hero is in at the end of the novel. What would he do then . . . ?

Ellison: Well, he certainly would learn to deal with himself. Whatever he did when he returns, so to speak, should be based on the knowledge gained before he went underground. This is a question of self-knowledge and ability to identify the processes of the world. Beyond that he has his freedom of choice. I wouldn't want to impose that upon anyone. I certainly would not suggest that he follow some plan which I thought would be good for me as an individual.

Interviewer: Agreed, it's not a plan or moral system that I ask about, but the psychological point at which your hero escapes the den. It is a large step from the underground den to creating the memoir. What springs him, releases him, and allows him to continue. Define the type of action he needs. He is obviously not going to go out and find a job, blend into society and be satisfied. He is now too aware an individual to—

Ellison: To want a job?

Interviewer: No, not to want a job but to dismiss the experiences he has gone through, to forget them.

Ellison: Well, he doesn't dismiss them. One of the things he recognizes is that he is responsible himself for so much of what he went through. He recognizes that had he not been so willing to do what other people wanted him to do he would have been saved so much of the agony of his experience. So it implies that when he gets back, doing whatever he's going to do, he will be more himself. He will not be so willing to be a good boy and he will have a better idea of how the individual functions creatively in society.

Interviewer: But he can't start off with an idea of what he is. All his experiences made him something. When he dismisses his early influences and ideals, does he get all his standards from himself?

Ellison: No, he does not get all his standards from himself. He gets them from a lot of people within the action. He even gets some things from the fellows who burn the apartment—Dupré and that crowd; he gets something from Mary, some knowledge of who he is and how he should live in the world and how to square his ambitions with his background. He's learning all the time.

Interviewer: There's never an emphasis on religion or the religious in *Invisible Man?*

Ellison: No, he isn't a religious individual.

Interviewer: Does the hero believe in God?

Ellison: I suppose he did at the beginning. There are religious moments in the book, but he was committed to a materialist solution finally—during his political activities.

Interviewer: But not finally; not at the very end while he's waiting in his underground den.

Ellison: While he's in his underground den he's trying to recreate the world as he discovered it.

Interviewer: Last night you stated that the main theme of American literature was the search for values, the individual's search for identity; and, of course, this is also the main theme of *Invisible Man*. Do you intend to continue this theme in your writing, in the new novel you're working on . . . ?

Ellison: Well, you don't choose the theme, the theme chooses you. But yes, that theme does come into it along with the theme of memory or the suppression of memory in the United States. One of the techniques which seems to have worked out for taking advantage of the high mobility which is possible in the States is forgetting what the past was, in the larger historical sense, but also in terms of the individual's immediate background. He is apt to make light of it. The immigrant will become ashamed of the language of the parents, the ways of the forefathers; and you have this, what I call 'passing for white', which refers to a form of rejecting one's own background in order to become that of some prestige group or to try to imitate the group which has prestige at a particular moment.

Interviewer: Well, isn't this the existentialist dilemma, the necessity to dismiss the past, to live in the present. What Mailer calls hipsterism?

Ellison: The hipster, although Mailer doesn't quite understand it, is not simply living in the present, he is living a very stylized life which implies a background because it takes a good while, a lot of living to stylize a pattern of conduct and an attitude. This goes back very deeply into certain levels of Negro life. That's why it has nuances and overtones which Mailer could never grasp. He is

appropriating it to make an existentialist point which doesn't seem
to me to be worth making.

Interviewer: Am I wrong to assume that Rinehart in *Invisible Man*
is a hipster?

Ellison: He's not a hipster in Mailer's sense. He is a kind of
opportunist who has learned to live in a world which is swiftly
changing and in which the society no longer has ways of bringing
pressure . . . or even identifying him. Thus he can act out many
roles. He's a descendant of Melville's 'Confidence Man' to that
extent.

Interviewer: In today's society, would this be an aim—to divorce
oneself from society in that way? This is what the grandfather of
your hero seems to be saying in the anarchic advice he gives in the
first chapter—to go along with the society on the surface only,
but actually to subtly undermine it, to act without it.

Ellison: Not to act without it but act against it, to collaborate with
its destruction of its own values. That's the way that a weak man,
that weak old grandfather—physically weak, that is—found for
dealing with a circumstance, but his grandson actually writes his
memoirs. *Invisible Man* is a memoir of a man who has gone through
that experience and now comes back and brings his message to
the world. It's a social act; it is not a resignation from society but
an attempt to come back and to be useful. There is an implied
change of role from that of a would-be politician and rabble-rouser
and orator to that of writer. No, there's no reason for him to lose his
sense of a social role. But I think the memoir, which is titled
Invisible Man, his memoir, is an attempt to describe reality as it really
exists rather than in terms of what he had assumed it to be. Because
it was the clash between his assumptions, his illusions about
reality, and its actual shape which made for his agony.

Interviewer: In this sense would you consider yourself an existentialist writer—since you dismiss all these myths as well? I know
the term has been abused. . . .

Ellison: Yes, the term has been so abused. Let's say that if I were
to identify myself as an existentialist writer, then it would be existentialism in the terms of André Malraux rather than Sartre. It would
be in terms of Unamuno, let's say, without the religious framework,
rather than Camus's emphasis.

Interviewer: Last night you expressed respect for Melville. Now in *Moby Dick,* in Ahab, you not only have an example of a social rebel such as you have in *Invisible Man,* but you also have what Camus calls a metaphysical rebel.

Ellison: Yes, you do have a metaphysical rebel.

Interviewer: In *Invisible Man?*

Ellison: No, not so much, because he doesn't have that level of conscious revolt. Ahab is a highly articulate individual and individualist who has gone through a conscious consideration of his philosophical position, who has broken through certain boundaries by having gone through them—even love of the family and so on. As he says, tells Starbuck, I guess, 'I do have my humanities.' Well, this is on a higher level than my character in *Invisible Man.*

Interviewer: What type of characters appear in your new novel? Do you examine the theme of rebellion to the extent that it becomes metaphysical, or are you dealing with people who have been integrated into the rhythm of society?

Ellison: Well, it's about a number of people. One man learns how to operate in society to the extent that he loses a great part of his capacity for, shall we say, poetry or for really dealing with life. And another man who seems caught at a very humble stage of society seems to have achieved quite a high level of humanity. But you see when I'm writing fiction I'm not thinking philosophy. These are tags which come later. I'll leave that to the critics. I won't try to classify my characters that way. You write to discover what you can, to make what you can of your intuitions, your themes, your talent, and so on. But if the great novels are novels which depict metaphysical rebels, then one hopes that these people will be metaphysical rebels. If you mean, however, characters who press the extremes of their situation, who try to make as much of what they will to do and what happens to them, the circumstances which they find themselves in—if you mean metaphysical to that extent, yes, these will be characters who move in that direction, to the extent of their given condition.

Interviewer: What I meant by metaphysical was extending the moral condemnation to the universe. A paradox, because man is the moral force and the universe amoral. For example, Ahab's anger at Moby Dick (a symbol for amoral force in the universe). Yet he wants to destroy the whale. Here Ahab is imposing a moral condemnation, condemning the world for what it is.

Ellison: Yes, he does. I guess we can approach this a little more specifically by pointing out that Melville was attempting to create a tragic hero. Certain things had happened to this man; for instance the whale had bitten off his leg. He had been a very successful captain—that is, financially successful. He was then pressed beyond the concern with simply slaughtering whales for their food and oil value and it became a matter of seeing in the whale the inscrutable nature of existence, of man's relationship to the total scheme. Well, is this moral or immoral? It's moral, it seems to me, as it embodies and expresses the individual's obligation to discover the extreme limits of his own possibilities, because through this, then, he discovers his true relationship to nature and society and so on—in this case to society and to nature, the society of the ship. He did everything he could to lead them into this reckless chase and to instil them with some of his own passion. He then goes on and threatens them; he uses the harpoon which is the symbol, shall we say, for technological development and skill, threatens them to make them follow Moby Dick and then discovers that he could not impose his will upon nature. Now you can call Moby Dick evil, you can call him a number of things. Melville has a lot to say about it (or Ishmael does) in the chapter called 'The Whiteness of the Whale'. Ahab as a tragic hero is sure to be destroyed because he has gone beyond the point where the individual can impose his will upon the chaos of the world.

Interviewer: Well, he has taken over the position of God in assuming the responsibility for the moral state of the world.

Ellison: I don't think he's taken over the position of God. I think he's acting as a god-like man, a man who would assume that it is possible to pierce through the mask and to discover ultimates. But that in itself is carrying out a very profound moral mission in terms of the obligation of human beings to learn as much as they can about the nature of life. The human being has the obligation to learn as much as he can about where he is and what he is for several reasons. The species can only continue to survive and to develop to the extent that this is done—in a disciplined way, one hopes, but if not it must be done anyway. Now that's one thing—a

man's relationship to the universe, to the chaos of nature and so on
which he tries to understand, tries to glean the laws. Secondly
there is the obligation of man as a member of society and there is
inevitably a clash between these two roles. Society sets up its
own ethics, its own moral system in order to make it possible to
survive and to render justice and to reduce chaos to a minimum.
This is not a God-constructed world. I don't think God constructed
society. I think it's man-made, and man plays it by ear far too
often. And it becomes quite a moral problem, an ethical problem as
to how man operates within that structure and what he does to
himself and to his fellow man, what he does to the resources
of society.

Interviewer: Must the individual persist even though it will destroy him?

Ellison: Well, he has to decide what does destroy. Good and evil,
destruction and creation, are so closely linked that you don't
always know what's going to happen. We know that up until the
discovery of the bomb and even as a result of that we have come
upon many life-saving techniques in many, many fields—techniques
of peacefully using and creatively using resources of this world.
We know that the industrial revolution was tied up with warfare,
chaotic disruptions of the existing social systems, and so on.

Interviewer: Well, to take a smaller segment of society, you say
that society is more or less an abstraction agreed upon to have a
large amount of people function as efficiently as possible—

Ellison: Let's not call it an abstraction because this is real life.
It's an arrangement. For all of the continuity of civilization, each
society is a sort of improvisation, especially when it's changing so
rapidly as most societies are now. There was a time, I guess the
Middle Ages, or even during the Renaissance, when there was a
slower degree of change and you could say that you had real
stability, but now that is impossible. Most societies are strictly
improvisations hoping to move toward a point of maximum stability. In the United States the change has been so abiding throughout
our history that we more or less accept it as given now, and you hear
fewer complaints about the change except when they start tearing
down a fine old building, or an especially attractive model of a car

goes out of production—you get complaints on that, but not about change itself.

Interviewer: What about another type of change? You say society is an arrangement. The arrangement in the U.S. supposedly says that the Negroes have had equality for a hundred years.

Ellison: No Negroes have had any illusions that we've had equality. In fact I don't think anyone has because we've been fighting in the courts for a long time, in the state and county courts and so on, for an increase in our participation as citizens. There's been no illusion about that in the States, but a very conscious fight between groups of men who say that we shouldn't have it and have the political power to frustrate our achieving full citizenship and a group of other men who have played ball with them from time to time, and another group of men who have not yet found ways of overlooking their own interests to work out this problem for the nation itself. That's not a system where a lot of people are pretending that something exists when it doesn't.

Interviewer: Well, I wasn't referring to the people, I was referring to the laws. The laws say yes, while reality says no.

Ellison: It's an interpretation of the laws. You can't deal with it in such bulk terms.

Interviewer: Granted that society is an arrangement. What means can a group within that society use to change the arrangement when they interpret a law in a certain way and see their right to certain civil liberties? What means should they employ to attain their ends? Up to now, as you say, they've been using the law courts. Here in Quebec, a separatist group has resorted to violence to gain what they deem their rights. Why hasn't the Negro used more aggressive means to gain his ends? Why hasn't he used violence, which is a traditional means of revolt? Why hasn't there been a riot similar to the one that ends *Invisible Man?*

Ellison: There were two riots like that in New York. I reported the riot on which that one is based for the *New York Post* in 1943. It was during the war and there was a lot of tension and after some altercation between a policeman and a Negro soldier and his mother and wife in a bar, Harlem just exploded and they rioted for a day and a night and destroyed many of the white businesses in Harlem from about 110th Street up until 145th Street. Most of the business area in Harlem, the neighborhood grocers and so on, was shattered, looted, burned. . . .

Interviewer: And that is where you gained the material for the riot scene in the novel?

Ellison: Well, some of it, but that's an imaginative construction which is based upon pattern, but the reality behind it was that a riot did occur, just as another similar riot occurred in 1935 when I was still living in Alabama. I hadn't been to New York yet. But violence as a means of achieving freedom in the United States has not been practical for Negroes—certainly not in the South where we are outnumbered and where the major instruments of destruction are in the hands of Whites. It would be foolish to have tried it that way. But there have been individual revolts and showdowns all along. These things are not publicized. But it seems to me far more effective, and there's no doubt but it has been effective, to work upon the basis of what is there and that is the Constitution of the United States. As long as the Supreme Court interpreted the 'separate but equal' clause as being the law of the land, then people who are citizens of that land, especially those who have very little power, had nothing to do but obey it. But that didn't stop them. They agitated to change the interpretation of the law, and in 1954 it was done. It takes far more courage for some of the children to walk on the streets of Birmingham, Alabama, with police dogs after them and with threats of tear gas and shootings—it takes far more courage to do that than to put a plastic bomb into a mailbox.

Interviewer: Isn't it also a matter of time? Many Negro leaders have said that the Negro wants his rights now, not in another fifty or seventy-five years.

Ellison: We do want our rights now. But you don't get rights by destroying them. No, when violence occurs, violence will be answered in some way, but if you are playing the long game—if you've learned the necessity of discipline. . . . What's happening in the United States is something far more complex than just a group of people and their allies challenging an existing horror. What you see happening, I think, is that the best of the American tradition is now finding its expression through these Negroes. That is what's important. That the moral and physical courage that has been typical of Americans, of America at its best, has now found roots among

my own people. This is a matter of time. This is a matter of knowing
the nature of your opposition. And you should recognize this:
most Negroes have never desired separation. Separation isn't the
question. Their goal was always to be a functioning part of the
governing apparatus with equal participation. This is our goal. If
the goal were to achieve separation or to seize control of the
government, then violence would be something to think about. But
intimidation can be imposed by marching barehanded before
police dogs and cattle prods and it requires physical and moral
courage. That intimidates, and it's a more subtle form of fighting
and a more effective one than I think you recognize.

Interviewer: James Baldwin has shifted his position from novelist
to spokesman for the Negro Revolt at present. Do you find your role
changing? Do you find that you are being asked to play the role
of spokesman?

Ellison: Well, you're asking me to play it right now, but it's a role
that I refuse because I recognize what Baldwin doesn't recognize—
that is, when you deal with political power you should have some
structure behind you and he doesn't. He has no way of imposing
his will. There's no apparatus, really, which is not to say that he is
not doing some good, but it's a limited good and he speaks with a
kind of freedom which is politically unrealistic.

Interviewer: Do you think he does a better job as spokesman than
as novelist?

Ellison: I'm not so sure. I prefer his essays to his novels as well
as to his pronouncements about the situation, but that isn't for me to
decide. If there are people who are moved and who are moved
toward changing their view of themselves and the world, I think this
is all to the good. The one thing I do know is that this is no role for
me. I'm not that kind of a speaker and I think I can best serve my
people and my nation by trying to write as well as I can.

Interviewer: Baldwin lately seems to have laid emphasis on his
being a Negro; you seem to consider yourself an American in—

Ellison: I consider myself both and I don't see a dichotomy. I'm
not an American because I arbitrarily decide so. I write in the
American tradition of fiction. My people have always been Americans. Any way you cut it, if you want to think in racist terms, the
blood lines were here before the Africans came over and blended

with them, as they were here before the Whites came over and blended. So racially, in terms of blood lines and so on, American Negroes are apt to be just as much something else as they are Africans. Now that's one thing. Culturally speaking, I inherited the language of Twain, Melville, and Emerson, after whom I'm named. No, it makes a very dramatic statement when you say, 'I am not American, I feel alienated.' But actually when you look at Mr. Baldwin's prose you see that he is not writing in the Negro idiom, even, not as much as I do. He's writing a mandarin prose, a Jamesian prose, which tips you off to where he really comes from.

I believe any novel becomes effective to the extent that it deals quite eloquently with its own material—that is, you move from the specific to the universal—and that there's no reason why any novel about a Negro background, about Negro characters, could not be effective as literature and in its effectiveness transcend its immediate background and speak eloquently for other people. I think that's the obligation, to try to write so truthfully and so well and eloquently about a specific background and about a specific form of humanity that it amplifies itself, becomes resonant and will speak to other people and speak *for* other people. This is an obligation. I feel that just as I feel this. It isn't a question of where I want to stand. When I decided to write fiction in the U.S., I committed myself to the obligation of all American novelists— which in no way contradicts my role as Negro. I am responsible to the extent that any individual can be responsible for at least continuing the best traditions of the American novel. I think Baldwin is faced with that too. . . . Now I might write a bad novel. Maybe this novel I am working on is a bad novel. If it fails it won't be because I decided that I was not an American but only a Negro or because I decided that I was not a Negro but only an American. There's no way of doing it. It would just be an instance of a failure. But the obligation is there. I think that certainly as an essayist Baldwin is speaking in an old American tradition and speaking very eloquently; which, again, contradicts in no way his role as Negro although his role as Negro does not really account, absolutely, for the quality of the essays.

Interviewer: You're saying that Baldwin is using an imposed style.

Ellison: I'm not saying that it's an imposed style. I'm saying the

emphasis upon the Negroness is an imposition, that he can't help
being a Negro any more than he can help being an American writer.
He was born here, he has been nourished on the forms of American
literature. To the extent that we can use these forms and techniques
and draw from the uniqueness of Negro speech and from the
uniqueness of our experience as Americans, we have something to
add to the general quality of American fiction, American literature, and so on. But beyond that it isn't a matter of making a choice;
you're just stuck with it. I could never be a French writer, for
instance. I could have gone to Paris and become involved in existentialist politics as Richard Wright did, but it didn't improve his
fiction; in fact it helped encourage some very bad tendencies in
his writing.

Interviewer: *The Outsider* is an example of this existentialist influence.

Ellison: Well, I think he was writing better existentialist fiction
when he was writing *Uncle Tom's Children*.

Interviewer: There is a large amount of theory in *The Outsider,* a
large amount of undisguised philosophy.

Ellison: Well, he talked ideas instead of dramatizing them. But
there *is* an existentialist tradition within American Negro life and,
of course, that comes out of the blues and spirituals.

Interviewer: Yes. One would think that the existentialist novel
would not be a novel of ideas, not the novels of Sartre, but a more
dramatic novel like *Invisible Man* which never mentions philosophy
yet presents the exact dilemma of existentialist man.

Ellison: Well, it's a matter of getting at the condition through the
resources of fiction rather than bootlegging in philosophy, in that
sense. That is, philosophy in art should be dramatized, it should be
part of the given situation, part of the motivations of the characters, a part of their way of confronting life. This is dramatized.
Thus, from that point of view you might say that much of the
great literature has been existentialist. Just as *Job* is an existentialist
fable, *Oedipus Rex* is existentialist, the 'How Long Blues' is existentialist.

Interviewer: Now, what position do you take in the Negro Revolt?

Ellison: Let's put it this way. I've always tried to express or to
create characters who were pretty forthright in stating what they

felt the society should be. And I've tried to present that. I've tried to present the moods of my people as I know them to be and I tried to present the potentialities within that situation as I could discover them through fiction. Ten years ago *Invisible Man* was published and people thought—well they always thought it was an interesting book. Now people are reading it and they think that I invented Malcolm X. What I'm trying to say is that each of us has his role to play and fiction is not a meringue; it is a serious and responsible form of social action itself.

Interviewer: What role are you playing politically?

Ellison: What do I do? I belong to the Committee of One Hundred which is an arm of the legal defence committee of the NAACP. I vote. I try to vote responsibly. I contribute whenever I can to efforts to improve things. Right now one of the things I'm trying to do is to point out that it's a more complex problem than that of simply thrusting out your chin and saying 'I'm defiant'. That's all right, but defiance has to have some real role. One of the big problems facing the country, facing my people specifically, is to prepare to take advantage of the breakdown in the old segregated system. One of the great failures of Negro education, education for Negroes in the U.S., is its failure to prepare the Negro student to understand the functioning of the larger American society. This was more or less planned right from the Reconstruction when the colleges were built. For one way of dealing with the Negro problem was to prepare Negroes to accept the status quo. This has changed, of course, over the years, but it's possible for a Negro student to grow up in the U.S. without having a real feeling of how the society outside of the Negro community operates. He might know how it operates politically, he might know how it operates in terms of social welfare and so on, but then there are other areas, and one of the obligations of the American writer who is Negro is not to simply say that this is no good, but to say why it isn't good, to give his Negro readers at least some insight into the processes of society as they actually exist. This is very important.

Interviewer: Even with this help there are few who will be able to escape this forced provincial system.

Ellison: I don't think it's forced. That's another distortion that

you are apt to get from reading some people. Negroes *like*
being Negroes.

Interviewer: But if they did want to take advantage of the larger
culture it would be a difficult process because the barriers still
remain. Now there may be one or two in a few thousand who—

Ellison: No, no, that isn't true. You have many, many, many who
are doing it, but the process is as the barriers go down to step up
the number of people who will find their way. . . .

Interviewer: Why shouldn't the barriers go down quicker?

Ellison: Why shouldn't they go down quicker? I want them to go
down quicker but it isn't that simple. Simply to take down a
barrier doesn't make a man free. He can only free himself and as he
learns how to operate within the broader society, he learns how to
detect the unwritten rules of the game, and so on. But this is what
any provincial does; this is what any white provincial has to learn.
It's just been easier for him to learn, that's all. Why shouldn't it be
easier for the Negro? The reason is because it's political, because
there's a great deal of fear involved, and so on. Should it be
changed? Yes. When? Today. The question is how.

An Interview with Ralph Ellison
Richard Kostelanetz / 1965

From the *Iowa Review*, (Fall 1989), 1–10. Copyright 1989. Reprinted by permission of Richard Kostelanetz.

RK: What follows is an interview that I did with Ralph Ellison for the BBC in the fall of 1965. Keep that date in mind when you hear some of these replies. His reputation as one of America's best writers is based on only one novel, which was published in 1952. *Invisible Man* received the National Book Award the following year and in 1965 a large poll of American critics and writers judged *Invisible Man* to be the best single novel of the post-war period.

Ellison, born in Oklahoma City, in 1914, once wrote that from his youth he has been haunted by the ideal of a renaissance man. He first studied music at Tuskegee University in Alabama, then sculpture in New York, before writing became his dominant interest. He has also worked in audio-electronics and as a professional photographer. In addition to fiction he has written criticism of jazz, literature, and culture. He has lectured at many American universities, and from 1970–79 was the Albert Schweitzer Professor at New York University. What is particularly impressive, if not awesome about Ellison, is not only the diversity of his cultural interests but the high excellence he achieves in those he chooses to favor.

RK: Your collection of essays *Shadow and Act* is dedicated to Morteza Sprague; and like others, I have wondered who is Morteza Sprague? Do you look at him as a hero or as a friend?

RE: Morteza Sprague, a graduate of Hamilton College, was a professor of English, and hardly older than several of his students. As a Tuskegee freshman I took his senior course in the nineteenth century English novel. He was an honest teacher, for when I went to him about Eliot and such people, he told me he hadn't given much attention to them and that they weren't taught at Tuskegee. But

he told me what to do about it: the places to find discussions
and criticism.

Although I didn't know Albert Murray at Tuskegee—it wasn't
until we made contact in New York City that we became
friends—he was also one of Sprague's students. Then, after graduat-
ing and pursuing graduate studies elsewhere, Murray joined
Sprague on the staff of the English department and they became
close friends. Yes, I consider Sprague a friend and dedicated my
essays to him because he was an honest teacher.

RK: You went to Tuskegee first as a composer . . .

RE: I went there as one who wanted to become a composer,
because they had a good band and an orchestra. I was a trumpeter. They had a rather thriving music school. They also had
William L. Dawson, a composer who had become quite famous
as a choir director. The Tuskegee choir opened Radio City Music
Hall when I was still in high school; this really got me excited! It
didn't seem possible that I might go to Julliard, but then I got the
offer of a scholarship at Tuskegee.

RK: Did you feel at all disadvantaged being in a Negro college in
the South?

RE: No, I didn't feel disadvantaged. Oddly enough, the library,
which was so important to me, was a rather well-rounded library.
I spent a lot of time there—worked there one year. I always hung
around the stacks; that was what I needed. I knew about Kittredge
of Harvard, and so on; those people's names were in the air. A few
of us used to talk about how nice it would have been, if we could have
attended Harvard, and to have studied under such teachers, but the
sense of being disadvantaged was nothing that bothered me. You got
there to study music and you studied music. It wasn't any easier
because you were at a Negro college. You always expected that a
little later on you would finish there and then go somewhere else;
perhaps to Julliard, where you were pretty certain that you would
get some of the best. But the teachers themselves held degrees from
Oberlin and the Boston Conservatory, and so on. Hazel Harrison had
been one of Busoni's prize pupils who lived in his Berlin house
along with a few others, like Percy Grainger, before the rise of Nazism
drove the non-Aryans out of Germany. She had Prokofiev manuscripts—I used to handle Prokofiev manuscripts at Tuskegee! I

didn't play the piano beyond the small technique needed to work on
one's harmonic exercises, but I learned a great deal about music
and the related arts from Miss Harrison.

Anyway, you don't think about the problems of being a Negro
when you're trying to get an education. When you're in the
classroom, you're thinking about the specific problem that is before
you, not the larger sociological problem—even though you are
quite aware that you are Negro, and that in leaving the sanctuary of
the college you're likely to run into possible discomfort, discourtesy,
and even violence . . .

RK: How did you turn to writing?

RE: Actually, I turned to writing before I realized what had
happened. Sometime during my high school days, it must've been
around the eleventh grade, I had a very bad cold that just clung to
me. The school nurse, Miss Waller, saw me on the street one
day—I was still coughing—and she made me go to a lung clinic at
one of the hospitals. I had to wait in a reception room with all
these obviously ill people. I was rather horrified and I began to try
to describe what was going on to some of the people who were
around me. I was doing it in the style, I thought, of O. O. McIntyre,
who was a syndicated columnist who used to appear in the
Oklahoma City papers. I remember that as a first doodling with
writing. The next thing I did was to set to verse a thing on the
swamp country by the Southern writer Albion Tourgée. I took this
to the American literature teacher and he looked at me as though I
had gone out of my mind, because I hadn't shown too much interest
in the class itself. I got passing grades but I had never tried to do any
writing or shown any real interest in literature as it was being
taught, although I read quite a lot; so you have that in the
background. It was nothing that I did consciously or with any
intensity, but those were the beginnings. The other thing was, reading
the prefaces of Shaw when I was in high school. A friend's parents'
library had all of Shaw and I thought those prefaces—I think the
first one I read was a preface to *Candida*—most incongruous, but
there it was. I remember that in my themes in school, I tried to
get some of the Shavian quality in my writing but there again, no
one paid any attention to it and I didn't take it seriously.

RK: What was the point after that?

RE: The point after that was that I became very, very much involved with modern letters after I read *The Waste Land*. I was so intrigued that I started reading all the commentaries that I could find. Among them Edmund Wilson's *Axel's Castle,* Harriet Monroe's book of criticism, and Babette Deutsch's book of criticism. I read a lot of Pound, and Eliot's essays. Evidently I was actually trying my hand at writing poetry during those days, because years later Al Murray pointed out to me that he had found some of my attempts in a library book. I suppose I blanked that out of my mind. Incidentally, I never wrote a decent poem, but the conscious concern with writing began there at Tuskegee: again without my being conscious that it was a forecast of what I was going to do. It was a kind of innocent wordplay. Then I came to New York during my junior year (1936) intending to work that summer and return. That didn't work out, but a few months after I'd been in New York I met Richard Wright. He asked me to review a book for the magazine, *New Challenge,* that he'd come to New York to edit. After my review was published, he asked me to do a short story. I had never tried to do a piece of fiction, never in my life! So I made my first attempt at a short story at Wright's suggestion. My story got to the galley proof stage, but then, thanks to a dispute between Wright and his fellow editors, the magazine was discontinued before my story could be published. Naturally, I was disappointed, but that's how I got started writing fiction.

RK: What did you find in Eliot?

RE: I found imagery for one thing; I found overtones of a sort of religious pattern which I could identify with my own background. I also saw a style of improvisation—that quality of improvising which is very close to jazz. Most people think I'm being pretentious when I say this but it grows out of a similar and quite American approach to the classics, just as Armstrong and any other jazz musician of that period would take a theme and start improvising. Then he would pay his respects to *Aïda,* to any number of operas, to light opera, or to religious music. All this came out in the course of the improvisation. It was these pinpoints of familiarity that made me want to solve the mystery. *The Waste Land* had the quality of a conundrum anyway, so you were really trying to trace the thing down and make it whole within your own mind.

RK: What's American about *The Waste Land?*

RE: Aside from its being the creation of an American, it's American in the rather ruthless assault it makes upon the literature of the past. It assumes possession, it abstracts, it recasts in terms of Eliot's sense of life and his sense of the possibility of language, of poetry, and of culture.

RK: Also American in its references. . . .

RE: Eliot is full of American folklore. He knew quite a lot about it. It would've been inescapable, coming from St. Louis, not to have been aware of the odd juxtapositions that you get in this country of cultural forces, cultural products; high culture, popular culture, it's all mixed. For the poet, he can mix them up any way he wants. Anything and everything is there to be used, and there is this kind of irreverent reverence which Americans are apt to have for the good products of the past. I think you get all of that in Eliot.

RK: So when Eliot speaks of the tradition, he means not only the classical tradition, but the tradition of cultural materials around him in St. Louis?

RE: I think so. This is often missed but I think it is very much there for the eye, and the ear that is willing to listen. It amuses me that "under the bam, under the boo" line comes out of a Negro song written by Cole and Johnson in one of their popular musicals of the 1890s, when a group of Negroes dominated the American musical stage.

RK: Unlike some other Afro-American writers, you choose to live in America, indeed, near Harlem. Why?

RE: Living here is the only living that I could do as a novelist. I lived in Italy for two years when I had the Rome Prize. But, for all of its difficulties, I had to face the challenge of the United States. Now that's one thing. Why do I live always close to other Negroes? Because I have to hear the language. My medium is language, and there is a Negro idiom, in fact there are many Negro idioms in the American language. I have to hear that sounding in my ears, I have to. A place like Harlem, or any American Negro community, has an expressiveness about it which is almost Elizabethan. Things are revealed in speech in the streets. There's a lot of humor and the language is always feeding back to the past;

it's throwing up wisdom, it's throwing up patterns and I never
know but when I'm going to hear something just in the street which
is going to be the making of some piece of fiction that I'm trying
to write.

RK: Is it fair then to speak of Harlem as a ghetto?

RE: I think that this is one of the most damaging misuses of a
concept that has ever come about in the United States. A ghetto
implies a cultural and religious distance. That's where the term
came from.

RK: It came to describe the Jewish neighborhoods . . .

RE: That's right.

RK: . . . on the Lower East Side . . .

RE: Not only the Lower East Side but it comes from Europe, as
we know, and it had a content there which obscures further the
relationships between American whites and American Negroes.
Language for one thing, for another the patterns of myth—of universal
myths, so to speak, of Christian myth, and so on as they have been
given embodiment in terms of Negro patterns. It's not too difficult
to look at John Henry and see the Hercules myth. If you are aware
of the connections, if you know where to look. It's not too
unusual to see that the rhetoric of a Negro sermon, for instance,
can be traced back to Shakespeare, if you know where to look,
or to the metaphysical poets. I'm not saying that these very often
unlettered ministers have read John Donne, but on the other hand
they are possessors of a living tradition.

RK: And have heard people who have read John Donne.

RE: That's right. Actually you find now that the great tradition of
nineteenth century eloquence in oratory is most alive within the
Negro community. We don't find it so much in Congress anymore,
but you find it among Negroes, especially right in the churches.

RK: This is because American Negro culture is more oral?

RE: Yes, it is still more oral than literary but it would be a mistake
to look upon it as primitive, because it is informed by the usual
American concerns.

RK: By this you mean that Negro culture can't be anything but
American culture?

RE: In the United States it's a part of the general American
culture, the language itself. The American English would not have

the same music in it if it were not for the existence of great numbers
of Negroes and great numbers of white Southerners, who have
learned their English partially from Negroes. This is not true on the
other hand where you have people who spoke or who speak a
different language. In Harlem, in fact in most so-called Negro
ghettos, a lot of Negroes do not spend most of their time there.
They work outside. They work as domestics in white homes; they're
cooking, they're taking care of children, they're teaching them their
manners, they're changing their diapers; they are completely involved in America on that level. The music, the dances that
Americans do are greatly determined by Negro American style, by
a Negro American sense of elegance, by an American Negro sense of
what the American experience should be, by what Negroes feel
about how an American should move, should express himself.
The ghetto concept obscures this. It's much better to say you have
slums. It's an old term and it doesn't cause as much confusion.
It's economic, not cultural.

    RK: One way in which the American tradition appears in *Invisible
Man* is in the tradition of story-telling. People are telling stories
about experiences.

    RE: Yes, that's true. And I connect this with certain problems in
the novel. James, for instance, had some negative things to say
about the first person point of view making for loose and baggy
monsters. And I happen to feel that one of the things I wanted to
prove, to myself at least, was that you could write a dramatic novel
using the first person.

    RK: But the blues singer sings in the first person, too.

    RE: Yes, and the blues singer is one of the most developed of
existentialist poets, but we never think about it in that way. It
wasn't until Sartre began to have his novels translated here that I
became aware that some of the blues were much better statements
of the existentialist position than he was able to embody, in *Nausea*
for instance . . .

    RK: For example?

    RE: Well, "Troublin' Mind" is an example, any number of Leroy
Carr's blues . . .

    RK: Would you say then analogously your book is to Western
literature as jazz is to Western music? And, in effect a product of

Negro American culture? Which is still American, which is still
Western?

RE: Yes, I would just point out that they are both Western, they
are both American precisely because they try to use any and
everything which has been developed by great music and great
literature. As for music, on the other hand, I suspect that the one
body of music which expresses the United States—which expresses
this continent—is jazz and the blues. What we have with Western
music, with so-called classical music, is an American version of
Western classical music.

RK: What do you mean when you say that many books written
by Negro writers are intended for a white audience?

RE: Well, I think that when you examine these books you will
find that in expressing Negro protest the writer directs his protest,
his emotion, even his plot toward a white audience. I suppose, what
I mean by this is that the books tend to be overly sociological, that
they are ultimately about civil rights, about sociological conditions
rather than an attempt to reveal personality living within certain conditions.

RK: Isn't there a sense in which the white audience expects a
Negro to be angry about the condition of being Negro in America?

RE: I'm afraid so, and if the conditions were good I think that
many white readers would expect the Negro writer to be angry
because he wasn't white. I mean you have that thing operating
underneath. More seriously, I try to use an approach which is
dictated not by my anger or my lack of anger, not by my protest or
any lack of feelings of protest, but by the logic of the art itself. I
write what my imagination throws up to me and I must feed this
back through my own critical sensibility. That critical sensibility
is informed by a sense of life which grows in its immediacy out of
my being part of the Negro American group. That's where I find
an oral tradition, that's where I found my closest friends who are a
great part of my life, that's where my parents were, that's where
my friends were. That's where emotion, that is the emotional
content of ideas and symbols and dreams, is to be found, where I
can release myself, release whatever creative capacity that I have.
There is a kind of ideal reader and that ideal reader would be a
Negro who was in full possession of all the subtleties of literature

and art and politics. You see what I mean? Not out of racist
motives do I imagine this ideal reader, but to give my own experience, both acquired and that which I was born with, its broadest
possibilities.

RK: Is there any particular person who is your ideal reader?

RE: No, I don't think so. The best reader of course is the person
who has the imagination, regardless of what his color is. Some
readers, I suspect bring more imagination to a work than the author
has put into it. And when you get that kind of reader you're very
fortunate because he gives you a stature, let's say, that you haven't
really earned.

RK: Well, there are ways of misreading *Invisible Man*. One way
is to think that it's autobiographical.

RE: Yes, that's true. It is not autobiographical.

RK: But the first person narrator?

RE: Yes, I did this, as I say, as an attempt to see whether I could
write in the first person and make it interesting, make it dramatic and
give it a strong dramatic drive.

RK: But there's a sense in which *Invisible Man* might first strike
a reader as a catalogue of adverse experiences of an innocent
Negro in America. Is this a correct interpretation?

RE: I would think that it was an incorrect and sentimental
interpretation inasmuch as the narrator of the book could have
stopped much of his experience had he been willing to accept the
harsh nature of reality. He creates much of his own fate. I don't
look upon him as heroic in that way. I think that he made a lot of
mistakes. But many white readers certainly are so sentimental
about the Negro thing that they can't see that.

RK: Isn't one of his more universal failures a failure of perception? He doesn't understand his own experience. He doesn't
understand why he fails.

RE: I think so. It's a failure of perception and it's a sort of wrong-
headed desire to summon up, to take on an identity imposed upon
him by the outside, when we know very well that each individual
has to discover himself and the world for himself. Usually this is
done through some sort of pain. But I must say that this is a tough
guy because he goes through many, many experiences which should
have driven him to himself and to his reality.

RK: In what sense does the title apply? How is the narrator or the Negro an invisible man?

RE: Well, I wasn't writing about *the* Negro. I was writing about a specific character, in specific circumstances, at a specific time. The invisibility, there is a joke about that which is tied up with the sociological dictum that Negroes in the United States have a rough time because we have *high* visibility.

RK: Your color is very apparent.

RE: High pigmentation, so the formula has it, which is true. No one will ever mistake me for white. But the problem for the narrator of *Invisible Man* is that he creates his own invisibility to a certain extent by not asserting himself. He does not do the thing which will break the pattern, which will reveal himself, until far along in the book. So he is not a victim. At least not merely a victim. He is a man who is wrong-headed.

RK: For some years now you have been working on a second novel. Parts have appeared to critical acclaim. Why does it take so long to write a novel?

RE: Well, it takes me a long time because I have a deep uncertainty about what I am doing. I try to deal with large bodies of experience which I see as quite complex. There is such a tendency to reduce the American experience, especially when it centers around the Negro experience. I'm constantly writing—I write a lot—but I have to put it aside. It has to gel, then I come back. If I still react positively to it, if I can still see possibilities of development, then I keep it.

RK: As a novelist, what do you think is the ultimate purpose of your profession?

RE: For me, I think it is to seize upon the abiding patterns of the American experience as they come up within my own part of the American nation, and project those patterns, those personality types, those versions of man's dilemmas, in terms of symbolic actions. Reduce it to eloquent form—that sounds perhaps pretentious but I think that's what the novel does—

RK: Oh, so modest!

RE: Oh, I don't mean to be too modest.

RK: Do you mean that you don't assume that the novelist can have any great social reforming power or have any great expansive power or any great power as a spokesman?

RE: I think that the good novelist tries to provide his reader with vivid depictions of certain crucial and abiding patterns of human existence. This he attempts to do by reducing the chaos of human experience to artistic form. And when successful he provides the reader with a fresh vision of reality. For then through the symbolic action of his characters and plot he enables the reader to share forms of experience not immediately his own. And thus the reader is able to recognize the meaning and value of the presented experience and the essential unity of human experience as a whole. This may, or may not, lead to social change or bring the novelist recognition as a spokesman. But it is, nevertheless, a form of social action, and an important task. Yes, and in its own right a form of social power.

An American Novelist Who
Sometimes Teaches
John Corry / 1966

From the *New York Times* Magazine, 20 November 1966. Copyright 1966 by the New York Times Company. Reprinted by permission.

Ralph Waldo Ellison, whose father read books and died when the boy was only 3, who grew up in Oklahoma City thinking he would be a Renaissance man, who bothered a neighborhood by doing great violence on a jazz trumpet, who wanted to compose a symphony before he was 26, or else to be a sculptor, take pictures or maybe even write, is today a reserved and slightly donnish man, who did, in fact, write. The book is called *Invisible Man,* and it is just possibly important, really and truly important.

At a recent windy seminar of the PEN Congress, when each poet, essayist and novelist there seemed compelled to introduce himself at length, Ellison distinguished himself by saying: "I am an American novelist. I sometimes teach." Then he sat down. He could have defined himself further: winner of a National Book Award for 1952, member of the American Academy of Arts and Letters, member of the National Arts Council, collector of honorary degrees, wanderer in academia, and member of the Carnegie Commission on Educational Television, on which he served with Oveta Culp Hobby of Texas, a couple of corporation presidents and a former governor of North Carolina.

Because he is all these things, and because he is a medium shade of brown, say the color of a worn penny, Ralph Ellison, of course, is an "Establishment Negro," an "Uncle Tom," perhaps, or maybe a "handkerchief head." Or he could also be, as the fight announcers simpered about Joe Louis, a credit to his race. These things depend on one's point of view. Ellison's is that he is an American novelist, who sometimes teaches.

Nonetheless, he is a Negro, and last year F. W. Dupee, the critic and teacher, called *Invisible Man* a "veritable *Moby Dick* of the racial crisis." The occasion of Professor Dupee's remark was a poll that the magazine *Book Week* conducted among 200 authors, critics and editors. These literati were asked to choose the most distinguished writers and the most distinguished novels between 1945 and 1965, and the most distinguished novel of all, they said, out of the 10,000 or so that were published, was *Invisible Man*. The No. 1 author, they said, was Saul Bellow. Ellison, because he had just that one book, was only No. 6, but that still put him one place above Norman Mailer and two above Hemingway.

"I failed of eloquence," Ellison says of the book, and perhaps he did; polls may have only a slight value. Still, in 14 years Random House has never had *Invisible Man* out of hard cover and it has gone through three editions in paperback and has been published by the Modern Library. None of these things positively make the book either an American or an underground classic, but there are signs that it could be either or both, and certainly it lives.

When the jury for the National Book Awards—Martha Foley, Irving Howe, Howard Mumford Jones and Alfred Kazin—awarded Ellison the prize, the citation said: "In it [the book] he shows us how invisible we all are to each other. With a positive exuberance of narrative gifts, he has broken away from the conventions and patterns of the tight 'well-made' novel. Mr. Ellison has the courage to take many literary risks, and he has succeeded with them."

Ellison did take literary risks, and it may be hopeless to try to summarize the plot. Between a Joycean prologue and epilogue, there is an unidentified narrator, a Southern Negro, who is introduced as a boy entertaining white businessmen by fighting nine other boys while all wear blindfolds. Then, still spitting blood, he gives a prepared address, full of racial uplift and gradualism, and is rewarded with a scholarship to a Negro college and a briefcase. That night he dreams that he opens the briefcase and finds an inscription, "To Whom It May Concern: Keep This Nigger Boy Running."

The hero goes to the college, but is expelled in his junior year; assigned as a driver for a visiting trustee, a white liberal from Boston, he makes the mistake of taking the trustee away from all

those well-adjusted colored kids on campus and into the back
country. There they meet Trueblood, a bizarre, comic and tragic
man who has committed incest and now finds that the white folks
for the first time look kindly on him. In fact, the trustee, Mr.
Norton, gives him a $100 bill.

But Mr. Norton is shocked and says he must have a stimulant.
Reluctantly the boy drives him to a Negro roadhouse, where the
psychotic inmates of a veterans' hospital, all former members of the
Negro *bourgeoisie,* are on their weekly visit to prostitutes. There
is a riot, and a patient, a former brain surgeon who was beaten by
whites after he saved a life (Trueblood had been rewarded for
depravity), tells Norton that he is a "lyncher of souls."

Norton has seen reality of a sort, and Bledsoe, the Negro president of the college, who is also a conspirator in race uplift, expels
the youth, telling him in a final betrayal that he is only being
suspended. Armed with sealed letters of reference from Bledsoe,
the youth goes to New York to find a job. The letters, in fact, turn
out to be suggestions to keep this nigger boy running.

Eventually, the youth gets a job with Liberty Paint, which makes
whitewash for national monuments. Its slogan is "Keep America
Pure With Liberty Paints," its symbol a screaming eagle. The youth
is told to measure 10 drops of black liquid into white paint and
stir until it becomes invisible. But he unwittingly sabotages the
paint and the black becomes visible. Banished to a lesser job
working for a grotesque Uncle Tom, he is hurt in an accident,
hospitalized in a strange aseptic place and strapped into a machine
that seeks to "produce the results of a prefrontal lobotomy without
the negative aspects of a knife." He is pronounced cured when
he is unable to remember his name.

Thus he is ready for a new life. The latter part of the book
touches, among other things, his involvement in the Brotherhood,
i.e., the Communist Party, his eventual disenchantment, a magnifi-
cently weird black nationalist, a riot in Harlem, and the hero's
retreat into a coal cellar. Here, he says, he can enjoy his invisibility.
Then he falls asleep, dreams that he meets all his antagonists and
that he tells them he is through running. "Not quite," one says, and
they advance on him with a knife. Then they castrate him, and he
is free of all illusion.

Fourteen years after the publication of the *Moby Dick* of the racial crisis, its author sits in the study of an apartment on the eighth floor of a building that is neither in nor out of Harlem, but on the fringe, along Riverside Drive, in an area distinguished more for its vitality than for its charm. He lives there quietly and well, thinking long thoughts that he sometimes puts into essays or reviews, and working on a novel that he has been writing and rewriting for 10 years.

"I am a novelist, not an activist," he says, "but I think that no one who reads what I write or who listens to my lectures can doubt that I am enlisted in the freedom movement. As an individual, I am primarily responsible for the health of American literature and culture. When I write, I am trying to make sense out of chaos. To think that a writer must think about his Negroness is to fall into a trap."

In a long and splendid exchange with the critic Irving Howe in the pages of *The New Leader,* Ellison accused Howe of trying to "designate the role which Negro writers are to play more rigidly than any Southern politician—and for the best of reasons. We must express 'black' anger and 'clenched militancy'; most of all we should not become too interested in the problems of the art of literature, even though it is through these that we seek our individual identities. And between writing well and being ideologically militant, we must choose militancy. Well, it all sounds quite familiar and I fear the social order which it forecasts more than I do that of Mississippi."

Furthermore, he is disturbed, Ellison says, by the increasing emphasis on Negroness, on *blackness,* in the Civil Rights movement. "It grows out of despair," he says. "It attempts to define Negroes by their pigmentation, not their culture. What makes you a Negro is having grown up under certain cultural conditions, of having undergone an experience that shapes your culture. There is a body of folklore, a certain sense of American history. There is our psychology and the peculiar circumstances under which we have lived. There is our cuisine, though we don't admit it, and our forms of expression. I speak certain idioms; this is also part of the concord that makes me a Negro."

Ellison, however, does not speak in idioms freely, which can also be part of the concord, just as there are certain jokes that are told only by Negroes to Negroes (sometimes they are very funny). Ellison measures his words very carefully and he does not gesture much beyond a little dab in the air with a long slender cigar. When he is annoyed he hunches his shoulders and his radio-announcer voice rises from about baritone to tenor. He can be idiomatic then, and when he is, he amuses himself. "The Moynihan report complained that Negroes don't strut any more." Annoyed, voice rising. "Why, Negro faggots are the struttingest people I know." Laughing at himself.

Nevertheless, he is annoyed by the Moynihan report. The report, which was prepared by Daniel P. Moynihan when he was Assistant Secretary of Labor, says that the Negro family is disintegrating and that, more and more, Negroes are living in a matriarchal society. "Moynihan looked at a fatherless family and interpreted it not in the context of Negro cultural patterns, but in a white cultural pattern," Ellison says. "He wasn't looking for the accommodations Negroes have worked out in dealing with fatherless families. Grandmothers very often look after the kids. The mother works or goes on relief. The kids identify with stepfathers, uncles, even the mother's boy friends. How children grow up is a cultural, not a statistical, pattern."

Boy and man, Ellison has had a multiplicity of cultural influences. First, there was Oklahoma City, where he was born in 1914, which was the year his mother canvassed for the Socialists. Later, his mother, who was a domestic, was thrown into jail with the utmost regularity for violating the segregation orders laid down by Gov. "Alfalfa" Bill Murray.

Nevertheless, Ellison recalls life in Oklahoma City as lush. For one thing, there was music. Ellison played the trumpet in high school and hung around the Blue Devils, which grew into Count Basie's band. He had an older friend, Jimmy Rushing, the blues singer, and he knew Hot Lips Paige, who used to borrow his mellophone. Ellison remembers Lester Young, the tenor sax man, who came to town in 1929 and jammed in Halley Richardson's shoeshine parlor, and he remembers reading Hemingway for the first time in Negro barbershops. There were also the discarded opera records and copies of *Vanity Fair* that his mother brought

him from the homes where she worked. There were the sights and
sounds of the Negro community, and there was T. S. Eliot, whom
he began to read in his second year at Tuskegee Institute in Alabama.

Ellison had gone to Tuskegee to study music in 1933, the year the
Scottsboro boys were being retried, and he got there after being
thrown off a freight train in Macon County, Ala. He stayed at
Tuskegee three years and then went to New York to study
sculpture. On his second day there he met Langston Hughes on the
steps of the Harlem Y.M.C.A., and through Hughes he met
Richard Wright. When Ellison decided to write, it was Wright who
encouraged him and then guided him to the works of Joseph
Conrad, to the letters of Dostoyevsky and the prefaces of Henry
James and told him that, above all, writing must be done consciously.

In *Shadow and Act,* a collection of his essays published by
Random House in 1964, Ellison said that when he began to write
he was forced "to stare down the deadly and hypnotic temptation
to interpret the world and all its devices in terms of race."

"Writers are writers," he says, "and if you're good, you're good,
and I don't think racial matters should enter." He also mourns
the fact that critics sometimes measure a Negro's output by lesser
standards than they do a white writer's. He finds this a peculiarly
depressing kind of patronage. "Bad art is bad art," he says.

Ellison is reminded of an article by a well-known liberal, a
liberal's liberal really, which said that American Negroes needed only
two things: jobs and self-respect. "I despise that business of self-
respect," he says. "It is a cliché that has been picked up from
the sociologists. I don't know any Negroes who don't respect
themselves. I can't imagine anyone who has such a shallow
conception of humanity as to think they don't."

This, of course, denies the conventional wisdom: Negroes are
supposed to be hung up in their psyches. Ellison recalls a night in
1950 when he and his wife were on vacation and met some whites
who sought to show their breadth and humanity by telling Ellison
just what it was, exactly, that Negroes felt. Annoyed, he retreated
to his room where he wrote the character of Ras the Destroyer,
the black nationalist in *Invisible Man.* If you accept Ras's premise

about whites, which is that they are no good, then his arguments
are unassailable.

That night was 16 years ago, and by then only about 100 novels by
American Negroes had ever been published. The first 30 or so
were written between 1853 and 1920. Many were about sad qua-
droons and many were about "passing." Most were terribly
genteel. It was not until about 1920 that Negro poets and novelists
began to sing about Negroness.

These poets and novelists were members of what was variously
called the Negro Renaissance, the "New Negro" movement, and,
finally, the Harlem School. The Harlem School wrote about exotics.
It celebrated things like rent parties and ran heavily to the use of
idiom. It had literary virtue and it was deplored by Negro intellectuals like W. E. B. Du Bois, who, whatever his other qualities, was
a prude. In *Home to Harlem,* Du Bois wrote of the novel by Claude
McKay, "for the most part nauseates me, and after the dirtier parts
of its filth, I feel distinctly like taking a bath." All this, of course,
was followed by the Depression, which in retrospect, though not
in fact, was dominated by Richard Wright, the Federal Writers'
Project, Marxism and the search for a black proletariat.

The motif of the Depression years was protest. Ellison wrote
Invisible Man in their aftermath, and it was published three years
before the Montgomery bus boycott became the first of quite
another kind of protest. Chronologically, *Invisible Man* hangs
between these two times and so, in a way, does Ellison.

"I rejected Marxism," he says, "because it cast the Negro as a
victim and looked at him through ideology. Furthermore, what was
written by proletarian writers was so empty that I could tell they
weren't interested in art at all." And of today, he says: "Some
civil rights leaders, for all their courage, have neglected to work out
an approach to society that goes beyond the level of protest. Civil
rights laws and agitation have changed the nation. They don't
recognize this. The moment of the apocalypse is past and they're
still trying to bring it about."

Ellison looks over a Mies van der Roche chair in his apartment (the
chair is his equivalent of a cadillac, he says), and at a stylized bronze

of a horse and rider that was done by Peter Berthold Schlwetz Jr.,
whom he calls Tex, and, he says, "One thing is certain: the Negro
cannot at this stage of the game stay outside the general complex of
American institutions, even if he cannot get into them. There is
no use talking about the white Establishment and the mainstream,
and there is no use saying, 'I don't want to be integrated into a
burning house.' When we first came to this country, we didn't have
the techniques or the skills. This is still true. Once Negro leaders
grasp this fact they will cease to be Negro leaders and be American
leaders. Far too often they are provincial in their approach, acting
as if all the problems were specifically Negro problems.

"The leaders who function most effectively are the ones who
grasp the complexities of American life, not those who simply
rant against it. This is still a racist society; but just recognizing this
and having the ability to bring crowds into the street is no
guarantee that a leader will know how to guide his followers or that
he has any real power. Real power comes from the mastery of
political technique plus the discovery of such organizational techniques as will win the support of followers, who, in turn, will
allow these leaders to achieve their will."

Ellison says that Adam Clayton Powell, despite his difficulties in
the House of Representatives, knows the relationships of power,
and, because he does, is an effective leader. (Ellison says he is
amused to see respectable publications damning Powell as a racist
while they praise certain Southern Senators.) "Martin Luther King
has limitations when he functions politically because he is a church-
man," he says. "Once the struggle is moved from the streets into
the elaborate process of politics, his framework restrains him."

Ellison adds that he is not nonviolent, but that he can only admire
King for adapting a very old Negro tradition. Ellison does not like
to talk personalities, which is unfortunate because he has views on
people as well as things. He is, for instance, clearly out of sympathy
with those who present themselves as the only true voice of the
ghetto, who insist that the only authentic sound is a long wail of
despair or of degradation. He says they are bragging. He also says
there have been no more than a half dozen good novels by
American Negroes, but he will not say which ones they are.

Ellison was at home the other day after returning from Washington where he had testified before a Senate subcommittee on what it called "the crisis of the cities." He had told the Senators that it was a mistake to assume that Negroes wanted simply to break out of Harlem. They want to transform it, he said, "the Harlems of their country."

"These places are precious to them. These places are where they have dreamed, where they have lived, where they have loved, where they have worked out life as they could. It isn't the desire to run to the suburbs or to invade white neighborhoods that is the main concern with my people in Harlem. They would just like to have a more human life there. A slum like Harlem isn't just a place of decay. It is also a form of historical and social memory."

The statement was consistent with things Ellison had said before, and he seemed a little surprised that it had been picked up, slightly bowdlerized, by a large part of the press.

That afternoon he began to talk about writing and about places he had lived, and he said that "if you try to discover what an American environment is, you find that it's more people than places, because people are connected by taste and sensibility. An intellectual's environment is shaped by other intellectuals."

He spoke about his own friends, and he mentioned Al Murray in Harlem, Stanley Edgar Hyman in Vermont, Robert Penn Warren in France and Jimmy Rushing in Queens. He visited Rushing every so often, he said, and it kept him close to his Oklahoma background. Hyman is an old intellectual sparring partner, and Murray, who lives between Fifth and Lenox in what is invariably called a ghetto, is a retired Air Force man who writes, teaches and shares Ellison's preoccupation with books and jazz. Murray, Ellison said, "reaffirms the general contours of my life."

Ellison talked about writing then and said that "if I give a negative picture of Negro life, if I demonstrate that everything in the Moynihan report is true, or write that all Negroes are rapists, then people will say, 'Yes, they really are like that. I don't have to worry about their condition.' "

Ellison paused, and a dignified Labrador named Tucka sauntered through the room. Tucka is the grandson of a dog owned by John Cheever; when Ellison was Alexander White Visiting Professor of

Literature at the University of Chicago, lecturing about the influence of the Civil War on American literature, Tucka was boarded with Vance Bourjaily in Iowa, which Ellison, the Oklahoman, pronounces something like "eye-way."

Ellison got to talking about Washington, and he said he thought that Lyndon Johnson was a good President and that he was being more forthright on some domestic issues than Franklin D. Roosevelt had been. "And as an Oklahoman," Ellison said, "I'm not bothered by his Texas accent."

He was asked about the White House Festival on the Arts last year and the petition Dwight MacDonald had circulated that was critical of American policy in Vietnam. Ellison said it had been "stupid of Dwight, not only stupid but in bad taste when we were guests of the President." He had been especially critical of Robert Lowell at the time, he said, because Lowell was the one who had introduced Vietnam as an issue.

Tucka lumbered through again and Ellison was reminded of hunting in Eye-way and of going after ducks on Long Island and pheasants in Dutchess County. There was also that bad time in Dayton, Ohio, in 1937 when he had supported himself and his brother by hunting and selling game. That winter, when the temperature had skidded toward zero, they had slept in a car in a garage that had both ends open. He had learned about wing shooting then by reading Hemingway on technique.

Ellison likes things of the earth, and he worries about the fungus on the African violets that he raises in his study. He likes to fish and he likes to bird-watch on Riverside Drive. He has spotted a mocking bird and a rose-breasted grosbeak there, and the largest woodcock he has ever seen came zooming in off 154th Street.

These are quiet pursuits, and Ellison leads, he said, a quiet life. He rises by 7, pads out to the hallway to pick up the paper and, if his wife, Fannie, is not up, he makes coffee. Then he reads the paper or watches the news on television. By 9 he is at his desk working, probably on the new novel, typing it on sheets of white or blue paper that he sticks into one of three big leather binders. If he is working hard, he will smoke cigars, and after a while they will make him sick and he will complain that his stomach feels dead. If the writing is going well he will be enjoying himself. It will seem to him that writing is not such a bad thing after all, and he will refuse to answer the phone. If he is going really well he will eat lunch at his desk. If he is having only a fair day, he will read after lunch or else tinker, which is his word for whatever it is that he does with the mass of hi-fi equipment he has stuffed into one closet. He is good at this kind of thing, and in the lean times just before *Invisible Man* was published he made money by building whole hi-fi systems.

Ellison also has a knack for color photography, and for a while he made a living at that, too. That afternoon he picked up and put down color photographs he had taken of his wife and of friends. He played a little on one of three recorders that stood with an old wooden flute in the corner of the study, and he showed off his collection of Kachina dolls from the Hopi and Zuñi Indians. He walked about his apartment, with its enormous collection of books, and into the bedroom, where there was a picture of a Negro girl, very romantic, and an etching of a Negro man, very black, by an Italian sculptor. There was also a photograph of Ellison, Bernard DeVoto and Archibald MacLeish at the National Book Awards ceremony, and a picture of Ellison's brother, who works for the city of Los Angeles.

Next to the bedroom was a smaller study, with more books, a desk greatly awash with pieces of paper, and a lot of black cardboard boxes with white letters on them: Malraux, Hemingway, Jazz and Sports, National Arts Council. He said that his wife looked after the boxes, just as she did the rest of his files.

Ellison said then that he had all the normal impediments of being a Negro, preferring, for example, to drive his 1960 Chrysler when he went out at night because he had what he called the normal amount of taxi trouble. "But if there is a rebuff, and I suspect many Negroes are like me, I consider it part of the environment," he said. "I am utterly amused when I go into a store to spend $100 and some little clerk is rude."

"You see," he said, "I don't allow anonymous people to give me a sense of my worth."

A Very Stern Discipline: An Interview with Ralph Ellison

Steve Cannon, Lennox Raphael, and James Thompson / 1967

From *Harper's Magazine*, March 1967, 76–95. Copyright © 1967 by *Harper's Magazine*. All rights reserved. Reproduced from the March issue by special permission.

Ralph Ellison's memorable first novel, Invisible Man, *winner of the National Book Award for 1952, brought him immediately to the front rank of American writers. His essay, "Harlem Is Nowhere," appeared in* Harper's *in 1964, and was included in his book of essays and reviews,* Shadow and Act. *Ellison is a native of Oklahoma City. In 1933 he went to the Deep South to Tuskegee Institute in Alabama, where he majored in music. Later he came to New York City to study sculpture, but he turned to writing and since 1939 his stories and articles have been widely published. This interview, which Ellison has revised from the original tapes, was conducted by three young Negro writers.*

Interviewers: *Do you think that one of the faults of the Negro writer is that he is unable to come to terms with the human condition—particularly that of the Negro in America?*

Ellison: Here I don't like to speak generally. The conception of the human condition varies for each and every writer just as it does for each and every individual. Each must live within the isolation of his own senses, dreams, and memories; each must die his own death. For the writer the problem is to project his own conception eloquently and artistically. Like all good artists, he stakes his talent against the world. But if a Negro writer is going to listen to sociologists—as too many of us do—who tell us that Negro life is thus-and-so in keeping with certain sociological theories, he is in trouble because he will have abandoned his task before he begins. If he accepts the clichés to the effect that the Negro family is usually a broken family, that it is matriarchal in form and that the

mother dominates and castrates the males, if he believes that Negro
males are having all of these alleged troubles with their sexuality, or
that Harlem is a "Negro ghetto"—which means to paraphrase one
of our writers, "piss in the halls and blood on the stairs"—well,
he'll never see the people of whom he wishes to write. He'll never
learn to use his own eyes and his own heart, and he'll never
master the art of fiction.

I don't deny that these sociological formulas are drawn from life,
but I do deny that they define the complexity of Harlem. They
only abstract it and reduce it to proportions which the sociologists
can manage. I simply don't recognize Harlem in them. And I
certainly don't recognize the people of Harlem whom I know.
Which is by no means to deny the ruggedness of life there, nor the
hardship, the poverty, the sordidness, the filth. But there is something else in Harlem, something subjective, willful, and complexly
and compellingly human. It is "that something else" that challenges
the sociologists who ignore it, and the society which would deny its
existence. It is that "something else" which makes for our strength,
which makes for our endurance and our promise. This is the
proper subject for the Negro American writer. Hell, he doesn't have
to spend all the tedious time required to write novels simply to
repeat what the sociologists and certain white intellectuals are
broadcasting like a zoo full of parrots—and getting much more
money for it than most Negro writers will ever see. If he does this
he'll not only go begging, but worse, he'll lie to his people,
discourage their interest in literature, and emasculate his own talent.

This is tricky terrain, because today the sociologists are up to
their necks in politics and have access to millions of governmental
dollars, which, I'm afraid, have been secured at the cost of propa-
gating an image of the Negro condition which is apt to destroy
our human conception of ourselves just at the moment when we are
becoming politically free. Those who buy this image are surely in
trouble, no matter the money it brings.

One of the saddest sights currently to be seen is that provided by
one of our most "angry" Negro writers who has allowed himself to
be enslaved by his acceptance of negative sociological data. He
rants and raves against society, but he's actually one of the safest
Negroes on the scene. Because he challenges nothing, he can only

shout "'taint" to some abstract white "'tis," countering lies with lies. The human condition? He thinks that white folks have ruled Negroes out of it.

A few years ago there was a drunk who collected newspapers from the shops along Broadway between 145th and 153rd Streets. He was a Negro who had fought the wine for a long time and who when drunk was capable of a metaphysical defiance. His favorite pastime was to take a stand near a stoplight and accost white people who stopped for the traffic signal with shouts of "Why don't you go back down town! I want all you white m . . . f . . . s—mens *and* womens—to go on back down town!" Our hate-mongering fellow writer reminds me very much of this man, for he is about as effective and no less obscene. Yes, we do have a terrible time in dealing with the human condition.

One critic has said that the Jewish writer went through a similar period. I think he was trying to say that the Negro writer would very soon get over this and become the major strength in American literature.

I hope he's right, but I wouldn't want to make a prediction. I think, however, that the parallel is much too facile. Jewish writers are more familiar with literature as a medium of expression. Their history provides for a close identification with writers who were, and are, Jewish even when they wrote or write in languages other than Yiddish or Hebrew; and this even when that identification rests simply on a shared religious tradition and hardly on any other cultural ground whatsoever. It reminds me of our attempts to claim Pushkin and Dumas as Negroes.

By contrast, neither Negro American expression nor religion has been primarily literary. We are by no means, as is said of the Jews, "people of the Book"—not that I see this as a matter for regret. For we have a wider freedom of selection. We took much from the ancient Hebrews and we do share, through Christianity, the values embodied in the literature of much of the world. But our expression has been oral as against "literary." And when it comes to the question of identifying those writers who have shaped American literature—the framers of the Declaration, the Constitution, and Lincoln excepted—we tend to project racial categories into the areas of artistic technique, form, insight; areas where race has no proper place. We seem to forget that one can identify with what a writer has written, with its form, its manner, techniques, while *rejecting* the writer's beliefs, his prejudices, philosophy, values.

The Jewish American writers have, on the other hand, identified with Eliot, Pound, Hemingway, and Joyce *as writers* while questioning and even rejecting their various attitudes toward the Jews, toward religion, politics, and many other matters. They have taken possession of that which they could use from such writers and converted it to express their own personal and group sense of reality; they have used it to express their own definitions of the American experience. But we Negro writers seem seldom to have grasped this process of acculturation. Too often we've been in such haste to express our anger and our pain as to allow the single tree of race to obscure our view of the magic forest of art.

If Negro writers ever become the mainstay of American literature, it will be because they have learned their craft and used the intensity, emotional and political, of their group experience to express a greater area of American experience than the writers of other groups. What the Jewish American writer had to learn before he could find his place was the American-ness of his experience. He had to see himself as American and project his Jewish experience as an experience unfolding within this pluralistic society. When this was done, it was possible to project this variant of the American experience as a metaphor for the whole.

However, I don't believe that any one group can speak for the whole experience—which isn't, perhaps, desirable. They can only reduce it to metaphor, and no one has yet forged a metaphor rich enough to reduce American diversity to form. Certainly the current group of Jewish writers—among whom there are several I admire—do not speak adequately for me or for Negroes generally. But during the Thirties Jewish writing, although more skillful, was as provincial as most Negro American writing is today. That's the way it was and we don't solve problems of history by running away from them. And what I mean by provincial is an inability to see beyond the confines, the constrictions, placed upon Jewish life by its religious and cultural differences with the larger society; by its being basically the experience of an immigrant people who were, by and large, far less cultured than their more representative members.

It took long years of living in this country, long years of being a unique part of American society and discovering that they were not *forced* to live on the East Side, of discovering that there *was* a place for the Jews in this society which did not depend upon their losing their group identity. They discovered that they possessed something precious to bring to the broader American culture, on the lowest as well as on the highest levels of human activity, and that it would have a creative impact far beyond the Jewish community. Many had not only to learn the language but, more wonderful, they had to discover that the Jewish American idiom would lend a whole new dimension to the American language.

How do the situations of the Negro and Jewish writers differ?
I think that Negro Americans as *writers* run into certain problems which the Jews don't have. One is that our lives, since slavery, have been described mainly in terms of our political, economic, and social conditions as measured by outside norms, seldom in terms of our *own* sense of life or our *own* sense of values gained from our *own* unique American experience. Nobody bothered to ask Negroes how they felt about their own lives. Southern whites used to tell the joke about the white employer who said to a Negro worker. "You're a good hand and I appreciate you. You make my business go much better. *But* although you work well every day, I can never get you to work on Saturday night, even if I offer to pay you overtime. Why is this?" Of course, you know the answer: "If you could just be a Negro one Saturday night you'd never want to be a white man again." Now this is a rather facile joke, and a white Southern joke on Negroes; nevertheless, it does indicate an awareness that there is an internality to Negro American life, that it possesses its own attractions and its own mystery.

Now, the pathetic element in the history of Negro American writing is that it started out by reflecting the styles popular at the time, styles uninterested in the human complexity of Negroes. These were the styles of dialect humor transfused into literature from the *white* stereotype of the Negro minstrel tradition. This was

Dunbar and Chesnutt. It helped them get published but it got in
the way of their subject matter and their goal of depicting Negro
personality. And let's face it, these were times when white
publishers and the white reading public only wished to encounter
certain types of Negroes in poetry and fiction.

Even so, it was not a Negro writer who created the most memorable character in this tradition but Mark Twain, whose Nigger Jim
is, I think, one of the important characters in our literature. Nevertheless, Jim is flawed by his relationship to the minstrel tradition.
Twain's drawing of Jim reflected the popular culture of the 1880s,
just as the Negro characters you get in much of current fiction are
influenced by the stereotypes presented by the movies and by
sociology—those even more powerful media of popular culture.

The Negro writers who appeared during the 1920s wished to
protest discrimination; some wished to show off their high regard
for respectability; they wished to express their new awareness of
the African background, and, as Americans trying to win a place
as writers, they were drawn to the going style of literary decadence
represented by Carl Van Vechten's work. This was an extremely
ironic development for a group whose written literature was still in
its infancy—as incongruous as the notion of a decadent baby.
More ironic, this was a time when Eliot, Pound, Hemingway, and
Stein were really tearing American literature apart and reshaping its
values and its styles in the "revolution of the word." We always
picked the moribund style. We took to dialect at a time when
Benito Cereno, Moby Dick, and *Leaves of Grass* were at hand to
point a more viable direction for a people whose demands were
revolutionary, and whose humanity had been badly distorted by the
accepted styles.

During the 1930s we were drawn, for more understandable reasons, to the theories of proletarian literature. So during the
Twenties we had wanted to be fashionable and this insured, even
more effectively than the approaching Depression, the failure of the
"New Negro" movement. We fell into that old trap by which the
segregated segregate themselves by trying to turn whatever the
whites said against us into its opposite. If they said Negroes loved
fried chicken (and why shouldn't we?), we replied, "We *hate* fried
chicken." If they said, "Negroes have no normal family life," we

replied, "We have a staider, more refined, more puritanical family life than you." If they said that Negroes love pork chops, we replied, "We despise them!" With few exceptions, our energies as writers have too often been focused upon outside definitions of reality, and we've used literature for racial polemics rather than as an agency through which we might define experience as we ourselves have seen and felt it. These are negative charges, I know, but they seem true to me.

Indeed, it's very difficult, even today, for younger Negro writers to come along and overcome these negative tendencies. Far too often they have been taught to think in Jim Crow terms: "I can do thus and so—not because human beings express themselves in these ways, but because such and such a *Negro* dared to do so." And if no other Negro has involved himself in the activity in question, then we tend to draw back and doubt that we might do very well even as pioneers. And so the younger writer comes along and tries to write on the models of other Negro writers rather than on the best writers regardless of race, class, or what have you—completely ignoring the fact that all other writers try to pattern themselves on the achievements of the greatest writers, regardless of who the hell they were.

This is how the Jim Crow experience has gotten into our attitudes and set us back. We have been exiled in our own land and, as for our efforts at writing, we have been little better than silent because we have not been cunning. I find this rather astounding, because I feel that Negro American folklore is very powerful, wonderful, and universal. And it became so by expressing a people who were assertive, eclectic, and irreverent before all the oral and written literature that came within its grasp. It took what it needed to express its sense of life and rejected what it couldn't use.

But what we've achieved in folklore has seldom been achieved in the novel, the short story, or poetry. In the folklore we tell what Negro experience really is. We back away from the chaos of experience and from ourselves, and we depict the humor as well as the horror of our living. We project Negro life in a metaphysical perspective and we have seen it with a complexity of vision that seldom gets into our writing. One reason for this lies in the poor teaching common to our schools and colleges, but the main failure

lies, I think, in our simpleminded attempt to reduce fiction to a
mere protest.

*I notice that you mentioned, quite some time ago, that you
learned a lot of skill under Richard Wright. Do you find that he
gauged his craft to the great writers of the world?*
He certainly tried to do so. He was constantly reading the great
masters, just as he read the philosophers, the political theorists, the
social and literary critics. He did not limit himself in the manner
that many Negro writers currently limit themselves. And he encouraged other writers—who usually rebuffed him—to become conscious craftsmen, to plunge into the world of conscious literature
and take their chances unafraid. He felt this to be one of the few
areas in which Negroes could be as free and as equal as their
minds and talents would allow. And like a good Negro athlete, he
believed in his ability to compete. In 1940 he was well aware that
Native Son was being published at a time when *The Grapes of
Wrath* and *For Whom the Bell Tolls* would be his main competition.
Nevertheless, he looked toward publication day nervously but ea-
gerly. He wished to be among the most advanced artists and was
willing to run the risk required.

*Earlier you referred to the minstrel as a stereotype. Is it possible
to treat such stereotypes as Sambo, or even Stepin Fetchit, as
archetypes or motives instead of using them in the usual format?*
Well, in fiction stereotypes partake of archetypes. And to the
extent that stereotypes point to something basically human, they
overlap. And yes, in literary form stereotypes function, as to other
forms of characterization, as motives. But the point is that they
act as *imposed* motives which treat reality and character arbitrarily.
Thus to redeem them as you suggest, the writer is challenged to
reveal the archetypical truth hidden within the stereotype. Here
archetypes are embodiments of abiding patterns of human existence which underlie racial, cultural, and religious differences. They
are, in their basic humanity, timeless and raceless; while stereotypes are malicious reductions of human complexity which seize
upon such characteristics as color, the shape of a nose, an accent,
hair texture, and convert them into emblems which render it unnec-

essary for the prejudiced individual to confront the humanity of those upon whom the stereotype has been imposed.

So in answer to your question as to whether it is possible to use such stereotypes as Sambo and Stepin Fetchit, I'd say that it depends upon the writer's vision. If I should use such stereotypes in fiction, I'd have to reveal their archetypical aspects because my own awareness *of,* and identification *with,* the human complexity which they deny would compel me to transform them into something more recognizably human. To do less would be to reveal a brutalization of my own sense of human personality.

On the other hand, let's take Faulkner. When Lucas Beauchamp first appears in Faulkner's work he appears as a stereotype, but as he was developed throughout the successive novels, he became one of Faulkner's highest representatives of human quality. Or again, when Ned in the last book, *The Reivers,* is seen superficially he appears to be the usual head-scratching, eye-rolling Negro stereotype. But beneath this mask, Ned is a version of John, the archetypical Negro slave of Negro folklore, who always outwits and outtalks his master. Ned masterminds the action of the novel and in so doing he is revealed as Faulkner's own persona. He is the artist disguised as Negro rogue and schemer.

This suggests that attempts to approach stereotypes strictly in racial terms is, for the Negro writer, very, very dangerous. We must first question what they conceal, otherwise we place ourselves in the position of rejecting the basic truth concealed in the stereotype along with its obvious falsehood. Truth is much too precious for that.

On the stage of Town Hall a few days before the 1964 Democratic Convention, a group from the Mississippi Freedom Democratic Party talked of their experiences. To the facile eye one of the men who talked there might well have been mistaken for the Sambo stereotype. He was Southern, rural; his speech was heavily idiomatic, his tempo slow. A number of his surface characteristics seemed to support the stereotype. But had you accepted him as an incarnation of Sambo you would have missed a very courageous man—a man who understood only too well that his activities in aiding and protecting the young Northern students working in the Freedom Movement placed his life in constant contact with death,

but who continued to act. Now I'm not going to reject that man
because some misinformed person, some prejudiced person, sees
him as the embodiment of Uncle Tom, or Sambo. What's inside
you, brother; what's your heart like? What are your real values?
What human qualities are hidden beneath your idiom?

*Do you think the reason for this is that Negroes in the U.S. are
caught, if they allow themselves to be, in a bind? Do you think
that the Negro writer then is forced, sometimes, to go away to gain
a perspective? Or can he transcend his situation by remaining
in it?*

Well, again, I would say that the individual must do that which is
necessary for him individually. However, I would also say that it
is not objectively necessary to go away. He might solve his problem
by leaving the Village or by leaving Harlem. Harlem has always
been a difficult place for Negroes to gain perspective on the national
experience, because it has sponsored a false sense of freedom. It
has also sponsored a false sense of superiority regarding Negroes
who live elsewhere. I remember getting into an argument during
World War II with a fellow who insisted that Southern Negroes had
no knowledge of boxing or baseball. This came from refusing to
use his eyes around New York.

One frees oneself, as a writer, by actually going in and trying to
get the shape of experience *from the writer's perspective*. I see
no other way. But this, unfortunately, requires a writer's type of
memory—which is strongly emotional and associative—and a certain
amount of technique. You must pay the Negro community the
respect of trying to see it through the enrichening perspectives provided by great literature—using your own intelligence to make up
for the differences in economy, in class background, in education,
in conscious culture, in manners and in attitude toward values.
Human beings are basically the same and differ mainly in lifestyle.
Here revelation is called for, not argument.

How do you mean, "argument"?

I mean that it's futile to argue our humanity with those who
willfully refuse to recognize it, when art can reveal on its own
terms more truth while providing pleasure, insight, and for Negro
readers at least, affirmation and a sense of direction. We must

assert our own sense of values, beginning with the given and the irrevocable, with the question of heroism and slavery.

Contrary to some, I feel that our experience as a people involves a great deal of heroism. From one perspective, slavery was horrible and brutalizing. It is said that "Those Africans were enslaved, they died in the 'middle passage,' they were abused, their families were separated, they were whipped, they were raped, ravaged, and emasculated." And the Negro writer is tempted to agree. "Yes! God damn it, wasn't that a horrible thing!" And he sometimes agrees to the next step, which holds that slaves had very little humanity because slavery destroyed it for them and their descendants. That's what the Stanley M. Elkins "Sambo" argument implies. But despite the historical past and the injustices of the present, there is from *my* perspective something further to say. I have to *affirm* my forefathers and I *must* affirm my parents or be reduced in my own mind to a white man's inadequate—even if unprejudiced—conception of human complexity. Yes, and I must affirm those unknown people who sacrificed for me. I'm speaking of those Negro Americans who never knew that a Ralph Ellison might exist, but who by living their own lives and refusing to be destroyed by social injustice and white supremacy, real or illusory, made it possible for me to live my own life with meaning. I am forced to look at these people and upon the history of life in the U.S. and conclude that there is another reality behind the appearance of reality which they would force upon us as truth.

Any people who could endure all of that brutalization and keep together, who could undergo such dismemberment and resuscitate itself, and endure until it could take the initiative in achieving its own freedom is obviously more than the sum of its brutalization. Seen in this perspective, theirs has been one of the great human experiences and one of the great triumphs of the human spirit in modern times. In fact, in the history of the world.

Some might say to your argument that you are expressing your own hopes and aspirations for Negroes, rather than reporting historical reality.

But hope and aspiration are indeed important aspects of the reality of Negro American history, no less than that of others. Be-

sides, it's one of our roles as writers to remind ourselves of such
matters, just as it is to make assertions tempered by the things of the
spirit. It might sound arrogant to say so, but writers, poets, help
create or reveal hidden realities by asserting their existence. Otherwise they might as well become social scientists.

I do not find it a strain to point to the heroic component of our
experience, for these seem to me truths which we have long lived
by but which we must now recognize consciously. And I am not
denying the negative things which have happened to us and which
continue to happen, but I am compelled to reject all condescending,
narrowly paternalistic interpretations of Negro American life and
personality from whatever quarters they come, whether white or
Negro. Such interpretations would take the negative details of our
existence and make them the whole of our life and personality. But
literature teaches us that mankind has always defined itself
against the negatives thrown it by both society and the universe. It
is human will, human hope, and human effort which make the
difference. Let's not forget that the great tragedies not only treat of
negative matters, of violence, brutalities, defeats, but they treat
them within a context of man's will to act, to challenge reality and
to snatch triumph from the teeth of destruction.

*You said it's unnecessary for one to leave the country to get a
perspective. We notice in some of your older writings that after
having come back from Rome you sat up in New Hampshire and
wrote* Invisible Man.

No, I started *Invisible Man*—that novel about a man characterized by what the sociologists term "high visibility"—in Vermont,
during the few months before the war came to an end. I was cooking
on merchant ships at the time and had been given shore leave, so
I accepted the invitation of a friend and went up there. I had no idea
that I was going to start a book. But maybe I should add this: it
isn't *where* you are that's important, but what you seek to depict,
and most important of all is perspective. And the main perspective
through which a writer looks at experience is that provided by
literature—just as the perspective through which a physician
looks at the human body is the discipline of medicine; an accumula-
tion of techniques, insights, instruments, and processes which

have been slowly developed over long periods of time. So when I
look at my material I'm not looking at it simply through the
concepts of sociology—and I do know something about sociology.
I look at it through literature; English, French, Spanish, Russian—especially 19th-century Russian literature. And Irish literature, Joyce and Yeats, and through the international literature of the
Twenties. And through the perspective of folklore. When I listen to
a folk story I'm looking for what it conceals as well as what it
states. I read it with the same fullness of attention I bring to
Finnegans Wake or *The Sound and the Fury* because I'm eager to
discover what it has to say to me personally.

Living abroad is very necessary for those Negro writers who feel
that they've been too cramped here and who wish to discover
how it feels to live free of racial restrictions. This is valid. I should
also say this: I came to New York from Tuskegee with the
intention of going back to finish college. I came up to work. I didn't
earn the money so I stayed. But while I lived at the Harlem
YMCA I did *not* come to New York to live in Harlem—even though
I thought of Harlem as a very romantic place. I'm pointing to an
attitude of mind; I was not exchanging Southern segregation for
Northern segregation, but seeking a wider world of opportunity.
And, most of all, the excitement and impersonality of a great city. I
wanted room in which to discover who I was.

So one of the first things I had to do was to enter places from
which I was afraid I might be rejected. I had to confront my own
fears of the unknown. I told myself, "Well, I might be hurt, but I
won't dodge until they throw a punch." Over and over again I
found that it was just this attitude (which finally became unselfcon-
sciously nondefensive) which made the difference between my
being accepted or rejected, and this during a time when many places
practiced discrimination.

This requires submitting oneself to personal ordeals, especially if
one grew up in the South and Southwest. Nor is this because you are
afraid of white people so much as a matter of not wishing to be
rebuffed. You don't wish to be upset when you're going to see a
play by having a racial hassle on your hands. This distaste is very
human. I've had a white Mississippian stop me on the streets of
Rome asking if he would be admitted to a certain place which had

caught his eye. I said, with a certain pleasurable irony, "Sure, go ahead; just tell them you're a friend of mine."

What do you consider the Negro writer's responsibility to American literature as a whole?

The writer, *any* American writer, becomes basically responsible for the health of American literature the moment he starts writing seriously. And this regardless of his race or religious background. This is no arbitrary matter. Just as there is implicit in the act of voting the responsibility of helping to govern, there is implicit in the act of writing a responsibility for the quality of the American language—its accuracy, its vividness, its simplicity, its expressiveness—and responsibility for preserving and extending the quality of the literature.

How do you regard President Johnson's statement that "Art is not a political weapon"? He made it at the White House in 1965.

I don't think you've got it complete; let's read it. He said, "Your art is not a political weapon, yet much of what you do is profoundly political, for you seek out the common pleasures and visions, the terrors and cruelties of man's day on this planet. And I would hope you would help dissolve the barriers of hatred and ignorance which are the source of so much of our pain and danger."

You think that he is far ahead of many people?

He is far ahead of most of the intellectuals—especially those Northern liberals who have become, in the name of the highest motives, the new apologists for segregation. Some of the *Commentary* writers, for instance. Let's put it this way. President Johnson's speech at Howard University spelled out the meaning of full integration for Negroes in a way that no one, no President, not Lincoln nor Roosevelt, no matter how much we love and respected them, has ever done before. There was no hedging in it, no escape clauses.

About Robert Lowell's refusal in 1965 to participate in the White House Art Festival, was this justly done, or do you think that he was engaged too much in politics? Do you think it was necessary?

I do not think it was necessary. When Lowell wrote to the

President—and it was a skillfully written letter—he stated his motives of conscience, his fear that his presence would commit him to the President's foreign policy. In other words, he feared the potency of his own presence in such a setting, a potency which would seem to rest in his person rather than in the poetry for which we praise him and consider him great. But he didn't stop there, the letter got to the press, and once this happened, it became a political act, a political gesture.

I think this was unfortunate. The President wasn't telling Lowell how to write his poetry, and I don't think he's in any position to tell the President how to run the government. Had I been running the Festival I'd simply have had an actor read from Lowell's poetry—with his permission, of course—for then not only would we have had the best of Lowell, but the question of his feelings concerning foreign policy wouldn't have come up.

Actually, no one was questioned as to his attitudes, political or otherwise—except by Dwight Macdonald. It wasn't that kind of occasion. Any and every opinion was represented there. Millard Lampell, who had been picketing the White House, had part of his play presented, and his background is no secret. So it was not in itself a political occasion, and all of the hullabaloo was beside the point. I was very much amazed, having gone through the political madness that marked the intellectual experience of the Thirties, to see so many of our leading American intellectuals, poets, novelists—free creative minds—once again running in a herd. One may take a personal position concerning a public issue which is much broader than his personal morality, and the others make a herd of free creative minds! Some of my best friends are mixed up in it—which leaves me all the more amazed.

Speaking of herd activity, do you think that writers, generally, band together for the added stimulation or appreciation that they need? Or do you think that it is a lack, on their part, of a certain kind of intelligence?

It depends upon their reason for coming together. I think it very important for writers to come together during the early stages of their careers, especially during the stage when they are learning their techniques, when they are struggling for that initial fund of knowledge upon which they form their tastes and upon which artistic choices are made. And it's good for artists to get together to eat and drink—for social activities. But when they get together in some sort of political effort it usually turns out that they are being manipulated by a person or group of persons who are not particularly interested in art.

In other words, are you denying what happened to you in the Thirties, during The New Masses *experience?*

No, I don't deny that at all; instead, I speak out of that experience. But what happened to me during the Thirties was part of a great swell of events which I plunged into when I came to town an undergraduate musician, and through which I gradually transformed myself into a writer. The stimulus that existed in New York during the Thirties was by no means limited to art; it was also connected with politics, it was part of the *esprit de corps* developed in the country after we had endured the Depression for a few years. It had to do with my discovering New York and the unfamiliar areas of the society newly available to me. It had to do with working on the New York Writers Project and getting to know white friends, and being around Richard Wright and around *The New Masses* and the League of American Writers crowd.

But, if you'll note—and the record is public—I never wrote the official type of fiction. I wrote what might be called propaganda— having to do with the Negro struggle—but my fiction was always trying to be something else; something different even from Wright's fiction. I never accepted the ideology which *The New Masses* attempted to impose on writers. They hated Dostoyevsky, but I was studying Dostoyevsky. They felt that Henry James was a decadent, some sort of snob who had nothing to teach a writer from the lower classes—I was studying James. I was also reading Marx, Gorki, Sholokhov, and Isaac Babel. I was reading everything, including the Bible. Most of all, I was reading Malraux. I thought so much of that little Modern Library edition of *Man's Fate* that I had it bound in leather. This is where I was really living at the time. So perhaps it is the writers whose work has most impact upon us that are important, not those with whom we congregate publicly. Anyway, I think style is more important than political ideologies.

Do you see, then, a parallel between the Thirties and the Sixties, with this new resurgence of young Negro writers, with this turning toward Africa and, shall we say again, the resurgence of a particular kind of provincialism in New Negro writing?

I think that we should be very careful in drawing parallels. This is a period of affluence as against the poverty of the Depression. True, during that period a lot of Negroes had the opportunity to work in WPA at clerical jobs and so on, so that for us the Depression represented in many ways a lunge forward. We were beneficiaries of the government's efforts toward national recovery. Thanks to the national chaos, we found new places for ourselves. Today, our lunges forward are facilitated by laws designed precisely to correct our condition as a group—by laws which start at the very top and which have the Supreme Court, the Executive Branch, and Congress behind them. This is quite different from the Thirties.

As to Africa, I think it probably true that more of the present crop of writers are concerned with Africa than was true during that period. In fact, quite a number who were concerned with communism are now fervid black nationalists. Oddly enough, however, their way of writing hasn't changed significantly. Of course, I might not know what I'm talking about, but there seem to be fewer Negro writers around who seem publishable at the moment. Surely there are fewer than the more favorable circumstances of today warrant.

Some people think that you should play a larger part in civil rights. . . . This is similar to Sartre's rebuttal to Camus in Situations, *this idea of "engagement."*

Well, I'm no Camus and they're no Sartres. But literature draws upon much deeper and much more slowly changing centers of the human personality than does politics. It draws mainly from literature itself, and upon the human experience which has abided long enough to have become organized and given significance through literature. I think that revolutionary political movements move much too rapidly to be treated as the subjects for literature in themselves. When Malraux drew upon revolution as the settings for his novels he drew for his real themes upon much deeper levels of his characters' consciousness than their concern with Marxism; and it is to these deeper concerns, to the realm of tragedy, that they turned when facing death. Besides, political movements arise and extend themselves, achieve themselves, through fostering myths which interpret their actions and their goals. And if you tell the truth about a politician, you're always going to encounter contradiction and barefaced lies—especially when you're dealing with left-wing politicians.

If I were to write an account of the swings and twitches of the U.S. Communist line during the Thirties and Forties, it would be a very revealing account, but I wouldn't attempt to do this in terms of fiction. It would have to be done in terms of political science, reportage. You would have to look up their positions, chart their moves, look at the directives handed down by the Communist International—whatever the overall body was called. And you would be in a muck and a mire of dead and futile activity—much of which had little to do with their ultimate goals or with American reality. They fostered the myth that Communism was twentieth-century Americanism, but to be a twentieth-century American meant, in their thinking, that you had to be more Russian than American and less Negro than either. That's how they lost the Negroes. The Communists recognized no plurality of interests and were really responding to the necessities of Soviet foreign policy, and when the war came, Negroes got caught and were made expedient in the shifting of policy. Just as Negroes who fool around with them today are going to get caught in the next turn of the screw.

Do you think there is too much pressure on the Negro writer to play the role of politician, instead of mastering his craft and acting as a professional writer?

Yes, and if he doesn't resist such pressure he's in a bad way. Because someone is always going to tell you that you can't write, and then they tell you *what* to write.

Among the first things the Negro writer has to resist is being told that he'll find it difficult to make a buck. I waded through tons of that. But I decided that I would make sacrifices, go without clothing and other necessities, in order to buy books, in order to be in

New York where I could talk to certain creative people and where I
could observe this or that phenomenon. Resisting these warnings
is most important. And if you deflect this particular pressure, there
will always be people who will tell you that you have no talent.
We understand the psychological dynamics of it—Booker T. Washington gave it the "crabs-in-a-basket" metaphor: if a Negro
threatens to succeed in a field outside the usual areas of Negro
professionals, others feel challenged. It's a protective reaction, a
heritage from slavery. We feel, "Well, my God, he has the nerve to
do that—*I* don't have the nerve to do that; what does he think
he's doing, endangering the whole group?" Nevertheless the writer
must endure the agony imposed by this group pessimism.

Why do you think this exists?
Because of our sense of security and our sense of who we are
depends upon our feeling that we can account for each and every
member of the group. And to this way of thinking any assertion of
individuality is dangerous. I'm reminded of a woman whom I met
at a party. We were discussing Negro life and I uttered opinions
indicating an approach unfamiliar to her. Her indignant response was,
"How do you come talking like that? I never even heard of you!"
In her opinion I had no right to express ideas which hadn't been
certified by her particular social group. Naturally she thought of
herself as a member of a Negro elite and in the position to know
what each and every Negro thought and should think. This is a
minority group phenomenon, and I won't nail it to Negroes
because it happens in the Jewish community as well.

In the interview that you had in Robert Penn Warren's Who
Speaks for the Negro? *he addressed a question to you that has
something to do with Negroes being culturally deprived, and you
answered that many of the white students whom you'd taught
were also culturally deprived. They were culturally deprived, you
said, because while they might have understood many things
intellectually, they were emotionally unprepared to deal with them.
But the Negro was being prepared emotionally, whether intellectually
or not, from the moment he was placed in the crib. Would you
expand that a bit?*
I think you've touched *the* important area that gets lost when we

hold such discussions. I get damn tired of critics writing of me as though I don't know how hard it is to be a Negro American. My point is that it isn't *only* hard, that there are many, many good things about it.

But they don't want you to say that. This is especially true of some of our Jewish critics. They get quite upset when I say: *I like this particular aspect of Negro life and would not surrender it. What I want is something else to go along with it.* And when I get the other things, I'm not going to try to invade the group life of anybody else. And of course they don't like the idea that I reject many of the aspects of life which they regard highly. But you know, white people can get terribly disturbed at the idea that Negroes are not simply being restricted from many areas of our national life, but that they are also judging certain aspects of our culture and rejecting their values. That's where assumptions of white superiority, conscious or unconscious, make for blindness and naïveté. For in fact we've rejected many of their values from the days before there were Jim Crow laws.

Only a narrowly sociological explanation of society could lead to the belief that we Negroes are what we are simply because whites would refuse us the right of choice through racial discrimination. Frequently Negroes are able to pay for commodities available in the stores, but we reject them as a matter of taste—not economics. There is no *de facto* Jim Crow in many areas of New York, but we don't frequent them, not because we think we won't be welcome—indeed many Negroes go to places precisely because they are unfairly and illegally rejected—but because they simply don't interest us. All this *we* know to be true.

Negro Americans had to learn to live under pressure—otherwise we'd have been wiped out, or in the position of the Indians, set on a reservation and rendered powerless by the opposing forces. Fortunately, our fate was different. We were forced into segregation, but within that situation we were able to live close to the larger society and to abstract from that society enough combinations of values—including religion and hope and art—which allowed us to endure and impose our own idea of what the world should be and of what man should be, and of what American society should be.

I'm not speaking of power here, but of vision, of values and dreams. Yes, and of will.

What is missing today is a corps of artists and intellectuals who would evaluate Negro American experience from the inside, and out of a broad knowledge of how people of other cultures live, deal with experience, and give significance to their experience. We do too little of this. Rather we depend upon outsiders—mainly sociologists—to interpret our lives for us. It doesn't seem to occur to us that our interpreters might well be not so much prejudiced as ignorant, insensitive, and arrogant. It doesn't occur to us that they might be of shallow personal culture, or innocent of the complexities of actual living.

It's ironic that we act this way, because over and over again when we find bunches of Negroes enjoying themselves, when they're feeling good and in a mood of communion, they sit around and marvel at what a damnable marvelous human being, what a confounding human type the Negro American really is. This is the underlying significance of so many of our bull sessions. We exchange accounts of what happened to someone whom the group once knew. "You know what that so-and-so did," we say; and then his story is told. His crimes, his loves, his outrages, his adventures, his transformations, his moments of courage, his heroism, buffooneries, defeats, and triumphs are recited with each participant joining in. And this catalogue soon becomes a brag, a very exciting chant celebrating the metamorphosis which this individual in question underwent within the limited circumstances available to us.

This is wonderful stuff; in the process the individual is enlarged. It's as though a transparent overlay of archetypal myth is being placed over the life of an individual, and through him we see ourselves. This, of course, is what literature does with life; these verbal jam sessions are indeed a form of folk literature and they help us to define our own experience.

But when we Negro Americans start *"writing,"* we lose this wonderful capacity for abstracting and enlarging life. Instead we ask, "How do we fit into the sociological terminology? Gunnar Myrdal said this experience means thus and so. And Dr. Kenneth Clark, or Dr. E. Franklin Frazier, says the same thing . . ." And we

try to fit our experience into their concepts. Well, whenever I
hear a Negro intellectual describing Negro life and personality with
a catalogue of negative definitions, my first question is, how did
you escape, is it that you were born exceptional and superior? If I
cannot look at the most brutalized Negro on the street, even when
he irritates me and makes me want to bash his head in because he's
goofing off, I must still say within myself, "Well, that's you too,
Ellison." And I'm not talking about guilt, but of an identification
which goes beyond race.

You have said that Hemingway tells us much more about how
Negroes feel than all the writings done by those people mixed up
in the Negro Renaissance.

What I meant was this: Hemingway's writing of the Twenties and
the Thirties—even of the Forties—evoked certain basic, deeply felt
moods and attitudes within his characters which closely approxi-
mated certain basic attitudes held by many Negroes in regard to their
position in American society, and in regard to their sense of the
human predicament. And he did this not only because he was a
greater writer than the participants in the Negro Renaissance, but
because he possessed a truer sense of what the valid areas of
perplexity were and more accurate sense of how to get life into
literature. He recognized that the so-called "Jazz Age" was a
phony, while most Negro writers jumped on that illusory band-
wagon when they, of all people, should have known better.

I was also referring to Hemingway's characters' attitude toward
society, to their morality, their code of technical excellence, to their
stoicism, their courage or "grace under pressure," to their skepticism as to the validity of political rhetoric and all those abstractions in the name of which our society was supposed to be governed,
but which Hemingway found highly questionable when measured
against our actual conduct. Theirs was an attitude springing from an
awareness that they lived outside the values of the larger society,
and *I* feel that their attitudes came close to the way Negroes felt
about the way the Constitution and the Bill of Rights were applied
to us.

Further, I believe that Hemingway, in depicting the attitudes of
athletes, expatriates, bullfighters, traumatized soldiers, and impo-

tent idealists, told us quite a lot about what was happening to that
most representative group of Negro Americans, the jazz musicians—who also lived by an extreme code of withdrawal, technical
and artistic excellence, rejection of the values of respectable
society. They replaced the abstract and much-betrayed ideals of
that society with the more physical values of eating, drinking,
copulating, loyalty to friends, and dedication to the discipline and
values of their art.

Now I say all this while fully aware that Hemingway seldom
depicted Negroes and that when he did they were seldom the
types we prefer to encounter in fiction. But to see what I mean one
has only to look upon the world of Hemingway's fiction as offering
a valid metaphor not only for the predicament of young whites, but
as a metaphor for the post-World War I period generally. Seen in
this inclusive light he tells us a hell of a lot about the way Negroes
were feeling and acting.

At any rate, this is how I use literature to come to an understanding of our situation. It doesn't have to be, thank God, *about* Negroes
in order to give us insights into our own predicament. You do not,
to my way of thinking, assume that a writer can treat of his times,
if he writes well, *without* revealing a larger segment of life than that
of the specific milieu which engaged his attention; for it must if it
is to be valid go beyond and touch the reality of other groups and
individuals. Faulkner tells us a great deal about many different
groups who were not his immediate concern because he wrote so
truthfully. If you would find the imaginative equivalents of certain
Civil Rights figures in American writing, Rosa Parks and James
Meredith say, you don't go to most fiction by Negroes, but
to Faulkner.

*You have said that you don't accept any theory which implies
that culture is transmitted through the genes. What, then, is your
reaction to the concept of "negritude"?*

To me it represents the reverse of that racism with which prejudiced whites approach Negroes. As a theory of art it implies
precisely that culture is transmitted through the genes. It is a
blood theory.

There are members of my family who are very black people, and there are some who are very white—which means that I am very much Negro, very much Negro American, and quite representative of that racial type with its mixture of African, European, and indigenous American blood. This is a biological fact; but recognizing this, and loving my family, and recognizing that I'm bound to them by blood and family tradition is by no means to agree with the proponents of negritude. Because even while I affirm our common blood line I recognize that we are bound less by blood than by our cultural and political circumstances.

Further, I don't believe that my form of expression springs from Africa, although it might be easier for me as an artist if it did, because then, perhaps, a massive transfusion of pure Nigerian blood would transform me into a great sculptor. I've been reading the classics of European and American literature since childhood, was born to the American tongue and to the language of the Bible and the Constitution; these, for better or worse, shaped my thought and attitudes and pointed the direction of my talent long before I became a conscious writer. I also inherited a group style originated by a "black" people, but it is Negro American, not African. And it was taught to me by Negroes or copied by me from those among whom I lived most intimately.

All this is similar to the notion that Negroes have a corner on soul. *Well, we don't.*

You're right, and anyone who listens to a Beethoven quartet or symphony and can't hear *soul* is in trouble. Maybe they can hear the sound of blackness, but they're deaf to *soul*.

Richard Wright was called a white man.

I've had something like that happen. When I was teaching at Bard College a young Negro girl approached one of my white colleagues and said, "Is this Mr. Ellison a Negro?" Now I can't understand that; it sounds like she was putting him on. Because there I was facing classes with my big African nose, teaching American literature and highlighting the frame so that they could become aware of the Negro experience in it—and she wants to know whether I'm Negro! I suppose the social patterns are changing faster than we can grasp.

Recently we had a woman from the South who helped my wife

with the house but who goofed off so frequently that she was
fired. We liked her and really wanted her to stay, but she simply
wouldn't do her work. My friend Albert Murray told me I
shouldn't be puzzled over the outcome. "You know how we can be
sometimes." Al said. "She saw the books and the furniture and
paintings, so she knew you were some kind of white man. You
couldn't possibly be a Negro. And so she figured she could get away
with a little boondoggling on general principles, because she'd
probably been getting away with a lot of stuff with Northern
whites. But what she didn't stop to notice was that you're a
Southern white man. . . ."

So you see, here culture and race and a preconception of how
Negroes are supposed to live—a question of taste—had come together
and caused a comic confusion. Such jokes as Al Murray's are
meaningful because in America culture is always cutting across racial
characteristics and social designations. Therefore, if a Negro
doesn't exhibit certain attitudes, or if he reveals a familiarity with
aspects of the culture, or possesses qualities of personal taste which
the observer has failed to note among Negroes, then such confusions in perception are apt to occur.

But the basic cause is, I think, that we are all members of a highly
pluralistic society. We possess two cultures—both American—and
many aspects of the broader American culture are available to
Negroes who possess the curiosity and taste—if not the
money—to cultivate them. It is often overlooked, especially in our
current state of accelerated mobility, that it is becoming increasingly necessary for Negroes themselves to *learn* who they are *as
Negroes*. Cultural influences have always outflanked racial discrimination—*wherever and whenever there were Negroes receptive
to them, even in slavery times*. I read the books which were free
to me for my work as a writer while studying at Tuskegee Institute,
Macon County, Alabama, during a time when most of the books
weren't even taught. Back in 1937 I knew a Negro who swept the
floors at Wright Field in Dayton, Ohio, who was nevertheless
designing planes and entering his designs in contests. He was
working as a porter but his mind, his ambitions, and his attitudes were
those of an engineer. He wasn't waiting for society to change, he
was changing it by himself.

What advice would you give to a young person of eighteen who was setting out to be a writer?

My first advice would be to make up his mind to the possibility that he might have to go through a period of depriving himself in order to write. I'd remind him that he was entering into a very stern discipline, and that he should be quite certain that he really wanted to do this to the extent of arranging his whole life so that he could get it done. He should regard writing very much as a young physician is required to regard his period of training. Next, I'd advise him to read everything, all the good books he can manage, especially those in the literary form in which he desires to become creative. Because books contain the culture of the chosen form and because one learns from the achievements of other writers. Here is contained the knowledge which he must have at his fingertips as he projects his own vision. And because without it, no matter how sensitive, intelligent or passionate he is, he will be incomplete.

Beyond that, he shouldn't take the easy escape of involving himself exclusively in *talking* about writing, or carrying picket signs, or sitting-in as a substitute activity. Because while he might become the best picket in the world, or the best sitter-inner, his writing will remain where he left it.

Finally, he should avoid the notion that writers require no education. Very often Hemingway and Faulkner are summoned up to support this argument, because they didn't finish college. What is overlooked is that these were very gifted, very brilliant men. And very well-read men of great intellectual capacity. So no matter how you acquire an education, you must have it. You must know your society and know it beyond your own neighborhood or region. You must know its manners and its ideals and its conduct. And you should know something of what's happening in the sciences, in religion, in government, and in the other arts.

I suppose what I'm saying is that he should have a working model of the society and of the national characteristics present within his mind. The problem of enriching that model and keeping it up-to-date is one of the greatest challenges to the Negro writer, who is, by definition, cut off from firsthand contact with large areas of the society—especially from those centers where power is translated into ideas and into manners and into values. Nevertheless, this can be an advantage, because in this country no writer should take anything for granted, but must use his imagination to question and penetrate the façade of things. Indeed, the integration of American society on the level of the imagination is one of his basic tasks. It is one way in which he is able to possess his world and, in his writings, help shape the values of large segments of the society which otherwise would not admit his existence, much less his right to participate or to judge.

A Dialogue with His Audience

Barat Review / 1968

From *Barat Review*, January 1968, 51–53. Copyright 1968 by *Barat Review*. Reprinted by permission.

Q: In a recent issue of the *New Republic* Stanley Kauffmann published an article on Negro literature in America in which he suggested that there have been several phases of Negro literature: a phase of subservience, a kind of *Uncle Tom's Cabin* phase; a phase of Negro reaction and Negro search for identity highlighted by *Native Son* and your own novel *Invisible Man*. He suggested further that the recent novel introduced a new phase of Negro adaptation to the given American culture. In other words, the Negro problem has become almost synonymous with typical white American problem. Mr. Ellison, would you care to comment on this?

Ellison: I didn't read Kauffmann's article, but I have a feeling that his is schematic thinking. American Negro literature, going back to the oral tradition, has perhaps been more a source for American literature written by whites than by Negroes. Negro literature has always been a universal and eclectic expression because no one was censoring what Negroes made of the oral tradition. Some of its magic was recognized by Joel Chandler Harris and others, and many writers have drawn from it. So you have *that* aspect. You've had bad writing by Negroes as well as some good writing by Negroes. When I say "bad," I mean writing which was as much concerned with how it said what it said as with what it was saying. One of the reasons why you've had very very bad writing by Negroes is not because of a lack of talent but because it is on the level of the word that Negroes have been most defeated by segregation. It has been on the level of the word that Negroes have accepted the idea which was imposed upon them by segregation, and they've tried to see themselves and to express themselves in those terms. To highlight what I mean: if you turn to something like jazz, you get this absolute Picasso-like experimentation, this sense of creative power. You have this with Negro athletes. It's us

136

Negro writers who have failed. But Mr. Kauffmann couldn't understand that. He isn't prepared to understand it—not because he's
white, but because he thinks schematically.

Q: Mr. Ellison, would you comment on the legitimacy of a
southern white's—namely William Styron's—attempting to enter
into the consciousness of a Negro revolutionary in his latest work,
The Confessions of Nat Turner?

Ellison: Yes, but I won't promise I have anything interesting to
say about it. Let me put it this way: human experiences are the
whole. There is no reason why William Styron or anyone else
should not confront the challenge of an unknown aspect of personality. The beginning (and he made the beginning because he was
willing to identify), and one of the best, most successful, meaningful and rich projections of a Negro in fiction was made by William
Faulkner. He made it possible for me to look at certain aspects of
Negro life. What is at stake here is the willingness of the artist to
surrender the prejudices of his background and to give himself to
his art. And art itself is no more prejudiced than science. If you
read the works of Dostoyevsky, if you read, especially, his diary,
he sounds like a raging maniac. He's a Slavic monster; he's anti-
Semitic; he's all these things. And yet—and here's the humanistic
core of his work—when he begins to write novels there comes into
being a dialectical, human willingness to let each side have its
say. There's an opportunism in it, but it's a built-in opportunism.
You cannot have a dynamics of personality and social classes and
so on without letting each have its say. This is one of the reasons
why I believe in the importance of the novel within the racial
situation. William Styron might fail, might have failed, but he has
every bit as much right to project himself into the character of
Nat Turner as I have the right to project myself into the dilemmas
of Abraham Lincoln or the Jew who became Klansman, or as Leon-
tine Price has a right to project herself into the roles of a heroine of
Italian drama. This is not a racial matter; it is a matter of
sensibility, of talent, and of willingness to become the other.

Q: In your creation of *Invisible Man,* do you feel you borrowed
at all from the Kafka idea of the alienation of the Jew in Europe?

Ellison: No, I had enough alienation of my own to draw on. I'm
not certain whether I had read Kafka before I wrote *Invisible*

Man, though I certainly have read a lot of him. But the most direct
treatment of alienation which I knew and which, in the very rhythm
of the epilogue, was Dostoyevsky's *Notes from the Underground.*
After Dostoyevsky you don't need Kafka.

Q: Mr. Ellison, you have suggested that the matter and purpose
of the novel cannot be legislated. At the same time you have
observed that many of the problems which the novel treats have
been dictated to the artist by the common faults in the construct
of our nation. It seems there is a paradox here. Would you comment
on it?

Ellison: There are always people who try to legislate, who try to
tell you what to write. But I would suggest, for example that it wasn't
until after the German occupation that existentialism became a
concern of the French. Here at home, I find existentialist consciousness to have been a property of the blues, for instance,
because there's always a kind of uncertainty within American
life. This matter isn't arbitrary. I suppose what I'm saying is that a
novelist doesn't have to be told what he's going to do. There are
certain realities within a given moment of history and society which
he must respond to. And then, from the outside, as it were, there
is the history of the novel as form itself or collectively of forms to
contend with. Part of the artist's role, part of the pleasure of being an
artist lies in fighting against what other people have done within
that form. If you are a painter, there's no way for you, whether
consciously or not, to ignore the fact that the Impressionists investi-
gated the possibilities of color. The paradox is in the situation.
It's the human paradox.

Q: Lately we have been hearing that the novel is definitely a
waning literary form. How do you feel about this kind of general
comment?

Ellison: For myself, I don't love death and I'm still trying to write
novels. But personal references aside, the novel dies as any other art
form dies until the next viable and vibrant example comes along.
The novel has been dying ever since it began, I suppose. If you
go back and look at the tons of fiction which have been turned
down, which no one reads any more, you begin to feel that it's
like Finnegan's wake (I mean the myth, not the novel) until a bottle
of booze—or whatever that metaphor can mean to a given

writer—is introduced. You have a wake and Finnegan comes alive again. Maybe that's one of the meanings of Joyce's choice. The novel will not only endure, it will be dominant. In society we learn to read it and to use the wisdom which is involved in these very entertaining forms.

Q: In your paper on "The Novel and American Democracy," you alluded to Whitman's optimism and to Crane's celebration of the "little man," and in your own novel *Invisible Man* you do give a sense of collaboration between reader and writer on the common man, the man who is striving to become human. I wonder if you would comment on the proliferation in our own day of heroes in novels who are *isolatoes*, rebels, Gile's Goat Boy types. It seems that there are a lot of these around; how would you explain them?

Ellison: I think we have to recognize that American literature is a part of Western literature and that we are living through a period in which there is a great questioning of the social identity of individuals. This is one of the things that Stephen Crane was writing about: that here was a "little man" who didn't even know that the big issues were there; he had his *own* special problem.

However, I feel that each diverse group within the United States has put forth its own novels, and somehow built into that production is a feeling that each background must be projected as a metaphor for the human tradition. But there is a mixture of bragging and affirmation in all this. And you have to read the negative heroes very carefully because sometimes an earlier tradition takes over—the tradition of the underdog, for instance, or of the holy fool. I would suggest that the real test of the novel is not the kind of hero that is presented but the quality of the work itself. It is the quality of the expressed talent which affirms no matter what the philosophical position of the main characters involved.

Q: What kind of a hero do you think Bigger Thomas is? And how do you think Richard Wright manages to create a hero who so dominates the novel?

Ellison: Through brute force. *Native Son* is a very powerful novel, but to my mind something is missing. In the end Wright has to condescend to Bigger because Bigger is reduced to a kind of lack of consciousness through which he could not have conceived of Wright. So the hero was brutalized by Wright. I say this not to put down my

friend, but rather to point to something about the nature of the
novel as humanist expression. In it we seek not status, not class,
but a reflecting consciousness—certainly in the hero who confronts the complexities of his situation. There is a dichotomy in
Native Son. Bigger goes through all his experience understanding
very little of it. He doesn't know how to dance. He doesn't possess
the culture of Chicago Negroes of his background of that period.
And then suddenly you've got a leap—and you have a Marxist,
white Jewish lawyer stating the meaning of the experience. Bigger
was a deprived character, but he was deprived by the author, not
by what was there. One has to use the novel, I think, to assert some
sort of ability to confront one's situation.

The Uses of History in Fiction: Ralph Ellison, William Styron, Robert Penn Warren, C. Vann Woodward

Southern Historical Association / 1968

From the *Southern Literary Journal* (Spring 1969), 57–90. Copyright 1969 by the *Southern Literary Journal*. Reprinted by permission.

Woodward: In introducing novelists into the formal deliberations of historians, I really feel no need to apologize, except perhaps to the novelists. For if apologies are due, they should come, I think, from the side of the historian. Historians have too long cultivated a rather priggish, nineteenth-century cult of fact, a creed that borrowed its tenets and prestige from the sciences and the heyday of their ascendency. Like scientists, we said, historians stuck to facts, preferably to hard facts. This conception, this prestige of hard facts, derives especially from the English. It was Oscar Wilde who said that the English are always degrading Truth into Fact, and he went on to say that when a Truth becomes a Fact, it loses all its intellectual value.

Since fiction was conceived to be, in this usage, the opposite of fact, and since novelists dealt exclusively in fiction, historians were inclined to be rather priggish about novelists, especially if they ventured into historical subjects. Historians have been much more eager to claim kinship with scientists, notably social scientists. When the social sciences turn to historical subjects, historians appear flattered rather than offended. We were, or have been, inclined to embrace them as cousins, to offer joint courses, to hold conferences. Our kinship is actually much closer to novelists. We are in fact siblings, historical siblings. The novel is the youngest of the literary forms—the only one the Greeks didn't invent. It was born only in the mid-eighteenth century, not long before professional historiography first saw the light of day in

Germany. Both sprang from a common parentage of storytellers. Both grew up together in an environment permeated with the growing historical consciousness of western man, and competed with each other to satisfy the demand for historical understanding.

In their mutual attitudes there has been a good deal of sibling rivalry—though, it is, I think, more manifest in the historians than in the novelists. Actually, I find among novelists more respect for and awareness of good history than I find among historians a proper respect for and awareness of good novels. Over the last two centuries novels have become increasingly saturated with history, and novelists have been becoming ever more deeply historically conscious.

In a sense, all novels are historical novels. They all seek to understand, to describe, to recapture the past, however remote, however recent. They might all be described by the title of Marcel Proust's great work, *Remembrance of Things Past*. In his own efforts to understand, describe, and recapture the past, the novelist uses no more specialized a vocabulary than the historian. As Isaiah Berlin has said, history employs few if any concepts or categories peculiar to itself, but broadly speaking, only those of common sense, or ordinary speech—in other words, the same speech the historian himself uses. If the historian feels free to borrow concepts and insights from the psychologist, the analyst, the sociologist, in his efforts to explain human motivation and behavior, the novelist is equally free to use the same resources in doing much the same thing.

An historian stands in no less need of imagination than the novelist; if anything he needs rather more. There are firm rules, of course, about what his discipline permits and forbids him to do with his imagination. He cannot, for example, as the novelist can, invent characters, or invent motives for his characters. I certainly have no wish to relax those rules or to confuse or blur the distinction between the historian and the novelist. But over the years, as I have watched my novelist friends at their work, as I have read their books and talked with them about their problems, I have learned to appreciate more and more how much we have in common in our uses of the past, our interest in it, our demands upon it, our concerns with it.

This is, I think, especially true of Southern writers, and particularly of the three who take part in this discussion. Allen Tate has spoken of the peculiar historical consciousness of Southern writers, and described their work as a literature conscious of the past in the present. Tate could hardly have called to witness a better illustration of his thesis than his friend Robert Penn Warren. Warren's books have dealt with virtually every period of American history since the time of Thomas Jefferson, including that time and including also the period of Jackson, the Civil War, the early years of the 20th Century, the 1920s, the 1930s, and on down to the present. These books constitute for some of us a good part of our intellectual autobiography. His first book was not fiction at all, but a biography of John Brown. It seems to me that in that book of "straight" history, he announced the basic themes of all his novels: man's confrontation with evil, and the conflict between good and evil within the human heart. Together, these books constitute a moral history of the South.

William Styron's early novels dealt with contemporary themes and characters, though never without a characteristic consciousness of the past in the present. Only in this latest novel, on Nat Turner, has he turned to the more remote past for his subject, and in this "meditation on history," as he calls his book, he comes very close indeed, given the license of the novelist, to doing what the historian does in reconstructing the past. Here he is concerned with the particular, rather than with the universal, which is, I believe, the distinction that Aristotle made between poetry and history.

Ralph Ellison has declared his allegiance to history, as well as his Southern identity, most clearly in his warning to a critic about the abstraction he would impose upon American reality. With characteristic Southern fear of abstraction, and abhorrence for it, he declared: "the Negro American consciousness is not a product (as so often seems true of so many other American groups) of a will to historical forgetfulness." Rather, it is the memory of slavery and the hope of emancipation, and the myths, both Southern and Northern.

I will call on these speakers in the order of seniority, and that will put Mr. Warren first.

Warren: I want to say that I am appalled and honored to be

invited to a group of historians. It makes you feel that the writing
of fiction is more important than you thought it was, and that your
writing is, too. I am honored to be here and it is a great pleasure
to be among my friends—three old and dear friends.

What I want to do now is simply to try to state a few principles
that occur to me about the relation between history and fiction—in
a way, between history and art, as I see the problem, as a background to what may happen later.

First I should like to say that the word History is a very ambiguous word. Clearly it means on one hand things that happened in
the past, the events of the past, the actions of the past. And the
word also means the record of the past that historians write. So
whenever the word is used, we have to sort out its meaning. I
myself use it differently, in each sense, as the occasion may
demand, and I'm afraid my friends do the same thing.

As Vann has said, history is in the past tense. That sounds simple
enough. It is about the past. But it is not simple, because it is not
merely about what happened in the past, it is also the imaginative
past. History and fiction are both in this past tense. History is the
literal past tense. The historian says, "It was in the past; I prove
that it happened." The fiction writer says, "I'll take it as it has
happened, if it happened at all—which it probably didn't." But the
mode of the past tense is the past tense of a state of mind—the feel of
the past, not the literal past itself. It is a mode of memories. It's the
mind working in terms of memory. The history of the past that the
historians write is the racial past, the national past, the sectional
past, all kinds of pasts, including economic history—but the past,
always. To the novelist, say Thackeray, writing about Becky Sharp,
the past may be merely a little personal past. But it is past. Even
science fiction is about the past; the writers tell about the future as
though it were past. In science fiction, you get yourself to a point
beyond the story that you are telling. It is never in the future tense.
It is in an assumed future which has become a past.

This fact points to a particular stance of mind: it has *happened*,
and we are trying to find its meaning. It's a mode of memory we are
dealing with, an actuality as remembered. History is concerned
with actuality; its past must be provable. The fiction writer's past
is not provable; it *may* be imagined. His characters *may* be imag-

ined. But historical characters are imagined, too. They are
brought into the picture of an imagined world. For how do we know
the world of "history," unless the historian has "imagined" it?

Now the big difference here between history and fiction is that
the historian does not know his imagined world; he knows *about*
it, and he must know all he can about it, because he wants to find
the facts *behind* that world. But the fiction writer must claim to
know the *inside* of his world for better or for worse. He mostly fails,
but he claims to know the inside of his characters, the undocu-
mentable inside. Historians are concerned with the truth *about,*
with knowledge *about,* the fiction writer with the knowledge *of.*
And neither of these "knowledges" is to be achieved in any perfect
form. But the kinds of "knowledge" *are.* This is a fundamental
difference, it seems to me.

This leads to another distinction. Fiction is an art, one of the
several arts. I want to read a little passage—the most radical passage
I could find—about art as distinguished from other human activities.
"Either art is a pure, irreducible activity, one that provides its
own peculiar content, its own morality—it includes itself in its own
meaning; or art is, on the other hand, a pleasanter form of
presenting facts, meanings and truths pertaining to other realms of
reality like history, sociology, morality, where they exist in purer
and fuller form." This states the distinction quite coldly. For fiction
is an art, like painting or music—with one difference. Its materials are
more charged with all the human commitments and recalcitrances
and roughnesses.

Now here is where the rub comes, I think. The materials that go
into a piece of fiction may be drawn from history or human
experience, but their factuality gives them no special privilege, as
contrasted with imagined materials. They have, as "materials"
for it, the same status, and nothing more than that. But they come
in with all the recalcitrances and the weights and the passions of
the real world. The simplest example I can think of is this. Take
Hamlet, or any tragedy we all admire and respond to. It is dealing
with the recalcitrances of human pain, confusion and error. We
know these things all too well: the pain, confusion, and error of
our own lives. But we come out of the play not weeping, but feeling
pretty good, and we go down to the beer parlor and talk about it.

Something's happened to the pain, confusion, error. It has happened only because we put the pain and error into perspective, and look at it—to see it and at the same time not quite feel it. We see it as if it had happened a long time ago—to us, but somebody else, too.

There is, however, always a point where the exigencies and the pains of the materials of fiction or drama or poetry are too great to be absorbed. This recalcitrancy, which is the basis of contention between the form and the content of literature, can become too great. The really bigoted Catholic cannot read Milton; the really bigoted Protestant can't read Dante. In reading literature we have to make allowances for our theologies and our beliefs. But there is a point where it cracks. Let's recognize that. There is a form in which the recalcitrant material—that is, the practical commitment in relation to it—violates the vision of humanity, the long-range beauty of contemplation that is art. Let's leave it there for the moment.

Ellison: I think I'll go back and try to talk about American historiography and American fiction. I would start by suggesting that they're both artificial; both are forms of literature, and I would suggest further that American history grows primarily out of the same attitudes of mind, and attitudes toward chronology, which gave birth to our great tall stories. Constance Rourke reminded us that we began to define ourselves and to create ourselves through the agency of the word, of the imagination, the fictional imagination—and that basically we are liars. I would suggest that historians are responsible liars. Liars are not bad people; I am by profession a liar. The role of lying is like the role of masquerading. Yeats has a quotation, which I have used somewhere, about the necessity of putting on the mask in order to achieve one's dreams, one's idea of one's self. So when I put a scar on my face or part my hair, you understand that I'm trying to achieve some idealistic image; or if I wear it in Afro-style or conk it, you understand that that too is simply a human assertion against the flux and flow of time and a desire to modify that which was given. And it is here that the novelist and the historian appear to part company. The historian is dedicated to chronology. He can suppress, he can emphasize, he can project, and he can carve out his artifact; and this helps us to imagine ourselves, to project ourselves, to achieve certain goals, certain identities; but he must obey the order of the calendar and the tides of political fortune. I can't, here in New Orleans, fail to point out that so much of American history has turned upon the racial situation in the country. This is a given and accepted fact now. It's argued over and over again. The problem that we have to deal with on the side of history is: How much did you choose to put in, how much did you leave out, what did it lead to, and how to interpret the results. I'm going to be a little nasty here and suggest that our written history has been as "official" as any produced in any communist country—only in a democratic way: individuals write it instead of committees. Written history is to social conduct and social arrangements in this country very much like the relationship between myth and ritual. And myth justifies and "explains" facts. Now it's all human, it is understandable and it has to be evaluated, because complex personal and political interests are involved in such intricate ways that arriving at objective evaluations is extremely difficult. But, thank God, there have been a few novelists who decided to tell the "truth" in their own unique and devious ways. Isn't that nasty?

For here the novelists have a special, though difficult, freedom. Time is their enemy, and while chronology is the ally of the historian, for the novelist it is something to manipulate or even to destroy. And this, I think, is why we wish that historians, within the limitations which they embrace and to which they dedicate themselves, could do a little better by chronology, by events as they actually unfold. Because in certain ways the historians have, thankfully, taken a broader cut of the American experience than the novelists. By nature they possess a greater patience before facts, before events. If you really want to find out what happened in the United States over all these years, you know that *some* historian has written something about it. That is one of the glories of historical writing in this country; there has always been somebody who, for some reason, has tried to say, "Well, the consequences of this fact actually exist, this event actually occurred, and I think it is related in such and such a way to the total reality." But too often history has been an official statement, and it has danced attendance to political arrangements.

Fiction, on the other hand, as it manipulates reality, as it tries to get at those abiding human predicaments which are ageless and timeless, has fought with time, has fought with the realities as envisioned by official history, and by rearranging experience in artful ways it has tried to tell us in small ways the symbolic significance of what actually happened. If you want to know something about the dynamics of the South, of interpersonal relationships in the South from, roughly, 1874 until today, you don't go to historians; not even to Negro historians. You go to William Faulkner and Robert Penn Warren, or you go to the popular arts. You have to read the latter very carefully of course, because they are the biggest liars of all. But somehow the novelists try to deal with unpleasant facts, difficult facts, and Faulkner dealt with the most unpleasant facts of race. I suppose that's why American history has not been ultimately concerned with tragedy, while literature, at its best, always has. It's always trying to find ways of dealing with the unpleasant facts, and the only way, the profoundest human way, of dealing with the unpleasant, is to place it in conjunction with the pleasant. Thus fiction, at its best, moves ever toward a blending of the tragic with the comic—or towards that mode which we know as the Blues.

I would suggest, then, that American novelists have a special role which should not be confused with the role of the writer of history; which for them is *verboten*. The moment you say something explicit about history in a novel, everybody's going to rise up and knock the hell out of you, because they suspect that you are trying to take advantage of a form of authority which is sacred. History is sacred, you see, and no matter how false to actual events it might be. But fiction is anything but sacred. By fact and by convention fiction is a projection from one man's mind, of one man's imagination. An American novelist tries to integrate all of the diversity of our people and our regions, our religions, and so on, into an imaginative whole. And through that imaginative integration he attempts to seize the abiding circumstances, the abiding problems, the abiding and time-tested forms of humanity—heroism, truth and failure and love and death—all of the ramifications of those experiences which make us human.

I think that we have something very important going here. We work the same side of the street. So keep us honest and we'll keep you historians honest. I think that Red Warren, who has always been concerned with history, has offered us an example of how to confront the problem of history as the novelist should. I think that when he wrote about a great American politician who governed his state and refused to intrude into the area of the historian, he refused because he was canny enough to realize that he could never get *that* particular man into fiction. And yet, I believe that he did use that man to bring into focus within his own mind many, many important facts about power, politics and class and loyalty. So today we possess an essence of that man presented in a highly imaginative, moving and enduring way, without the novelist having taken anything away from that man. And without his having added anything to one who we know was an important historical figure—except the art-created possibility of looking at him through the enriching eyes of Red Warren's imagination. Thanks to Warren's art we may now view that man through that heightened sense of the past which both history and literature grant to all who are truly involved with the mystery of human existence.

Styron: I have never talked much in public. I don't mean to sound shy, but I haven't, nor have I taught, and I admire the eloquence that has preceded me, and only wish that I were able to speak in an impromptu manner as well as my good friends have done. As a consequence, I have resorted to a composition, fairly brief, some of it composed on Eastern Airlines today, with a terrible and ominous post-election traumatic blues all over me. So I'm going to read it, and if you shut your eyes, perhaps I can give you a subtle feeling that I am not reading it.

Last spring in an exchange in the *Nation,* I quoted at some length from a volume called *The Historical Novel,* by the great Hungarian Marxist critic, Georg Lukács, in an effort to explain my attitude toward the freedom of movement and choice any good novelist must exercise when writing historical fiction. Historical fiction has been largely discredited in this country, doubtless due to the fact that its practitioners, most of them, have aimed at titillating a predominantly female audience, an audience one hopes that has now been preempted by the Late, Late show. What I am speaking about, of course, is the serious historical novel: literature in the tradition of Scott, Stendhal, Tolstoy, Pushkin, Faulkner, and Warren, and it is to this great genre that Lukács has addressed himself, in my opinion, with more intelligence, passion, and penetration than any other modern literary critic. As Irving Howe has written of Lukács, "Unlike so many Marxist critics, Lukács turns to literature not because it provides him with political opportunities but because he has been involved with it for a lifetime and has experienced the passion of the true scholar. . . . Repeatedly Lukács turns to 'the increasing concreteness of the novel in its grasp of the historical peculiarity of characters and events,' repeatedly to that self-reflectiveness in the dominant characters of the modern novel, which he sees as the sense of history become part of experience and thereby transformed into a dynamic agent reflecting and acting upon the dialectal contradictions of the outer world."[1]

It seemed to me that some of Lukács' observations on the historical novel and the novelist's responsibility are more trenchant and wise than any I could make about the matter, and certainly record as well as I could my own feelings about the intricate and subtle relationship between historical fact and fanciful conjecture, between historical faithfulness and literary license, along with other troubling problems that beset the unhappy wretch who dares tackle this literary form. Let me then quote again from Lukács, hoping that these maxims will serve as representative of my own sentiments regarding the fiction writer's very difficult obligation to make sense out of history.

"The deeper and more genuinely historical a writer's knowledge of a period," Lukács says, "the more freely will he be able to move about inside his subject and the less tied will he feel to individual historical data." Speaking of Sir Walter Scott, for instance, he observes: "Scott's extraordinary genius lay in the fact that he gave the historical novel just such themes as would allow for this 'free movement,' and so cleared the way for its development; whereas the earlier traditions of his so-called predecessors had

---

[1]Irving Howe, "Preface to the American Edition," Georg Lukács, *The Historical Novel* (Beacon Press, 1962), pp. 9–10.

obstructed all such freedom of movement, preventing even a genuine talent from developing. Naturally, a special difficulty is involved in the treatment of specifically historical subject-matter. Every really original writer who portrays a new outlook upon a certain field has to contend with the prejudices of his readers. But the image which the public has of any familiar historical figure need not necessarily be a false one. Indeed, with the growth of a real historical sense and of real historical knowledge it becomes more and more accurate. But even this correct image may in certain circumstances be a hindrance to the writer who wishes to reproduce the spirit of an age faithfully and authentically. It would require a particularly happy accident for all the well-known and attested actions of a familiar historical figure to correspond to the purposes of literature. . . ."

In another context, Lukács expands on this theme of what is not merely the likelihood but the necessity of the writer being allowed great latitude in structuring his vision of the past. He says, "What matters in the novel is fidelity in the reproduction of the material foundations of the life of a given period, its manners and the feelings and thoughts deriving from these. This means, as we have also seen, that the novel is much more closely bound to the specifically historical, individual moments of a period than is drama. But this never means being tied to any particular historical facts. On the contrary, the novelist must be at liberty to treat these as he likes,"—and this is an important phrase, I think—"if he is to reproduce the much more complex and ramifying totality with historical faithfulness. From the standpoint of the historical novel, too, it is always a matter of chance whether an actual, historical fact, character or story will lend itself to the particular method by which a great novelist conveys his historical faithfulness."

Finally, quoting Pushkin, Lukács remarks: "Truth of passions, verisimilitude of feelings in imagined circumstances—that is what our mind demands of the dramatic writer." And he declares, "the writer's historical fidelity consists in the faithful artistic reproduction of the great collisions, the great crises and turning-points in history. To express this *historical* conception in an adequate artistic form the writer may treat individual facts with as much license as he likes, for mere fidelity to the individual facts of history without this connection is utterly valueless."[2]

Needless to say, the foregoing thoughts merely skim part of the surface of Lukács philosophy of history and its relation to literature. Yet in his unyielding insistence that a writer's responsibility is not to the dead baggage of facts, but to the unfettering and replenishing power of his own imagination, that imagination which at its best can alone reveal ultimate truths, Lukács' observations seem to me enormously provocative, and I hope they provide substance for further discussion this evening.

Woodward: Thank you very much, gentlemen. As an historian, I gather from the comments of Mr. Warren that the novelists deal with the inside of history, leaving the outside, I suppose, to the historian; from Mr. Ellison, that historians are essentially liars, and this leaves the truth to the novelists; from Mr. Styron that fidelity to fact is not an obligation of novelists, and this *emancipates* them. Am I too far off base, gentlemen, in saying that it seems to me that you are saying you are going to write a "super-history," or at least a better history than historians can write?

Ellison: No. I'm suggesting that we have reached a great crisis in American history, and we are now going to have a full American history. You, Vann, began to initiate this movement, as far as I am concerned. We're beginning to go back and to evaluate those realities of American historical experience which were ruled out officially. Henry Steele Commager and a lot of other people, such as Samuel Morison, have turned flip-flops in recent years. I used to be outraged when I read some of the stuff that they wrote, because there is, certainly in the Negro part of the country and in the Southern part of the country, a stream of history which is still as tightly connected with folklore and the oral tradition as official history is connected with the tall tale. I think that we are beginning to realize that.

For instance, the only public school I ever attended was named after Frederick Douglass. The people who walked there from Tennessee and the Carolinas have a sense of history which is only

---

[2]All quotations are from Georg Lukács, *The Historical Novel,* trans. from the German by Hannah and Stanley Mitchell (Beacon Press, 1962), pp. 166–168.

now beginning to get into the history books. Part of this is legend. Part of this is myth. But so much of it—so very much of it—is what actually happened, happened to them. And if official history, if conscious historians do not take cognizance of this experience, then what a critic like Lukács says has very little validity. He was, after all, writing about European countries, with no divided history. Of course I know that the Owen Glendower that Shakespeare gives us in the historical plays is certainly not the Owen Glendower of the Welsh, it's the Shakespearean and Elizabethan notion of Owen Glendower. But here we are dedicated to a different kind of democracy. We have all of these things which happened, and they happened in such great variety. I'm afraid to say what Louisiana experience is, what Louisiana history is, even of the period of Huey Long, because I used to hear things—and highly favorable things, about Long, for instance—from Negro students that I attended college with at Tuskegee.

I think that one of the things that we want to discuss here is the rhetoric of fiction. If you project in fiction a version of history, then you have an obligation to think about these other feed-ins from the common experience which are going to put to question your particular projection of history. I don't think that history is Truth. I think it's another form of man trying to find himself, and to come to grips with his own complexity, but within the frame of chronology and time. Here in the United States we have had a political system which wouldn't allow me to tell my story officially. Much of it is not in the history textbooks. Certain historians and untrained observers did their jobs, often very faithfully, but many of them have been forgotten except by scholars and historians, and the story they recorded was altered to justify racial attitudes and practices. But somehow, through our Negro American oral tradition and through the names given to children and to public institutions—those places with which white society was not too concerned as long as they did not challenge the public order—these reminders of the past as *Negroes* recalled it found existence and were passed along. Historical figures continued to live in stories of and theories about the human and social dynamics of slavery, and about the effects of political decisions rendered during the Reconstruction. Assertions of freedom and revolts were recalled along with triumphs of labor in the fields and on the dance floor; feats of eating and drinking and of fornication, of religious conversion and physical endurance, and of artistic and athletic achievements. In brief, the broad ramifications of human life as Negroes have experienced it were marked and passed along. This record exists in oral form and it constitutes the internal history of values by which my people lived even as they were being forced to accommodate themselves to those forces and arrangements of society that were sanctioned by official history. The result has imposed upon Negroes a high sensitivity to the ironies of historical writing and created a profound skepticism concerning the validity of most reports on what the past was like.

And so, when a novelist moves into the arena of history and takes on the obligations of the historian he has to be aware that he faces a tough rhetorical problem. He has to sell *me,* convince me, that despite the racial divisions and antagonisms in the U. S., his received version of history is not drastically opposed to mine. Because I am conditioned to assume that his idea of the heroic individual is apt to violate my sense of heroism;—for instance, Bedford Forrest is considered a hero by many whites but it would be an heroic task for me, or for most blacks, to see him so. I can, however, accept Sam Feathers or Lucas Beauchamp in Faulkner, in ways that I couldn't accept Jim in *Huckleberry Finn.* For me, Jim was not rounded enough. And yet, he was involved fictionally with serious historical matters. But Lucas Beauchamp was involved with serious historical and personal matters—*but* (and this is an important *but*) he was mainly involved in those things which historians would not talk about, and this is one of the important roles which fiction has played, especially the fiction of southern writers: it has tried to tell that part of the human truth which we could not accept or face up to in much historical writing because of social, racial and political considerations.

Warren: Our little girl, who is about 11 years old, was studying for an exam in American History, and she said to me, "hear my lesson." I heard her lesson and she said things I thought were pretty preposterous, but I didn't say anything about it, because I knew she was saying her lesson for an exam. I was too smart to say anything about it, but she was watching my face. "Oh, poppy!"

she said, "this is for an exam; this is not the truth. I know better
than this."

Now this is not the historians' fault. This is the people who write
textbooks of history. It's very different. Official histories may be
tests, or orators at the Fourth of July, or textbook makers, but not
historians. They are very different, you see. And girls of ten years
old get this point quickly; they understand it perfectly. By the time
they are seventeen or eighteen, in college, they may lose it. But they
know it at ten years old. They watch things much more shrewdly
than their elders; they have no stake in it except truth—truth, and
grades. They are quite different: they know this, you see.

The historian is after this truth, and it's a good truth. So is the
novelist. They are both trying to say what life feels like to them.
They have different ground rules for it. Let's assume that both are
conditioned by their societies at every given moment—at every
moment in history, in time. Now, the breaking out process is always
an act of imagination both for the historian and the novelist. The
rules are different, though, in this sense: the historian must prove
points, document points, that the novelist doesn't have to document. Yet without that sense of documentation, the knowledge that
It Is Possible, the novelist can't operate either. He is conditioned
always by the sense of this documentation—that it is historically
possible. He himself is tied to the facts of life. He must respect them.
Insofar as he departs from them by imagination, he departs in terms
of the possibilities laid down by these ground rules of fact—
psychological fact, historical fact, sociological fact, all the various
kinds of fact. Those are his ground rules. He can take a new view
of them, but he cannot violate any one of them to a point which
invalidates acceptance. That's the big proviso here. It varies a
great deal. The materials that go into his work come from the rough-
textured life around him, made up of beliefs and facts and attitudes of
all kinds. A bigoted Catholic can't read Milton, and a bigoted
Protestant can't read Dante, but a civilized Catholic can read
Milton with joy. There's a point, though, where one's commitment
to basic ideas and basic materials, by reason of bigotry or something else, makes one incapable of accepting the total vision of an
art—of a novel or a poem, or whatever. Let's face this fact. The

autonomy of the art is always subject to the recalcitrance of the
materials and to your own lack of self-understanding.

Styron: I don't know what I'm going to say to add to this
confusion. We've been dealing in very intelligent abstractions, all
of which make me feel that maybe we should get a little bit more
concrete. I like that phrase of Red Warren's just now: "the
autonomy of the art is subject to the recalcitrance of the materials."
This is something that I have had preying on my mind for some
time, in regard to a private argument, which became extraordinarily
public, having to do with a book I wrote not too long ago. It occurred
to me in thinking of this particular book, *The Confessions of Nat
Turner,* that in all of the extraordinary flak and anti-anti-missile
barrage that has surrounded it, no one, insofar as I know (and I
don't mean only people who criticized it from the black point of
view, but a number of my white commentators as well; and I bring
this up not out of any immodesty, but simply because I'm more
comfortable in talking about particulars rather than aesthetic abstractions)—no one has conceived of this book, which does deal
with history indeed, as a separate entity which has its own autonomy, to use Red Warren's phrase, its own metaphysics, its own
reason for being as an aesthetic object. No one has ventured, except
for several people in private (bright people, whom I admire), to
suggest that a work which deals with history can at the same time
be a metaphorical plan, a metaphorical diagram for a writer's attitude
toward human existence, which presumably is one of the writer's
preoccupations anyway—that, despite all the obfuscation which surrounds the really incredible controversy about the rightness and
wrongness of racial attitudes, wrong readings of Ulrich B. Phil-
lips, Stanley Elkins, and so forth, a work of literature might have
its own being, its own fountain, its own reality, its own power, its
own appeal, which derive from factors that don't really relate to
history. And this is why, again, I'm intrigued by Red Warren's
phrase, "the autonomy of the art is subject to the recalcitrance of
the materials."

I would like to suggest that, in the endless rancor and bitterness
which tends to collect and coalesce around controversial literary
works, it might also be wise to pause and step back (I'm not
speaking of my own work alone)—and regard a work as containing

many metaphors, many reasons for being. This is true for all the literary works I admire. They are works (and I would include, among modern works, books by my distinguished contemporaries to my right) which do exist outside of history, which gain their power from history, to be sure, which are fed by a passionate comprehension of what history does to people and to things, but which have to have other levels of understanding, and have to be judged by other levels of understanding. It may be that in our perhaps overly modern and desperate preoccupation with history, which can be so valuable, we lose sight of the ineffable othernesses which go to make a work of art. At the risk of repeating myself once more, I would like to say that these factors have been forgotten.

Warren: May I say something, Vann? It strikes me that the question is one of the basic tensions of our whole lives. We can't have an easy formulation for this, an easy way out of the question. We are stuck with the fact that life involves passions and concerns and antipathies and anguish about the materials of life itself—whatever goes on in our hearts and outside of ourselves. This is what good literature involves. If you couldn't carry these things into literature, literature would be meaningless. It would be a mere parlor trick. All this—the concerns, the confusion—goes into literature; it goes into the arts. It exists in terms of the experience that the writer describes in literature, presented there in and of himself. They are not the same thing for everybody; a little different, you know, for each person, frequently quite different. But they all go in as passion, as commitments of various kinds. Yet at the same time the thing described must be made objectively itself. Now take Glendower, to whom Ralph was referring. Now nobody here is a Welsh nationalist, I trust. If there is one here . . .

Ellison: Ralph Ellison is.

Warren: No, you're not; *you* aren't Welsh.

Ellison: I'm a Welsh nationalist. But I also admire art.

Warren: I'm a Confederate. So here we are. We have personal loyalties and problems, you see. But in *Henry IV, Part One,* Glendower didn't bother us in terms of the great theme of the play. People are not living and dying over Glendower today. This is a purely pragmatic approach to it, you see; what can we surrender,

what immediate needs can we give up, how can we withdraw our
commitments in a given region of this play—in materials of the
play—to gain a larger view? Now I couldn't care less who won
the battle, at Shrewsbury, personally. It was a long time ago, and it
isn't very important now. . . .

What I care about is the pattern of the human struggle there—as
we know it in relation to Hotspur on one hand, and to the cold
calculators on the other hand, and to Hal, as a kind of Golden
Mean, and then, at last, to Falstaff, with all of his great tummy
and great wit, and his ironic view of history and morality—outside
of all schematic views. We are seeing a pattern of human possibility that bears on all of our lives, a pattern there that we see every
day—the Hotspurs, or those cold calculators like Westmoreland,
and then the people like Hal, who try to ride it through and in their
perfect adaptability be all things to all men, and drink with Falstaff
and kick him out at the end (in the next play, of course). We see
this happening all the time. Shakespeare wrote a great vision of
human life, but it's not about Welsh nationalism.

Ellison: Yes. And I'm all for the autonomy of fiction; that's why I
say that novelists should leave history alone. But I would also remind
us that the work of fiction comes alive through a collaboration
between the reader and the writer. This is where the rhetoric
comes in. If you move far enough into the historical past, you don't
have that problem. I don't give a damn what happened to Owen
Glendower, actually, but as a writer, if I were to write a fiction
based upon a great hero, a military man, whose name is Robert E.
Lee, I'd damn well be very careful about what I fed my reader, in
order for him to recreate in his imagination and through his sense
of history what that gentleman was. Because Lee is no longer
simply an historical figure. He is a figure who lives within us. He
is a figure which shapes ideals of conduct and of forebearance and
of skill, military and so on. This is *inside,* and not something that
writers can merely be arbitrary about. The freedom of the fiction
writer, the novelist, is one of the great freedoms possible for the
individual to exercise. But it is not absolute. Thus, one, without
hedging his bets, has to be aware that he does operate within an
area dense with prior assumptions.

Warren: Quite right.

Ellison: This I say without any discussion of Bill's personal problem. I haven't read his book, and he knows that—well, maybe he doesn't. Our house burned down so I didn't get to read it at first, and after the controversy I deliberately did not read it. One thing that I know is that he isn't a bigot, he isn't a racist, and all of that. That's beside the point. But there are very serious problems involved. I am known as a bastard by certain of my militant friends because I am not what they call a part of the Movement. That is, they figure I don't cuss out white folks enough. All right; I cuss them out in my own ways. But this isn't the real problem. The real problem is to create symbolic actions which are viable specifically, and which move across all of our differences and all of the diversities, of the atmosphere, and allow us to say, "yes," just as Red is saying about Shakespeare. This tells us something of what it means to be a man under these particular circumstances. But at the same time you don't have the freedom to snatch any and everybody, and completely recreate them. This is why you must lie and disguise a historical figure. You cannot move into the area, or impose yourself into the authority, of the historian, because he is dealing with chronology. The moment you put yourself in a book, the moment you put any known figures into the book, then somebody is going to say, "But he didn't have that mole on that side of his face; it was on *that* side. You said that he had a wife; he didn't have a wife. You said that he beat his wife at three o'clock in the afternoon; no, he beat her before breakfast, and they got up at five." Facts are a tyranny for the novelist. Facts get you into all of this trouble. On the other hand, Bill, I would suggest that whether you like the dissonance you picked up, you've written a very powerful novel, and it's very self-evident. Don't kick it. Don't knock it. Just leave history alone.

Styron: I'm not kicking, Ralph. I'm not. No. I'm glad you authenticate what I said through the voice of Lukács, that facts *per se* are preposterous. They are like the fuzz that collects in the top of dirty closets. They don't really mean anything.

Warren: I wouldn't go that far.

Ellison: They *mean* something. That's why you're in trouble.

Styron: I'll dispute that.

Ellison: Okay.

Styron: It depends on what facts you're talking about. Let's pare this down. Obviously when somebody like Lukács, or somebody like myself, claims that it's necessary to dispense with facts, it's not to say that promiscuous blindness, a disavowal of evidence, is what the novelist has as a dirty little secret all of his own. It's not that at all. It's simply to say that with a certain absolute boldness, a novelist dealing with history has to be able to say that such and such a fact is totally irrelevant, and to Hell with the person who insists that it has any real, utmost relevance. It's not to say that, in any bland or even dishonest way, a novelist is free to go about his task of rendering history with a complete shrugging off of the facts. This is not what Lukács says; it is not what I say. It is simply that certain facts which history presents us with are, on the one hand, either unimportant, or else they can be dispensed with out of hand, because to yield to them would be to yield or to compromise the novelist's own aesthetic honesty. Certain things won't fit into a novel, won't go in simply because the story won't tell itself if such a fact is there. This is what Lukács meant. It's what I mean when I say that a brute, an idiotic preoccupation with crude fact is death to a novel, and death to the novelist. The primary thing is the free use and the bold use of the liberating imagination which, dispensing with useless fact, will clear the cobwebs away and will show how it really was. This is all I mean about fact and its use or misuse.

Ellison: You mean really what was in your imagination, not in historical reality, don't you, Bill?

Styron: Well isn't that what we're talking about? I mean, when we read *War and Peace* we are reading about Tolstoy's imagination. I don't want to make any invidious comparisons; I'm just saying that anybody who deals, any creative imagination which deals with the fabric of history leaves you, if he's a good novelist, with a sense of an imaginative truth which transcends, in this case, what the historian can give you. An historian can tell you just what happened at Borodino, but only Tolstoy, often dispensing with facts, can tell you what it really was to be a soldier at Borodino. This is what the distinction is, and this is what I insist is the novelist's prerogative when he is faced with the materials of history.

Woodward: I'm interested in this question of fact myself. One of our distinguished novelists present, Red Warren, has written a novel about an historian. I think that Jack Burden was an historian, really. At least he was the narrator of *All the King's Men,* and he had two historical investigations in his career. One of them, you'll remember, was the investigation of the truth about an ancestor, I believe a great-uncle named Cass Mastern, and he said that the investigation was a failure. It was a failure because he was simply looking for the truth. The second investigation was about a man who turned out (though he didn't know it at the time) to be his father, Judge Irwin, and this investigation proved to be a great success. And he said that the reason for that success was that he was only looking for facts. The facts resulted in the suicide of his father, and a tragedy. So an interesting distinction was made there between facts and truth. Jack Burden, incidentally, was an historian, a seeker for a Ph.D., as some of us have been.

Warren: He didn't get it.

Woodward: He didn't get it, and the reason, as you say, was he did not have to know Cass Mastern to get the degree. He only had to know the facts about Cass Mastern's world. I would be interested in hearing you discuss this distinction between fact and truth. I think it's to the nub of our discussion, perhaps.

Warren: I'll tell you how it happened. I'll do it in two ways. One is how it happened to me, and the other is what could be said about it afterwards; they are quite different things. Jack Burden himself was a pure technical accident, a way to tell the story. And you stumble into that, because you are stuck with your problem of telling a story; you have to make him up as you go along. But that's another problem. The question about his peculiar researches, as I look back on them, is simply this. Being a very badly disorganized young fellow, he really didn't want the Ph.D. anyway. He stumbled on his family history, involving a character in his family, a couple of generations back, who had devoted his life to trying to find a moral position for himself. And this young man, without any moral orientation at all that I could figure out (he's an old-fashioned lost boy, not the new kind—there have always been these lost boys), didn't want his Ph.D., and he didn't know what to do with himself. He didn't know his mother, he didn't like his father, and so forth. At first he couldn't face the fact that in his own blood, there was a man who *had* faced up to a moral problem in a

deep way. He couldn't follow it through, could not bear to face the
comparison to the other young man. Then, he couldn't face the
truth otherwise, without this piece of research. Later, when he had
the job of getting the dirt on a character in the novel, he did get all the
facts. He gets all the facts, and the guy turns out to be his father,
who commits suicide. It's a parable, I didn't mean it to be one; I
wasn't trying to make a parable of truth and fact. It just worked out
that way. You sort of stumble into these things. It's a parable, as
you pointed out to me tonight; I hadn't thought about this before.
Well, the facts Jack Burden gets are deadly things. Facts may kill.
For one thing, they can kill myths.

Woodward: We're working here toward a distinction between fact
and fiction. Fact comes, I believe, from the Latin: *factum est,* a
thing done, an event. It has acquired a lot of prestige in historical
circles; it gets talked about all the time—facts, something you dig up
like gold, you unearth. Fiction is something that's created, something that's made, something that is made up perhaps of facts and a
lot of guesses. I think of two protagonists in Faulkner's *Absalom,
Absalom!,* Shreve McCannon and Quentin Compson, who are
really seeking historical truth, and they are doing it with facts and
evidence, and bits and pieces, and they go on and on, trying to create
this image and to discover the truth about Colonel Sutpen. What
they are trying to do seems to me very similar to what the historian is
trying to do. He gets together a lot of evidence, and he "creates"
the truth.

Ellison: But they are characters in a fiction, Vann, not historians.
So there's a difference.

Woodward: Yes, but the historian seems to me to be doing much
the same thing with the evidence he gathers. He puts it together.
Cleanth Brooks has put page after page of the evidence of *Absalom,
Absalom!* together to show how this truth is arrived at.

There are some people here who came to ask questions of these
writers, and I think we ought to give them an opportunity.

First Questioner: I would like to direct my question to Mr. Styron.
Mr. Styron, Mr. Ellison said that the novelist doesn't have the right
to distort facts completely. He said his power is not absolute when
it comes to fact. Then you also talked about imaginative truth,
and that certain things don't fit into a novel. I'd like to know about

the fact that Nat Turner was married—didn't that fit into your novel?

Styron: It seems to me I've heard this before. I can only reiterate what I have said despairingly in public and even more despairingly in cold print, that in the evidence which was available to me when some years ago I began to collect the few basic materials to write this book, there was no evidence which told me he had such a wife.

First Questioner: Didn't Thomas Gray's *Confessions* say that?

Styron: No. I'm very sorry. Or is that a rhetorical question?

First Questioner: No, I read an article in *Ebony* by Lerone Bennett.

Styron: I read it, too. He's wrong. No, if you read the *Confessions* yourself, the original *Confessions,* this is one of the amazing things about it. He mentions all the rest of his family, but mentions no wife. Once again, in an essay I wrote about this controversy, I said that, without laying aside my belief in the irrelevance of certain facts, this on the other hand would have been so important that if I had been given any kind of substantial evidence that he had a wife, then as a novelist I would have felt compelled to create a wife for him. But I only ask again, certainly not for the last time, that people who, like yourself, constantly castigate me for leaving his wife out, consult the evidence yourself, and use a little reason.

First Questioner: Is Margaret Whitehead, in the evidence, completely obsessed in his mind?

Styron: Margaret Whitehead is a part of my fictional imagination. I have no apologies for her. But as for the fact of a black wife, I submit to you, humbly, that the evidence does not show that he had one; and therefore, I think reason dictates that it was perfectly all right for me to leave her out.

First Questioner: I have a number of other questions, but I'm only going to ask one more. You said that a novel has its own reason for being. What's the reason for being for *The Confessions of Nat Turner?* Because I read it and I couldn't find any.

Styron: Well, I don't know how to answer a question like that. In fact, I don't think I'll try. It's so majestic a question that I don't think I'm able to answer it.

Second Questioner: Seeing as though calling historians liars tonight has been quite popular, I can remember that the last time I called you a liar, it became very bitter. It seems as though we confront each other from the North to the South. I met you in Massachusetts this summer, and now all the way down in New Orleans I'm here to call you a liar again.

Ellison: Which one of us, please?

Second Questioner: I'm primarily concerned with Styron. I met him this summer at Harvard. I think possibly we need to take a look at the revolutionary black figure, Nat Turner, to see what he actually represents to black people. I think when we talk about slavery and revolution that it has to be looked at from a psychiatric or a psychological viewpoint. Okay, we take a look at the ten blacks who responded to your book on *The Confessions of Nat Turner*. In this group we have C. V. Hamilton, we have Alvin Poussaint. These men have really delved into the thing; they have looked at it from a psychological viewpoint.

I heard Warren say a few minutes ago that fact can destroy, that fact can be deadly. I contend that imagination and lying can also be deadly and can also destroy. Now let's take a look at this a bit further. First of all we see two major bases from which this book was written. We see some religious ties with Nat Turner—that he was a preacher or something, who had some vision about killing white folk. Secondly, I remember your statement that the white woman was a higher symbol or goal for the black man or the black slave—something that he looked up to and wanted and desired. Okay, I remember asking you that question up North, and I want you to tell these Southern whites this same thing. I want to know this: if the white woman was the symbol for Nat Turner to look up to and this was why he wanted sexual relations, and had all these desires, then, since that black woman [in the novel] was below the white man, what kind of image was she?

Styron: Have you paused for a question now? Well, let me tackle all of these again, one by one. Indeed you have haunted me. You're my *bête noire*, I'm afraid. I recall you from Harvard Summer School with terror. Now here you are again. I won't reply to your *ad hominem* remarks about my "lies," and so on, but I will try to reply directly to you about what I conceive to be the essential truth about Nat Turner's relationship with white women. Forgive me if I paraphrase you badly, but I think you are asking me if I sincerely believe that Nat Turner really yearned, carnally and otherwise, for a white girl. Am I right?

Second Questioner: No, you're wrong.

Styron: Well then, would you please rephrase it?

Second Questioner: My thing was, if you placed the white woman above the black slave—the male slave, and said that this was something that he wanted because she was above or higher than him, then how do you explain the white man reaching below him to go back in the quarters, to get the black women out of those slave quarters, which is the cause of many of my brothers and sisters sitting here tonight being of different pigmentation of skin?

Styron: I don't think at any place in the book did I for an instant deny the very implicit fact that white men were down in the quarters at all times. The reason that I didn't necessarily describe this happening in any great detail is simply that it didn't suit my artistic needs. But if you are implying that somewhere in the book there is a vacuum, that somewhere in the book there is an implication that Negro women were not violated more or less systematically by white men who ruthlessly went down in the cabins, then you have totally misread the book. Because it's there.

Second Questioner: You see, the facts you included would *sell*. The whites *wanted* to read that Nat Turner was not a strong, black, revolutionary figure, but that he had certain sexual desires that drove him on. All right, you talk about his killing women and children. Let's take a look at the *Ten Black Writers* and how they analyze that. It seems that most of the men were away at a meeting. This made no difference. You talk about children; you make me believe that Nat Turner walked up and just stabbed babies or beat them in the head—which possibly would have been all right, because possibly he had the insight to know that these same little white babies would one day be the slave masters of his children, wherever they were. So wiping out the white children would be the very same thing as wiping out those adult honkies. When he burned down a house, he got white women and children and anybody else who was in the house. It made no difference who was in the house; when the house went up in flames, everybody and everything in the house went up, not just women and children.

Styron: What is your complaint?

Second Questioner: My complaint is this: don't just say he killed women and children, like the man had a hang-up or was afraid of white men, because explicitly the ten blacks tell you how he knocked some honky down and beat him to death, and then laid his wife down and killed her, right next to him. He wasn't afraid of white men; he killed white men, white babies, white women, white cats, white dogs, everything that was in the neighborhood.

Styron: Indeed he did. I tried to point out something to you, I think. I shall try again. (You reappear in my dreams; I knew somehow that you'd find me here. From Cambridge to New Orleans; it's more than the mind can encompass.) Anyway, if I may quote, in a sort of contradistinction to your ten black critics, one of the people who criticized the ten black critics, in this case Eugene Genovese. I think he pointed out, at least to my satisfaction, that if you will read the evidence—if you read the crude evidence of Nat Turner and his insurrection, and you can read it in twenty minutes— you will get the impression, and any rational person will get the impression when he is finished, of a ruthless and perhaps psychotic fanatic, a religious fanatic who, lacking any plan or purpose— admittedly, because it is in the testimony, lacking any plan or purpose—takes five or six rather bedraggled followers and goes off on a ruthless, directionless, aimless forty-eight-hour rampage of total destruction, in which the victims are, by a large majority, women and little children.

Second Questioner: But *white*.

Styron: No. Wait a minute. This is the crude evidence; this is what Lukács would say. These are the facts. Deal with them. I submit to you—I submit to any rational intelligence in this room who would allow himself twenty minutes—that this is the impression you would get. A deranged—

Second Questioner: It isn't the impression that I got.

Styron: Well, I'm sorry.

Second Questioner: It may be a white impression.

Styron: I don't think so.

Second Questioner: Quite clearly.

Styron: I don't think so. What Genovese was generous enough to grant me, in my dealings with this man, was that I supplied him

with the motivation. I gave him a rationale. I gave him all of the
confusions and desperations, troubles, worries.

Second Questioner: But look. Let's stop here.

Styron: Excuse me. Will you hear me out?

Second Questioner: He was a slave, and that gave him enough
reason.

Styron: All right. Listen to me, will you, please?

Second Questioner: That gave him enough reason, right there.

Styron: All right.

Second Questioner: You didn't have to create anything for him.
He saw brothers and sisters being killed all around him. He saw
families being broken up.

Styron: The evidence . . .

Second Questioner: I notice your other point, that these were kind
slavemasters. It doesn't matter how kind they were; they were
slavemasters.

Styron: I'm sorry, you haven't read it carefully. The evidence
doesn't show any . . .

Second Questioner: I've read it quite carefully.

Styron: Well, then, we're at an impasse, my friend, because you
say it's one way, and I say it's another.

Second Questioner: Yes, but everytime we meet, you always jibe,
and say that I miss your point. You ought to stop lying.

Woodward: Are there other people who want to ask questions?

Third Questioner: I have a question about another Southern
novel, an older one. Perhaps I have read you, the panel, wrong,
but I gather you would be willing to predict that in a hundred years
Gone with the Wind will be an obscure or forgotten novel. From
listening to what you have said about using historical facts and
about catching the essence, I gather that you would think that
Gone with the Wind has failed.

Styron: You must be crazy; I didn't say any such thing. I admire
Gone with the Wind very, very much. I reread it about four years
ago. It's a remarkable novel. I don't think it's a great novel, but it's
a remarkable novel, precisely because this little woman from
Atlanta had a fire of an imagination, which captured her and
somehow allowed her to breathe some kind of miraculous spirit
through and around the rather threadbare facts about antebellum

Georgia. I certainly would not say that it's going to be dead in a
hundred years. If I led you to believe that, you misunderstood me.

Woodward: Yes sir?

Fourth Questioner: As long as we call ourselves black and white,
then even if we gain black power, unless we censor that movie
I'm sure all white folks will go to it. They love that myth. But I
think it's slightly beside the point. [*to Styron*] I would suggest, by
the way, that I'm very sorry that Mr. Ellison didn't read your book.
I'm extremely sorry, because of the putdown that you did on the
young man. I think that intellectually you would have had a little bit
more trouble with Mr. Ellison. I didn't stand up here for a putdown,
so I'm not going to ask you anything at all. I have a whole lot of
trouble with that book. I must say that, like every other black
man, I resented it. I do think that the book must not be valid if all
the black intellectuals put it down. If it salves the conscience (salves;
how do you spell that word?)—if it salves the conscience of whites,
and they want to read it, well, then you can make some money.
But in view of this, I want to ask Mr. Warren this: since we all felt
that *All the King's Men* had to do with Huey Long, why didn't *he*
say Huey Long, or King Fish, or something like that? I wonder
what would have happened to *The Confessions of Nat Turner* had
it just been called the *Confessions of a Revolt Leader,* or something
like that. I doubt if anybody would even have paid any attention
to it. So I'd like to ask Mr. Ellison—he disguises his characters—

Ellison: I made them up; they were all me.

Fourth Questioner: Yes, I know, but you've lived through [the
period] since Rinehart, you've lived through Malcolm—

Ellison: Yes.

Fourth Questioner: We've had some different experiences [since
then]. I don't suggest that you follow in the footsteps of Leroi
[Jones] really, as a lot of my militant friends would suggest, but
since you are older, and you did live through something, I'd like to
know—I mean, it was different, you know; everybody was trying
to get along with whitey during that time, and now it's kind of six
one way, half-a-dozen the other. But since you've lived through
Malcolm, and I've heard that you are writing now, how do you
see guys like Rinehart? Would you fictionalize Malcolm, disguise
him, or would you feel free to say, well. . . .'

Ellison: I would be ashamed to tell the truth about Malcolm in fiction.

Fourth Questioner: Ashamed to tell the truth about him?

Ellison: Yes. Well, I think you're getting at a much more important problem which . . .

Fourth Questioner: You see, I'm concerned with *using* work . . . , Malcolm versus fiction for instance. I'm saying, leave off the word Nat Turner on that book, and just make it the *Confessions of a Slave Leader,* and nobody would read it. (Which I don't think they should, anyway.) But what would you do with Malcolm?

Ellison: Well, wait a minute. You throw too many things at me at once, when you're really bouncing them off me to hit Bill.

Fourth Questioner: Yes, I'm trying very hard.

Ellison: All right . . .

Fourth Questioner: He [Styron] put down that other young man so skillfully. I think I'd be a little bit more trouble because I don't think that that young man was aware of the fact that Mr. Styron was trying to put him down.

Ellison: Maybe the young man . . .

Fourth Questioner: I thought that was cute and extremely unfair. Nine million people in this country voted for Wallace—I take that rather seriously. A fascist. I mean, you see, we haven't accomplished the revolution—

Ellison: May I . . .

Fourth Questioner: Yes, please.

Ellison: I think that there is a basic question of what all arts attempt to do, or what art should attempt to do. Through depicting the real, fictionally, imaginatively, by abstracting from the historical process, reducing it to a controlled situation where the imagination can load each character, each scene, each mood, even each punctuation mark with the individual writer's sense of life, art can give man some transcendent sense of his complexity and his potentiality—of his possibilities—and convey something of the wonder of human life, and I must say, without reducing man to what Malraux would call a handful of secrets . . .

Fourth Questioner: That's why I'm sorry you didn't read the book.

Ellison: . . . posited in his negative potentialities. I think that

there is something else here which *you* might think about. I don't
know whether you are a writer, or whether you should write, intend
to write, or what not. But I think that there is a world of art, a
world of fiction, and this must be protected against assaults. Not
because we are black or white, or because we are oppressed and
fighting for more freedom in this country, but because we seek to
express ourselves. I want to say, I want the freedom to depict, to
recreate Robert E. Lee in terms of my own vision of human
possibility, human failure, and so on. So we cannot reduce this
thing, really, to the struggle, which is very important on the political
level. This distinction is very important, and I point out that two
of the ten critics tried to stick to the literary, to the artistic problems
involved. Beyond this, of course, as you and the other young man
have dramatized so vividly for us, there *is* a problem. Damn it,
there is a *problem* about recreating historical figures. That's why
I said it's poison to the novelist; he shouldn't bother them. Don't
appropriate the names. Don't move into the historian's arena, because
you can only be slaughtered there. But you can also be very, very
powerful, and I think that this should not be missed: this book,
whatever its literary qualities—and I will stand up for Bill's personal
qualities and his . . .

   Fourth Questioner: Malcolm said that most whites in America,
deep down in their toes, are racists, even when they don't
think so.

   Ellison: I would suspect that all Americans, black and white,
are racists.

   Fourth Questioner: Well, we . . .

   Ellison: That isn't the problem here, you see. You asked me then
what would I make of Malcolm. Well I wouldn't dare to tell the
truth about him, because it would destroy the same myth, and this
myth is a valuable myth. But I don't want Malcolm telling me what
American history is, and I don't want him to tell me what my
experience has been, and so on, any more than I want or I would
allow Bill or anybody else to do that. You see, there is a world of
fiction, and there's a world of politics. I think it's very important for
your own position that you keep these things in clear perspective.

   Fourth Questioner: Are you suggesting that we are still invisible?

   Ellison: I am by no means. I was not invisible, and I would think that you, speaking with your inclination, would remember that old joke: The Negro is unseen because of his high visibility.

Woodward: Well, I hope that enigma will satisfy questions. There are people here who have been standing patiently for over two hours, and I feel that I am obliged to bring the meeting to a close after one more question.

Fifth Questioner: I was going to ask two questions, but I'll condense them. Mr. Styron has stressed several times what I think is probably the quintessential bone of contention this evening; he said—I think I quote him accurately—that the fiction writer's obligation is to make sense out of history. I was going to ask, whether he thinks that is the fiction writer's primary, or one of his primary, obligations. I'd like to address my central question to Mr. Ellison, and step back to a novel that is not as recent and, at present I assume, not as controversial as *The Confessions of Nat Turner*. Mr. Ellison, you said that Jim of *Huckleberry Finn* was not grounded enough, and I think many of us would probably agree with that, but I'd like to ask whether you feel that this was because of a failure of creative imagination, or a failure of historical imagination, on the novelist's part. Or do you see the two as one problem?

Ellison: I think the author was too much a victim of the history of his times. Artistically, you see, fiction isn't written out of history, it's written out of other art forms. The going art form for depicting Negroes, the one freshest on the minds of people during Mark Twain's time, was the popular art form of the blackfaced minstrel, and it was that tradition which Mark Twain was very much involved in. His own values managed to project through Jim, but I still insist that it was not grounded enough in the reality of Negro American personality. I know of no black—Negro—critics (I'm a Negro, by the way) who wrote criticisms of *Huckleberry Finn* when it appeared. It was all a dialogue between, a recreation, a collaboration, between a white American novelist of good heart, of democratic vision, one dedicated to values—I know much of Mark Twain's writing—and white readers, primarily. What is going on is that now you have more literate Negroes, and they are questioning themselves, and questioning everything which has occurred and been written in the country.

Fifth Questioner: Well, then, in a sense his creative imagination was limited in fact by the historical moment, and that is what has changed.

Ellison: Limited, too, by his being not quite as literary a man as he was required to be. Because he could have gone to Walter Scott, to the Russians, to any number of places, and found touchstones for filling out the complex humanity of that man who appeared in his book out of his own imagination, and who was known as Jim.

Fifth Questioner: But were any of the, let's say, less socially favored characters of novelists who were his contemporaries or his predecessors any more fully recreated historically than he managed to do with Jim? You know, with someone with whom he could not directly identify?

Ellison: Aren't you making this too much of an objective matter? It's a collaboration. It was a successful book. I read it years ago. In fact, it was so successful and so painful that they made it a boy's book, a children's book, in order to be able to deal with the moral pain which it aroused. Nevertheless, part of the discomfort which we feel—and the questions which those slaves (when was this? the 80s), those people of my background, would have asked about it—was not Mark Twain's central concern. What I am suggesting is that *everybody* reads now. *Everybody* is American whether they call themselves separatists, black separatists, secessionists or what not. And everybody is saying: Damn it, tell it like *I* think it is. And this is a real problem for the novelist.

Woodward: Ladies and gentlemen, we are limited to two hours and we have exceeded our limit. Let me thank you for your patience and good humor, and our fellow members for their contribution.

Indivisible Man

James Alan McPherson / 1969

From *Speaking for You,* edited by Kimberly M. Bentson, How-
ard University Press, 1987. Copyright 1970 by James Alan
McPherson. Reprinted by permission of James Alan Mc-
Pherson.

July 1969

Ralph Ellison, a pair of high-powered binoculars close to his eyes,
sits by the window of his eighth-floor Riverside Drive apartment,
looking down. Across the street, in the long strip of green park
which parallels the Hudson River, two black boys are playing
basketball. "I watch them every afternoon," he says, and offers the
binoculars to me. I look down and recognize the hope of at least
two major teams, ten years hence, developing. Perhaps future
sociologists will say that they possess superior athletic abilities
because of biological advantages peculiar to blacks; but perhaps by
then each of these black boys will have gained enough of a sense
of who he is to reply: "I'm good at what I do because I practiced it
all my life." The encouragement of this sort of self-definition has
become almost a crusade with Ellison. But I also recognize that if I
ran down and waved my arms and shouted to them: "Did you
know that Ralph Ellison watches you playing every afternoon?"
they would continue to shoot at the basket and answer: "Who is
Ralph Ellison?"

*   *   *

"He spoke at Tougaloo last year," a black exchange student at
Santa Cruz told me. "I can't stand the man."

"Why?"

Originally published in *Atlantic Monthly,* 226, December 1970, 45–60. Copyright ©
1970, Epilogue © 1984 by James Alan McPherson. Reprinted by permission of
James Alan McPherson. The remarks in the Epilogue were delivered by James Alan
McPherson at the first Langston Hughes Festival at the City College of New York on
April 11, 1984, and appear in print for the first time here.—Ed. [Kimberly W.
Bentson]

"I couldn't understand what he was saying. He wasn't talking to *us*."

"Did you read his book."

"No. And I don't think I will, either. I can't stand the man."

If you ask him about the Tougaloo experience, Ellison will laugh and then tell an anecdote about the stuttering black student who said: "Mr. E-l-li-s-s-s-*on*, I r-r-*ead* your b-b-*ook The* Inv-v-v-si-b-b-*ble* M-m-*man*. B-b-but after he-e-e-ar*ing* you tonight I f-f-*feel* like I j-j-ju-*ust* hear-r-*rd* J-j-je-*sus* C-c-ch-r-r-*rist* d-d-d-runk on *Thunderbird Wine!*" And if you laugh along with him, and if you watch Ellison's eyes as you laugh, you will realize that he is only testing a deep scar to see if it has healed.

*   *   *

Ellison's difficulty, one cause of all the cuts, is that matter of self-definition. At a time when many blacks, especially the young, are denying all influences of American culture, Ellison, as always, doggedly affirms his identity as a Negro American, a product of the blending of both cultures. But more than this, he attempts to explore most of the complex implications of this burden in his fiction, his essays, his speeches, and his private life. He is nothing as simple as a "brown-skinned aristocrat" (as Richard Kostelanetz characterized him in a *Shenandoah* essay-portrait); rather, he is a thinking black man who has integrated his homework into the fabrics of his private life. "I don't recognize any white culture," he says. "I recognize no American culture which is not the partial creation of black people. I recognize no American style in literature, in dance, in music, even in assembly-line processes, which does not bear the mark of the American Negro." And he means it. For this reason he has difficulty reconciling some of the ideas of black nationalists, who would view black culture as separate from the broader American culture. To these people he says: "I don't recognize any black culture the way many people use the expression." And Ellison is one of the few black intellectuals who have struggled to assess the influence of the black on American culture and the relationships between the two. But, until fairly recently, not many blacks—perhaps even college-educated blacks—knew that he existed.

In 1952 he published his first novel, *Invisible Man,* which won a

National Book Award, and this at a time when the white critical
establishment was less eager to recognize literary achievement by
black Americans. Now, almost nineteen years later, he is still the
only black American who has received this honor. The novel has
gone through twenty paperback printings and was judged, in a
1965 *Book Week* poll of two hundred authors, critics, and editors,
"the most distinguished single work published in the last twenty
years." A second book, a collection of essays and interviews called
Shadow and Act, was published in 1964 and is essential reading
for any attempt at understanding Ellison, the man or the artist.
While *Invisible Man* is a story of one man's attempt to understand
his society and himself, the essays outline Ellison's own successful
struggle to master the craft of the writer and to understand, and
then affirm, the complexities of his own rich cultural experience.

He likes to call himself a college dropout because he completed
only three years of a music major at Tuskegee Institute before
coming to New York in 1936. Before that he was a shoeshine boy, a
jazz musician, a janitor, a free-lance photographer, and a man
who hunted game during the Depression to keep himself alive.

Today he is a member, and a former vice president, of the
National Institute of Arts and Letters; a member of New York's
Century Club and the American Academy of Arts and Sciences;
and a trustee of the John F. Kennedy Center for the Performing
Arts. He is a former teacher at Bard, Rutgers, and Chicago and was
Albert Schweitzer Professor in the Humanities at New York Univer-
sity. He has an interest in noncommercial television, which began
with his work on the Carnegie Commission on Educational Television,
and continues with his trusteeships in the Educational Broadcasting
Corporation, and the National Citizens' Committee for Broadcasting.
Among his awards are listed the Russwurm Award, the Medal of
Freedom (awarded by President Johnson), five honorary Ph.D.'s, and
one of the highest honors which France can bestow on a foreign
writer: Chevalier de l'Ordre des Arts et Lettres, awarded to him
in 1970 by the French Minister of Cultural Affairs, André Malraux.
But all these experiences seem to have equal weight in his mind;
all seem to have given equal access to information, equal opportunity for observation of the culture. And he is as likely to begin a
discussion with some observation made when he was a shoeshine

boy as he is to mention the first names of some of America's most respected writers and critics.

His success does not prove, as one writer says, that "a fatherless American Negro really does have the opportunity to become the author of one of America's greatest novels as well as an aristocratic presence and an all but universally respected literary figure." Ellison's achievements are too enormous to be reduced to a sociological cliché, a rhetorical formulation. If anything, his success proves that intelligence, perseverance, discipline, and love for one's work are, together, too great a combination to be contained, or even defined, in terms of race.

Although he lives in New York and has access to literary and intellectual areas, Ellison seems to have very limited contact with the black writers who also live there. Yet his shadow lies over all their writers' conferences, and his name is likely to be invoked, and defamed, by any number of the participants at any conference. One man has said that he would like to shoot Ellison. Another, whom Ellison has never met, has for almost ten years blamed Ellison for his not receiving the last Prix de Rome Award, given by the American Academy of Arts and Letters. On the other hand, a growing number of young black writers, among them Ernest J. Gaines, Cecil Brown, Michael Harper, Ishmael Reed, and Al Young, are quick to admit their respect for him.

He reads the work of black writers, dismisses some of it, and is always willing to give an endorsement. And although he is very protective of his time, his telephone number is listed in the Manhattan directory, and he will usually grant an interview or a few hours of conversation in the afternoon (his working day usually ends at 4:00 P.M.) to anyone who is insistent.

"A fellow called me one morning," Ellison chuckles, lighting up a cigar, "said he just had to see me. So I consented. I went to the door, and there was a brown-skinned fellow from the Village. He brought a bottle of wine, several records, and four attempts at short stories. I looked at these things, and they weren't really stories. So I asked: 'What do you want me to tell you?' He said: 'Well, what I want you to do is tell me, should I just write, or should I tell the truth?'" Ellison pauses to laugh deep in his chest, "I said: 'Tell the truth.'"

*   *   *

"He came to Oberlin in April of 1969," a black girl in Seattle
recalled. "His speech was about how American black culture had
blended into American white culture. But at the meeting with the
black caucus after the speech, the black students said: 'You don't
have anything to tell us.' "

"What did he say?"

"He just accepted it very calmly. One girl said to him: 'Your
book doesn't mean anything because in it you're shooting down
Ras the Destroyer, a rebel leader of black people.' "

"What was his answer?"

"He said: 'Remember now, this book was written a long time
ago. This is just one man's view of what he saw, how he interpreted what he saw. I don't make any apologies for it.' Well, she went
on to tell him: 'That just proves that you're an Uncle Tom.' "

*   *   *

Another of Ellison's problems, one peculiar to any black who
attempts to assert his own individuality in his own terms, is that
he challenges the defense mechanisms of the black community.
Because of a history of enforced cohesiveness, some blacks have
come to believe in a common denominator of understanding, even
a set number of roles and ideas which are assumed to be useful to
the community. Doctors, lawyers, teachers, social workers, some
orthodox thinkers, some orthodox writers are accepted—as long
as they do not insist on ideas which are foreign to the community's
own sense of itself. But when a black man attempts to think beyond
what has been thought before, or when he asserts a vision of reality
which conflicts with or challenges the community's conception,
there is a movement, sometimes unconscious, to bring him back
into line or, failing that, to ostracize him. The "mass man" of
sociological terminology is the "right-on man" of black slang,
gliding smoothly and simplistically, and perhaps more comfort-
ably, over questionable assumptions, and reducing himself to a
cliché in the process. For a black thinker, such as Ellison, this
assertion of individual vision is especially painful because the
resultant ostracism carries with it the charge of "selling out" or
"trying to be white." Yet a white thinker who challenges assumptions held by whites about themselves is not charged with "trying

to be black." The underlying assumption is that whites have a
monopoly on individuality and intelligence, and in order for a
black man to lay claim to his own he must, necessarily, change
color.

In response to charges by attackers that he is a "token Negro"
because he is very often the only black serving on cultural
commissions, Ellison says: "All right, if you don't want me on, I'll
resign. But you had better put a *cardboard Negro* in my place
because when decisions are made which will affect black people
you had better make sure that those people who make the
decisions remember that you exist and are forced to make sure that
some of your interests are being met."

This impulse toward leveling, however, is not confined to the
black community. It is a minority-group reaction. And while
Ellison remembers a black professor at Tuskegee who tore up a
leather-bound volume of Shakespeare's plays to discourage his
interest in literature, he also remembers a white professor friend
who said: "Ah, here's Ralph again, talking about America.
There's no goddamn America out there."

                    *   *   *

"At Oberlin," the Seattle girl said, "one of the ideas they
couldn't accept was Ellison's statement that black styles had
historically been incorporated into American life. He went on to say
that in the future, don't be surprised if white people begin to wear
Afros because that's now a part of American popular culture. Well,
the kids went out screaming, 'Who is he to insult what we wear?
No honky could wear an Afro. They're stealing what is ours.'"

One year later disenchanted white youth, on both coasts and in
between, are sporting their versions of the Afro. . . .

                    *   *   *

He is as practiced a listener as he is a speaker, and gives even the
most naively put question thorough consideration before responding.
He is a bit guarded at first, perhaps unwinding from a day at his
desk, perhaps adjusting to the intellectual level of his guest. Then
he begins talking, occasionally pausing to light a cigar, occasionally
glancing out the window at the street, the park, the river beyond.
After a while you both are trading stories and laughing while Mrs.
Ellison makes noises in the kitchen, just off the living room. A

parakeet flutters into the room. Ellison calls it, imitating its chirps, and the bird comes and hovers near his hand. "Have you ever heard a dog talk?" he asks.

"No."

We go into his study, and he plays a tape of a dog clearly imitating the rhythm and pitch of a human voice saying "hello." We listen again, and laugh again. Mrs. Ellison calls us to dinner. It is difficult enjoying the food and digesting his conversation at the same time.

"Ralph, stop talking and let him eat," Mrs. Ellison says.

After dinner we move back into the living room and continue the conversation. Finally Ellison's dog, Tucka Tarby, comes into the room and walks back and forth between us. Then you realize that it is well after midnight and that you have put a serious dent in the essential personal rhythm of a writer's day. Tucka has been patient, waiting for his evening walk. Ellison puts on an army jacket, and we go down in the elevator. This is an old building, just on the edge of Harlem, and most of the tenants are black. The lobby has colored tiles, a high ceiling, and live flowers protected by glass. "I've lived here for eighteen years," he says. "But it wasn't until 1964 that some of the people found out I was a writer." Tucka pulls us up 150th Street toward Broadway. We shake hands, and he and the dog walk off into the Harlem night.

*   *   *

"I think that what made it hard for him," the Seattle girl said, "was that LeRoi Jones was coming to Oberlin that next day. The kids figured that Jones the Master is coming, so let's get rid of this cat. But I think he's very gutsy, in a day like today with all these so-called militants trying to run him into the ground, coming to Oberlin saying to the kids: 'You are American, not African.' "

"Did anyone come to his defense?"

"One of the teachers stopped the meeting at one point and said: 'Would you please listen to what the man has to say? You're sitting here criticizing, and some of you haven't even read the damn book.' "

*   *   *

Among his peers Ellison's presence or even the mention of his name causes the immediate arming of intellectual equipment. There can be no soft-pedaling, no relaxation of intellect where he is involved. At Brown University in November of 1969, novelists and critics gathered at the annual Wetmore Lecture to discuss form, the future of the novel, and each other. Critic Robert Scholes opened one discussion on form by reading from Ellison's acceptance speech before the National Book Award Committee. "Ah, Ellison," Leslie Fiedler said, throwing his arm out in a gesture of dismissal. "He's a black Jew."

Ellison chuckles. "Leslie's been trying to make me a Jew for years," he says. "I have to look at these things with a Cold Oklahoma Negro Eye. But someone should have said that *all* us old-fashioned Negroes are Jews."

* * *

Ellison is not only interested in the fiction written by young black writers; he is concerned about young black people in general: what they are thinking, what they are doing, what their ambitions are. But his knowledge of them is limited to sessions during speaking engagements, letters, and what he hears from the media. "A hell of a lot of them are reading my book," he observes with obvious pleasure. "I have a way of checking this. And for a long time they didn't read much of anything."

Yet he worries that despite the increased educational opportunities available to them, young black people are becoming too involved in, and almost symbolic of, the campus reactions against intellectual discipline, the life of the mind. "It's too damn bad," he says. "You see that men are now analyzing the song of the whales, the talk of dolphins, planning to go to the moon; computer technology is becoming more and more humanized and miniaturized; great efforts are being made to predetermine sex, to analyze cells, to control the life process in the human animal. And all of this is done with the *mind*. And indeed," he goes on, "the irony is that we've never really gotten away from that old *body* business; the Negro as symbolic of *instinctual* man. Part of my pride in being what I am is that as a dancer, as a physical man"—and again that distant chuckle comes from deep within his chest—"I bet you I can outdance, outriff most of these intellectuals who're supposed to have come back." Now he is serious again. "*But that isn't the problem, dammit!* I was *born* doing *this!* It's a glorious thing to know the uses of the body and not to be afraid of it. But *that has to be linked to the mind.* I don't see any solution for literary art. If you're a dancer, fine. If you're a musician, fine. But what are you going to do as a writer, or what are you going to do as a critic?'' He sighs, as if he were weighed down by these considerations.

"I find this very interesting," he continues, "but not new. When I think about Tuskegee and people with whom I went to school, I know that over and over again they really did not extend themselves because they didn't have the imagination to look thirty years ahead to a point where there would be a place for them in the broader American society, had they been prepared."

He says: "I understand ambition; I understand the rejection of goals because they're not self-fulfilling. I've turned down too many things starting as a youngster."

He looks out the window toward the Hudson, then continues in a lower tone. "I was married once before, and one reason that marriage came to an end was that my in-laws were disgusted with me, thought I had no ambition, because I didn't want a job in the Post Office. And here I was with a dream of myself writing the symphony at twenty-six which would equal anything Wagner had done at twenty-six. This is where my ambitions were. So I can understand people getting turned off on that level. But what I can't understand is people who do not master a technique or discipline which will get them to a point where they can actually see that it's not what they want or that something else is demanded. But over and over again I see black kids who are dropping out or rejecting intellectual discipline as though what exists now will always exist and as though they don't have the possibility of changing it by using these disciplines as techniques to affirm *their* sense of what a human life should be. It's there where I get upset."

He has a habit of pausing whenever the discussion begins to touch areas pregnant with emotion, as if careful of remaining within a certain context. But on some subjects he is likely to continue. "I also get upset when I see announcements of prizes and medical discoveries and scientific advances, and I don't see any black names or black faces. I believe that we are *capable*," he says. "I believe that there are enough unique features in our background to suggest solutions to problems which seem very, very far removed from our social situation."

The duality of cultural experience which Ellison insists on in his writing is acted out in his professional and personal life. He is just as much at home, just as comfortable, in a Harlem barbershop as he is as a panelist before the Southern Historical Association exchanging arguments with C. Vann Woodward, Robert Penn Warren, and William Styron. He is a novelist well respected by his peers (when his name is mentioned in almost any literary circle, there will be invariably an inquiry about his current project), and he brings to bear the same respect for craft in an introduction to the stories of Stephen Crane as he uses to evaluate the work of black artist Romare Bearden. Yet, precisely because of his racial identity, he is also the leading black writer in American letters. And while he disclaims this position as "an accident, part luck and part a product of the confusion over what a black writer is and what an American writer is," the reality is there, nevertheless, and has to be coped with.

Before he accepted the professorship at New York University, Ellison earned a good part of his income from college speaking engagements. He accepted around twenty each year. He tends to favor the East Coast or Midwest and avoids the West Coast, partially because of the great distance and partially because of the political nature of the West. He is very much in demand, although his fee is usually $1,500 to $2,000. In the past year he has spoken at such colleges as Millsaps, East Texas State, Rockland, Illinois, West Point, and Iowa State University at Ames.

He takes pride in being able to deliver a ninety-minute speech without the aid of notes. He will make some few digressions to illuminate his points, but will always pick up the major thread and carry it through to its preconceived end.

*   *   *

March 1970
Ralph Ellison stands on a stage broad enough to seat a full symphony orchestra. Before him, packed into a massive new auditorium of gray concrete and glass and deep red carpets, 2,700 Ames students strain to hear the words of the man billed as "Ralph Ellison: Writer." Ames is almost an agricultural school, and its students still have fraternity rows, beer parties, rat pins and ties, white shirts and jackets. Most of them are the beardless sons of farmers and

girls whose ambitions extend only as far as engagement by the
senior year. The American Dream still lingers here, the simple
living, the snow, the hamburgers and milk shakes, the country
music and crickets and corn. This is the breadbasket of the country,
the middle of Middle America. And yet, ninety miles away in
Iowa City, students torn from these same roots are about to burn
buildings. "When the pioneers got to your part of the country,"
he tells them, speaking again of the vernacular, the functional level
of the American language, "there was no word for 'prairie' in the
Oxford English Dictionary." His speech is on "The Concept of
Race in American Literature." And he delivers just that. But it is
abstract, perhaps over the heads of many of the students there
(even though parts of it later appeared as a *Time* essay in the
issue on "Black America"). Still, the students are quiet, respectful,
attempting to digest. Speaking of the ethnic blending which began
with the formation of the country, he says: "And, to make it brief,
there was a whole bunch of people from Africa who were not introduced by the British, but quite some time before were introduced
into what later became South Carolina by the Spanish. Where-
upon they immediately began to revolt—" Here loud applause floats
down to the lower audience from black students in the second
balcony. Ellison pauses. Then continues: "—and went wild, and
started passing for Indians. I hear a lot about black people passing
for white, but remember, they first started passing for Indians."
There is some giggling and laughter at this. But, behind me, I notice a
black student cringing.

During the question-and-answer session afterwards, the students
ask the usual things: the conflict between Richard Wright and
James Baldwin, the order of symbols in *Invisible Man.* One girl
wants to know if racial miscegenation is a necessary ingredient of
racial integration. He laughs. "Where'd you get that word?" he
says. And answers: "I don't think that any of us Americans wants to
lose his ethnic identity. This is another thing which has been used
to manipulate the society in terms of race. Some few people might
want to lose their identities; this has happened. But I would think
that the very existence of such strong Negro American influences in
the society, the style, the way things are done, would indicate that
there's never been the desire to lose that. There's just too much

self-congratulation in so much of Negro American expression. They wouldn't want to give that up." He says: "The thing that black people have been fighting for for so long was the opportunity to decide whether they *wanted* to give it up or not. And the proof is that in this period when there is absolutely more racial freedom than has ever existed before, you have the most militant rejection of integration. These are individual decisions which will be made by a few people. But if I know anything about the human being, what *attracts* a man to a woman has usually been picked up very early from the first woman he's had contact with. There is enough of a hold of tradition, of ways of cooking, of ways of just relaxing, which comes right out of the family circle, to keep us in certain groups."

At the reception after the speech, the whites dominate all three rooms; the few black students cluster together in one. Ellison moves between the two, sometimes almost tearing himself away from the whites. He talks to the black students about books, LeRoi Jones, Malcolm X, color, their personal interests. They do not say much. A white woman brings a book for his autograph; a professor gives a nervous explanation of the source of the miscegenation question: the girl has been reading Norman Podhoretz's essay "My Negro Problem and Ours" in his course. Ellison smiles and shifts back and forth on his feet like a boxer. Everyone is pleasantly high. The black students, still in a corner, are drinking Coke. I am leaving, eager to be out in the Iowa snow. We shake hands. "This is awkward," he says. "Call me Ralph and I'll call you Jim."

Santa Cruz, California
April 1970

Dear Amelia:

I was very pleased to have met you during my stay in Ames. Now, before the Spring Holidays begin, I wish you would tell me your impressions of Ellison as an artist, as a black man in touch with young black people, as a man of ideas. . . .

There are thousands and thousands of books in the rooms of his apartment; and besides the pieces of sculpture, paintings, African violets, self-designed furniture, and other symbols of a highly cultivated sensibility, are deep drawers and file cabinets which, if opened, reveal thick sheaves of notes and manuscripts. Ellison's huge desk, which sits in a study just off the living room, is covered with books, a red electric typewriter, well-thumbed manuscripts, and tape equipment. In conversation he always sits in the leatherstrap chair by the window, looking out on the Hudson and the street below.

He is a very direct and open man, even though there are silent levels of intimidating intelligence and unexpressed feeling beneath much of what he says. And he tends to approach even the most abstract idea from a personal point of view, usually including in any observation some supportive incident drawn from his own experience.

He talks freely of his mother, who died when he was in his early twenties, his relatives in Oklahoma, his professional relationships with other writers and critics, conversations with people on the subway or in the streets of Harlem; a recent chance meeting with Kurt Vonnegut in the streets of Manhattan; his respect for Saul Bellow as an extremely well-read novelist. And there is not an unkind, unprofessional, or imperceptive word for anyone, not even his most rabid critics. But he does become irritated if you question too closely his sense of identity as an American writer as opposed to a black writer, and he is likely to react when he senses a too containing category being projected onto him. "Let's put it this way, Jim," he says, irritation in his voice. "You see, I *work* out of American literature. In order to write the kind of fiction that I write I would *have* to be in touch with a broader literary culture than our own particular culture." He pauses, and then says: "This is not to denigrate what we have done, but in all *candor* we haven't begun to do what we can do or what we should have done. I think one reason why we haven't is that we've looked at our relationship to American literature in a rather negative way. That is, we've looked at it in terms of our trying to break into it. Well, damn it"—and his voice rises, and his hand hits the arm of the chair—"*that literature is built off our folklore to a large extent!*" And then he laughs that deep honest chuckle, and says: "I ain't conceding that to *nobody!*"

Ames, Iowa
April 1970

Dear James:

As an artist the man is beautiful. I think that is what was so captivating about his book. The symbolism that he uses and the combination of literary mechanics that he employs will probably make his work much more lasting than that of his black contemporaries. *Invisible Man* is a classic, and to say any more or less about it would be an understatement.

As for being in touch with the ideas of young people today, I think that he is quite aware, but he doesn't have the charisma that one would expect after hearing his reputation as a speaker and taking into account the acclaim his book has received. Part of my feeling is due to the disappointment of hearing him explain the figure in *Invisible Man*. So many concerned blacks had read the plight of the Afro-American into this figure with no face and no name. So many people saw the author riding to champion the cause of the black man. Those same people heard him say that the symbol was representative of a universal man. I found that most disheartening.

We are unfortunate at Ames, as well as at many other places across this nation, to have a group of young people who have been introduced to new ideologies and a new rhetoric and are attempting to adopt both when they do not understand either. Therefore, when they see or hear anyone who does not speak in their rhetoric they cannot, do not, and will not try to communicate with him. This was very true of Ellison.

He has a lot to say to a people who will listen to him. Today's youth are angry, and many times this anger closes their ears to a different rationale. Ellison's language and approach, I fear, attach to him the stigma of black bourgeois and conservatism. This figure does not communicate well with the vocal black youth.

Ellison is still a first-novelist, despite his reputation. And that one novel was published over eighteen years ago. He contributes a steady flow of articles to intellectual journals and periodicals, and scholars and critics are rapidly making a permanent place for him in the archives of American literary criticism. But while students continue to read and his critics continue to write, there is the expectation of his long-awaited second novel. So far he has read from it in universities and on public television, published sections of it in intellectual journals, allowed a few close friends to read some of it, and has remained strangely silent about publication of the rest. Inestimable numbers of people, black and white, in and out of universities, friends and enemies, await the publication of the complete novel. Whenever his name is mentioned among a group of writers or literati, the immediate response is: "When is his novel coming out?" One man has heard that he has pulled it back from his publisher again for more revisions; another says that

Ellison worries about its being dated, a third man says he has heard
that Ellison cannot finish it.

Concerning that novel there are many other stories. Perhaps the
best one is that which some friends of the Ellisons supposedly
heard from the writer's wife. "She says she hears him in his study
at night turning pages and laughing to himself. He enjoys the book
so much that he isn't in a hurry to share it with the public."

Whether or not this is true, Ellison is extremely reluctant, at first,
to discuss the book. A fire in his summer home in Plainfield, Massachusetts, destroyed a year's worth of revisions, he says, and he is
presently in the process of revising it again. "I want what I do to
be good," he says.

"Are you worried about the quality of it?"

"No," he says. "But you want to be sure when you write so
slowly, because if it's not good, if it's just passable, they'll be
terribly disappointed."

He has enough typed manuscripts to publish three novels, but is
worried about how the work will hold up as a total structure. He
does not want to publish three separate books, but then he does not
want to compromise on anything essential. "If I find that it is better
to make it a three-section book, to issue it in three volumes, I would
do that as long as I thought that each volume had a compelling
interest in itself. But it seems to me that one of the decisions one
has to make about long fiction is whether the effect of *reading* it
is lengthy. If you don't get the impression that you're reading a long
thing, then you've licked the problem of the battle of time."

The setting of the novel, he says, is roughly around 1955. The
form of it, he says, chuckling to himself, is in the direction of a
"realism extended beyond realism." There are several time
schemes operating within it, and the sections already published
heavily suggest that it is complexly involved with the Negro church
and its ritual. In fact, three of its major characters, Bliss, Eat-
more, and Hickman, are ministers.

On an afternoon, after a martini and before dinner, if the flow of
conversation has been relaxing, and if the mood is right, Ellison
might read a few sections from the book. It may take him a while to
thumb through several huge black-bound manuscripts, perhaps
numbering thousands of pages, to find an appropriate section. But

when he does begin to read there is the impression, from the way the
rhythms rise and fall and blend and flow out of him, that he is proud
of every word. He chuckles as he reads, stops to explain certain
references, certain connections, certain subtle jokes about the
minister whose sermon he is reading. And in those sermons his
voice becomes that of a highly sophisticated black minister, merging
sharp biblical images with the deep music of his voice, playing
with your ears, evoking latent memories of heated southern
churches and foot-stomping and fanning ladies in long white
dresses, and sweating elders swaying in the front rows. And suddenly the sermons are no longer comic, and there is no writer
reading from his work. You see a minister, and you feel the depth
of his religion, and you are only one soul in a huge congregation
of wandering souls hearing him ask, over and over: *"Oh Yes, Yes,
Yes, Yes, Yes. DO You Love, Ah DO You Love?"*

"Stephen's [Dedalus] problem," he wrote in *Invisible Man,* "like
ours, was not actually one of creating the uncreated conscience of his
race, but of creating the *uncreated features of his face."* Ellison is
fifty-six. His face does not show very much of it, but enough is
visible. He has a receding hairline, a broad forehead, and deep
curved lines on either side of his nose running down to the corners
of his mouth. It is a handsome brown face, from either point of
view, and there is a healthy stubbornness, besides all else inside that
forehead, which helps him to protect it. The face can be cold,
severe, analytical, pensive, even smiling. But it is not going
to change.

Epilogue

In the early 1970s I gained access to the Langston Hughes papers,
then just acquired by the Sterling Library at Yale University. One
letter in particular I remember. It was from Ralph Ellison, written
sometime in the 1940s. "Dear Lang," it began, and went on to
describe the beauty of the intellectual experience Ellison had just
derived from his reading of Thomas Mann's *Joseph and His Brothers.*
Hughes had apparently encouraged Ellison to read the novel. In
many respects, it was a love letter to the ideas of Thomas Mann.
What struck me was the great importance that Ellison, and possibly

Hughes, must have placed on the life of the intellect. This was, after all, in the 1940s, a time when, given certain social and economic realities, ideas must have seemed of little use to an American classified as black.

I had met Ralph Ellison, and Fanny, several years before. My interest, during that highly polarized time, was in incorporating into my own thinking some of his insights into the relationship of black Americans to what is sometimes called, with embarrassment, American Culture. Statements by him such as "Uncle Remus was teaching that white boy calculus" would embarrass my imagination into action. He would force me to make imaginative leaps.

For fifteen years now I have been trying to complete the reading necessary for such leaps of the imagination. I assure you that such insights, such creative ideas as his, are of fundamental importance. They chart new directions, for individuals and for nations. But they are, unfortunately, the stock and trade of a very few—an elite, if you will. The average person will not and cannot be comfortable with abstractions. He demands something close to his own experience, something concrete. And yet the idea, the imaginative shadow, is an essential prelude to the *act*. For example, but for the creative use of ideas derived from Roman Civil Law by a man named Charles Hamilton Houston, there might not have been a Civil Rights Movement in this country or a Thurgood Marshall. But for the imaginative leap made by Martin Luther King, Jr., there would be no practical platform on which Jesse Jackson could run. Good ideas, no matter how wild they seem at first, have a way of making their practical impression.

Rome, in Julius Caesar's time, was content with the tradition of the city-state inherited from the Greeks. Rome was said to be "blind" to the future because it could not move forward without first looking back for a precedent. Caesar's genius led him to *imagine* that by making the provinces equal with the city of Rome, authority would no longer have to flow outward from the city square. The concept of the nation-state appeared first in Caesar's imagination. The price he paid for his imaginative leap was assassination. It was left to Augustus to impose, consciously, the psychological habits that made ideas and institutions, and not blood, the basis of membership in a community. Perry Miller has remarked that only two nations in the history of the world—Rome under Augustus and America under Jefferson—came consciously into existence. He also noted that black Americans and Indians were the only wild cards in the *ethnic* equation. The cultural factors imposed by these two groups were the only elements that kept this country from becoming a mere extension of Europe. Of these two, black Americans made up the only group that *could not* look back to a time before the very earliest colonial period, the only group on this continent which created itself, consciously, out of the raw materials indigenous to this country's basic tradition: European, African, and Indian. I admire Ralph Ellison because he had the courage, when it was not fashionable, to stick to his guns—to affirm the complexity of his ethnic and cultural background. Sometimes I wish we were merely Africans. Life would be easier and romances are fun to write. And I am aware of the price, political and personal, that must be paid for this stance. One runs the risk of not seeming "pure" to all other ideologies and "races." And allies are few and far between. Worse, one runs the risk of alienating one's own group, often on the merest chance that someone, sometime in the future, will understand the implications of one's thought. It is to Ralph Ellison's credit that he has stood up for the complexity and the integrity of an entire culture that has sometimes been too "blind" to appreciate the universal implications of his thought. He has very painstakingly cultivated the psychological habits that could help make his countrymen something more than mere expressions of this group or that. His work has been involved with exploring the cultural foundations of a nation-state. Perhaps it is ironic that the implications of his work are just beginning to be realized, at a time when the institution of the nation-state is becoming obsolete.

Much has been said about Ralph's projected novel. I expect that much more will be said about it. I have never read the book, but I remember one night, back in the summer of 1969, when he read a section of it to me. The prose was unlike anything I had ever heard before, a combination of Count Basie's sense of time and early American minstrelsy and Negro Baptist preaching. And the narrator was riffing everything, from coffins to the Book of Numbers. I have been thinking about those five or ten minutes for many years now, and what I think is that, in his novel, Ellison was trying to solve the central problem of American literature. He was trying to find forms invested with enough familiarity to reinvent a much broader and much more diverse world for those who take their provisional identities from groups. I think he was trying to *Negro-Americanize* the novel form, at the same time he was attempting to move beyond it. There are a lot of us who are waiting, patiently, for him to make that leap.

An old friend of his, a man named Virgil Branam, who grew up with Ellison in Oklahoma, told me once, "Ralph's the same way he was when he was a boy. He ain't changed." I think that, for a long time now, he has been trying to teach all of us a little calculus.

Ralph Ellison: Twenty Years After

David L. Carson / 1971

From *Studies in American Fiction*, 1 (1973), 1–23. Copyright 1973 by *Studies in American Fiction*, Northeastern University Press. Reprinted by permission.

The following conversation took place in the New York City residence of Ralph Ellison on 30 September 1971. Mr. Ellison published his novel, *Invisible Man*, in 1952. Winner of a National Book Award at the time of its publication, the novel continues to hold its position of high esteem for both the popular and the critical audience. In 1965 it was judged "the most distinguished single work" published after 1945 by a *Book Week* poll of prominent authors, critics, and editors. A similar survey conducted by Professors John K. Crane and Daniel Walden of the Pennsylvania State University during the summer of 1972 shows that the nation's leading critics still place *Invisible Man* at the head of the list of two dozen American novels (1945–1972) "most likely to endure."

Mr. Ellison published a collection of his own critical essays, *Shadow and Act,* in 1964, and he is currently finishing his second novel. He holds the Presidential Medal of Freedom and the *Chevalier de l'Ordre des Arts et Lettres;* he is presently Albert Schweitzer Professor of Humanities at New York University.

C: Is there a future for the American novel, Mr. Ellison? Most young people don't really seem to like to read. Those who do would rather read Cleaver than Ellison, McKuen rather than Frost.

E: Well, the novel will be here, I think, and the experience of electronic culture notwithstanding, a few people will continue to read, and those who seek to achieve their identities and fulfillment of self through the writing of fiction will continue to write. I think that this attitude is a phase. I have students who haven't read as much as I would have expected them to read, but as a teacher I find that I can get to them if I start wherever it is they are at and try

to work back. I think the novel is going to be here because it is
one of the literary forms that can deal with the great diversity of the
experience in this country, and it can grapple with the essential
loneliness which our very numbers impose upon us and which the
character of the culture, the unifying agency of the big media,
forces upon us. I think people are going to have to start reading in
order to escape some of the pressure from television.

C: You think television may force us full-cycle the other way?

E: I think so. I think that the country has once again to look at
where it came from and what it promised itself, then, you're going
to have to go to fiction for any sort of insight into the complexity of
passion and action that goes into being American. I think that the
form is tied up, in a way that we don't pay enough attention to, with
the nature of the society.

C: What specifically do you mean by that?

E: Well, I think fiction has a way of dealing with the complexities
of a democratic egalitarian society wherein there are so many things
that you can't say, so many ambivalences toward values, toward
status, toward the concept of equality itself, toward class. All of these
things we live with; we swim with them. Our politics are made up
of manipulating these ambiguities; and the individual, if he thinks
at all about what he is and what he is doing, has to come back to
them somehow. And I don't think that soul-searching editorials in
newspapers are enough.

C: I think this ties in with a comment you made once before. You
said that one of the problems of young people today was that they
were unaware that they had yet to learn the rules by which the game
was played. I think this would apply to all young Americans, and
it may be their most difficult adjustment.

E: I think so. Over and over again you find people making
assumptions about the nature of this society on levels which, I won't
say surpass, but which are different from the levels from which they
come. The assumption that there is a conscious conspiracy in
progress all the time forgets that the country is still improvising
itself.

C: Playing it by ear?

E: Yes, by ear. And I know of certain levels of society where I
assumed that there was a rigid plan through which people of a certain

quality of mind and experience had things all worked out. Well it wasn't that way at all.

C: This parallels Henry Adams' experiences with the Grant administration. The corruption was so great that he assumed there had to be a conspiracy, but he found there was none.

E: Yes, everybody was grabbing anything that wasn't nailed down, to see if he could haul it off.

C: This leads me to ask, because of the many similarities of ideas between *Invisible Man* and Adams' *Education,* if his concepts influenced you.

E: No, and I must confess—although I guess I shouldn't—that I have made several stabs at reading the *Education* and have never finished it.

C: Well, I thought I had found strong parallels between your use of the forces of the dynamo and the virgin and his, particularly in the Trueblood episode.

E: Well, all I can say is that it was just a matter of working with what was there in the fictional situation.

C: Is there a connection in idea?

E: I would have to say, yes. I was, though, working consciously out of my idea of tragedy as it becomes entangled with notions of race in the South, but I haven't been able to convince many people that Trueblood is a tragic man. Of course I tell the story using the resources of vernacular humor, but I felt that Trueblood, after becoming half-consciously involved in this kind of chaos, lived up to his obligations as head of a family, although ironically the tragedy was turned into scandal and comedy by the people around him. Now in writing the dream (and, incidentally, I haven't read this book in a long time, so I might be off of it), I felt that I was dealing not only with racial taboos but with taboos which undercut race and go back to the ways society is structured. And once you get into that area, I think you get a blending of power sources, concepts of time, animal imagery, and so on.

C: I have always read Trueblood as both tragic and comic, but is he a trickster? Is he making the most of telling his story because he has learned that white society will pay him well for telling it?

E: Let's put it this way. He is a story teller and a singer, so underneath he is some kind of half-assed artist. Maybe he is me,

I don't know. No one says: "Are you Trueblood?" They always
ask me if I'm not the narrator, and I have to say no, and then they
don't believe me.

C: Well ever since you observed that Ned, in *The Reivers,* was
Faulkner's persona—and I think he is—I've not been at all certain
that Trueblood wasn't yours.

E: [Laughter.]

C: It seems to me that one of the messages which your narrator
is constantly confronted with but never understands until he is in
the coal hole is that one must face up to one's responsibility in the
existential sense as Trueblood does.

E: Yes, I think so. I was improvising, trying to make meaning of
a lot of things as I told the story, but I would think that it was
inevitable that this guy would end up underground. He's a dumb
sonofabitch, you know.

C: This seems to relate to your affirmation of Constance Rourke's
idea that all Americans wear masks, that we are all Arkansas Travel-
ers. But I sense that city folk are not as guilty of this as country
folk.

E: Well, it applies to all of us, but in the city it is less conscious,
except when you get on the level of someone like Rinehart, who
is consciously exploiting it. Maybe we had better talk about generations too, because there was a time when so much of the rural
southern and southwestern humor and strategies of existence was
being imported to the city so fast that you didn't know who you
were talking to most of the time. I'm beginning to think now, just
from some of the Black kids I meet, that they have lost the
continuity between that kind of American shiftiness and the sense
of humor that goes with it.

C: It does seem that we have become more innocent despite the
fact that we are so much more sophisticated in some ways.

E: That's right, and that can get you into all kinds of trouble
because you are assuming a sort of stability, both of character
and of motive and of every damned thing else, which cannot
possibly exist in this sort of society. This can just get you
thrown off.

C: You once mentioned that you were reading Lord Raglan's

Hero as you began to write *Invisible Man*. Am I right in finding the
heroic quest pattern operating repeatedly at all levels of the novel?
    E: Of course.
    C: Well, it seems to be shown quite effectively in your original
version of the novel's hospital passage. Did you use a model
for this?
    E: Now I have to show my hand. I had to invent the medicine just
as I invented the machinery. The critics describe what was
happening to him, the therapy, as "shock therapy," but it wasn't.
[Laughter.] I deliberately did not consult physicians, nor medical
technicians, for a direct model. I just felt that what I was going to
do would, perhaps, carry more power if it weren't spelled out too
specifically. I followed the same assumption which James used
when he discusses creating a ghost. If you make it too explicit
you kill it.
    C: Of course, but I suspect that the doctors are trying to recreate
a man, to create an Uncle Tom, who will know his place and not
want to work at Liberty Paint.
    E: That's right.
    C: But their plans backfire and he loses his fear, everafter, of the
Nortons. This happens during his stay at Mary Rambo's.
    E: Yes.
    C: Well, since we are on to Mary Rambo, I'd like to ask you
about your women. In your early fiction some critics find you
treating your women, in terms of the modern sociological interpretation of the woman's role in the Black family, as creatures of
emasculation.
    E: I hope I haven't been feeding anything into that sociological
business. Well in "Did You Ever Dream Lucky" you have a Mary
type figure who tells a story about her own greenness (naivete). The
point of it is, I think, that in that story the treatment of Mary as a
dominant figure is natural for me. I was raised by my mother, my
father died quite early, so she had to be strong, but I never felt
that she emasculated me because she always insisted upon my
achieving manliness and responsibility. So, I'd say that you would be
closer to the truth if you saw the early women in my fiction from
the perspective of Mark Twain; in terms of the symbolism of
woman standing for established values rather than as, in Freudian

terms, castraters. I would say that they were "circumcisers."
[Laughs.]

C: Of course, the Battle Royal as a false initiation rite (circumcision) is then really a castration rite.

E: [Laughs.] That's right.

C: But I think your analysis of the women's role rings true, not only for Black society, but for American society as a whole.

E: It's an American thing. That's the ultimate point because suddenly you see something about the general society, but the sociologist says: "The Black mother does this, the Black family castrates and maims psychologically." But nine times out of ten, in the lower class Black family, the mother is telling the boy he had better do his homework if he is going to get anywhere with a woman.

C: I know you have never had much faith in the sociologists' approach to Black problems. Are you still against them?

E: Not all. [Chuckles.]

C: Well, when you reviewed Gunnar Myrdal's book in the forties you didn't think much of it. Do you still feel that way? I thought Herskovits' book was a fair job for 1941.

E: *The Myth of the Negro Past?*

C: Yes.

E: I would say that I rejected it then and later found some validity in it. Stanley Edgar Hyman, who was my friend from 1942 until he died, thought quite a lot of Herskovits. And my problem with Herskovits is a problem that I have with many sociologists, and it was not that I denied that we were from Africa, but that the context—and the way he put it—seemed to imply that we needed to apologize—that we needed a past. I believed then, and I think I still believe, that one of the costs of being an American, a conscious American, is an acceptance of the fact that the past does not have the relevancy that it had in Europe. That's the reason for democracy. And this goes on today. You get all of these apologies. You get Negro-Americans walking around top-heavy from trying to Africanize themselves when that which is authentically African in them has come down to us through more subtle ways, and we are not the only inheritors of it. I'm afraid white southerners inherit a hell of a lot of it too.

C: We all do.

E: Yes, this is one of the ingredients of the American style. Now I collect African art, but I've never been an Africanist, nor have I been any number of other things that have been faddish. But I've never had any questions but that I'm part African. Usually they say the other thing: "You're part white."

C: Well we are all mongrels in America, I guess, and yet an awareness of our past seems important. Not in the sense of an aristocratic heritage, but in terms of what our ancestors thought and hoped.

E: Yes. How did they conduct themselves? What did they try to pass on, even when they were failing? This is what gets missed. Some drunk in Oklahoma City could say to me: "Raf, you don't want to get around and do like I do. You don't want to do like those sonsabitches over there. You got a chance." What more can you ask? We are all going to get ground down by time and circumstance, but it is the principle, it is the hope that counts.

C: And yet you are sometimes criticized, as was Faulkner, for advocating endurance.

E: But Faulkner was a great artist and Faulkner knew, just as my mother knew, just as many people I grew up with knew, that there ain't a goddam thing you can do *but* endure. The question is: "*How* do you endure?" Some people are going to have more, some are going to have less, but the moment you say that living has no meaning, that's when you're lost. Some critics demonstrate a special lack of perception in terms of American reality.

C: You once talked about critics finding a homosexual theme in *Huckleberry Finn*. I suppose this is the same sort of thing.

E: Yes, you wonder sometimes what kind of society we have?

C: Is this the city kid having lost track with what goes on in the real world—where the milk and the beef come from, the smell of hay, manure, and grain?

E: Often it's a city Jewish kid. That's why it is so ironic for a critic of that type to lecture me about endurance. You look at them and you bend over, and you say: "Well, goddam! Don't you know where *you* come from? I'm simply speaking out of where *I* came from."

C: I find it interesting that you sometimes partially unmask

yourself by writing literary criticism. We have not had much of
this from our novelists except James.

E: Well, you know, as I said about Baldwin, you don't achieve a
certain level of literary competency in the pool hall or the picket
line. Goddamn it you're born in the library. I played varsity football
in high school but they wouldn't let me play in college because I
was a music major. The bandmaster, an old army man, said: "Here,
I'm teaching you to use your lips and fingers and you want to go
out there and get the shit kicked out of you." He was once
bandmaster of the Tenth Cavalry back when it was a segregated
outfit. I wanted to go out for college football, but, I started to say
this: In high school even during off season, I would want very much
to be out on the front lawn throwing and kicking a football, showing
off in front of the girls, but, more likely than not, I was either
upstairs reading or looking out while I did exercises on my trumpet.
There was always that division of interest and desire but it's the
literary thing, the library, the reading that makes the writer, and
people are confused by this. I have a lot of young, would-be-
writers, who feel that they don't have to read anything. I say,
"What the hell do you think you write out of?" Books are written
out of other books just as battle plans are made out of earlier
strategies and tactics.

C: Alfred Kazin in a recent *Saturday Review* article also points
out that activism isn't enough. But you are often taken to task by
critics for not being more so.

E: Well, you know, I was an activist during the thirties and part
of the forties. That's easy; it's easy to be on picket lines. I was in
some of the first sit-ins which involved WPA. I have carried picket
signs, I have helped block off Fifth Avenue, I was in on the
agitation which led to the creation of the National Maritime Union,
when broken bottles and bricks and every damn thing else were being
thrown down on South Street; I've gone through that. I have written
protest letters and articles. One of the articles was for the *New
Masses,* back in 1939, and against Father Coghlan's Christian Front.
That was a time when Negroes couldn't cross Amsterdam Avenue
(which is only two blocks east of here) without a battle, and many
of the police officers simply stood back and let the kids raise hell.
Harlem has a long history of Irish-Negro antagonism, not to mention

the other ethnic antagonisms that existed, and there was intense
anti-Negro feeling. So that if you came over here you'd get yourself
knocked in the head and thrown into the river. The article in the *New
Masses* caused much protest to be directed at the police precinct
and one day I answered the door (on Hamilton Terrace) to find the
chiefs of the station and the detective squad staring at me. At first I
was upset, but then I realized that since these guys had come to
my *apartment* instead of having me dragged to the *station,* they
were not out to beat me up. It meant that my writing had been
effective and they had come to me for information.

Now one of the facile ideas which was being encouraged in this
country by leftists, especially the Stalinist Communists, was that
the writer owed only a second level allegiance to the art through
which he found his identity. This I never liked, and never believed. A jazz musician who allowed other activity to cut into his
performance as a jazz musician was just nowhere. A minister who
spent most of his time plastering or plumbing, might be a dedicated
man, but this wouldn't help him become the eloquent minister
that people wanted. Well, you can see where I'm going with this.
Now, I believe that I have contributed more to the general struggle
by trying to write the things that I write as well as I can than I could
by being a propagandist. I don't want to be a political leader. It
ain't my kind of thing. So I leave it to other people.

C: Yes.

E: I leave that to people who believe in it, but I am also true to
myself, because I became myself by being stubborn and fighting
against people who were telling me what to do. Today I would still
be a guy stumbling around Oklahoma City if I had let some of the
people out there tell me what to do before I discovered what the
hell I *wanted* to do. So now it is looked down upon, it's called
individualism, ego trips, and so on. Well, if you aren't on an ego
trip from the cradle to the grave you ain't nobody. So I feel that
my writing (although there isn't enough of it to satisfy me), the
quality of it, aims, I hope, high. I certainly have dedicated my life
to dealing with truth and to projecting it eloquently and artistically.

But there is another side to this whole question. I haven't been
socially inactive, even in non-literary terms. I was one of the original
appointees to the National Council on the Arts, which is now the

Foundation on the Arts. You ask Roger Stevens, its first chairman,
(or anybody else who was there during those first years) what I
contributed to its efforts. I wasn't simply sitting there being your
"black boy" who was there for publicity purposes. When given that
opportunity I discovered that I had something to contribute
precisely because my thinking hadn't been channelized into the
usual grooves. Hell, I know a lot from being outside. This is one
of the accidents that happen in this crazy country where all kinds
of ideas are in the public domain, and because a man is ruled out
of its organizations it doesn't mean that he stops living or thinking.
I had been on the WPA Writers Project and I became interested
in the government's participation in the arts and in the relationship
between the government and its artists and its cultural institutions
years ago. André Malraux was always concerned with this. I suppose that is why De Gaulle made him his Minister of Cultural
Affairs. I was an old admirer of Malraux, whom I have been reading
since I first came to New York.

C: *Man's Fate* is, if I recall correctly, one of your favorite books.

E: It is. And so is his *The Psychology of Art*. Before the book
was published, I used to go into the book shops in the Village and
buy the excerpts from it that were being published in the English
edition of the French magazine *Verve*. It was an expensive magazine
which published high quality color plates, and the booksellers would
dismantle the back issues and sell them to artists. But I would go
in and buy the essays, usually for a quarter. So that when Malraux's
Psychology of Art came out in three volumes at twenty-five bucks
a volume I had already read a lot of the material.

And there are other things. Today there is something called
"public television," The Corporation for Public Television, which
is a semi-private governmental agency. I was a member of the
Carnegie Commission which hammered out its basic concept, and
if anyone wants to know what I was doing there, let them ask the
members with whom I served. Its report contains much of my
thinking and turns of phrase.

C: This is something many people don't suspect.

E: Oh, I know. When you say to them: "You have to have more
than one string to your bow," they don't understand. I have an
identity as a writer, but I do other things. You don't see me out

making pronouncements; very often I don't believe in the pronouncements that are made. But as a novelist—and here is the other
consideration—I believe that novelists have an integrity imposed
upon them, or at least a moral standard, and a discipline imposed
upon them by the form in which they find their expression. One
of the things which I've learned about that form is that you must
look at your brother, your mother, your father, your wife, and
everything else with a certain kind of imposed objectivity. I am not
saying that the novelist should be a god, but when I look at
politics and some of the moves that are made, I wouldn't want to be
out there saying: "Look goddamn it you're a fool." I wouldn't
want to be out there saying: "You're feeling good saying this and
doing this, but you're being unrealistic, and there will be blood flowing
from this action." I have seen this happen over and over again.
What do you do? You don't want to discourage a surge toward greater
democracy in this country, but you don't have to be a part of foolishness.

C: Before I had read much criticism on *Invisible Man* I sensed it
was a novel in the American vernacular tradition. I saw something
of Melville and Twain in it, but I'm hard pressed to get down to
specifics, although I do find some correspondence between your
"Prologue" and that of *Moby Dick*.

E: Let me test something on you. [Reads from Dostoyevsky's
Notes from the Underground, Modern Library Series, the opening lines from Chapter I.] That ain't Melville. [Chuckles.]

C: Critics often seem confused by your use of Jungian archetypes
while at the same time you also seem to follow Freud. Did you
intend to mix the two?

E: Let's put it this way. You speak of my psychology as confusing
critics because they didn't know whether it was Freudian or
Jungian. It's neither. I'm a rhetorician and as far as I'm concerned
as a novelist, as a fiction writer, the terminologies of both become
rhetorically useful. If I can make a point, if I can structure a scene
by drawing out the thread of Freud or Jung in the fabric, very
good. If I can make people respond (and with Supercargo I was
very consciously, as you know, playing with the Freudian concept of
Ego, Id and Superego) by striking these notes, I'll do it because it
makes for a richness of texture. But I was also having fun with it

because when you dramatize such a psychoanalytic concept it just seems to make it a little more human, or at least humorous.

C: I find it interesting that many of your critics have missed the fact that the man who tells the tale isn't Ralph Ellison and that he has also changed since he experienced the Golden Day business.

E: Oh, they don't understand. They don't even understand that the book is the fictional autobiography of the man who relates it.

C: That's what I meant, and that's why those who charge that the ending is a copout are wrong.

E: Yes, because in writing the book he is no longer underground; he has come out. Most writers aren't worth anything, and I'm probably one of them, but critics have the arrogance which comes from not knowing too much of the diversity of actual experience. They have the arrogance of the academy, the arrogance of the library, for them everything is symbolic, and you say: "For God's sake man, when a fart gets loose in a crowd, things happen; that isn't a symbol!"

C: Like in *1601?*

E: Oh God, how constrained poor Mark Twain had to be. But what shapes my attitude toward many of the critics is that coming from out there where I come from, from that background, racial and otherwise (and I don't know *what* my class identification is because it's too vague, I only know that we were poor as hell) gave me the feeling that too many of our critics rose to prominence too quickly through their brilliance of mind. Their knowledge is not tempered by experience, and especially if they come from the lower classes. As a result, they know little about the *other* many lower classes or even about the middle classes. They are defensively provincial and view every other group as enemies or unworthy opponents. It's very strange and it gets in the way of their perception.

C: But isn't that the difference between a novelist and a critic?

E: I suppose so. The novelist has a certain advantage through the more restricted collaboration required of his reader. He creates meaning out of absurd realities, as James would say. If he captures an image of reality and presents it graphically enough, vividly enough, the reader assumes that you, the novelist, knows what *he* knows. So the fiction comes alive. It works. The problem for so

many novelists and especially young Black novelists is that they're
writing in a society that is divided not only along racial lines but
along class lines. But, ironically, as the racial lines give way the
class lines become more rigid and the ideology of Blackness gets
in the way of communication and observation. So the young Black
novelist probably finds it more difficult to get even as close to the
mores and manners of those classes of society which exist beyond
his own than it was for me. I have been a waiter, and I know that
all millionaires do not have good manners, nor are they all men of
taste. Their lives can be as untidy or as tragic as any Black man's.
Most older Negro waiters know this very well. We Negroes are the
most ironic observers of the American scene. Those of us who
are waiters, maids, nursemaids and cooks are close and concerned
observers; and they are not always putting down what they see or
fighting the class or the race war. Too much of their fate is tied up
with the fate of their employers as it is with the rest of society.

C: Like Dilsey?

E: That's right. Dilsey is a great character, a great woman. There
is no question that she is one of the greatest figures in American
fiction.

C: Do I sense you working within some kind of a time dichotomy
in *Invisible Man*—the Bergsonian concept of *durée* as opposed to
clock time?

E: Well, you know that it was inevitable that I would do so. Because—

C: CPT?

E: Yes, that's right, and the ironic way in which the whole
question of who is with it or who isn't, as structured by social
class and race, would make you conscious of time. Now I was
playing very consciously with time, and I had read Bergson, at
least *On Laughter,* and had read other Bergson. But the very fact
that the concept of Colored Peoples' Time, which is a great comic
thing in Negro institutions, got me. But then, you see, the important
thing is that time is determined by mode of production and
technology. In *Invisible Man* this is an abiding concern. When the
narrator comes from the South into the industrialized North, all
of that business at the factory is bound up with the concept of time

and process having an effect on individual personality as well as on race.

C: Well, when the narrator reminiscently travels back to the college he strolls across the campus, and sees a series of things which seem to be more or less repeated on every quest throughout the rest of the novel. In other words he establishes a pattern of quest symbols: a bird, a time symbol. . . .

E: Yes.

C: Sex, a dynamo. . . .

E: Yes.

C: A façade of some sort, followed by a bridge, crossing over to a wasteland. . . .

E: Yes.

C: With broken glass, followed by disillusionment, hysteria.

E: Well, when you write a book, you write what you can, but you see a book isn't written linearly. . . .

C: Conceptually?

E: That's right. It's back and forth, and you're discovering it all the time, and the images themselves (even images or symbols of which you yourself are not aware) breed others because your mind is in that groove. It's grabbing and snatching ruthlessly at anything that might help it achieve its purpose and achieve a form. At this distance, I can't say what came first, the concept or the image itself.

C: But the most important cluster of symbols (the woman, the clock, and the dynamo) seem to be saying again and again that industrial society has set up substitutes for all three of the real things. Modern sex is an abstraction used as a façade to cover time and the dynamo, American society's substitute for real sex. We have moved from the real time of the menstrual cycle to. . . .

E: Yes, into a mechanical and electronic and technologically influenced sense of time. I don't know to what extent I was consciously concerned with this, but if you step away a bit and get back to something I said earlier about my being aware that place and mode of production have a *tremendous* impact upon personality and with one's sense of social hierarchy, with one's social identifications and sense of value. And thus with one's sense of personal identity. I was trying very consciously to use the scene in the factory hospital (which is concerned with the symbolic and technological manipulation of personality, and implicitly so) because the narrator was undergoing a major pattern of rebirth.

But one of the things that you haven't asked me about is the dramatization of history as intertwined with the other themes. That is, the contrast between the narrator's tempo of movement and perception of action in the South as against that he encountered and experienced in the North. Because in this are gathered together the symbols of technology and race, the contrast between rural and industrial society, and other themes that come together in the action. I don't know to what extent the effect of the Civil War is objectively there in the book, but, certainly, it is there.

C: How do you see the Civil War as tying in to the novel?

E: It was one of the unstated themes, one of the realities, historical events, which I assumed to feed our awareness and help shape our perceptions and emotions in relation to most fiction of a certain scale, written by American novelists who deal with the South. It might be that a great part of the thinness of some of the writing by young Blacks of northern experience is due to the fact that they do not possess that tragic dimension. Anyway, it doesn't have to be spelled out; it just has to be there and it resonates like the deep notes of a pipe organ, which are less heard than felt. As Hemingway says, if you are aware of an unstated theme it works its effect even if you don't write it down in detail because it helps shape your principle of selection, your detail, your configuration of action, image, and theme.

C: Again this goes back to roots.

E: Yes, to *conscious* roots.

C: Should I see parallels between Ike McCaslin and the narrator of *Invisible Man*? For instance, Faulkner always claimed, as you do about your narrator, that Ike was a damned fool.

E: Well, they are both portraits of Candide, and when you put them into all of the complexities of their background and options they are fools who have the advantage of teaching us wisdom even as the author flatters us into believing that we would never have made their mistakes. Isn't that true? But in a new paperback study of *The Bear* which I received the other day, one critic wrote about Ike McCaslin as a copout because he wanted to renounce his patrimony. Well, copout or not, whatever you call him, Ike engaged himself so deeply in the human experience that we are all a part of him and he is a part of all of us. It would seem to me that if I tried to do anything with the narrator of *Invisible Man,* it was certainly *not* to make him a great hero, but to present him in such a way that in his curiosity and blundering he would transcend any narrow concepts of race and hit us all where we live.

C: I think he does.

E: That was the challenge, and of course I felt that he should be comic. Most people forget that he is a comic figure.

C: Does this have something to do with the double critical standard, the fact that I at first, along with so many whites, could not read that book objectively because I had not been properly conditioned to receive what it had to say? This must be terribly frustrating. Does it bother you?

E: It bothers me in this way. Obviously I am an American Negro, and I use Negro American as a cultural concept; I use it as a description of both my mixed racial heritage and my pluralistic cultural background, but the form in which I try to express myself is not a "racial" form; the novel is universal. I write out of a pretty conscious awareness of American literature, as well as an awareness of Russian, French, English, and German literature. Perhaps I should have started with English literature, but unless we are going to allow questions of pigmentation to completely hypnotize us, and I'm afraid that in this country we do that too often on both sides of the racial line, we'd better look at our cultural complexity. If we don't we are on the wrong track. The tendency to avoid what is so obvious becomes a little bit boring to me. What am I going to do? I mean why does anyone (not you, David) want to waste my time by approaching me as though I am a total victim of my race? I couldn't have written certain sentences but for the fact that certain white writers wrote certain sentences, and I'll say the reverse: William Faulkner couldn't have written certain dialogues but for having heard certain *black* Mississippians expressing themselves in certain succinct ways. Hell, on the level of *culture,* everybody's out breathing in the air that's around him, and when it's good, goddamn it, to the writers it's irresistible!

C: It has always struck me that American literature follows in the long English tradition of Chaucer, Skelton, Shakespeare, Donne,

Swift, Fielding, and Sterne. Then while the English novel became
Victorian we came up with Cooper and a new tradition.

E: Cooper was a great writer. I outrage people by saying that as
a kid I read *The Last of the Mohicans* ten times, and they say:
"What?" Then I say: "What were *you* reading when you were
a kid?"

C: And then there is Hawthorne, Melville, and Twain.

E: And James! I learned so much from him.

C: But he is so effete.

E: He is effete, but he is so canny. I suggest that we all take a
look again at his criticism, at his prefaces. James is *the* aesthetician,
the best theorist of the aesthetics of the novel. There is no question
about it. Somebody could make a great contribution if he went
back and gave us a little book, even, on what James knew about
what Mark Twain knew from James' particular background. Because James, in *The American,* dealt extensively with the American
vernacular tradition. And he is a man who fell in love with the
European tradition because he felt that he didn't have enough here
to sustain him. And yet his first published story was about the
Civil War. One of James' older brothers was an officer in Colonel
Shaw's Massachusetts Regiment which was made up of freed
Negroes. Of course, many of the leading abolitionists were in and
out of James' father's home, so during the abolitionist period
James knew a great deal about what was going on in the country.
There is no way for it *not* to have gotten into his fiction. The
goddamn critics, new arrivals, who were "making it" on the basis
of James' effeteness, and who didn't know a goddamn thing about
American history, were all wet. This is what a local Negro out of
Oklahoma says about it, and I'm probably as prejudiced about it
as anybody, but for a long time now I've tried to find someone
putting this stuff together. Leon Edel has done a lot but there is
so much to James.

C: Can we go back to the American vernacular tradition for
a moment?

E: That's exactly where American independence lies. In this
course I give down at NYU, it is one of the things I keep pointing
out: through our vernacular speech we made a counter-assertion
which at first we accepted in a self-effacing way, and then we
grew conscious by affirmation and we realized that it was an

assertion of a separate identity. This is how our language, the
American language, got started. We still remain respectful and
bemused, some of us, and stand in awe of proper English usage,
but it was the vernacular we used, always, when asserting our
"felt" identity. In this country the vernacular tradition is the
basis of our revolutionary tradition. You know all this.

C: And yet here in this city we teach prescriptive grammar in
English-as-a-second-language courses. I wonder if we aren't going
about it in the wrong way?

E: Well, I've had to tell some critics: "Well alright, buddy, you're
telling me what this is all about, and you can't even understand
the language." This whole business of language and trying to
assume an identity through linguistic style very often leads people to
betray themselves and to lose their heritage.

C: Right on. [Laughs.] Can we talk about birds for a moment?
You always have seemed fascinated by birds and the imagery of
flight. Why?

E: I like birds. When I was a child my mother raised chickens
and guinea fowl. One of my earliest memories of birds goes back
to when I was about two and a half years old when my father was
dying and my brother Herbert (who was only sixteen weeks old
when my father died) was on the way. This day I had my little
tricycle and I had a little lard bucket filled with water hanging on
the handle bars and I was pedalling like mad to put out a fire that
I'd set to the paper in the backyard trash burner. I was playing
fire department and making the sound of a fire engine to the best
capabilities of my high, shrill voice. Well, across the fence between our yard and the next there was one of these fighting roosters
which belonged to Dr. E. W. Perry (a minister who became
distinguished in black Baptist circles) and as I played and was busy
throwing water and raising hell, this rooster flew over the fence
throwing spurs and attacked me. Then, as I tried to get away, a
woman stepped out of the kitchen of the house next door and told
me to be quiet because Lina, our neighbor, was having a baby.
Shortly thereafter Lina, who was my mother's friend, gave birth,
and so did my mother, and all this within a few hours. So as you
can see right there, and without benefit of Freud, birds, fire, play,
excitement, birth and chastisement became associated in my mind.

But beyond that I'm simply curious about birds. I love to watch
them. Just now there is a flock of migratory blue jays in the area
and at this time of year we get great batches of many species. They
roost up here in Trinity Church Cemetery and then fly out early in the
morning to Central Park and then work their way South. The
Freudian concept of birds gets into my work both in a serious and
kidding way. Somehow birds just seem to be more aesthetic than
many Freudians would allow. For me they are not only sexual
objects. Sometimes they are symbols for other things: the furies,
the doves of peace; in my work they are deliberately ambiguous.
Besides, a writer doesn't have to accept all the interpretations
which are handed down. He can play upon the ambivalent feelings
which individuals bring to birds, and upon the ambiguous connotations that go with them. Usually when birds appear in *Invisible
Man* there is death, shooting, and so on, in the offing.

C: Are they heralds?

E: Heralds? Yes, as in the Norse myths.

C: As the hero crosses the rooftops escaping from the police after
the eviction speech, he runs into a flock of white pigeons.

E: That should tell the reader something, that there is going to be
a little trouble. But I'm a pretty good wing shot and I've learned
a lot about bird's habits from hunting.

C: That leads to another question. In 1937 you say you hunted
birds in Ohio for a livelihood, and you say you learned how to do it
from Hemingway. What did you mean?

E: I had shot many a quail before, but no one had ever broken it
down so well as Hemingway did, and I became a better shot by
just having read his description of how you led a bird, how you got
on him. You came behind him, got on him, and kept swinging. I
had been doing that, but to have someone tell me was very important. It meant the difference between eating and going hungry.

C: I understand, but since we're on to a Hemingway matter, let
me go astray for a moment. It seems that neither he nor Faulkner
felt any need to be a leader, a patron, of young writers, and yet it
also seems that you, because of your Black heritage, are expected
by someone to provide this sort of service.

E: I've never tried to lead anybody and never wanted to be a
leader. In fact, it would be a disadvantage to have a lot of

sycophants or imitators. The thing that I would like to pass on is simply a respect for the art, a respect for ideas, and, ultimately, a respect for the truth of American experience with all of its complexities. If you can get that across, then everybody can have a toe-hold or handgrip on tradition even while he is still doing his own thing. What bothers me about so many of these new, loud-mouthed guys is that they have no sense of what came before themselves. They have little sense of what their parents are really like, and absolutely *no* sense of what their grandparents were like. Thus in their most militant assertions they turn out to have less respect for their Black forefathers than some of the whites who held their forefathers in slavery.

C: This seems to touch on the theme of "Flying Home," which was published in the 1944 *Cross Section* along with Mailer. . . .

E: That was quite a significant anthology. Norman Mailer, Shirley Jackson, and a bunch of us appeared for the first time between hard covers.

C: And with Richard Wright's "Man Who Lived Underground." Many critics suggest that *Invisible Man* comes from Wright's story, which appeared there, but I can see little connection.

E: No, no, Wright's approach was Dreiserian, from the Chicago school.

C: By the way, does the title, "Flying Home," come from the jazz piece of the same name?

E: Yes. [Sings.]

C: I suspect old dirt farmer Jefferson, and not Todd the aviator, is your persona.

E: Yes. Yes, he's also Thomas Jefferson. [Laughs.]

C: This sort of allusion has its ties with *Invisible Man*. You use an introductory verse, some lines from Eliot's *Family Reunion,* as a prefatory passage to the novel. Is this supposed to parallel Apollo's judgment at Delphi?

E: That was when the change from a matriarchal to a patriarchal society came about. Yes, it's true; although, again, I don't know to what extent I was conscious of drawing upon it. But I *was* exposed to that classical lore. So perhaps I was doing what Mark Twain and Eliot did. I was taking a vernacular motive and bouncing it off a related classical incident.

C: Is this what produces a visceral reaction, a gut feeling in the reader, about a work of art, perhaps a Gestalt, before conscious understanding occurs?

E: Yes, it has to do with the Gestalt, the tendency of the mind to make wholes out of a collectivity of parts; and it also has to do, basically, with art. But goddamn it, in an "inside dopester" society like ours, if the reader doesn't get the point immediately, if it doesn't hit his conscious knowledge, he says: "Hey, what's happening? Why don't you *do* something." But I'd say that if your tongue sticks out and your eyes bug out, you should know that something is going on beneath the surface, and start thinking it through. On the other hand, there is always some brainy sonofabitch around who can tell you what you are doing, what you're manipulating; all you have to do is dramatize and project your conception. Coming as we do out of the European, Asian and African traditions (through language, drama, technology, medicine, and so on) Americans, at least those who are alert, are capable of grabbing hold of anything. Thus, in my work, symbolism isn't just a peccadillo; it is there as a hook to snare errant fish, and to make them realize something about our experience. At its best American folklore, drama, the novel, literature, have always been concerned with teaching Americans how to accept their goddamned fate and then to go on to overcome it. And if a writer doesn't want to help them do that, then he should go into politics! [Laughs.]

C: Mark Twain said, but only in material written for the *Autobiography,* that he had lasted because he had always preached, that there was always a didactic purpose under his humor. But I guess all the good ones were this way.

E: They are didactic in their special way, and the great novelists have had a grasp of the philosophical implications of what they are doing. That includes Mark Twain, who was, as the academics say, an auto-didactic (whatever that term is) and as such he had probably read more philosophy than most American philosophers. What do you say? Literature is to entertain; it is also to instruct, and it instructs, just as a television commercial instructs, in ways that are not always intended: by presenting patterns and details of things and experience vividly and in such a manner that the viewer gives them extension through his own experience. Litera-

ture shapes taste and values, it conveys information, and it sets the
arrows of fate but as it structures fictional actions it enlarges our
sense of the drama of man's fate. So we can kid ourselves about
where learning takes place, but it takes place anywhere and
through anything which engages the conscious mind. It's like energy; it is never dissipated. In fact, it is a form of energy through
which experience is transformed into consciousness. Back in the
early days of this country when there was no radio, television, or
magazines, it was understood that stories were a means of preparing
you for life in a new society. Stories turned one ever again to the
details of the new world, and they cautioned the listener to stand on
his own feet, to come to grips with this experience, and *this* nature,
climate, terrain; with these Indians, with *these* Negroes, French-
men, Germans, and so on. Such stories dwelled with specific
details and nuances of American experience because it was with
these that one had to come to grips if one wished to survive and
fulfill the American promise.

C: Yes.

E: This is why the most vigorous American literature is based
upon American folklore.

C: You found the basis for your novel in the myth and ritual of
the so-called frontier life of the South. Can we find the same kind
of thing in the cities? Can the young novelist find myth and ritual,
in the city, which reaches the broad American audience?

E: Kenneth Burke in an unpublished essay talks about that
something which goes beyond the act. And what goes beyond the
act is a matter of language. The language gives the act back to us;
the language structures the act; the language humanizes the act:
this is my interpretation of an essay which is not too fresh in my
mind. Now the business of dealing with American experience is
so confused by the selling techniques which use the same channels,
so to speak. They use language, they use images, they use
symbolism. And this confuses that great part of the population
which has a weak sense of its past, of its identity. It confuses
them by imposing pseudo realities, pseudo values, pseudo myths.
This is Hollywood. This is the Hollywood which for years could give
us cowboys without showing a Black cowboy. As I've written
somewhere, Griffith was a great technician, a great artist, but, as

a political factor in the rhetoric of American equality, he did a hell
of a lot of damage to people like me. When he did that he hurt in
a reverse way the South and he also hurt the nation. I'm not going
to make him a villain because I don't think he was. I think this is
an instance of a great man coming along, learning to manipulate a
new rhetorical, narrative tool without fully understanding the implications of what he had developed as it related to the American
democratic equalitarian commitment. So you look at the myths
which are being created. Even the drug addicts can spin powerful
myths. All they have to do is get a few professors, or jet-set
figures, to say: "Well, smoking pot, or taking LSD, is O.K." and it
catches on. So, in this country, which reinvents itself every ten
days such myths catch on. But, just as the human body matures in
an ancient cycle and dies in an ancient cycle, great and enduring
and abiding questions always come up. A great part of the American
literary energy today is used in giving false answers to these
abiding questions.

A Conversation with Ralph Ellison

Leon Forrest / 1972

From *Muhammed Speaks*, 15 December 1972, 29–31. Copyright by *Muhammed Speaks*. Reprinted by permission of Leon Forrest.

"In a city of a million and a half Blacks, I'll bet there aren't 100 who know or care about the art of writing, in the way you insist on using that term, Forrest. It's not relevant, nor is Ellison, I am afraid," the Chicago street corner friend declared.

Yet I had just spun my friend upside-down, with the joyous news that we had a pending interview with Ralph Ellison, the man generally considered the greatest living Black writer in the Western World. My friend's dual reaction to the Ellison news expresses a not uncommon ambivalence, for he was actually very proud that we had obtained an interview with the man who wrote, according to 200 top critics, in 1965, the most important novel published in this country, since World War II, *Invisible Man,* 1952.

Ralph Ellison has been working for the last 17 years on what I believe is yet another major orchestra of a novel, actually going far past *Invisible Man,* in its larger than life dimensions concerning the American ethos. I have read perhaps five published chapters of the work-in-progress of this monumental work, reportedly measuring more than 1500 pages, that he published in various magazines over the years. It is a work-in-progress that looks into patterns of sanity and continuity, the ruptured and chaotic memory of the national consciousness, and the moral responsibility for the past.

During a period of cheap, vogue-sustained Black writing, and patti-cake Jewish writing, and gross pornography, Ellison has been taking on the very deepest moral questions of the Union. The book involves a Senator who is passing for white, who was raised by Black church people, and becomes something of the brutalized metaphor himself of what happened to the baby Democracy, tossed from hand to hand and born out of wedlock (ala Fielding's Tom Jones, to

say nothing of some of the leading people in the U.S.). The
Senator at the height of one of his tirades against Blacks on the floor
of the congress is shot down by a Black assassin. And he cries out
after being shot down for Daddy Hickman, the father-figure minis-
ter-musician, who raised him. This is only a fragment of work-in-
progress, that this terrifically proud, consummately developed, college drop-out from Tuskegee has conjured into overwhelming writing
and enriching experience.

> "It is because we have had such great writers in the past, that a writer is
> driven far out, past where he can go, out to where no one can
> help him."
>
> Ernest Hemingway

Forrest: "Could you explain what you believe to be the role of
literature, the contribution of literary art to a people over the
long haul?"

Ellison: "Literature is a form of art wherein time can be reduced
to manageable proportions; and the diversity of experience can
be assembled to show an immediate pattern: to conserve memory,
focus energies, ideals and to give us some idea of the cost and
glories of those ideals. Art unites the people, and extracts that
which is meaningful, rendering a heightened sense of value through
its attention to details, which unite the members of a group, into a
concord of sensibilities. . . . Literature is a form through which a
group recognizes its values—values from without and values from
within. . . ."

Ellison feels that because so much of the fiction by Black and
white authors is written in terms of the clichés, not the humanity,
of the Afro-American, it often goes "from Sambo to Nat Turner,
which of course means, you've left out most of us." His faith in
the ranging possibilities of the novel form have to do with its
"resonance, because through that form you can deal with complexities, but it exacts a price; it demands that the writer refuse the
easy opportunity to publicize or make public power out of his perspectives of the world." Much of the psyche the writer brings to his
desk has to do with the "tendency to deny the humanity and the
diversity of slaves—that a slave was a man—and possessed complexities. . . . And what of the slaves who were skilled? That
always gets left out."

Forrest: "What constitutes the universal-literary shaping and terrain of the 'writer's' kind of mind?"

Ellison: "I suspect it is the type of mind, while not losing sight of the factual nature of reality, is obsessed with extracting those characters, nuances, and rhetoric, which as he re-combines them in terms of literary forms, he conveys what he considers most important in life. . . . The life of the imagination leads him to combine those images he has extracted from reality. The writer trains the imagination by reading imaginative writers, reading biography and autobiography of certain writers' lives and what they have to say about their own work."

We talked of the meaning of Hemingway for a time, and he says that Hemingway was a writer who employed the organizing principle of how the many task–memories of his life fitted into the vocation of his life, fiction . . . journalism for instance.

Forrest: "What is the role of reading in the shaping of the writer's mind?"

Ellison: "The sense of form comes from a great deal of reading, o that a variety of structures are constantly informing the intelli-ence centers or nourishing the imagination."

Forrest: "It is a highly associative mind, is it not?"

Ellison: "Yes. And the writer develops a sense of the literary ssibility and a special alertness, in many areas, from the sea-ns and their changes to a football game, and of course the drama erent in both."

e Quest for Excellence

Ellison sees the processes of the novel, at its best, as an "attempt to make an eloquent form, so that the sections are true." He is constantly elaborating on the many themes that come up in the course of our conversation. He places a high value on good, meaningful conversation, and as he shapes and hones his thinking, he often makes a statement so noble and memorable, that the statement itself, is literature. "Art has to do with the process of reaching down into repressed values and giving it some luminosity," he says.

Forrest: "Would you discuss the role of re-writing in the craft?

Perhaps it would be meaningful for the very young writer, if you would?"

Ellison: "For me writing is re-writing. I sketch out an idea and it tends to grow. The image of blowing on a flame comes to mind here. The process of the novel has to do with the attempt to make an eloquent form, so that the sections are true." He warns the immediately successful young writers "to be careful lest you are praised for the wrong things."

Underneath all of the conversation is the quest for the mastery of craft, discipline and the continuity of memory within diverse history. . . . And underneath that, is something very old, timeless and absolutely Black and it has to do with the way a Black drop-out uncle, who has become very successful in his own business, might say to a young Nephew, home from college for the summer (taking the mop away from the student) and declaring: *"Now Nephew let me show you how to properly scrub that floor. There is a right way and a wrong way to do everything. And I'm not about to allow you to run the family (race) business until you've mastered all phases of it—lest you give me the business and yourself the shaft."*
And another kind of relative, underneath that:

> "Son, after I'm gone I want you to keep up the good fight. I never told, but our life is a war and I have been a traitor all my born days, a spy in the enemy's country ever since I give up my gun back in the Reconstruction. Live with you head in the lion's mouth. I want you to overcome 'em with yeses, undermine 'em with grins, agree 'em to death and destruction, let 'em swoller you till they vomit or bust wide open." They thought the old man had gone out of his mind. He had been the meekest of men. The younger children were rushed from the room.
> . . . "Learn it to the younguns," he whispered fiercely; then he died.—From *Invisible Man*

He is profoundly concerned with the escalating crisis in our schools. Part of the problem he believes has to do with the "teacher's capacity to maintain a sense of hope in his vocation." The teacher must believe in the miracle of education, Ellison said. "The intelligence of our young people is there. But the teachers must orient and motivate the young and present them with viable models to follow. But when you glamourize the pimp and the prostitute on the one hand and on the other make the man who works hard for a living and the craftsmen seem insignificant to the life of the community, you are building a terrible situation."

Forrest: "I have been personally shocked and dismayed about the way a man like Gordon Parks, was taken in by the hustling joke rhetoric of Eldrige Cleaver, who represents a terrible image for young people to follow. And the general waywardness of Parks, who is a great photographer, in his current movie-making fiascos."

Ellison: "But you must understand Mr. Forrest that because a person has standards in one area of culture, doesn't mean that it is going to be carried over in other areas at all."

But in Ellison there is a continuity of standard across the board. He ranges in first-rate lecturing from the impact of the U.S. Civil War upon literature to the heavy terrain of the mighty Russian novels; he has written the best study of the top Black painter, Roman Bearden, and the finest panoramic view of the musician Charlie Parker; he has supported himself by building whole Hi-Fi systems; Ellison is one of very real experts on U.S. jazz living today, he was a first rate trumpeter. Virtuosity of craft is a hallmark on his life.

Ellison is very sensitive to the forms that merchandising of social crisis takes, and how this is all reflected within the larger reviberations of society and those who play on society's hunger for that which is novel, or the novelties syndrome. He comes down hard on certain sociologists of the last two decades, "who have become the power brokers and experts on our dilemma; they spell it out, how it is, and where it is." Moynihan, for instance, with his 'benign neglect theories', which of course were preceded by his notion of the destroyed, ruptured Black family and the Black matriarchy.

The very narrow and small-minded Black press comes in for a wholesome analysis from Ellison. He stated: "There is every reason why the Black newspapers should be cracking the great stories. We should be the people to affirm the people's right to know." For instance, Ellison explained, "It was Adam Clayton Powell, not the reform Democrats—Mrs. Roosevelt's group—who broke the power of Carmine De Sapio, in Tammy Hall (in New York). You don't need the white newspapers to do this." DeSapio recently was released from prison and Ellison was referring to a slant on the news that the Black news media might have used. He was referring to much more of course; he was talking about a whole way of approaching the news, a whole shape of the reporter-writer's mind.

Forrest: "You have spoken of the possible uses of folk art of the sermon. But what is the process, the metamorphosis that goes into re-making a speech or sermon into art?"

Ellison: "It is a blending of forms: church, congregation and drama. It is involved with re-birth and trans-cendence . . . It is involved with themes of consciousness of characters; theology and any other literary consideration."

Ralph Ellison is actually a very easy man to interview. I do not use a tape recorder. We are sitting in the front room of his large apartment. There are many fine pieces of African sculpture and Romare Bearden paintings across from where we are sitting. There are thousands of books in his Riverside Drive apartment. But it is not the lavish pad many have described, rather it is a well-lived-in apartment of a writer who is a cultured man. Different from many other Black writers, Ellison lives in a building that is basically Black.

Even his rambling is controlled, and part of his search for the right word, or phrase, just as he says the life of the imagination of the writer must be, whereas fantasy is more "life-dreaming." There is that kind of precision. And although he has been asked all of these questions hundreds of times before, in the hundreds of lectures he has given, Ellison re-creates each question, as he once again tests and reexamines his thinking about the world.

A hard-headed and enormously proud man, Ellison surprisingly is always in search for precision and clarity. It is related—one suspects—to his obsession with hitting the highest mark in literature, in his private work, and to make reality (which is constantly shifting, yet ever constant for him) clean and true and just. And in this sense he is also a very humble man, before the great ranges of "felt-life" experiences that he has touched, and for those things that are awesome, or that he doesn't know about.

Ralph Ellison is one of the most river-deep militant race men I have ever met. His very soul is anchored to Black pride and excellence. He is as likely to use the word "Negro" as "Black." . . . Yet his pride-filled pronunciation for the Afro-American is Nee-GROW. The performance of Alvin Ailey Dancers makes him weep, because of the baptizing, compelling, memories it evokes and affirms. He has developed an epic file of memories, and he always relates questions posed to those memories. But the public memories are recalled with much of the same zeal, humor, or fury, that he brings to many of his own personal memories. But when he speaks of his mother—whom he apotheosized—the ringing tragedy that he feels over her death, at the hands of an incompetent Negro medic, is telling, with regard to his fury about excellence, "Because you see Mr. Forrest this was a man who did not do his homework, and the consequence of all of this incompetence, at every level, is indeed life-destroying."

Peripheral, perhaps this segment of the conversation, was the joy he expressed over the celebration of the Black woman as depicted by Miss Judith Jameson, and her tribute to the all Black women in her dance-solo rendering of "Cry," in the Alvin Ailey troupe program.

Ellison is married to a Black woman, who is highly devoted to him and his work.

Literature and the humanities have disciplined and ordered the fundamental fires and passions of his days. But in his call for an understanding of the continuity of history, he understands that life is based in tragic rhythms and movements.

He is a man bent on artistic deliverance, who accepts the fundamental role of literature as an agent that renders harmony and lucidity out of the ever constant fires of chaos in man, and in the ever erupting world about him.

Interview with Ralph Ellison

John O'Brien / 1972

From *Interview with Black Writers,* edited by John O'Brien,
(Liveright Publishing Corporation, 1973), 63–77. Reprinted by
permission of Liveright Publishing Corporation.

Ralph Ellison has acted as a pivotal figure in the development of the
concept of black American literature. He was the first black
American writer to be taken seriously by critics. His first, and so
far only novel, *Invisible Man,* was credited as not only being the most
important piece of fiction by a black writer, but also as being one of
the great novels of twentieth century literature. As a result,
Ellison has been pointed to by critics as a model for other black
writers, as an example of what could be done with the "black
experience" if it were handled with imagination and control. This
role, which Ellison talks about with some degree of amused irony,
has caused unfair criticism from more militant black writers.

In addition to a great novel, Ellison has written some of the most
stirring and perceptive essays in recent American criticism. Collected
with a few interviews and book reviews in *Shadow and Act,* the
essays analyze trends in American literature in the light of America's racial conflicts. In one essay Ellison suggests that it was the
nineteenth-century novelist, such as Melville or Twain, who attempted to come to terms with what Ellison sees as the central
moral dilemma in America—racism. In the figure of Hemingway
he saw the refusal of the twentieth-century author to forge a vision
that would address itself to the relationships between blacks and
whites. Instead, he points out, Hemingway went to foreign and
distant forms of rituals of violence rather than choosing those of
America. Ellison interprets this as the effort of the American writer
to turn from social to personal concerns as the drama of his fiction.

Although Ellison has published parts of his second novel, which
has been rumored to be three volumes long, his reputation rests
upon *Invisible Man,* despite the fact that it was published almost

twenty-five years ago. It has never been out of print and continues
to be widely used in American literature classes. The stature that
the novel has achieved is well deserved. Breaking loose from the
limiting notion that racial themes could be handled only in a naturalistic novel, Ellison molded a style which moves, as he has suggested
elsewhere, from naturalism, to expressionism, to surrealism. And
as with other American classics, the novel endures because it
locates and brilliantly explores truths of the American experience.

The interview was conducted in December, 1972. We met on a
Saturday afternoon in Ellison's New York apartment which looks
out onto the Hudson River. We talked steadily for almost three
hours. Unlike most of the other interviews, I avoided asking him
specific questions about his novel and essays because he has in
other places already addressed himself to these matters. Instead
I hoped to have him develop some of the informing ideas of his
work which might help to illuminate his fictional concerns.

Interviewer: I have been re-reading your essays recently, especially
"Twentieth-Century Fiction and the Black Mask of Humanity."
In that essay you explain all of American literature in terms of racial
attitudes and conflicts in America. It is a very original and very
perceptive essay.

Ellison: That essay was written but wasn't published for a number
of years. Then an editor of something called *Confluence* up at Harvard
asked me if I had something for them and I sent them that essay.
That editor (laughing) turned out to be Henry Kissinger.

Interviewer: Had you tried to get it published before?

Ellison: I don't recall but I suspect that I did. I suspect that I
wrote it for something but that it was turned down. The essay
itself is very vague in my mind. I *do* know that I wrote it (laughing).

Interviewer: You interpret American literature by applying your
own moral framework.

Ellison: There is a moral obligation for the critic to recognize
what is rich and what is viable in criticism and then apply it and
play it back through his own experience, through his sense of what
is important not simply about criticism, but about life. I look at
criticism as a corrective, as a moral act, as well as an act of
appreciation. The critic should try to give as much as he has

gained. In doing this, of course, you run the risk of making a fool of
yourself. For instance, I was told, "You're out of your mind,
Ellison. This had nothing to do with what you're saying." But I
always felt that if it didn't have anything to do with what I was
saying, then something was wrong either with me or with criticism.

Interviewer: There is a certain amount of daring in your essays.
Because you are concerned with large trends you often are forced
to speak in sweeping generalities. I don't think that this invalidates
what you say but it certainly makes it easy for other critics to
attack you.

Ellison: Well, (laughing) that's the advantage of being outside the
academy, at least in my training. Also, it's the advantage of not being
primarily a critic and of having written such an essay at a time when
I had nothing to lose. I could say any kind of thing that I felt was
valid. I had no board of examiners asking me to substantiate it. I
did have friends, however, who said I was a damned fool. But
there was no problem of advancement. I was just trying to make as
much from the insights I had gained from reading good criticism
and trying to say what American literature looked like from where
I stood. Whatever is valid in it comes from that particular freedom
and whatever is invalid comes from the same source.

Interviewer: One of your points was that a writer like Melville
was consciously aware of the American democratic ideals and
was looking forward to the time when they would be fulfilled. It
seems to me that such a writer necessarily feels alienated from
the society about him because it has not yet reached that point in
the future. You argue that Melville did not feel this tension
between himself and his society.

Ellison: No, he was not writing about a future but about a
futuristic society, a society that was always moving toward the
materialization of ideals that were stated in an ideal document.
That's what I mean by futuristic. Tragedy always involves making
the ideal manifest in the real world. The whole drama of man against
nature in *Moby Dick* is a tragic story because Ahab is using the
resources of technology and his great courage in a misdirected way.
His enemy was not nature but his own wild ambition, his own
uncontrolled obsession which made him pick a quarrel with a whale.
You can call the whale evil, or call it nature, or call it good. It

amounts to the same thing. Americans are called upon to regulate
themselves. God is not going to stop us and no foreign enemy is
going to stop us. We have to stop ourselves. We have to define what
is human and see that we live within it without creating a stultify-
ing atmosphere, and see that within it human ingenuity will not
be discouraged.

Interviewer: Then you would read a novel like *Moby Dick* and
feel that Ahab acts as an example to us of what must be avoided?

Ellison: What must be done and what must be avoided. We need
an example like Ahab. Ahab was a philosopher, Ahab was a man
who was determined to define his humanity against all of the
dangers of nature, and he went to his death doing so. But it was
the role of the writer within the book to record in a meticulous way
all of the nuances of that drama.

Interviewer: You see, I don't think that the heroes of the great
American novels act as a warning to us as much as they show us
what is inevitable in our American experience. And that experience
is almost always one of defeat. You can think of Young Goodman
Brown, Ahab, Hemingway's heroes, Jay Gatsby, and—though I am
sure he wouldn't agree—Faulkner's heroes. This experience of
the hero seems to me to be opposed to that of the hero in many
novels by black writers. For instance, the hero at the end of
Toomer's *Cane,* although he has not fully realized himself, is about
to gain his manhood and enter life. The hero of *Invisible Man*
suggests the same thing. Then in a novel like LeRoi Jones' *Tales*
you have a character who triumphs over his experience, masters
environment, and is ready to begin living. On the other hand, the
hero in most American novels, and perhaps even in most Western
literature, ends in either alienation or death.

Ellison: I don't think that I can go along with your analysis.
Oedipus is defeated and Christ is defeated; they're both defeated
in one sense, and yet they live. Raskolnikov is defeated; he's found
out and sent to Siberia. But there's a promise of redemption. So,
just take those instances. You've got an ambiguous movement from
defeat to transcendence in those works. Ahab is defeated but
Ishmael isn't. Ishmael brings back the story and the lesson; he's
gone to the underworld and has returned. Gatsby ends up dead
but the narrator does not; he gives us the account. So, you don't

have absolute defeat or absolute victory. You have these ambiguous defeats and survivals which constitute the pattern of all literature. The reason for that is that literature is an affirmative act, but, being specifically concerned with moral values and reality, it has to deal with the possibility of defeat. Underlying it most profoundly is the sense that man dies but his values continue. The mediating role of literature is to leave the successors with the sense of what is dangerous in the human predicament and what is glorious. That's why we must judge literature, not on the basis of its thematic content or its technical innovations, but on its vision of the human condition.

Interviewer: Then you would say that the heroes of Hemingway's later novels reached such an affirmation?

Ellison: Well, I would even think that about his earlier novels. Jake Barnes survives, precisely because Jake Barnes is the writer of *The Sun Also Rises*. Ball-less, humiliated, malicious, even masochistic, he still has a steady eye upon it all and has the most eloquent ability to convey the texture of the experience.

Interviewer: It is what they survive with that interests me. I think that our real concern in the novel is with what happens to the protagonist, with whether or not he will be able to handle his experience. I can't understand why the American novelist, with the exception of certain black writers, appears unable at most times to show transcendence or triumph. The narrators who are left behind will not be any better able to tackle the moral problems that faced the protagonists.

Ellison: I think they will. They shared the experience and their moral sense interprets the story. This is where their moral thrust comes in. You can say that's having it easy, but after all, a novel is only a novel, and the characters in novels have to go by the conventions of novels. At that point we have to leave the characters in the novels and look at the creator of the novel. And there again you have to come back to asking how much reality did he make us feel and what was the breadth of his vision of life. And that's something that changes as we come back to a book as we grow older, and as times change.

Interviewer: Would works like *The Odyssey* and *The Aeneid* represent to you what literature should be?

Ellison: Yes, yes, yes, indeed.

Interviewer: Do you find that there is a preoccupation with evil in American literature as a whole that is not as pronounced in the works of many black American writers?

Ellison: I think the difference is how people from these two backgrounds designate evil. One of Faulkner's labors, as was true of some other white Southern writers, was to redefine evil. And when you redefine evil you redefine human quality. That's why Lucas Beauchamp is one of the heroes of Faulkner's work. Faulkner had to see Lucas Beauchamp through the lens of the stereotype. When Lucas first appears in Faulkner he's a lecher. He's always goosing and feeling the maids in the kitchen and he's eating ice cream and collard greens, which is a terrible way of pointing out that this is a negative son of a bitch. But when he ends up Lucas is one of the great examples of humanity. So, how you define evil has been a major preoccupation of American literature because in the larger political context the symbolism of evil has always been racial, and basically the evil within the American body politic has been designated black. That's where the difference comes and that's why there's this conflict between blacks and whites over the nature of reality. I carry on the fight to get us to see reality in a more realistic manner and to designate evil in terms of human unpredictability, rather than in terms of racial prejudice.

Interviewer: *Invisible Man* comes down strongly on the side of the ideal of democracy and that in the future the ideal may be fulfilled. But I wonder whether there isn't something in the American experience which necessitates that we have someone as a victim—to designate someone as evil—whether or not he be black. I see no reason to believe that we will ever come any closer to living the ideal than we have in the last few hundred years. We change in superficial ways but remain essentially the same.

Ellison: I see what you mean. I would suggest that all societies are hierarchal either through the inheritance of wealth and authority or through genetic inheritance of talent or intelligence. By the nature of things you are always going to have those inequities, those ills in society that can be ameliorated but never cured. Some people are going to have less than others whether it's in a democracy, a socialistic society, or a communistic one. Some people are going to have more talent or more ambition than others. This also involves the values of the society. You are going to have people who feel guilty because they have more, and you're going to have people who feel guilty because they have less. In order to have a human society you are going to have to have some form of victimization. Somebody is always going to be designated as the symbol of evil. They may be lynched in a realistic rite of scapegoating, or scapegoated verbally, or scapegoated in terms of where they can live, or how high they can rise in the society. This is the human way. I suspect that as this society matures we're going to find ways of designating the scapegoat on a basis other than race. We no longer designate him on the basis of his late entry into the society, as with the Irish migrants in the late nineteenth and early twentieth centuries. Just as the Irish are no longer designated as scapegoats and have even become a cult because of the Kennedys, you are going to have other modifications. And I am hoping as this society matures that whatever the scapegoat is going to be, he's not going to be black and it's not going to be based upon race. And I think that as that happens we are going to come to grips with the fact that we are a class society but that the possession of culture is much more important in the scheme of things than a man's skin or his background.

Interviewer: But rather than this natural kind of hierarchy, we have always had an irrational method for deciding how the system of power should be put together.

Ellison: What do you mean by natural?

Interviewer: The possibility of ascendancy because of the innate abilities of the individual would seem to me to be a natural hierarchy as opposed to one in which race was used as the criterion for who would get what, and where.

Ellison: Well, I think human life is a move toward the rational. Whatever man must do in order to bring order to the society is what he considers rational. For a moralist, the problem is to point out that such order is not imposed by nature and it is not imposed by God. It's a human thing. Some of the most moral men supported slavery. They rationalized it and in rationalizing it they accepted the most vicious practices and the most brutal forms of violence in order to keep the structure going. But this happens in France, it happens in England, it happens all over. What is significant in America is that at some point a group of men said that they were going to do something about this, they were going to change it, at least idealistically. So, now we have a Constitution which gives all of us a ground to fight on. And it works, though it doesn't work fast enough.

Interviewer: What I wonder is whether, even if we do manage to stop using blacks as the scapegoat in this country, we will not simply replace them with another. Perhaps our scapegoating will go on internationally. This does not appear to me to be a movement toward the ideal.

Ellison: Well, that's a whole other thing. I know of no country that has been less involved internationally, and we certainly have been involved. It started with taking over this continent from the Indians.

Interviewer: But we have been less involved?

Ellison: I think we've been less involved. Certainly less involved than the French and the British. We never colonized Africa. We haven't colonized Southeast Asia. We have had people fight in these places but we were never over there to colonize. We certainly have exploited these countries, but I don't think that these wars come about as a solution or a stopgap measure for our problems here. They come about because we belong to a family of nations and we are a very powerful and influential one. And we will continue to be involved no matter what we decide as a part of national or international policy.

Interviewer: It's that I don't see why—because we live with this myth of democracy—we should assume that we will ever really become a true democracy. We have the myth on the one hand and the reality on the other. They move along side by side, and we don't really seem to care.

Ellison: But all societies have scapegoats. You're scapegoating right now; I'm scapegoating right now. That's the way language works; it's built in. The moment you begin structuring values, some are going to be ideal and some are going to be less ideal. If you extend it, you are going to end up with God on the one hand and the devil on the other, or a term for God and a term for the devil. And in a political system you are going to end up with some form of

inequality. But in just the very nature of things there are going to
be some who are more equal than others and some who are less
equal. The human challenge is to moderate this and you can only
do this by consciously keeping the ideal alive, by not treating it as a
folly, but by treating it as Thoreau and Emerson were treating it, as a
conscious discipline which imposed upon you a conscientiousness
which made you aware, every hour and every day. To impose a
human vision upon the world . . . but it's so easy to drift. All right,
we don't have the stability of an England, but England isn't as stable
as it used to be. In England, the grandeur of language and the
grandeur of ceremony, both of the state and the church, have
been geared to impose values upon the populace and to make the
system work. These are human systems. They work at a cost.
America's works at a cost. What standards you view them with
determines your judgment. I'm stuck with democracy.

Interviewer: There are a few questions I want to ask you about
Invisible Man. According to the way you define blues, in your
essay on Richard Wright, as "an autobiographical chronicle of
personal catastrophe expressed lyrically," would you say that
your novel is a blues novel?

Ellison: I think of blues as a tragi-comic form. Stanley Hyman
has said that it's a blues novel. I'm not able to judge. I just wish
that it were as resonant and elegant as some of the blues. I tried to
use blues elements as well as I could.

Interviewer: Jonathan Baumbach has suggested that the novel is
structured according to episodes of death and rebirth. At the end
he argues that the invisible man may be metaphorically returning to
the womb by his descent into the basement.

Ellison: I certainly structured it on patterns of rebirth. That is a
pattern that is implicit in tragedy, in the blues, and in Christian
mythology. But I didn't think of his going underground as returning
to the womb. That's imposing (laughing) Freudian symbolism without
thinking too much about what a womb is. After all, that novel is a
man's memoir. He gets out of there. The fact that you can read
the narrator's memoirs means that he has come out of that hole.

Interviewer: I guess I understood that he was writing it while he
was still underground.

Ellison: The fact that you can read it (laughing) means that he went out to mail it to a publisher. You couldn't read it if he were still in there. But that's a form beyond the form.

Interviewer: The image of history that you use in the novel is that of a boomerang. How does this differ from other geometric figures that are used to explain the shape of history?

Ellison: Vico, whom Joyce used in his great novels, described history as circling. I described it as a boomerang because a boomerang moves in a parabola. It goes and it comes. It is never the same thing. There is implicit in the image the old idea that those who do not learn from history are doomed to repeat its mistakes. History comes back and hits you. But you really cannot break down a symbol rationally. It allows you to say things that cannot really be said.

Interviewer: When I read Reverend Barbee's speech I was re-minded of the sermon that Stephen Daedalus hears when he's on retreat in *A Portrait of the Artist as a Young Man*. Did you perhaps have Joyce's satire in mind when you composed Barbee's speech?

Ellison: Sure, I had read Joyce. I had read *Portrait* any number of times before I thought that I would write a novel. But I was also concerned with the problem of heroism and with the mythology of the hero. I had read Rank's *The Myth of the Birth of the Hero*. I wasn't using these things consciously, but they are just a part of my sense of how myth structures certain human activities. Barbee's speech had a great deal of irony in it but it was not simply a projection of irony. Barbee believed in certain things and I be-lieved in certain things. Myth has a viable function in human life and I don't think that we can escape it. But what I was trying to show was that this is how Barbee saw the Founder, who was by now idealized and whose influence was shaping the pattern of the narrator's life. And, of course, the hero was not going to deal with the myths; he was going to deal with the realities of growing up. He was not going to deal with abstractions of literature or theology, but with the real obstacles in the real world.

Interviewer: I am interested in the assumption you seem to make in the novel about identity. Unlike what I find in many contemporary novels where characters must invent their identity, you seem to suggest that the invisible man must find the identity that was always there but hidden from him.

Ellison: I think it has to be created too. However, man does not pick his parents or the place in the world where he begins his journey. His problem is to recognize himself through recognizing where he comes from, recognizing his parents and his inherited values. This is a very active, self-creating process. The way to create a false identity is to think that you can ignore what went before.

Interviewer: I think it's valid to ask why he doesn't settle for an identity that will be less painful.

Ellison: I suppose he had to go through it because (laughing) I had to write a novel. I feel that a novel should contain joys and sorrows and that an encounter with experience is important for readers, especially those who want to compromise. It's like asking why Oedipus decided to have a fight with that old bastard on the road, why he didn't just move aside and let him go. He might well have done this but then you wouldn't have had this great tragedy.

Interviewer: Maybe that's just my point. Why shouldn't a person avoid those things that seem to cause him pain? Why doesn't the invisible man find a way of life that will not result in alienation from his society?

Ellison: But what else was there to settle for? Being embittered like Clifton? Consciousness is all! The reason that the hero cannot settle for less is, as he says, that the mind didn't let him. He says that explicitly. The mind kept driving him.

Interviewer: Yet Bledsoe seems to understand all that the invisible man does and he is not driven to do the same things. Is it just that Bledsoe was able to be cynical about all this?

Ellison: Bledsoe is cynical, but Bledsoe never lied to this guy. And Bledsoe's acceptance was based upon rebellion too. He bawled out the invisible man because he had allowed Norton to get a glimpse of the chaos of reality and the tragic nature of life. Bledsoe expected him to be a man who could equivocate because Bledsoe looked upon equivocation as, what we now call (laughing), the "credibility gap." Bledsoe lived within and manipulated the credibility gap. But this young man is an idealist. He went through the agony of "the battle royal" because he wanted to go on following an ideal, wanted to become a leader; and this experience is an initiation into the difficulties of an heroic role, especially given his background and place in society. Finally, if there's any lesson for him to learn, it's that he has to make sense of the past before he can move toward the future. Now, if people feel that this wasn't worthwhile, I have to accept that. But then I would have to ask whether they found it an interesting book. Did they read it through?

Interviewer: And his sense of himself as an individual is tied to his sense of the past?

Ellison: His problem is to create an individuality based upon an awareness of how it relates to his past and the values of the past. He's constantly puzzled by his grandfather, puzzled and angered over Bledsoe and his various compromises, bewildered by Trueblood. His experience is a warning against easy abstractions and easy individualism because no one was allowing him to be an individual. Everybody was giving him a name, telling him what to do. He finally exhausted that and got down to the bedrock where he had to come to grips with himself and with his past.

Interviewer: I also wanted to ask you about the lobotomy. . . .

Ellison: It wasn't a lobotomy, but I left that purposely vague. Some people say lobotomy, some people say shock treatment. It's probably closer to shock treatment, but I deliberately did not make it definitely one or the other.

Interviewer: It seems to be the reason for the great change in the invisible man that immediately follows his experience in the hospital.

Ellison: No. You have to take these things in sequence. It happened after he had gone North, after he had gone through certain experiences there, after he had been introduced to the world of technology and labor unions. It's a metaphor for a new birth, wherein assumptions that he had about the North and assumptions that he had about himself had to be reversed.

Interviewer: What bothers me, though, is the method of the change. Perhaps what I am asking is whether or not the metaphor implies things which you really did not intend. After the hospital he is very much changed and one is forced to wonder whether this operation did not cause it.

Ellison: Well, he could have accepted the effects of the lobotomy and have become a vegetable; but he didn't. He continued to press on toward his ideal of becoming a leader.

Interviewer: The last question I wanted to ask concerns the novel you are working on. In an interview with James McPherson that appeared about two years ago, you said that it was nearing completion. Do you want to say anything about it now.

Ellison: (laughing) The only thing I'll say is that in the next issue of *New American Review* there will be a section of the work-in-progress. I am very pressed now because I will have to start working with my editor on my novel. It's not quite finished, but it's getting there.

Interviewer: You seem to have had the misfortune of having written a classic American novel the first time out.

Ellison: That's something other people decided. I didn't (laughing). It was just a book I wrote. I didn't have anything to lose. I didn't think that I was writing a classic. I didn't think the book would sell. I hope that this new book will be good. I've published some sections which I like very much, but the problem is to make a total functioning whole. If I make it function, it should be an interesting book.

Ellison: Exploring the Life of a Not So Visible Man

Hollie I. West / 1973

From the *Washington Post,* 19, 20, 21 August 1973. Copyright © 1973 by the *Washington Post.* Reprinted by permission.

"I'll Be My Kind of Militant"

Q: How do you feel about the criticism you sometimes get from black students who feel you haven't been militant enough?

A: I say, "You'd be your kind of militant and I'll be my kind of militant."

Q: Do you still get as much of that as you did several years ago, in the 1960s, when there was an incident involving students shouting at you at the University of Iowa?

A: I don't know what the attitudes are. I get a lot of letters from students. I know that my books are still being read and presumably by some of the blacks, because I've been told by some who have attacked me in print that they "love" this and they "love" that" and so on. Anyway, if you have any sort of effectiveness, if you make any kind of impact, you're going to polarize people. I never felt it necessary to go out and justify my militancy. My writings are there. I'm not an ideologist. I reject a lot of what they have stood for in the movement, and as it turned out: Where are they today? Many of them are in exile. Many of them are exhausted because they had very little to go on. They were not rooted in what they could have been rooted into, which by inheritance they should have been rooted into. I'm not a separatist. The imagination is integrative. That's how you make the new—by putting something else with what you've got. And I'm unashamedly an American integrationist.

I come out of fighting people—people who took broad responsibility for things. I try to do it in my own way. It might not satisfy many people, but it satisfies me. It's the best that I can do. You see I've been doing other things. While the complaints have gone on

235

about my militancy, I've been trying to build other things—or help
build them. I was a member of the commission that set up public
television. It's not going the way I wanted it to go, or the way we
conceived it. However, the political situation around that has
improved recently. I was a part of that and not just a person sitting
on the board. I was working and my language is in there.

Some of the point of view of the original Council on the Arts is
mine. Roger Stevens and people like that can tell you that I was one
of the most active people on that thing because I do have a
responsibility to culture in the country. Not just black culture. I
am an American and because I am black these things are very, very
precious to me. I know that so much has been lost within our
own creativity, the products of our own creativity—lost or distorted
or degraded through commercialization and so on. So that's been
taking up quite a lot of energy. I have an active side.

Q: You've criticized young black writers for taking the ideological
route. Could part of the reason for these black writers attempting
to be political spokesmen be that there are so few politicians
writing?

A: Politicians don't write.

Q: Few black politicians have books ghost-written for them.

A: Yes. And why is that?

Q: Perhaps some of this can be traced back to the oral tradition
among blacks. Maybe they feel they can be more effective in
speeches.

A: Are they?

Q: They're effective in being reelected, I suppose.

A: That hasn't been going on for very long, you know.

Q: There's just not much literary tradition among blacks generally, and this is quite obvious among black politicians.

A: It's true. We haven't even been a reading people—until very
recently. I had a student get terribly angry with me for having
reminded him of this out at Oberlin a few years ago. These are facts
we have to deal with. The other thing I would suggest: You don't
find black politicians writing books, or having them ghost-written,
because they do not take responsibility for the total society.
They're trying to work with a small segment of the society. We're a
great part of the American society and its culture, but politically

they have been men of narrow vision. We do not initiate or articulate
enough issues.

Q: The electorate is partly responsible for this, isn't it?

A: The electorate does have to be led as well as followed. There're
just too many issues in American life which we should have been
talking about. We should have been talking about ecology—in the
broadest sense. You see, during my time I've seen people burning
kerosene lamps, and that's not been too long ago right here in
Harlem. And there're still too many people in the so-called
ghetto—what I call slums—who have toilets in the hall or who're
using water toilets in the back of buildings. Now you talk about
ecology—that's enough to start you thinking about ecology.

Beyond the question of the decaying of buildings, you put it in a
broad perspective, then you have other parts of the population
you can respond to. Much of—this is off the top of my head—the
so-called resentment of the blue collar whites has come about
precisely because we have not defined our issues in broad enough
terms. We've allowed them to be too racial in motivation, rather
than basing them on the general interest of a much broader group
of people. Now I'm not a politician. I don't know how you can
use that to structure a program, but I do know you have to think in
those terms.

Q: But hasn't this been tried? Are you referring to reaching a
broad spectrum of the electorate—blue collar workers, blacks,
whites—in the labor movement? That was the cross-section of
groups that supported Roosevelt in the '30s, wasn't it?

A: Along with lynchers and all kinds of people. That's right. It
was a coalition. Now speaking as a Democrat, we became so
damn self-righteous that we gave up the possibility of making these
accommodations, these alliances, coalitions—because everyone
has to accommodate them. So you have a lot of people who should
be united on a number of issues—just sprawling all over the place.

What I'm saying, and this is the best way I can put it, is that a
Negro leader must understand that he is not simply the leader of
black Americans. To be *effective* he must lead and he must be
concerned with broader issues, and he is in the position of seeing the
broader issue and anticipating it precisely because we catch so
much of the hell.

Q: I wonder if Negro people are ready for that sort of leader. If you look at [Sen.] Edward Brooke [R-Mass.] who tries to appeal to a broad segment of the population, he doesn't command the admiration of blacks nationally.

A: Well, who's responsible for that? The press is partially responsible and a lot of black militants and so-called separatists who cannot see that he is a leader and if they don't like what he's doing, the way to affect his policy certainly isn't to attack him and refuse to have anything to do with him, because obviously the man has a constituency. You know, there are American leaders who are black, who lead constituencies that are not predominantly black. There're others who could not be anywhere in politics but for the suffering of black America.

Q: Perhaps black voters have been conditioned to think a black politician or black leader should only lead black people. Perhaps many black leaders themselves do not have the vision to go beyond just wanting to lead blacks.

A: Well, that should be corrected. But I should also point to you the contradiction there. They considered—I mean the masses of blacks—Franklin Roosevelt their President. They considered Jack Kennedy their President. And they should consider Lyndon Johnson their President because he certainly did more to change the patterns of racial relationships from the Supreme Court to the Cabinet on down—than any other President.

American Negroes are capable of seeing leaders and recognizing as leaders men who are not black. Just as they would be willing to see a black leader who is a wise and perceptive leader lead others than themselves, I think we would like to see a black President. I would—if we had a man who was up to it. And considering what's happened, there must be some who're up to it.

Q: But I'm suggesting that blacks are less willing to accept a black leader who is a leader of all people than a white leader of all people. They put special demands on a black leader.

A: This has to be tested. I don't know the statistics about Brooke's district in Massachusetts, but he won reelection. He must have had some black people voting for him. They're not going to reject him just because white people voted for him. We have a whole group of young politicians in the South who're getting in precisely because whites do vote for them and they are supported by blacks. So I would not accept that generalization. I would just go back and say, "Damn it, we're in a new period and politicians are going to have to learn how to deal with it."

And they're going to have to learn how to deal with it without the easy rhetoric of black separatism or of racial chauvinism. If you're a politician, your object is power. And if to get the power, you must build a constituency beyond the black community, then damn it, it's up to you to come up with ways of doing that.

Now this has been understood in the big machine cities like Chicago, wherein the blacks were supporting the machine because it did something for them, while the alderman and a number of the district leaders were all white. Well, that pattern is changing, and as it changes, the structure of political parties has to change. But still the black leader who's going to take over [Mayor Richard] Daley's place is going to have to be at least as smart a man as Daley; and Daley is a very smart politician.

Q: He'll probably have to be a much better man, a much smarter politician than Daley ever thought of being.

A: Yea, that's right. But that's the penalty placed upon us for being down at the bottom of the social hierarchy. It's a challenge and it should make us give up the excuses for our second-rate stance and go on and develop people who are able to deal with a very complex situation.

Q: In view of the present administration's stand on school busing, its attempts to place antiblack Southerners on the Supreme Court and its general strategy of making a pitch to Southern voters, what do you think the effect of Richard Nixon has been on the American racial situation? Do you think his administration represents a setback to racial progress?

A: Let's put it this way: I certainly think he has had a chilling effect upon our optimism, but I also think the policies which they seem to be following calls upon us to be a little more realistic about where we have come from and it should force us to reassess the progress made and not made under Kennedy and Johnson.

Quite a lot has happened to this country since the end of the Second World War and the election of Richard Nixon. And too much was distorted when the black movement began to attack

Johnson over Vietnam and got ourselves all involved in that
particular struggle, and we began to downgrade and badmouth a
President who had done quite a lot to change patterns of American
racial relationships which had existed since the Reconstruction.
That sort of second look had to come: One, we had patterns of
social structuring, terminology, language, conception of justice,
conception of who an American was and what he was, and what
a Negro was, where he could go.

All of that has been changed. Attitudes and values which had
been built so thoroughly into the society that people had signs up
telling you where you could go to the toilet have been changed.
Clerical systems, bureaucracies, wherein your racial background
determined how you were rated—that's been changed to a large
extent. All of that came about. People were able to go into schools
where they were not accepted before. We have certain jobs available
to us which were never available before. And instead of meeting
the challenge of these new opportunities, many of us—and especially the youths—recalled in a kind of despair.

I think we've gone through a period of desperation where many
young blacks became separatists because they were frightened by
the need to compete. I think that's part of the phenomena on these
college campuses. Somebody tells me, "Oh, they do this because
they feel lonely and isolated when they first go to college," I felt it
at Tuskegee.

Q: But how does this follow—Negro students being frightened by
the need to compete? How does this follow what happened in the
early 1960s—the sit-ins, the thrust for desegregation?

A: It isn't the thrust—which was a highly successful campaign
and absolutely admirable. It was how they responded. They asked
for something, evidently thinking that it was all going to be sweet-
ness and light. But they just found they had moved onto another
level of struggle. That is America, and it happens for all people.

It's rougher for us, perhaps. We have reached a point where we
really have to reexamine where we stand and not seize the easiest
explanation and fall into despair. If you go to a college where
students have had certain advantages over you in educational
background or in training, or the quality of training, you shouldn't
get upset about it because you've been told about it. You know

that one of the motives for integrating the white colleges and schools
was because we were not getting the same quality of education.
So what you do is bide your time—go consciously about making up
what you did not have because there's no question but that you
can compete.

Q: What role do you think the brutality, the murders, the dehu-
manization of black students in the South played in this whole
picture?

A: Well, look, Hollie West—for God's sake, man, we'd been
protesting against brutalization and discrimination and every damn
thing else for years before the '60s. Talk about reaction. We were
reacting when it was very costly to react. My wife was in protest at
Fisk (University) over lynching years before that.

Q: But these kids went down there with such high expectations
and when things didn't work out, they were bitterly disappointed.

A: This is the kind of reaction I'm talking about. They reacted in
the same way when blacks got into colleges and found out it
wasn't going to be an easy thing. They just became aware of how
entrapable reality can be. I think that's what happened. You talk
about Stokely Carmichael. Stokely Carmichael with his predominantly West Indian background, and I don't hold that against him,
but I'm talking about culture. I'm talking about what a person
expects, what he is conditioned to understand. He was not. And
when you talk about the despair and brutalization, a hell of a lot of
the students who went through that are going back South to live.

Q: Perhaps it was naive of them to think they could change things
overnight, but I got the feeling from talking with some of these people
afterward that they believed they would make instant impact and
life would be nice and sweet.

A: Well, life ain't like that. I'm sorry. I wish it were, but life is
not like that. And, of course, something else which I don't
say—so many of them burnt themselves up in the effort and they
were the sacrificial troops. And I don't think they realized they
were sacrificing themselves.

So there's a heroism involved in that. The shootings that happened at Southern University (in November 1972) are not quite
the same things that were happening in the '50s, even though people

were killed. It's not quite the same struggle. It's not the same Baton Rouge or New Orleans that existed 10 or 20 years ago.

Q: But we saw killings four or five years ago, at South Carolina State.

A: And you saw them at Kent State, and you're going to see more of them.

Q: Why?

A: Because until we learn that it's one thing to use violent rhetoric and it's another thing to deal with the violence which is released by that rhetoric; and that Americans, when they get panicky, will kill you. Now the slaves understood that. Your parents and my parents understood that. And there're a few people today who understand it—that there never was a simple matter of frightening the white man.

It was always a question of what to do when he got frightened, and our history has taught us he gets frightened awfully easy. Now a lot of white students had no sense of that, and evidently a lot of ours still don't understand that very often there are guys who just want the excuse to kill you. I had to live with that throughout my experience in Alabama. I had to learn that it was not important for me to meet every challenge some peckerwood came along with, because that's all he had. He had one motive: to put me in my place, while my motive was to create a place for myself.

Q: You say that some young blacks have not learned that. Perhaps they haven't learned it because they haven't been taught it by their parents.

A: I think that built into the Negro American community—as is built into a great part of the white American community—is an instinct not to draw the line too sharply for its children, lest attitudes of adventure and courage will be dampened. You see what I'm trying to say?

Q: I think so. Is an example of this the tendency for many Negro parents not to tell their children about segregation?

A: Or not to tell them about slavery. Sometimes you'd have to pull information out of older people. I remember going through this myself. "What happened, what happened?" Now I understand that what happened in many instances was so discouraging that they did not want to discourage me, as they used to say, "Don't do what I did. You're young boy. You have a chance."

And I think part of the motivation is to keep that hope alive, to let you discover the world for yourself, and beneath that there is that feeling, that awareness, that reality changes very rapidly in the United States. And that you must change with it. You cannot let the past keep blinding you to the new configuration of the present.

And certainly black Americans, especially those from the South, have a reason to take this very seriously because they watched for years and years, and they suffered the white South as it sought to see the present in terms of the past. And if we have a new South now it is because they're no longer trying to do that so violently and because part of this, to go back, was due to their activities on the part of the young blacks during the '50s and '60s.

Q: Something related to all this happening in the South is the life of Martin Luther King. Have we recovered from his death? He was the last Negro American to claim a mass following among blacks and had moral leadership among all Americans.

A: I don't know whether we've recovered. I know that he hasn't really been replaced. I recall, though, that there were a lot of people who were not following Martin Luther King. It's another instance of martyrdom endowing the martyr with a hell of lot more following than he had during his struggles when he was difficult to deal with.

Q: But many of these people who say they didn't follow him perhaps applauded what he did even though they didn't agree with his techniques, his methods or even some of his goals. But they may have generally agreed with his intentions.

A: They're pleased to applaud a black leader who gets his name into the papers. That comes into it too. But there was a great division. A lot of people now who talk about Martin Luther King despised him because his rhetoric was not violent. King hasn't been dealt with yet either—I mean his significance.

Q: Is it too early?

A: It's not for me to say it's too early. I think it depends upon the person who's prepared to do it. I think that someone is really going to have to go into the wisdom of our tying our struggle too closely with the Vietnam War.

Q: But he did that late in his career.

A: Late in his career? That's a relative remark. Late because it

was shortly before he was killed so what can you say. He certainly
had reached a point where he had to come up with new directions.
I myself think that Martin Luther King had reached the point
where he should have become a politician. I mean a professional
politician because he was moving in that direction—at least events
were moving him in that direction.

Q: But if he had done that he would have lost some of the
backdrop of ritual.

A: Well, he might have lost the backdrop of that ritual, but Adam
Clayton Powell never lost his and he was as good a Baptist.
There're certain things you cannot do without the apparatus to do
it with.

Q: But King's approach was different from Powell's. King's
approach was unified. I mean the morals and ethics were tied in
directly with everyday life.

A: So it seems. Well this is true of all leaders. You have a role,
you have an image there and you have a human being behind it. I
think that the desire to function as a moral leader became confused
in his mind because he *was* a moral leader and he got into an area
where his morality was too simplistic. Because when you get on the
level of a state, of a nation and war, the questions of morality
become quite difficult. Because a state is based upon power and the
exercise of power and that involves violence. There's always some
violence in the offing—whether it's day-to-day stress between man
and nature or between armed contingents of the various interests
and aspects of authority.

Q: But you can't very easily separate political power from morality.

A: No you don't. But it's quite different depending upon where
you stand. In a pulpit it's one thing. When you're leading a nation
it's something else again.

Q: Is this why you reject his tying the Vietnam War into the civil
rights movement?

A: Well, I reject it because I think it led to a diffusion of interests
and it allowed a lot of nonblack people who were part of his
support to focus their energies elsewhere. It let them off the hook
when the going got hot in the racial arena. I trace some of the
defection of energies to ecology and antiwar protest back to people

who realized when blacks started moving into their neighborhoods and their schools that they were dealing with something more
difficult than just taking a high moral position as they looked
toward the South.

Travels with Ralph Ellison Through Time and Thought

Q: You once wrote that American literature was built partly from
Negro folklore.

A: Yes. There's never been a time when we—our expression, our
symbols, our turns of face—were not finding our way into the
products of other Americans who were consciously or unconsciously creating. After all, "Turkey in the Straw" is a Negro
tune, but it is identified with whites just as is "Carry Me Back to
Ole Virginny," by a black Virginia composer. Very early, I guess in
the 1830s, Whitman was suggesting that in the dialect of the American Negro was a basis of an American form of grand opera. You
see, this is overlooked. Americans had to create themselves. We
had to be conscious of language in a way that English people did
not have to be. It was their mother tongue. It was our mother tongue
but we were in rebellion against it—against the values on which it
was based, which were those of kinship. We didn't reject the great
traditions of British literature, the King James version of the
Bible, Shakespeare or the great poets, but we rejected the values
which enspirited that language and we began to try to discover
how to create an American literature. This was consciously stated
over and over by many people. What was more American than Mose,
and who was more expressive, more artistically inventive in dancing, making jokes, telling stories? Mark Twain delighted in telling
Negro ghost stories and used to do it on public stage, public
platforms. He knew very consciously that he was using the moral
predicament surrounding the racial conflict in this country to give
structure to his imagination and his stories. This was inescapable.
So when I say that we are always there, it isn't just an idle assertion.
All you have to do is look and say, My God, when would the white
man have had that particular insight? How could he have had the
insight if there had been no racial conflict? How could he have

had this particular kind of conception of humanity if there had been no blacks within the society?

Q: Well, much of this sort of thing is oral. Much of folklore, for that matter, is oral.

A: The study of folklore tends to be literary, but folklore is usually the expression of a preliterate society. Of course it continues even after literature develops because it's tradition.

Q: In that connection, do you see the study of oral history as a valid way of interpreting and understanding American history?

A: I would think that a great part of American history has been lost precisely because those people who wrote the history structured it to their own conceptions. We could just take the Negro part of American history. Much of that was lost because it was not written down but passed along from individual to individual.

Yet there doubtless still remains a lot of correspondence written by blacks as they moved about the country, which would tell us quite a lot about American history as it actually unfolded. But until recently historians haven't bothered with this material. Quite a lot of work was done during the WPA [Works Progress, later Works Projects Administration] days when many ex-slaves were interviewed. I was reading recently some accounts collected during the Writers Project in Oklahoma. I read the statement of this man and looked at his name and then realized that I had known him. He was in his eighties when I was a little kid out there, but he was very much alive. And it had never occurred to me that he had been a slave. In fact, many of the people who went to Oklahoma had had some slavery experience.

Q: In case you saw folklore developing in Oklahoma, and by that I mean you saw certain lifestyles and traditions being created. Was this crucial to the development of your later interest in folklore, and how it was interwoven into culture generally?

A: Well, folklore was interwoven. I wasn't aware that I was seeing it develop. I was just a part of a community in which you had an extension of folklore patterns from the South and into the Southwest. After all, many of the people came from Alabama, North Carolina, Mississippi, South Carolina, and Georgia. And they brought along stories. As with any situation where folkloristic pattern is adapted to new situations, the people who were involved

with it were not aware of it unless they were scholars. I was not a
scholar, but I delighted in stories and lyrics. As one who wanted to
be a musician and a composer I was getting it on all sides:
classical music as well as jazz and the blues and spirituals. But one
thing I can say that was important in this connection was that I very
early began to read Shaw. I was reading Shaw when I was ten, and
I came across a number of these Haldeman Julius blue and gray
books, and I read some of Nietzsche, and I understood the relationship between Nietzsche and Shaw. Nietzsche was, of course,
concerned not with folklore but with the underlying ritual patterns.
Years later when I began to try to understand Eliot and Pound,
and so on, to see how they worked putting these things together, I
began to look back and understand, "Oh yes, I was involved with
folklore," but this was the result of certain sorts of conscious
experience based upon literature. I discovered the folklore because I had become a literary person.

Q: Sterling Brown has written that the urbanization of blacks is
helping to break up rural folk culture. Is there such a thing as
urban folklore?

A: Yes, I think so. But it isn't a thing in itself. The traditions are
modified in the city. I worked on a folklore project here in New
York City under WPA collecting children's rhymes and things. But
I went beyond that to get older people to tell me stories, and very
often a word or a concept would have just become a mumble.
Usually a word becomes some nonsense phrase because it was
out of the rural context in which the rhyme or story had originated.
It continued because that's what the people have to work out of.
This tradition goes way back to the South, and some of it goes back
to Africa.

Q: The tradition may continue, may be modified in the urban
setting, but is some of the vitality lost?

A: The vitality is lost in some ways. Some patterns drop out. But
what is it that gives life to folklore or any kind of literature? It's the
experience of people. And as the experience maintains a continuity
where issues and motives remain alive and there's an audience
for it, you get a vitality. You're not going to keep life from changing.
You can't do that. One of the things that tends to throw people
off is that they don't go looking for folklore, they don't go places

where folklore is still alive. I'm sure that the Afro [hair style] has killed off more folklore than anything else, because guys don't have to go to the barbership or stay there long enough for the lying to start. But there're still plenty of people around who know the stories.

Q: I'm not asking that life stand still, but I have questions about whether much of the vitality of Negro life is being retained.

A: I think the vitality is maintained, but you just have to know where it is. Here the great emphasis is on writing. I'd like to feel that all my fiction has themes, motives, and images from folklore. That's my way of keeping it alive. I'm just conscious of literature generally, to see how to structure it with similar patterns. And I think that that's happening with a number of the younger writers. I think that they realize that this heritage is a valuable one. But the trick is how to use it.

I might write a decent blues lyric, but for me to write a blues lyric is quite different from some guy who knows no other form of expression. You can see that it is more immediately native to him than it is to me, although it is my tradition, too.

Q: In a sense you took direct part in some folk traditions: the tradition of hoboing, for one.

A: Well, that sure ain't Negro—that's American! Yes, I did. But you must remember this: My father's people built railroad trestles for the Southern Railroad during the Reconstruction period, and my people were railroad people to an extent. That's part of it. So much of folklore is mixed up with traveling, with freight trains, with the sounds of trains and so on. That's the advantage of having lived close to the railroads. One reason I live here [on Riverside Drive in Upper Manhattan] is that there's a railroad track right down there. I've got a river, a highway, and a railroad track. I like to hear those cars bumping along there.

Yes, I did hobo. That's how I got to school during the Depression. I was able to get to Tuskegee by riding freight trains rather than going across Arkansas where they were pretty rough on you. They had chain gangs. I went North—went up to East St. Louis, over to Evansville, got the L & N, and went down South. I was taken off the train at Decatur when the Scottsboro case was being tried.

They were just shaking the train down. They didn't bother us. I ran and got away from whatever was going to happen.

Q: Do you miss the trains?

A: Yes, I do, because they were a vehicle of folklore. I miss them very much. Mark Twain understood the importance of the Mississippi River (as did T.S. Eliot and others) to the fluidity of American literature and folklore. Where you get people going back and forth you get literature, art. Kansas City and Chicago were great towns for jazz because they were great railroad towns. People would come up and tell their stories. Sometimes they would go back. The Pullman porter was a great agent of that type of culture, the waiter and so on. You miss that. You miss the sound, the romance of the railroad. There's something very valuable that has been lost.

Q: I've been told that someone taught you to hobo, to hop freights. Is that right?

A: Yes, I made notes on that, and I will write about it. It was a friend of my parents, a little white-looking, blue-eyed, light-haired Negro fellow. Whenever he was outside Oklahoma he was a white man. He used to come back and forth, stay a few days, and take off. He happened to be there when I had the scholarship at Tuskegee.

They needed a trumpet player, but I got word that I'd have to be there at a certain time and I didn't have the money to do it because I was buying clothing and I was buying a horn, and so on. So I approached him and said, "Charlie, why don't you teach me to hobo?" I got my mother's reluctant permission and we took off. I had thirty-two bucks and he had very little. He taught me who to avoid, how to get on trains, and how to protect myself. It was quite a nice thing to have done.

Q: Was it an involved technique?

A: You had to be able to read a manifest which was nailed on the side of the car to know where a train was going and when it was scheduled to be there. You had to know how to avoid railroad bulls [detectives]. You had to know what to do when a train got into town where there were difficult police or sheriffs. You had to know where you could buy things in a racial situation. It was quite a bit involved.

You had to know the best route to take. I wouldn't have known
to have gone north. And as it was, I was taken off the train. I
wasn't allowed to go into St. Louis. I was stopped because they
were turning boys around who were going up to the World's Fair.
Charlie went across into East St. Louis. He told me to see what I
could do with the guard. I walked across the Mississippi River
bridge and convinced the guard that I wasn't going to the fair, that
I was going to college, and this was the only way I could do it.
And he let me through.

Q: Do you see any special problems in the study of Negro
folklore, distinguishing it from the folklore of white America—
say, Appalachian whites or whites in the Ozarks?

A: Well, you just have to find out where Negroes are and you
have to give up the idea that culture exists in neat pockets.
Culture is exchange. A slave could be in the yard looking in at
whites dancing and come out and imitate that dance, and then put
his own riffs to it, and you've got something else. That's how
American choreography developed.

Remember there was an exchange. Just as they looked at polite
forms of dancing, European dancing as adopted by American
whites—many of whom were going back and forth to Europe during
colonial times—those slaves looked at that, they learned from
that and put something of their own with it, and later on whites
looked at what the [slaves] did and put something of their own to
it, and you get this interchange.

It's a dialectical process. You tell me a story, or I hear you telling
your child a story. I'm a cook or a maid or a butler. I go back
home and tell my kids the story. Since there's an element of rhetoric
involved, I change it to fit in with the background of my child, and
then I enspirit it with my own motives for freedom or my own sense
of humanity, my own sense of the complexity of human experience. And so you've got a modification.

You can look and say, "This is a Negro story." You look at
"John Henry"—that seems absolutely black. But you look a little
closer and you remember the tales of Hercules, you recognize the
modification. I'm not saying it's not ours. But I'm saying it was
not created out of the empty air but out of the long tradition of
storytelling, out of myth.

Q: I know that you have laid great emphasis on the give-and-take process in our culture. Do you see it working as effectively now as it was when the main thrust of blacks was to integrate with whites?

A: It isn't an arbitrary matter. You cannot control integration by setting up an ideological structure and saying, "We're separatists." I still watch the guys walking around. They may be wearing dashikis, but who makes the cloth? They don't. The Africans don't, for the most part. Maybe a few do.

It's too damn expensive to cloak a political movement. They're still looking at American TV, listening to American news, using European cameras, American cameras, drinking the best Scotch whiskey. You see, that's to kid themselves. But to get back to the question.

I think there is a more conscious interchange of cultural styles between the races in this country now than ever before. When did you ever hear blonde, blue-eyed white girls shouting like Holy Roller sisters and making millions out of it? When did you ever see young white boys singing in the style that used to be common to backwoods Negro entertainers? This, too, was in churches: all that falsetto singing and shrieking and going on. This is being exploited not simply by people in show business but by middle-class kids who have heard it and liked it, and decided it was easy to do. They couldn't do that with jazz, and it got so for a while there you couldn't hear any decent music, even on an FM station.

In literature, and I'm not going to call any names, but we have our guys who—in the name of black power—are picking up some of the sleaziest attitudinizing of whites.

Q: Let's consider one of your statements from an essay in *Shadow and Act.* You said you feared the commercialization and banalization of Negro culture.

A: I still do. And I wish there could be some control of it, but there cannot be control of it, except in this way: through those of us who write and who create using what is there to use in a most eloquent and transcendent way. You cannot control Tin Pan Alley—too many people are making money off it—any more than you can control a tenor saxophone player who, instead of playing music, found he could make more money and go further commercially by rolling on the floor and shrieking. And we had quite a lot of that.

But at the same time Johnny Hodges and Coleman Hawkins and God knows who else just kept on developing the possibilities which were implicit in the style of saxophone jazz from way, way back, beyond Sidney Bechet. It's one thing for a commercial group to go out and exploit the possibilities of gospel music and quite a different thing for a serious composer who sees something which is valuable in that style and uses it to realize his own artistic vision.

Q: But what you mentioned earlier—the blue-eyed blonde wearing her hair in Afro style, shrieking and shouting like a backwoods Baptist—is happening more frequently than a serious composer utilizing the resources of Negro music.

A: It always does. The vulgar tongue is spoken by more people than the refined tongue. The task of the artist is always to refine that which is the vulgar speech—to make it sharper and make it more transcendent and more eloquent. As I said, Negroes cannot control that any more than we can control the economy. But we don't have to play the game and we can set our own fashions as we did with jazz.

Back in the twenties and thirties most white people were not dancing to jazz. And the musicians did not need great commercial success among whites to determine artistic values for them, I suppose, because that avenue was closed to them. They determined their own artistic values in the academy of the dance hall and jam session. That's the kind of self-determination which is needed to preserve not only the artistic values of jazz but all American culture.

Q: I'd like to go back to your earlier statement about there being more cultural exchange than before. You cite the example of young whites taking on the lifestyles of blacks. But I don't see young blacks being influenced so much by the lifestyle of young whites. Take rock music. Many blacks have been reluctant to embrace it. But there have been some: Jimi Hendrix, for one.

A: I was going to say that. Keep on talking.

Q: But I think he's more of an exception than a Janis Joplin or many of the other young white rock performers.

A: What about Chuck Berry? You see, here you have to watch

the circling—the back-and-forth play. Chuck Berry was doing
some of this stuff a long time ago. They took it up and did their
version of it. He's done his version of it. He fits into that slot.

Q: We spoke earlier about the commercialization and banalization
of Negro-American cultural expression. You said this was happening, but at the same time in the portion of *Shadow and Act,* "Some
Questions and Some Answers," you said at one point that you did
not believe that as we win our struggle for full participation in
American life we abandon our group expression. Do you still
believe that today, in light of what's happened since. . . ?

A: No. I don't think that we will abandon it. That's all we have.
You see, you might have people on a certain cultural level who
will seek to abandon our expression, but tradition is more devious
than that. It isn't an arbitrary matter.

You watch a little Negro kid try to dance. He's going to dance
like a little Negro American kid. And why is that? Beyond any
physical question or articulation of the limbs there is a spirit of the
dance which is around him, and he observes and absorbs it before he
is aware of what he is absorbing. It's very interesting to watch little
white and Negro kids dance on television and observe the difference between them. Now some of those little white kids can dance
and some of them have been very much influenced by Negro
American style, but I think that this is a part of the culture that
moves from individual to individual in the context of the community
and you don't have to be altogether aware of it. You are doing what
comes naturally.

You are not going to lose a certain way with words because it is
built into the way we speak. What we call rapping or riffing—you
are going to hear your daddy talking or your uncle or your older
brothers and sisters. This is preserved in speech and its informed
attitudes, which can range from the most explicit to that which is
implicit and subtle. So you're not going to get away from that.
What will happen, I think, is that as you become conscious as an
artist, you will begin to exploit it consciously. You will work it in
terms of what others have done in other cultures. You will abstract
motives from there and impose them within your own scheme.

But it's a give-and-take human thing rather than a racial thing,
and at some point we're going to have to realize that simply by having

the same skin we're not all the same people. There are many cultural levels within the Negro group. There are people who are on the folk level in their cultural lives, even though they might be operating computers. And there are people who shine shoes who, in their cultural lives, are on the high level of articulate culture.

Q: It's this give-and-take that's so important, I suppose. This reminds me of something that Duke Ellington said to me in an interview. He said the pull of American culture was so strong that no one could resist it.

A: Not only that, but it's in artifacts, you see. You put on a pair of shoes, a hat. Negroes thought they were going to isolate themselves by putting on an Afro. The Jewish kids, the blonde kids—they're wearing them too. Why? Because it's irresistible. It's a style. It's a new way of making the human body do something; and that operates over and beyond any question of race.

Growing Up Black in Frontier Oklahoma

Q: We were talking earlier about your growing up in Oklahoma City, and you said that your parents came from South Carolina and Georgia. Oklahoma was part of the frontier shortly before you were born. Did this create any special meaning for people growing up there at that time?

A: I think so. I think that the people were aggressive. They had a sense of what it meant to come to the frontier because they had come looking for better conditions for themselves and for their children. They were quite aware—those who had come early—of the struggle to keep the new state of Oklahoma as liberal as possible. They had actively fought against the adoption of the Texas segregationist laws as a model for the Oklahoma constitution; and they had failed in that. But someone has said geography is fate, and it is fate for black Americans as well as for white.

The people who went out there were trying to determine their fate. And they did this quite actively. There were such all-black towns as Boley, as an example of a place where they were trying to determine that fate. In Oklahoma City you had constant struggles to keep the bigoted whites—and not all were bigoted—from imposing the old patterns of the segregationist South upon the racial

relationships there. I know that a great number of the people I grew
up with were armed, and during the 1920s, when there was a lot
of trouble, I've seen them produce those arms and stand waiting.

A man was lynched in Chickasha, and his body was brought over
to Oklahoma City for burial. The members of the white mob
telephoned to Oklahoma City that they were coming over to drag
this body back. And the Negroes sent word: "Come on. We'll be
waiting." And they were waiting. Jack Walton was mayor at the
time. I was out there when he came out and took a stand with the
Negroes to keep this thing from exploding.

You had segregation in Oklahoma City. But you had no tradition
of slavery. So those old patterns were not imposed as successfully
as they might have been. There was never a time that we didn't
have white friends. The neighborhood was mixed. But there were
friends of my father who would come by to see him, and he'd go by
to see them.

Q: Did this spirit pervade the entire Southwest—Texas and Arkansas?

A: It did not pervade Texas or Arkansas because both states were
older and they had been involved in the Civil War and had a
tradition of slavery. But Oklahoma was rather fresh and had been
conceived of by various Negro leaders as an all-black state. Sojourner
Truth thought of the old Indian Territory as an all-black state. It
was feared that Negroes were actively trying to convert it into
such an entity—early, in fact, just before statehood (1907).

Q: Wasn't there a duality of sorts in Oklahoma? The state was
both South and West. It had some of the traditions of the South,
but it was also a frontier state. Did this cause any conflict?

A: It caused conflict. But when you speak of something like
tradition, you must remember that tradition is not something
abstract. Tradition is within the attitudes of individuals, especially
on a frontier. Say, in the South—the traditions of the slave South
are inspired in buildings, patterns of movement about the cities, in
manners, in signs, in monuments, in all kinds of things. And
especially in the memories and attitudes of people.

But on a frontier the tradition—at a given point—is apt to be
more in the attitudes and memories of individuals. When you run
into a person who has an antiblack tradition, and you meet some

black who isn't going to accept it, who has determined to confront it head on—then you have conflict. Certainly it made for a conflict, but what was good about it was the constant jockeying to assert a different pattern of relationships, and that was very, very important for the people that I grew up with. And certainly it was important for me.

In the atmosphere of the place there was a sense that you had to determine your own fate, and that you had a chance to do it.

Q: Does this mean that there was a special set of circumstances surrounding Oklahoma because it was a frontier state? I don't know if I had that same feeling growing up in Oklahoma in the fifties. Maybe the frontier tradition had dried up by that time?

A: Well, what did you have by the fifties? My God, man, what did you have? Just consider what was happening during the forties. The tremendous changes that occurred when they were building liberty ships out that way. You know, in parts—then shipping them to a sea coast and riveting them together.

The influx of labor, of different traditions, the growth of the business community with its investment in maintaining discrimination and so on. You would get changes. Also, you got a great influx of people who had not shared that sense of promise that your people and my people had shared. They were in Oklahoma, but Oklahoma was not in them.

We have to look at this thing in the perspective of time. Given the late 1890s and the early 1900s, you had a heck of a period there—say, thirty years in which to feel enthusiastic and hopeful and during which you could build something for yourself.

For instance, people are surprised when I tell them I knew a few millionaires who were black. Some had made their fortunes in farming, one man in making cosmetics. There were a number of wealthy doctors who were land poor and then had oil discovered. People who traveled and had a lifestyle that was rather elegant considering that they lived much better than many of the whites and they possessed a higher degree of culture than many of the whites who had an opportunity to make more money, because you did have discrimination and you did have whites who were trying to keep Negroes under control.

Q: Were there any literary developments in Oklahoma that made any impact on you?

A: No. Where literature came into my life, I guess, was through my father's having been a reader; he read all the time and I don't even remember when I learned to read. I learned to read very early. I loved books. One year after my father died, the members of the church decided that my mother would work as the janitor of Avery Chapel Church and that since the new minister had his own home, we would live in the parsonage.

So for a couple of years, maybe three years, I lived in the church parsonage, the Methodist parsonage, and there were plenty of books there that had been left. Some of these were novels. I remember reading Rex Beach, such people, and then at some point a black Episcopalian priest went to the library to work on some sermons and was told it was against the law, that it was segregated. And he said, "Who says so?" and they looked around and discovered there was no ordinance refusing admittance to Negroes. It was just a custom. So immediately they rented a couple of rooms, big rooms out in the Slaughter Building, and put in some shelves, and dumped all kinds of books in there, and appointed a lady as librarian. So we had a library and I quickly began to read through those books, along with a few of my friends.

Incidentally, last year, last fall, I got word that the city council had voted six to one to name a new branch library after me.

Q: Is that right. Did they follow through with that?

A: Well, they are going to. They haven't broken the ground, but we had a letter from the mayor recently saying that when the ceremony comes he wants us to come out, and of course we will, if at all possible.

But I'm saying this puts things in perspective. I should also say that as early as the fifties when I went home after publishing a book, I was given a reception in the big downtown library and the segregation was over. One reason that segregation and certain of its aspects ended so easily in Oklahoma was that it was in the Deep South. [Segregation] hadn't been practical so long, nor were there the social structures that would support it in the same way.

Q: Did you know Roscoe Dunjee, the editor of the *Black Dispatch* [a black weekly newspaper in Oklahoma City]?

A: I knew Roscoe Dunjee. I used to sell the papers when I was going barefoot and I used to talk with him a lot. It never occurred to me that I would be a writer or anything, so I didn't know him or hadn't been interested in him in that way. I was a musician, I thought. But I used to see him daily. He used to come across the street to Randolph's Drugstore where I worked. I jerked sodas and was the delivery boy.

Dunjee was very well known for his attitudes, his forthrightness, and his leadership. He was one of those men in the neighborhood—the community we would call it now—who was always stressing the political. He was a constitutionalist and understood the possibilities of the Constitution long before the forties and fifties, when we got around to tackling the thing head-on. His paper would carry on editorial controversy with the writers and editors of the *Daily Oklahoma* and the *Oklahoma City Times*.

He was always involved in politics and he was always writing editorials about the historical implications of events and the historical background of the black struggle. So he was very important to me in terms of putting events into perspective.

He was an example of a man who did not approach events in some sort of stylized, second-class citizen's way but who spoke to the main issue, always fighting for us but seeing that his responsibility went far beyond the racial aspect. What was good for Oklahoma was good for us.

He had a tremendous impact because he was very articulate and a number of white people read what he had to say. He was handicapped because for a good while Negroes did not have the vote in Oklahoma.

Interview with Ralph Ellison

Arlene Crewdson and Rita Thomson / 1974

This interview was conducted on WTTW, Channel 11 and appears in "Invisibility: A Study of the Works of Toomer, Wright, and Ellison" by Arlene Crewdson, Master's Thesis Loyola University 1974. Reprinted by permission.

Crewdson: In an interview called "The Art of Fiction," you said the book, *Invisible Man,* was divided into three main divisions with three minor sections in each division and that each one was begun by an important letter or paper of some type. Would you perhaps clarify that a little bit for us?

Ellison: It has been a long time since I have read the book, but the first paper would have been his diploma from high school which was connected with his entrance into college. And the second would have been the paper on which his Brotherhood name was scribbled. No, I am out of sequence. The second name would have been involved with those letters which Dr. Bledsoe gave him to present to people in the North and the third, of course, would have been his Brotherhood name.

Thomson: Then each time he has faith in one of these letters or one of these pieces of paper, then eventually he is disillusioned. His faith is completely torn apart.

Ellison: Yes, each time he allows someone else to define him, to give him an identity or an identity which he tries to assume, he runs into difficulty. And so in the last chapter when he falls into the darkness, he becomes aware of this when he starts burning all these papers to make light for himself.

Thomson: And the paper then that is the anonymous threatening letter isn't really one of the major papers because it doesn't give an identity, because it is a different . . .

Ellison: Well, let's try not to make this too neat; when you are giving an interview you don't always remember how many tags

This interview was conducted by Arlene Crewdson and Rita Thomson on WTTW, Channel 11.

and errors you leave as you structure your plot. Yes, the anonymous letter was significant and perhaps no less than these others because always it has to do with identity and the misconception or the misconceiving of identities.

Crewdson: May I ask you, did you start out, sir, with this idea or did it develop as you went on writing?

Ellison: Oh, I started out by writing a phrase, "I'm an invisible man." I spent the next five years discovering what I meant by it. I did make an outline, a conceptual outline; I knew certain incidents, but as I put it together I discovered that certain things began to happen which seemed to have no direct connection with the concept which lay behind me. And that's part of the excitement of trying to write something.

Thomson: In one of the interviews, "The Art of Fiction," when you were talking about *Invisible Man,* you mentioned something about the ritual understructure of fiction, and you said that this helps to guide the creation of characters. I was wondering if you could explain to us, perhaps, what you mean by the sense of ritual in the book.

Ellison: Ritual is a sense of the correct way of doing things. It is usually involved with a myth which explains the actions. I do not want to get too technical here because I'm not competent to do so. But it becomes detached in society, and we have many, many rites, some comic, some quite serious. They are connected with taboos; they are connected with growing up in some way and keeping alive, and sometimes they are connected with intimidating. So I became aware after studying Eliot's use of Ulysses and other myths in his poetry that perhaps I could do the same thing if I studied the significance of little social forms which we usually engage ourselves in but not too consciously. The battle royal, for instance, is a form which turns up among Boy Scouts; among all peoples, and has no necessary unpleasant violence concerned with it. But it is, if you know a little anthropology, a way of introducing the young to the chaos which is implicit in darkness, and they fight their way through. And, of course, a boy who wins is somehow heroic because he has gone through the darkness; he has fought his enemies, opposing forces, blindfolded so he comes out of it. In the South the battle royal is benignly, or it used to be benignly fought

among Negro kids themselves. But it is when the racial thing
enters, the concept of white superiority and the concept of, well the
notion of a hierarchy based upon race is introduced, that this turns
into something else, and at that point I thought it did tell us
something quite meaningful about the structure of racial relationships.

Crewdson: If I can go back to that same interview, you said in
that that action is the thing, that what we are and what we do and
what we don't do is what is important. And you went on to say,
". . . the problem for me is to get from A to B to C and my
anxiety about transitions greatly prolonged the writing of my
work." Now, for you as a writer, do you feel therefore that the
plot is perhaps the basic element to work with and maybe the
characters come out of the plot?

Ellison: No, I think that as you can conceive a character as
implicit in the scene, or if you conceive a character in any sort of
active way, in any situation where he has to act, then the scene
becomes implicit. Kenneth Burke has a pentab which he uses as a
critical instrument; he calls it act, scene, agent, agency and purpose
and they are very useful when you want to analyze the relationship between background, character, scene, mood, agents and so
on. I am, in a strange kind of way, and I don't want to give myself
airs, an Aristotelian because I think in drama it is character which
is determined by plot, and this gets us back to the notion of rites.
Rites are there before character; rites are there to form and to test
character and I believe speaking abstractly that this is the way I
want my fiction to work.

Thomson: One of the very interesting things, too, I think in the
book are what you called surrealistic elements, impressionistic
elements in the book, and I think in the interview you said that the
part that takes place in the College really is very naturalistic
because it is extremely appropriate and then from the time of the
Brotherhood some scenes become very surrealistic, and I wonder
if you could explain to us what you mean by this and how you have
used it?

Ellison: Well, I thought I was just being true to reality. I was not
trying to impose the theories of surrealism upon my plot. In those
days the time, remember this has been fifteen years ago, I assumed

that when a Negro character moved across the Mason-Dixon line,
he was not simply taking a trip geographically but he was moving
through certain historical stratifications of time. He was moving
from a primarily rural environment with all of the slow paced tempo
of the South, and then when he moved North he was snatched up into
a more rapid tempo, a tempo not so closely related to the seasons
but to the Stock Market, to the existence of certain kinds of
highways, a density of automobiles and so on. Thus, he did move
into something which seemed to be surrealistic but which is only
a normal American juxtaposition of times and places and elements
from the past. I might add here I was in New Orleans recently
and was talking to a young friend, and he said, "Ellison, I thought
that you were just playing around with surrealism until the other
day, and I looked at television, and I saw all of that garbage,
millions of tons of garbage, on the streets of New York." So I
understood what you meant. It's not surreal at all; it's just what
happens in a society which is so rapid and so fluid and so given to
juxtaposing of diverse elements in peoples and so on. Customs,
for instance.

Crewdson: This point struck me toward the end of the book for
example, on page 112 the protagonist states, "The day's events
flowed past. Trueblood, Mr. Norton, Dr. Bledsoe and Golden Day
swept around my mind in a mad surreal whirl." I wondered as I read
that later on if you weren't trying to make that artistically work in
the way that we saw how he saw it in this world?

Ellison: That was the challenge and, yes, that is what I tried to
do to subject his particular consciousness to this multiplicity of
time levels, of ritual levels and of manners because he was always
challenged, as I think most of us Americans are challenged, to be
very, very conscious of where we are and that's not an easy thing
to do, and I do believe that knowing where we are, has a lot to do
with our knowing who we are and this gets back to the theme, I
hope, of identity with which he was sometimes involved.

Crewdson: I think you make the point very well at the end where
he meets Mr. Norton, and he tells him you don't know where you are
and if you don't know where you are, how do you know who
you are.

Ellison: Yes.

Thomson: That's the part of the epilogue, and I wonder if you
would tell us about the purpose of the prologue and the epilogue.
Did you feel that they sort of pointed the reader in a direction?
They are quite different, of course, from the rest of the story but
they seem to sum up so beautifully the theme.

Ellison: Well, actually they're the first parts written. Not all the
epilogue, but I conceived and felt, . . . because I don't want to
make this too conscious a process, but I wrote the first line and
then I was involved. As I became more conscious of what I had to do
I felt it necessary to prepare the reader through the prologue,
through the pitch, through the tonality, through the general crazi-
ness of the sensibility of the narrator for the kinds of experience
which would be unfolded as the novel progressed. So, then when I
got to the end, I had to find a way of rounding it out, so I just made
an envelope, and it was to work that way, I think, because for all my
long efforts to make this a novel, it is not really my book, it is a
memoir of this narrator, and to cut it off at some point, I had to
have the epilogue, so I just put it between the two and so it tells you
how he conceived of himself, how he came to conceive of himself,
and it ends with his falling into the hole where he would begin to
write the memoir which I call my novel but which is really
his memoir.

Crewdson: This leads to another question. Why did you choose
to write the novel as a first person "I" narration and perhaps
limited view?

Ellison: Well, for a number of reasons. I felt that I had to test my
own abilities, and I wanted to test certain theories of a writer
whom I admire very much and that was Henry James, who felt that
Dostoevski was not much of a novelist because he wrote in the
first person, and novels in the first person tend to be great baggy
monsters, and I also admired Ernest Hemingway, and he had
written two very wonderful, moving and, I think, great novels in the
first person, and so had Scott Fitzgerald and so had Melville in
Moby Dick. So I wanted to see if I could do that. Now that's one
part of it. I also felt that I could achieve certain types of intensity and
vividness if I wrote in the first person, and I also wanted to
challenge myself to see if I could create a dramatic action while
being narrated in the first person and at the same time make that an

integral part of the experience because you notice that the man
moves from someone who talks all the time (the exact reversal of
what has happened to me, I now talk all the time) but he started
out as an orator in school, and he really ends up, though he doesn't
say so, by writing a book.

Thomson: I imagine, too, that writing the book in the first person
has led so many people to ask if it is autobiographical, and I know
in "The Art of Fiction" that you say, no, it is not autobiographical.
What do you tell people when they ask about that?

Ellison: Well, I say that if they will grant me that I'm all the men
and all the women and all the children and animals and the black
people and the white people, yes, it's all me. But it has very little
to do with the factual biography of Ralph Ellison. It does have a
lot to do with the shape of his imagination.

Crewdson: On those lines, too, you said in an interview in
Harper's of March 1967, "Free one's self as a writer by actually
going in and trying to get the shape of the experience from the
writer's perspective and the writer's type of memory." Now, how
does this actually work in your case as a writer?

Ellison: Well, I was referring to the internalization of technique.
With novelists, with fiction writers, as with poets, I believe that
technique is not just an abstract set of tools of formulas, but it
becomes a way of feeling, hearing and sensing and smelling and
evoking reality. It's a way of putting the imagination to work,
moving beyond the given to one's own most intimate and hopeful
sense of human value and possibly human predicament. So that's
pretty much of what I must have been trying to say there.

Thomson: Well, I think I would like to go to the epigraphs in
Invisible Man, and ask Mr. Ellison perhaps what relation they
have to the theme of the story. The first one is from Melville,
" 'You are saved,' cried Captain Delano, more and more astonished and pained; 'you are saved: what has cast such a shadow
upon you?' " Is this to mean that the man at the end, our narrator
in the story, is saved?

Ellison: No, no, I purposely did not give the reply that Benito
Cereno gave the Captain because the answer is the Negro, and
the Negro in that sense becomes more than the African slaves, the
captured Africans, on board that ship. It becomes a matter of the

ambiguity of life and our involvement in it—indeed our involvement
in those forces which seem to oppose us or which we seem to
dominate. I was aiming for a general sense of that ambiguity and
also there is a prayer involved there. I was hoping the readers
seeing that would say maybe if we read this book with the same
quality of attention that we have read *Benito Cereno,* it will be a
better book.

Thomson: The other quote is from *Family Reunion* by T. S. Eliot,
and this one

> I tell you, it is not me you are looking at, not me you are grinning at, not
> me your confidential looks incriminate, but that other person, if
> person, you thought I was: let your necrophilia feed upon that
> carcase. . . .

Now, is this again . . . ?

Ellison: Well, yes that is calling attention to mistaken identities
and the assertion of identity which Harry was making and which
fondly I hoped this memoir of my narrator would be. You see you
didn't see me is what you were saying while you were saying this
and you will find references to that theme throughout.

Crewdson: I think something else that interested me in reading
the novel is your use of dreams very often to reveal present inner
thoughts of the characters or in some cases events that are to come.
Why did you choose to use this media, any particular reason?

Ellison: When I was about ten I went to a friend's home in
Oklahoma City—the father was a dentist and the mother a
teacher—and I came across a book called *Interpretation of Dreams,*
and I thought it was the kind of dream book that you saw around.
But that was my first contact with Freud, and I read quite a lot of
Freudian psychology, and my first job, a very temporary job,
when I came to New York, was to work with Dr. Harry Stack
Sullivan. I was his receptionist for a few months, and I also filed
case histories. And so, in glancing through the case histories of
some very famous people, I began to get an understanding of how
important dreams were. This was long before I decided to write,
but as I began to write and call upon those works which had been
so meaningful to me, I realized that I had read fairy tales far into
my teens, which was rather abnormal given the other things I was

doing, but I also have been strongly influenced by Dostoyevsky, and he has taught the novelist how to use the dream. And so, you see, there is this level where you are just having fun in seeing whether you can do what has been done, and this is the secret joy of the novelist when he can bring something off.

Thomson: One other element that you seem to use quite a bit is music in the novel, and I know you have been, of course, very interested in music yourself. Is this the reason or is it again kind of artistic experimenting?

Ellison: No, I love music but at this time when I realized I was going to write I deliberately stayed away from it. But fortunately I was writing about a milieu and a people who were intimately involved with music so I could bootleg it in.

Crewdson: Do you think there is any connection between the art of writing and the art of music?

Ellison: I think so. I think that the novel which has been most attractive to me, that is the nineteenth-century novel, moved toward tragic form and the form of the symphony. Symphonic form is basically a play upon tragic form so you have your big, your three movements, the intermixing of the tragic with the comic, the light with the solemn and so on. I should say the only form that I studied as a student both in high school and in college, was musical form. I was kind of stuck with that. Even if I hadn't been writing about Negroes I probably would have gotten it in there somewhere.

Crewdson: I would like to ask you something about a section that doesn't appear in *Invisible Man* that you published separately in a collection calling it "Out of the Hospital and Into Harlem." You mentioned in introducing the section that it was due to space that this section does not appear in the novel as we have it. Do you ever regret that, or would you like to see it in the novel?

Ellison: No, this book is no longer so much a part of my ambition. I was unhappy that I couldn't include some of the things. I guess this happens to any writer. You know you write scenes which you are just terribly taken with, but there is no place. This book did have to be shortened and rather than trying to do a mechanical cutting job, I reconceived it so "Out of the Hospital and Under the Bar" is the original version of how I managed to get the narrator out of the hospital and into Mary's house because in that version

Mary worked in the hospital and she, in my idea of what happens
to the folk Negro in Harlem, was a direct agent in his release from
this electro-mechanical device.

Crewdson: And that was the reason for the use of the folk medicine?

Ellison: Yes, yes, of course. I feel that even today much of what
seems strange to us about the eruption in our big cities among
Negroes is surprising because we don't really know enough about
the South, not only the black South but the white South, and we don't
know the folkways. I'm hoping that the televising of the funeral of
Martin Luther King gave millions of non-southerners an opportunity to see the mixture of lifestyles and cultural forms which are
present and very much a part of the Southern Negro community.

Thomson: You said, too, in publishing this middle section that
you had left out, that you felt that it could stand by itself on its
own, and it struck me when I read this that I think perhaps other
parts of the book could also stand by themselves such as the riot
scene at the end of the novel. Do you think parts of it really form
small wholes?

Ellison: I don't think so. I rather hoped that they would, but you
know you are ambivalent about this because a tightly structured
work should not allow for cutting. You could just have samples; you
could not have fully rounded actions. I wish I could interest my
editor to looking into that file of stuff that I cut out to see whether
there wouldn't be something to stand alone. But if you want to create
an organic form, you have to take the disadvantages which means
you can't chop it up so easily and make extra money by publishing
a separate section.

Crewdson: I have one other question, too, concerning what you
said in introducing that section. Talking about the hero, you wrote in
parenthesis, "the hero who is somewhat of a liar," and I was
interested in knowing did you intend him to be so in the novel or
was this statement the result of a later change in your attitude
toward the protagonist?

Ellison: I felt that the reader was getting a report from his point
of view. That's what you have to be alert to whenever you read fiction
in the first person. Ford Maddox Ford wrote a very wonderful novel
which turned, I mean, on the fact that the narrator was not being

truthful, and when we look at this man you have to question just
what he is reporting. You see he is a bit of a fool. If he had been
a little bit more alert he wouldn't have had to go through all those
repetitions of the same pattern. Of course, I would not have had
a book to write either.

Thomson: In addition you said that the hero's invisibility is not a
matter of being seen but a refusal to run the risk of his own
humanity, and so this at the same time seems as though society
isn't to blame, and I think in the book that society, too, makes it
very difficult for him to have his own humanity. Isn't that part of
the theme? He may be at fault, but, I think that the book said
society is at fault too.

Ellison: Yes, *too*, as long as we don't make it all one way because
wherever you are born, under whatever circumstance and whoever you are, whatever color you are, you do have an obligation to
try to make your way because they are not going to grease the skids
for you. You still have to find ways of asserting your own humanity.
Of course, society is much against it, and his great fault was
saying or was trying to say "yes" too often to the society, but not
"yes" in that ambiguous way that his grandfather was advising
him but just "yes, let me be—I am willing to do the right thing. You
want me to be good; I'll be good, and I'll advance." But this
didn't help him very much.

Crewdson: You also said in the *Harper's* interview that this
invisible man has been characterized by what the sociologists
term "high visibility." Now, not being a sociologist, what did you
mean by that?

Ellison: Sociologists used to say—for example Park and Burgess
published right here in Chicago, you know, which is one of the
centers for American sociology—used to say that the great problem
of the American Negro is caused because of his high visibility. After
all, we have more pigment than most people so if you put us in a
crowd you can always pick us out. It's not so easy anymore
but. . . .

Thomson: Do you agree with that definition of him?

Ellison: It wasn't whether I agreed or disagreed. I saw it as
ironic, and I could play upon it, you see. If Negroes were all as
white and as blue-eyed as Danes, and they insisted upon being

Negroes, the same things would happen to us. The racism is a source of great political power and of great psychological security to people who need a victim, people who must feel that there are some people who are not so fortunate as they are. So, it becomes pretty complex business.

Crewdson: Also, when you speak about the fact that one of the problems concerning his withdrawal from society was that this humanity involved a type of guilt, could you explain that in terms of the invisible man?

Ellison: No, I don't understand that question.

Crewdson: Well, let's put it this way. He said he was irresponsible in the beginning but he accepts a possible social responsibility in the end. Is this where he sees the guilt in himself? He is not as responsible as he can be?

Ellison: Is this the beginning of the prologue?

Crewdson: Yes, in the prologue and the epilogue.

Ellison: Well, the prologue is the end, you see. So he is teasing; he is preparing the reader by this time for a kind of responsibility which is the responsibility of the man who writes a memoir not of the boy who went through the experience out of which he wrote the memoir. He was saying that this is the only way that he could make a statement and thus be responsible, and he had to start with fundamental things by asserting the complexity of this personality as based upon the complexity of his experience.

Thomson: Perhaps I should talk about some of the imagery and symbols that you used in the book. We mentioned the music, I think, that runs through it. Too, it seems that you use quite a lot of animal imagery in the book, hostile animals like the bear.

Crewdson: And, the dog imagery for instance, did you purposely choose animal symbols that were hostile?

Ellison: No. I didn't purposely choose them. Well, not because they were hostile, but, I can't really account for some of the things which go on there. Jack the Bear—Jack the Rabbit—are ambiguous animal images. They usually are connected with folklore, and they always appear in the context of where he has moved backwards or forward to his folk tradition. So they are not necessarily, for him, antagonistic and when the young man who is pushing the paper cart confronts him with the dog, I think he is reminding him. He's a kind of messenger such as you get in Greek tragedy who points the eras of the plot and reminds the hero in an ambiguous way of the time of day or the tonality that experience is turning into.

Crewdson: Isn't the man with the yams something like that?

Ellison: No. This is the man with the blueprints.

Crewdson: But isn't the man with the yams also a messenger?

Ellison: The man with the yams, that was food, and this was a moment of nostalgia and self-acceptance which also announced a turn in his approach to his experience. I use every and anything I can.

Thomson: Some of the other things that, too, seem to have more meaning and become sort of symbolic, I think, are the bank that he finds in the room and then carries with him and can't seem to get rid of, and the dolls that Tod is selling. Would you say these are symbols?

Ellison: Well, they are symbols; they are ambivalent symbols, but when Tod begins to sell those dolls after his strong hope and investment in the Brotherhood, he is turning against that part of himself and trying to kill it off. You have seen these figures, haven't you? They are real burlesque golliwogg types, and if you put dark glasses on them you might have something quite the contemporary. But I think that is what my imagination was trying to get at, this rejection of a role which had been assumed in great hope and then released, feeling that this had been an act of betrayal.

Crewdson: Also, I think the use of biblical symbols is very interesting. I am sure you intended it to appear as such, such as the campus and the Garden of Eden and the apple on Trueblood's step.

Ellison: Was there an apple there? I had forgotten.

Crewdson: Yes, there was.

Ellison: Well, so much of this just comes into the imagination because of the density of the western literary and religious tradition. All these symbols have passed back and forth for years and years, and you don't have to be conscious when you put them down; you only have to be conscious as you structure them.

Thomson: I wonder too about Trueblood. What significance does he have? Does he tend to sort of be symbolic, too, in the story?

Ellison: Well, Trueblood involved himself in incest, which is always a tragic action, and the point was, involving himself, he accepted the consequences of his act and tried to act manly about it, but his tragedy became a kind of entertainment for Mr. Norton and an embarrassment for the narrator. I put it up to the reader to take his own choice as to the quality of Trueblood's action, and I am hoping that more and more readers will understand there was a little bit of the hero in this fellow, who was right in the center of the context of irony in which the whole action of that part of the book unfolded.

Crewdson: You mentioned in one interview you were surprised the interviewer didn't see the humor in the work, and I think that we can see the humor in it. I wondered if you had any particular passage you enjoyed?

Ellison: I rather enjoyed when he goes into the Chthonian Hotel to this meeting and the man wants him to sing, and he can't sing. But the overall business of running so hard to get somewhere and always being sent on these fools' journeys, errands rather, amused me and in a wry sort of way. The humor is not unmixed, but I guess if I had longer to think about it, I could think of other specific passages which amused me.

Thomson: Well, we're running out of time. Maybe we have time for one short question. I know you were influenced by many authors. I wonder if just on the spur of the moment you could say whom you would advise a young person today who wanted to write to read? What writers would you advise them to read?

Ellison: Well, I would advise them to read as many good writers as they possibly could. Writing comes out of earlier writing; it doesn't come out of feeling in any immediate way. It's an expression of a sensibility which has been shaped by the mastery of certain artistic skills. And so I would say read Melville, read André Malraux, read Hemingway, read Mark Twain, read Raymond Chandler.

Thomson & Crewdson: Thank you very much, Mr. Ellison. It has been our pleasure.

Ellison: Thank you.

"A Completion of Personality": A Talk with Ralph Ellison

John Hersey / 1974

From *Ralph Ellison: A Collection of Critical Essays*, edited by John Hersey. Copyright © 1974. Used by permission of the publisher, Prentice Hall/A Division of Simon & Schuster, Englewood Cliffs, N.J. The following is the version of the interview that appeared in *Speaking For You* ed. Kimberly Benston.

One of the most significant views of the work of Ralph Ellison happens to be his own. He is, as he himself says, a slow worker, and over the course of the years, while he was writing away at his second novel—and while Invisible Man *paradoxically refused to drop out of sight—Ellison granted a number of interviews, each of which offered some telling comments on the situation of a novelist who had been thrust into more gnawing fame than most writers would want in their own time. He reproduced three of the interviews in* Shadow and Act. *Two other valuable ones are noted in the bibliography of this book, and the vivid picture of Ellison by a younger writer, James Alan McPherson, also in this collection, originally included an exchange of letters between the two authors, in which Ellison further elaborated his predicament.*

For predicament it has been, and what is forced upon a reader of these interviews is a sense that the polemic-versus-artistic argument—the argument, as old as art itself, over the question: "What use has art?"—hounds Ellison perhaps more than any other first-rank novelist of our time, unless it be Alexander Solzhenitsyn. That argument dominates several of the essays in this book, and it hums in harmonic overtones over the rest of them.

It occurred to me as I assembled and read these various views that in the din of this argument we had never had a chance to hear much from Ellison about his attitude toward the actuality of his craft, about the processes of his creative ordeal, about what he thinks actually happens *when he writes, about the deep familial sources of his ways of being and doing, about how his mind works through problems of shape and dream and sound, and about the particular, idiosyncratic inner workings of his art which may have been molded by his existential past. Although it is entitled "The Art of Fiction," not even the* Paris Review *interview, reprinted in* Shadow and Act, *goes beneath the surface of his struggle to achieve an art worth arguing about as much as his has been.*

And so, on a weekend that Ellison and his wife spent in my home, we talked late into one night about all these matters, and in the cool light of the next morning we had a conversation in which Ellison, with extraordinary finish and economy, and yet with a fabulist's deceptive randomness, too, synthesized and compressed his views of his labor of choice. Here is what we said:

Hersey: You were talking about your mother last night, and as you talked I wondered how much she had been a force in moving you toward your calling as a writer, and even in supplying materials that you have drawn on.

Ellison: She certainly had something to do with encouraging my interest in reading. She had no idea that I was going to become a writer, or if she did, she had more insight into me than I had into myself, because I thought I was going to be a musician. My mother always encouraged me to do *something,* and to be good at it—she insisted upon that.

It was my father who wanted me to be a writer. I didn't discover that until many years later—he died when I was three—until after I had written *Invisible Man* and talked with an older cousin, who told me that my father used to say, "I'm raising this boy to be a poet." Of course he had given me the name [Ralph Waldo].

But my mother did feed my passion for reading. She brought home books and magazines. My concern with the Picassos and Stravinskys of this world started at an earlier age than usual because she brought home *Vanity Fair.* Here was a world so far from Oklahoma City, in any expected sense, yet it was shaping my sense of what was possible. And she understood that that was what was going on.

And what I did get from my mother was an understanding of people. I was very quick-tempered and impatient, and things began to happen when I reached adolescence—and she would just talk about how people acted, what motives were, and why things were sometimes done. I remember being so outraged by something one of her friends had said that I didn't want to see her or her husband anymore. At thirteen I went to work as the husband's office boy, and this close friend of my father was so delighted with having me around that his childless wife was upset. Her reaction was to spread the word around that she suspected that I was actually her husband's child—Oh, boy! When the gossip reached me I was outraged—and not only over what it implied about my mother, but because of my love for my father. I had learned to walk at six months and had been his companion from that time until his death, and I was so far from accepting the reality of his death that I was still telling myself that any day he would reappear to take his place as the head of our family. Now I suspect that my fondness for my employer-friend and my vague awareness that he was, in fact, something of a father-figure added to my shock and outrage. At any rate, when I went to my mother about this matter she proceeded to calm me down.

"Well now," she said, "you should understand what's happening. You remember your daddy and you've been around and seen a few people and have some idea how they act. You've been working in drugstores and barbershops and at that office and since you've been around . . . and . . . as much as you have, you must know that she's crazy. So use your head. She doesn't have to be put in an institution, but you have to understand and accept the fact that she isn't responsible."

It was a rather shocking notion for me and I didn't want to surrender my anger, but I realized that my mother was right. What's more, I realized that very often I could save myself a lot of wear and tear with people if I just learned to understand them.

Beyond that, although she was religious, my mother had a great tolerance for the affairs of the world which had nothing to do with religion, and I think that that helped me to sort of balance things out, so to speak. The great emphasis in my school was upon classical music, but such great jazz musicians as Hot Lips Paige, Jimmy Rushing, and Lester Young were living in Oklahoma City, and through her allowing me to attend public dances and to maintain a certain friendship with some of them, even though she watched what I was doing, she made it possible to approach the life of the

Negro community there with some sense of its wholeness instead
of trying to distort it into some hoped-for religion-conceived perfection. As it turned out, the perfection, the artistic dedication which
helped me as a writer, was not so much in the classical emphasis as
within the jazz itself.

She also helped me to escape the limitations of trying to impose
any ingroup class distinctions upon the people of my community. We
were very poor, but my father had been a small businessman who
sold ice and coal to both whites and blacks, and since he and my
mother were pioneers in a young state, my mother knew some of
the city's leaders; they were my father's friends and remained as my
mother's after his death. So she didn't strive to be part of the social
leadership of the black community; that was left to the wives of
professional men, to teachers and preachers. Her background and
attitudes were such that all kinds of people came into the house,
or we visited their houses. That was one of the enriching parts of
my experience, because I knew people who went right back to
the farm and plantation, along with those who had gone to college
and medical school. Thus, my sense of their stories and lifestyles, and so on, was never very far from mind. My mother had
grown up on a Georgia plantation herself, she was a farm girl; and
then she left and went to live in Atlanta. It gave me a sense of a past
which was far from narrow.

She liked to talk. She never allowed me to lose the vividness of
my father, and she told me all kinds of things that he had done—that
he had run away from his own father in South Carolina when he
was quite young, and had become a professional soldier, and had
been in Cuba and in the Philippines and in China. He was with our
troops that fought against the Boxer Rebellion. Afterwards, he and
his brother had operated a candy kitchen in Chattanooga. He had
also operated a restaurant—always trying to get at something—
and then had become a construction foreman; that was how they
came West to Oklahoma.

There was also her overt and explicit concern with political
conditions. There was never a time when I was not aware of what
these were all about. When I was in college, my mother broke a
segregated-housing ordinance in Oklahoma City, and they were
throwing her in jail, and the NAACP would get her out, and they'd

come back and throw her in jail again. This went on until my brother beat up one of the white inspectors, then she decided that it was about time to get out of that situation before he got himself shot. She had that kind of forthrightness, and I like to think that that was much more valuable than anything literary that she gave me.

Hersey: The creative drive seems always to have been strong in you, ever since childhood. You said once that you couldn't remember a time when you hadn't wanted to make something—a one-tube radio, a crystal set, a toy; a little later you had an urge to compose music. Where do you think this drive came from?

Ellison: I don't know where it comes from. Maybe it had something to do with my father's working as a construction foreman, building buildings. It certainly came from some of the boys that I grew up with, as a child. They were always *doing* things. I always admired the guys who could make things, who could draw. This was something that gave me a great deal of pleasure.

But maybe the desire to write goes back to a Christmas gift. One Christmas my mother gave me—I must have been five—a little roll-top desk and a chair, not a swivel chair but a little straight chair, oak, and a little toy typewriter. I had forgotten that. We were living in the parsonage of the old A.M.E. Church, Avery Chapel, which the leaders of the congregation turned over to my mother after the new minister turned out to have his own home. "Why don't you be the janitress of the church and live in the parsonage?" they said. And we did, and that's where I got the desk and the little typewriter. I was also given a chemistry set. Now this might have been unusual in such relatively uneducated families—I think my mother went to the eighth grade in school—but she felt that these were the kinds of things that her boys should have. She was also very explicit, as we grew older, about our economic condition. We knew why we could not have a bicycle, why we could not have this, that, or the other. She explained that we could not have such things because she didn't have the money, and we had to accept that fact. So what did we do? We learned to do other things. Instead of playing with store-bought toys, you made your own. You fished and hunted, you listened to music, you danced and you spent a great amount of time reading and dreaming over books.

When Mr. Mead, next door, taught me the fundamentals of playing an old brass alto horn, my mother bought me a pawnshop cornet. She could afford that, and owning the instrument made it possible for me to acquire enough skill to get into the school band. So she did what she could, and in addition to encouraging my interest in reading she encouraged my interest in music, and so on.

But the desire to make something out of my imagination and to experiment was constant. In one story of mine there is an incident taken from life, where my brother and I took baby chickens and made little parachutes and got up on top of the chicken house and dropped them down. The lady next door told my mother, and we caught hell for that. We didn't kill the chickens, understand, we just floated them down. We did that, you see, because we had learned to take iron taps and tie strings to them and then attach the strings to pieces of cloth. When we threw these into the air we'd get a parachute effect and imagine that the taps were parachutists. We just took it a step further.

Hersey: What would you say was the starting point for your new novel?

Ellison: I guess it started with the idea of an old man being so outraged by his life that he goes poking around in the cellar to find a forgotten coffin, which he had bought years before to insure against his possible ruin. He discovers that he has lived so long that the coffin is full of termites, and that even the things he had stored in the coffin have fallen apart. Somehow, this said something to my imagination and got me started. You can see that it could go in *any* direction. But then it led to the other idea, which I wrote first, of a little boy being placed in a coffin, in a ritual of death and transcendence, celebrated by a Negro evangelist who was unsure whether he was simply exploiting the circus sideshow shock set off by the sight of a child rising up out of a coffin, or had hit upon an inspired way of presenting the sacred drama of the Resurrection. In my mind all of this is tied up in some way with the significance of being a Negro in America and at the same time with the problem of our democratic faith as a whole. Anyway, as a product of the

imagination it's like a big sponge, maybe, or a waterbed, with a lot
of needles sticking in it at various points. You don't know what is
being touched, where the needles are going to end up once you get
them threaded and penetrated, but somehow I kept trying to tie those
threads together and the needle points pressing home without letting
whatever lies in the center leak out.

Hersey: How soon after *Invisible Man* was published [1952] did
you start working on the new novel?

Ellison: I was pretty depleted by *Invisible Man*, so I didn't start
on another book immediately. I played around with various ideas
and spent some time trying to salvage material I had edited out of
Invisible Man. It was in Rome, during 1956, that I began to think
vaguely about this book and conceived the basic situation, which
had to do with a political assassination; this was involved with the
other patterns—the coffin business.

Hersey: This was before the Kennedys and King were assassi-
nated, of course.

Ellison: Yes, this was before. Almost eight years before. One of
the things which really chilled me—slowed down the writing—was
that eruption of assassinations, especially the first. Because, you
see, much of the mood of this book was conceived as comic. Not that
the assassination was treated comically, but there is humor involved, and that was rather chilling for me, because suddenly life
was stepping in and imposing itself upon my fiction. Anyway, I
managed to keep going with it, I guess because there was nothing
else to do. I know that it led me to try to give the book a richer
structuring, so that the tragic elements could contain the comic
and the comic the tragic, without violating our national pieties—if
there are any left. Americans have always been divided in their
pieties, but today there is such a deliberate flaunting of the pieties
and traditions—of others, anyway—that it's become rather difficult to distinguish what is admissible from that which is inadmissi-
ble. Even the flag and motherhood are under attack.

Hersey: With such fast-moving reality so close at hand, how
much in control of your fictional characters can you feel that
you are?

Ellison: Once a logic is set up for a character, once he begins to
move, then that which is implicit within him tends to realize itself,

and for you to discover the *form* of the fiction, you have to go where
he takes you, you have to follow him. In the process you change your
ideas. You remember, Dostoyevsky wrote about eight versions of a
certain scene in *The Brothers Karamazov,* and in some instances
the original incidents were retained but the characters who performed them were changed. I find that happens with me. I get to the
point where something has to be done and discover that it isn't
logical for the character who started out to do it, to do it; and
suddenly another character pops up. In this book there is an
instance wherein McIntyre has to interview the man who burns
his Cadillac. This man is being held in the observation cell of a
hospital because the authorities believe that a Negro who burns
his own Cadillac has to be crazy. So for McIntyre to see the man
there has to be an intermediary—so suddenly I found myself
dealing with a new character, a Negro employed by the hospital,
who gets McIntyre past the barriers and to the car-burner. This
fellow wasn't foreseen; he simply appeared to help me get on with
the form.

Hersey: About motive—what gives you the psychic energy to
take on a massive work and keep at it for a very long time?

Ellison: I guess it is the writing itself. I am terribly stubborn, and
once I get engaged in that kind of project, I just have to keep
going until I finally make something out of it. I don't know what the
something is going to be, but the process is one through which I make
a good part of my own experience meaningful. I don't mean in any
easy autobiographical sense, but the matter of drawing actual
experience, thought, and emotion together in a way that creates an
artifact through which I can reach other people. Maybe that's
vanity; I don't know. Still I believe that fiction does help create
value, and I regard this as a very serious—I almost said "sacred"—function of the writer.

Psychic energy? I don't know, I think of myself as kind of lazy.
And yet, I do find that working slowly, which is the only way I
seem able to work—although I write fast much of the time—the
problem is one of being able to receive from my work that sense
of tension, that sense of high purpose being realized, that keeps me
going. This is a crazy area that I don't understand—none of the
Freudian explanations seem adequate.

Hersey: As to the short range, you used a phrase last night that interested me. You said you wanted to keep the early morning free "in case the night before had generated something that could be put to good use." What did you mean by that?

Ellison: I never know quite what has gone on in my subconscious in the night, I dream vividly, and all kinds of things happen; by morning they have fallen below the threshold again. But I like to feel that whatever takes place becomes active in some way in what I do at the typewriter. In other words, I believe that a human being's life is of a whole, and that he lives the full twenty-four hours. And if he is a writer or an artist, what happens during the night feeds back, in some way, into what he does consciously during the day—that is, when he is doing that which is self-achieving, so to speak. Part of the pleasure of writing, as well as the pain, is involved in pouring into that thing which is being created all of what he cannot understand and cannot say and cannot deal with, or cannot even admit, in any other way. The artifact is a completion of personality.

Hersey: Do you experience anything like daydreaming or dreaming when you are writing? Do you feel that the writing process may involve a somewhat altered state of consciousness in itself?

Ellison: I think a writer learns to be as conscious about his craft as he can possibly be—not because this will make him absolutely lucid about what he does, but because it prepares the stage for structuring his daydreaming and allows him to draw upon the various irrational elements involved in writing. You know that when you begin to structure literary forms you are going to have to play variations on your themes, and you are going to have to make everything vivid, so that the reader can see and hear and feel and smell, and, if you're lucky, even taste. All that is on a conscious level and very, very important. But then, once you get going, strange things occur. There are things in *Invisible Man,* for instance, that I can't *imagine* my having consciously planned. They materialized as I worked consciously at other things. Take three of the speeches: the speech made at the eviction, the funeral address in Mount Morris Park, and the one that Barbee made in chapel. Now, I realized consciously, or I *discovered* as I wrote, that I was playing variations on what Otto Rank identified as the myth of the birth and death of the hero. So in the rewriting that conscious knowledge, that insight, made it possible to come back and add elements to the design which I had written myself into under the passion of telling a story.

What should also be said in this connection is that somewhere—it doesn't have to be right in the front of the mind, of the consciousness—writers, like other artists, are involved in a process of comparative culture. I looked at the copy of *The Lower Depths* on the table there this morning, and I remembered how much of Gorki I had read, and how I was always—not putting his characters into blackface, but finding equivalents for the experience he depicted; the equivalents for turns of phrase, for parables and proverbs, which existed within the various backgrounds that I knew. And I think that something of that goes on when a conscious writer goes about creating a fiction. It's part of his workshop, his possession of the culture of the form in which he works.

Hersey: You once said that it took you a long time to learn how to adapt myth and ritual into your work. Faulkner speaks of a "lumber room in the subconscious," where old things are kept. How do you get at the sources of these things deep down in your mind?

Ellison: I think I get at them through sheer work, converting incidents into patterns—and also by simply continuing at a thing when I don't seem to be getting anywhere. For instance, I wrote a scene in which Hickman is thinking about the difficulty of communicating with someone as constituting a "wall"; he thinks this as he is drifting off to sleep. Well, later in my work I suddenly realized that the damn wall had turned up again in another form. And that's when that voice in my unconscious finally said, "Hey, *this* is what you've been getting at." And looking back, I saw that I had worked up a little pattern of these walls. What the unconscious mind does is to put all manner of things into juxtaposition. The conscious mind has to provide the logical structure of narrative and incident through which these unconscious patterns can be allowed to radiate by throwing them into artful juxtaposition on the page.

Hersey: Do you, as some writers do, have a sense of standing in a magic circle when you write?

Ellison: To the extent that unexpected things occur, that characters say things or see things which, for all my attempts to be conscious and to work out of what I call a conceptual outline, are suddenly just *there*. That *is* magical, because such things seem to emerge out of the empty air. And yet, you know that somehow the dreams, emotions, ironies, and hidden implications of your material often find ways of making themselves manifest. You work to make them reveal themselves.

Hersey: Do you, when you are writing, sometimes find yourself so totally engaged by a character that you are carried away outside yourself by *his* feelings—are literally beside yourself?

Ellison: I find myself carried away and emotionally moved, sometimes quite unexpectedly, and my tendency is to distrust it, feeling that perhaps I'm being sentimental, being caught in a situation which I am not adequately transforming into art. So I put it aside and wait awhile, maybe months, and then go back, and if it still works after I've examined it as well as I can, as objectively as I can, I then perhaps read it to Fanny, and if she doesn't indicate that it's slobbering sentimentality, in bad taste, or just poorly achieved—then I leave it in.

Hersey: Would you say that, by and large, when you have had these surges of feeling the writing does hold up in the long run?

Ellison: Sometimes it does, sometimes it doesn't. I won't be able to say about this book until it has been read by enough objective readers. I won't be able to judge until then because it has some crazy developments.

I found myself writing a scene in which Hickman and Wilhite, his deacon, go into a strange house in Washington, and find a bunch of people in the hallway who are very upset because the police won't tell them what has happened in the apartment of one of their neighbors. Then one of the women goes hysterical and pretty soon she's outraging the crowd by talking about the most personal matters as she addresses herself to a bewildered Wilhite and Hickman. Not only was I shocked to discover myself writing this un-planned scene, but I still have questions about how it functions. Yet, for all its wild, tragicomic emotion—there it is! Now when your material takes over like that you are really being pushed. Thus, when this woman started confessing, she forced *me* to think about

Hickman's role as minister on a different level; I mean on the
theological level, which was something I hadn't planned, since I
wasn't writing an essay but a novel. Finally, Hickman came to my
aid by recognizing that the woman had been unfolding a distorted
and highly personalized dream-version of the immaculate birth. To
me she sounded merely irrational and comic, but Hickman, being
a minister, forced himself to look beneath her raving, even though
she is without question a most unacceptable surrogate for the
Virgin. After that, I was forced to realize that this crazy development was really tied in with the central situation of the novel: that
of an old man searching throughout the years for a little boy who
ran away. So I guess it sprang from that magic circle you referred to,
from that amorphous level which lies somewhere between the
emotions and the intellect, between the consciousness and the
unconscious, which supports our creative powers but which we
cannot control.

Hersey: I have wondered about the ways in which your musical
experience had fed into your writing.

Ellison: My sense of form, my basic sense of artistic form, is
musical. As a boy I tried to write songs, marches, exercises in
symphonic form, really before I received any training, and then I
studied it. I listened constantly to music, trying to learn the
processes of developing a theme, of expanding and contracting and
turning it inside out, of making bridges, and working with techniques
of musical continuity, and so on. I think that basically my instinctive
approach to writing is through *sound*. A change of mood and
mode comes to me in terms of sound. That's one part of it, in the
sense of composing the architecture of a fiction.

On the other hand, one of the things I work for is to make a line
of prose *sound* right, or for a bit of dialogue to fall on the page in
the way I hear it, aurally, in my mind. The same goes for the sound
and intonation of a character's voice. When I am writing of
characters who speak in the Negro idiom, in the vernacular, it is
still a real problem for me to make their accents fall in the proper
place in the visual line.

Hersey: Which comes first for you in writing, hearing or seeing?

Ellison: I might conceive of a thing aurally, but to realize it you
have got to make it vivid. The two things must operate together. What

is the old phrase—"the planned dislocation of the senses"? That *is* the condition of fiction, I think. Here is where sound becomes sight and sight becomes sound, and where sign becomes symbol and symbol becomes sign; where fact and idea must not just be hanging there but must become a functioning part of the total design, involving itself in the reader as idea as well as drama. You do this by providing the reader with as much detail as is possible in terms of the visual *and* the aural, *and* the rhythmic—to allow him to involve himself, to attach himself, and then begin to collaborate in the creation of the fictional spell. Because you simply cannot put it all there on the page, you can only evoke it—or evoke what is already there, implicity, in the reader's head: his sense of life.

Hersey: You mentioned "making bridges" a minute ago. I remember that you once said that your anxiety about transitions greatly prolonged the writing of *Invisible Man.*

Ellison: Yes, that has continued to be something of a problem. I try to tell myself that it is irrational, but it is what happens when you're making something, and you know that you are *making* something rather than simply relating an anecdote that actually happened. But at the same time you have to strike a balance between that which you can imply and that which you must make explicit, so that the reader can follow you. One source of this anxiety comes, I think, from my sense of the variations in American backgrounds—especially as imposed by the racial situation. I can't always be certain that what I write is going to be understood. Now, this doesn't mean that I am writing for whites, but that I realize that as an American writer I have a problem of communicating across our various social divisions, whether of race, class, education, region, or religion—and much of this holds true even within my own racial group. It's dangerous to take things for granted.

This reminds me of something that happened out at a northwestern university. A young white professor said to me, "Mr. Ellison, how does it feel to be able to go to places where most Negroes can't go?" Before I could think to be polite I answered, "What you mean is: 'How does it feel to be able to go places where most *white* men can't go?" He was shocked and turned red, and I was embarrassed; nevertheless, it was a teaching situation so I told him

the truth. I wanted him to understand that individuality is still
operative beyond the racial structuring of American society. And
that, conversely, there are many areas of black society that are
closed to *me* while open to certain whites. Friendship and shared
interests make the difference.

When you are writing fiction out of your individual sense of
American life it's difficult to know what to take for granted. For
instance, I don't know whether I can simply refer to an element of
decor and communicate the social values it stands for, because so
much depends upon the way a reader makes associations. I am
more confident in such matters than I was when writing *Invisible
Man,* but for such an allusion—say, to a certain type of chair or
vase or painting—to function, the reader must not be allowed to
limit his understanding of what is implied simply because the
experience you are presenting is, in its immediate sense, that of
blacks. So the writer must be aware that the reality of race conceals
a complex of manners and culture, because such matters influence
the shaping of fictional form and govern, to a large extent, the
writer's sense of proportion, and determine what he feels obligated to render as well as what he feels he can simply imply.

I had to learn, for instance, that in dramatic scenes, if you got the
reader going along with your own rhythm, you could omit any
number of explanations. You could leave great gaps, because in his
sense of urgency the reader would say, "Hell, don't waste time
telling me how many steps he walked to get there, I want to know
what he *did* once he got there!" An ellipsis was possible and the
reader would fill the gap.

Still, I have uncertainty about some of the things I'm doing, and
especially when I'm using more than one main voice, and with a
time scheme that is much more fragmented than in *Invisible Man.*
There I was using a more tidy dramatic form. This novel is
dramatic within its incidents, but it moves back and forth in time.
In such a case I guess an act of faith is necessary, a faith that if
what you are writing is of social and artistic importance and its
diverse parts are presented vividly in the light of its overall
conception, and if you *render* the story rather than just tell it, then
the reader will go along. That's a lot of "ifs," but if you can involve

him in the process his reading becomes a pleasurable act of discovery.

Hersey: Do you have in mind an image of some actualized reader to whom you are communicating as you write?

Ellison: There is no *specific* person there, but there is a sort of ideal reader, or informed persona, who has some immediate sense of the material that I'm working with. Beyond that there is my sense of the rhetorical levers within American society, and these attach to all kinds of experiences and values. I don't want to be a behaviorist here, but I'm referring to the systems of values, the beliefs and customs and sense of the past, and that hope for the future, which have evolved through the history of the Republic. These do provide a medium of communication.

For instance, the old underdog pattern. It turns up in many guises, and it allows the writer to communicate with the public over and beyond whatever the immediate issues of his fiction happen to be. That is, deep down we believe in the underdog, even though we give him hell; and this provides a rhetoric through which the writer can communicate with a reader beyond any questions of their disagreements over class values, race, or anything else. But the writer must be aware that that is what is there. At the same time, I do not think he can manipulate his readers too directly; it must be an oblique process, if for no other reason than that to do it too directly throws you into propaganda, as against that brooding, questioning stance that is necessary for fiction.

Hersey: How do literary influences make themselves felt concretely in your work? You have spoken often of Joyce, Eliot, Dostoyevsky, Hemingway, Stein, Malraux, and others as having influenced you early. How do the influences manifest themselves? How have you transformed them for your own ends?

Ellison: It is best, of course, when they don't show themselves directly, but they are there in many ways. Joyce and Eliot, for instance, made me aware of the playful possibilities of language. You look at a page of *Finnegans Wake* and see references to all sorts of American popular music, yet the context gives it an extension from the popular back to the classical and beyond. This is just something that Joyce teaches you that you can do, and you can abstract the process and apply it to a frame of reference which is

American and historical, and it can refer to class, it can refer to the fractions and frictions of color, to popular and folk culture—it can do many things.

A writer makes himself present in your work through allowing you to focus upon certain aspects of experience. Malraux's concern with the individual caught up consciously in a historical situation, a revolutionary situation, provided insights which allowed me to understand certain possibilities in the fictional material around me. From him I learned that the condition of that type of individual is essentially the same, regardless of his culture or the political climate in which he finds his existence.

Or again, some writers—say, Dostoyevsky, or even Tolstoy—will make you very much aware of what is possible in depicting a society in which class lines either are fluid or have broken down without the cultural style and values on either extreme of society being dissipated. From such writers you learn to explore the rich fictional possibilities to be achieved in juxtaposing the peasant's consciousness with that of the aristocrat and the aristocrat's with the peasant's. This insight is useful when you are dealing with American society. For years, white people went through Grand Central Station having their luggage carried by Ph.D.'s. They couldn't see the Ph.D.'s because their race and class attitudes had trained them to see only the uniforms and the dark faces, but the Ph.D.'s could see them and judged them on any number of levels. This makes for drama, and it is a drama which goes right to the core of the democratic faith. So you get your moral perception of the contradictions of American class and personality from such literature, even more, perhaps, than from psychiatry or sociology, because such novelists have always dealt with the drama of social living.

Hersey: You once had some very interesting things to say about the similarities and differences of the stances of black and Jewish writers in this country. It seems clear that Russian novelists have had a special kind of access to the deeper resources we were talking about earlier, access to primary feelings. Do you think there are particular ways in which Negro writers have had a corresponding access to those deeper resources—different in kind or degree

from that of the Jewish writer, or the white Protestant writer in
America, say, or the Russian writer, or the English writer?

Ellison: You will have to be very careful about that, because
writers are individuals, each unique in his own way. But I would think
that the access to primary feelings that the great Russian novelists
had grew out of the nature of their society and the extreme
disruption of hierarchal relationships which occurred during the
nineteenth century. Then you had a great declassed aristocracy,
with the Tsar still at the top, and an awakening peasantry at the
bottom. On one hand, society was plunging headlong into chaos,
and on the other there was a growing identification on the part of
many declassed aristocrats with the peasantry, an identification
across traditional hierarchal divisions which was sustained by the
unifying force of Russian Greek Orthodox Christianity. The fric-
tion generated by these social unities and divisions in that chaotic
scene made possible all kinds of intensities of emotion and aggra-
vations of sensibility. The belief in the Tsar as a sacred "Little
Father" remained a unifying force, but was no longer strong
enough to rationalize and impose order upon the expression of
primary emotions—class hate, greed, ambition, and so on. Such
disruption of the traditional ordering of society, as in our own
country since 1954, made for an atmosphere of irrationality, and
this created a situation of unrestrained expressiveness. Eyeballs
were peeled, nerves were laid bare, and private sensibilities were
subjected to public laceration. In fact, life became so theatrical (not
to say nightmarish) that even Dostoevski's smoking imagination
was barely able to keep a step ahead of what was actually happening
in the garrets and streets. Today, here in the United States, we
have something similar, but there's no point in my trying to explain
Russian extremism, or the genius of the great nineteenth-century
Russian novelists. Not even Dostoyevsky was able to do that.

Anyway, for all its expressiveness and chaos, the Negro American situation is something else, both in degree and source. Except
for the brief period of Reconstruction, when we helped create the
new constitutions of the southern states and attempted to restructure society so as to provide a more equal set of relationships
between the classes and races, we were *below* the threshold of
social hierarchy. Our social mobility was strictly, and violently,

limited—and in a way that neither our Christianity nor belief in
the principles of the Constitution could change. As the sociologists
say, we were indeed disadvantaged, both by law and by custom.
And yet, our actual position was ambiguous. For although we were
outside the social compact, we were existentially right in the middle
of the social drama. I mean that as servants we were right in the
bedroom, so to speak. Thus we saw things, and we understood
the difference between ideal assertions and crude realities. Much of
the rhetorical and political energy of white society went toward
proving to itself that we were not human and that we had no sense
of the refinement of human values. But this in itself pressured
you, motivated you, to make even finer distinctions, both as to
personality and value. You *had* to, because your life depended
upon it and your sense of your own humanity demanded that you
do so. You had to identify those values which were human and
preserving of your life and interests as against those which were
inhuman and destructive. So we were thrown upon our own
resources and sense of life. We were forced to define and act out
our own idea of the heights and depths of the human condition.
Because human beings cannot live in a situation where violence can
be visited upon them without any concern for justice—and in
many instances without possibility of redress—without developing
a very intense sense of the precariousness of all human life, not
to mention the frailty and arbitrariness of human institutions. So
you were forced to be existential in your outlook, and this gives a
poignancy and added value to little things and you discover the
value of modes and attitudes that are rejected by the larger
society. It also makes you terribly brutal and thick-skinned toward
some values while ultrasensitive to others.

Now this background provides the black writer with much to
write about. As fictional material it rivals that of the nineteenth-
century Russians. But to the extent that other American writers,
writers of different backgrounds, understand this material, or can
implicate it in their own experience, they too have a way into what
is currently known as "the black experience"—which I prefer to
call "the *Negro* American experience"—because for it to be worthy
of fictional treatment, worthy of art, it has to be meaningful to
others who do not share in its immediacy. I'll add that since it is

both my own and an irrevocable part of the basic experience of
the United States, *I* think that it is not only worthy but indispensable
to any profoundly *American* depiction of reality.

To repeat myself, this society has structured itself so as to be
unaware of what it owes in both the positive and negative sense to the
condition of inhumanity that it has imposed upon a great mass of its
citizens. The fact that many whites refuse to recognize this is
responsible for much of the anger erupting among young blacks
today. It makes them furious when whites respond to their complaints with, "Yes, but *I* had nothing to do with any of that," or
reply to their demands for equal opportuinty in a racially rigged
society with, "We're against a quota system because *we* made it on
our individual merits"—because this not only sidesteps a pressing
reality, but it is only partially true. Perhaps they *did* make it on
their own, but if that's true the way was made easier because
their parents did not have to contend with *my* parents, who were
ruled out of the competition. They had their troubles too, but the
relative benevolence of democracy shared by their parents, and
now by them, was paid for by *somebody* other than themselves,
and was being paid long before many of them arrived on these
shores. *We* know that as the nation's unwilling scapegoat we paid
for much of it. Nor is this knowledge a matter of saying, "Pay us
off," or saying, in the words of the old joke, "Your granddaddy
kicked my granddaddy a hundred years ago, so now I've come to
collect the debt, bend over." That's not the point. The point is
one of moral perception, the perception of the wholeness of American life and the cost of its successes and its failures. What makes
for a great deal of black fury is the refusal of many Americans to
understand that somebody paid for the nation's peace and pros-
perity in terms of blood and frustrated dreams; that somebody now
denied his proper share helped convert the raw materials into the
sophisticated gadgetry. I don't mean to imply that only the blacks
did this; the poor southern whites, the Irish, numbers of people
did. They, too, underwent the crudities and inequities of democracy
so that the high rhetoric could retain some resonance of possibility
and truth.

Hersey: How much is anger a motive force for novelists of all kinds? Does the artist start with anger more than with other emotions?

Ellison: I don't think that he necessarily starts with anger. Indeed, anger can get in the way, as it does for a fighter. If the writer starts with anger, then if he is truly writing he immediately translates it through his craft into consciousness, and thus into understanding, into insight, perception. Perhaps, that's where the morality of fiction lies. You see a situation which outrages you, but as you write about the characters who embody that which outrages, your sense of craft and the moral role of your craft demands that you depict those characters in the breadth of their humanity. You try to give them the density of the human rather than the narrow intensity of the demonic. That means that you try to delineate them as men and women who possess feelings and ideals, no matter how much you reject their feelings and ideals. Anyway, I find this happening in my own work; it humanizes *me*. So the main motive is not to express raw anger, but to present—as sentimental as it might sound—the wonder of life, in the fullness of which all these outrageous things occur.

Hersey: Have you felt some defiance of death as a writer—in the sense that what you are making may possibly circumvent death?

Ellison: No, I dare not. (*He laughs*) No, you just write for your own time, while trying to write in terms of the density of experience, knowing perfectly well that life repeats itself. Even in this rapidly changing United States it repeats itself. The mystery is that while repeating itself it always manages slightly to change its mask. To be able to grasp a little of that change within continuity and to communicate it across all these divisions of background and individual experience seems enough for me. If you're lucky, of course, if you splice into one of the deeper currents of life, then you have a chance of having your work last a little bit longer.

Ellison and I resumed this conversation, some time later, in Key West, where he and I are off-and-on next-door neighbors in small "conch" houses. This time I began asking him to tell me about his formative years.

Hersey: Could we talk a bit about your fledgling years in writing? Would you tell about how you got started?

Ellison: Well, it was kind of play, at first. I had begun to read Eliot and Pound and Hemingway and others—I think I read my first Hemingway in *Esquire* in barbershops in my home city, but it was Eliot's *Waste Land,* with its footnotes, that made me become fascinated with how writing was written. I always read a lot; I took a course in the nineteenth-century English novel at Tuskegee.

Hersey: Who put *The Waste Land* in your way?

Ellison: It was in the library at Tuskegee—a good library, even though it wasn't enough used. In fact, you could find most of the anthropological and geological references in that library. I worked in the library one year, just prowling the stacks, and reading. No one taught Eliot there. I think I got one professor interested in that area, although he was a very good man with a very good mind.

Hersey: You've told me in the past about Richard Wright's taking you under his wing when you moved to New York. When did you meet him?

Ellison: When I got to New York, I happened to have seen a copy of the *New Masses,* which had a poem by Wright. I was interested, because I did not see the techniques of modern poetry in the work of Afro-American poets. I happened to meet Langston Hughes the first morning that I was in New York. Staying at the Harlem Annex of the YMCA, I went across the street to get breakfast, and he was talking there with Alain Locke who was professor of philosophy at Howard, one of the theorists of the Negro Renaissance. I had read Locke's work, and I had met him a few weeks before, when he had been at Tuskegee to visit Hazel Harrison. So I introduced myself to him, and he introduced me to Hughes. Hughes put me to work immediately to return some books to the library. They happened to be Malraux's *Days of Wrath* and *Man's Fate.* He said, "You can read these before you return them, if you like," and of course I read them. I had read some Marxism even at Tuskegee—that, too, was in the library! I was quite excited by these books of Malraux's, and I asked Hughes if he knew a Negro writer by the name of Wright. He said, "Yes, he'll be here next week," and he dropped Wright a card. When Wright got to New York, he sent me a card telling me where I could meet

him. We hit it off, because I was, I guess, one of the few Afro-
Americans at that point who could talk about writing. At that
time I had no thought of becoming a writer myself—my world was
music. I had tried to write some poetry at Tuskegee, but just for
myself, just playing around with it. One poem was published; my
first publication was a poem, which I wrote after a friend of mine
died. He hadn't attended Tuskegee but had gone to some other
university, and coming home, he had had an attack of appendici-
tis; they wouldn't accept him at a white hospital and peritonitis had
set in.

One of Wright's reasons for coming to New York was to work in
the Harlem bureau of *The Daily Worker* and to edit a magazine
which they were trying to resuscitate. It had been called *Challenge*
during the Harlem Renaissance; they now called it *New Challenge*. He was editing this with two women, and he wanted a book
review, so I wrote my first book review—not a very good one. I later
reviewed the same book for the *Times,* and I think I did a *little*
better! And then as he planned his next issue, he didn't have any
short fiction, and he asked me to write a story. I said, "I don't
know anything about writing a story." He said, "You talk well
about stories. Why don't you try? You've had some experiences."
I had ridden freight trains, so I wrote a story about an incident
occurring on a hobo trip. He accepted it. I still have the galleys
somewhere. But the magazine folded; the girls didn't get along.
But by that time, I was caught, hooked. I began to write little
stories, and the *New Masses* published them; and I began to write
book reviews for them. In some of the issues I wrote most of the
unsigned reviews. They encouraged me. Some of the people there
didn't particularly care for Wright. I guess he was rising too fast.
They told me, "Oh, you're going to be a better writer than he
is." I said, "You're crazy." I just let that go. But I kept writing.

There's something of a misunderstanding about Wright and my
fiction. I met him in 1936 and I was writing a lot of fiction, but I
approached writing as I approached music. I'd been playing since I
was eight years old, and I knew you didn't just reach a capable
performance in whatever craft without *work*. I'd play one set of
scales over and over again. In Tuskegee I'd get up early in the
morning—and this was required of brass instrument players—and

I'd blow sustained tones for an hour. I knew the other students
used to hate it, but this developed embouchure, breath control, and
so on. And I approached writing in the same way. I wrote a hell of a
lot of stuff that I didn't submit to anybody. At first I showed some
of my things to Wright, and then by 1940 I wrote a story which
had to do with some fight that broke out between a chef and a
hallboy in a club, basing it upon a club where I had worked in
Oklahoma City; I'd worked there as a bread-and-butter boy and
then as an extra waiter—and I showed this to Dick, and he kept it and
kept it and didn't say anything. I let a few weeks go by and then I
finally said, "Well, what *about* it? What *about* it?" And he said,
"This is *my* stuff." And I said, "O.K., but what do you expect? I
thought I was taking your advice." So after that I never showed him
another piece of fiction.

Hersey: What kind of advice had he been giving you?

Ellison: Well, he'd suggest how to tighten, that kind of thing.
Wright did not have the kind of experience I'd had and was not
familiar with it; but generally he gave me suggestions on structure.
I was struggling with the problem of how to render Afro-American
speech without resorting to misspellings—to give a *suggestion* of
the idiom. Of course I had a musician's ear; and I kept working
with that. Some of the first things were embarrassing. You go from
something that you've read, until you find out about how *you*
really feel about it. But after 1940, I'd show him some of my essays
and book reviews, and very often he felt that I had too many
ideas in the pieces, and I told myself, "Well, there may be too many
ideas, but I guess the real problem is in articulating them"—
because by then I was reading a hell of a lot of Malraux, and I knew
that I didn't have enough ideas to cause confusion; it was a matter
of writing with clarity. So I kept working for that. I started to come
in contact with writer-intellectuals in New York—on the [New
York Federal] Writers Project and because Wright introduced me to
people in the League of American Writers. I began to meet people.
They were so available during those days! And, you know, you
began to *measure* yourself. In trying to learn something I talked to
very well-known Afro-American writers, and I found that they did
not know consciously what was going on in literature. I could not
discuss technique with them, and even though we shared some

points of ideology, because a number of them were leftists, they couldn't talk to me about technical matters.

Hersey: Who might some of them have been?

Ellison: Well, Hughes was one, Claude McKay was another, and there were lesser writers, some newspapermen. But they were all on the Project. Some of the stuff I worked on back then has recently been published.

Hersey: What sorts of things did you do with the Project?

Ellison: I did several things. But the main thing was a book to be titled *Negroes in New York.* When I got into the research, I realized I was dealing with American history. It was an education in itself. I also worked on a projected book of folklore—B. A. Botkin was at the top somewhere, I didn't work directly under him; I collected kids' rhymes and game songs and so on, but I'd take the opportunity to question old people and get them to tell me stories. It was a rich harvest. It was just tremendous. And it fitted right into some of the things I was reading. By this time I was rereading Mark Twain, and I'd started reading Henry James. And it was this kind of thing where Wright was important. He introduced me to the Henry James prefaces, which were edited by Dick Blackmur. I used to repunctuate James's prose, so that I could get the most out of it! I had to teach myself to read him. And I was reading Conrad's essays—any writer who wrote about the craft. The Goncourt brothers, the Russians. I was also reading essays on the cinema by Eisenstein and Pudovkin. I would collect old copies of *Hound and Horn,* copies of *International Literature;* and I had a hell of a lot of Gorki's works; and the pamphlets on literature which were published by the Communists. And I was reading *Partisan Review,* even though I disagreed with the politics. Hell, I could read Eliot in the *Partisan Review;* I used to say, "I wonder why these guys are publishing people whose politics disagree with theirs." But I was glad that they did, because what Eliot had to say was far more interesting than what Philip Rahv had to say.

Hersey: There is one other thing about those early days I'd like to explore with you. In my previous interview with you, we talked about family influences, and you told me how your mother and your father had helped to shape what you have become. You've often talked about Fanny's role in your literary life. Would

you talk about that a little? She must have come into your life
about that time.

Ellison: As I said in the introduction to the thirtieth-anniversary
edition of *Invisible Man,* when I met Fanny, she had a steady job. I
had been working on the *Negro Quarterly,* and sometimes you got
paid, and sometimes you didn't. Angelo Herndon had set up the
Negro Quarterly and wanted someone who was familiar with literature to work with him. I was doing very well on the Writers
Project—it wasn't much money, but it *came* on payday. And finally
I said, "All right, Angelo, if you'll pay me what I make on the
Writers Project, I'll come on there." I'd gone on the Project in 1938,
and this was 1942; and of course the money was not always there.
I guess I should say that I had been married once before.

Hersey: Yes I know.

Ellison: By the time I met Fanny I was going to sea—in 1944.
She worked for the Urban League. Of course I had money from
my voyages; you got a bonus whenever you went into the war zone.
So that was fine, but by the time we were married in 1944, the war
was still on, and I was going to sea. In 1945, I started *Invisible Man.*
I had come back from the sea and had no job. She was working. I
began building high-fidelity amplifiers and installing sound systems
with a friend of mine who knew more about such things than I
did. And I took photographs and sold a few pieces, and so on. But
the main—and secure—financial support was Fanny. Beyond that,
she would read the damn stuff—and type it!—and correct the
spelling! We laugh now, because I've become a much better
speller, just by giving my attention to it.

Hersey: Does she still help in these ways?

Ellison: She still types final drafts; I type my rough stuff. I read
aloud to her, over and over again.

Hersey: Do her responses make a difference to you?

Ellison: Yes, they do, very definitely. I don't always agree, because in an oral reading, you don't always get the nuances, you
don't get the visual rhythm. But she knows quite a bit. Fanny
studied drama and speech at the University of Iowa; so she's had her
training. She directed a little in Chicago, before she was married. I
think one of the reasons we became attracted to each other was that
we both liked books. We combined our libraries. One of the things

which always struck me is that we both had the same copy of *Vanity Fair,* which we'd kept; it had a cover with a Balinese woman by Covarrubias. I'd begun reading *Vanity Fair* when I was a kid; when I was able, I'd buy it. What you were exposed to in the magazine was the avantgarde. I was familiar with names that didn't turn up in college courses until many years later—even if it had been at Harvard! That's what I mean when I speak of "free-floating educational possibilities." If you're attuned, the stuff is there.

Hersey: And then, of course, in 1952 you published *Invisible Man,* and everything must have changed in your life; all your relationships must have changed. What about your relationship with your former mentor, Wright, for instance?

Ellison: Dick and I remained friends, although of course it had not been so close after he had gone to live in Paris. Fanny and I went over to Europe first in 1954, when I lectured at the Salzburg Seminars; then in 1955 when we went to Rome, we stopped in Paris and saw him; then I think I saw him again in 1956 when I went to Mexico for a conference and went by to see him as we passed through. There was some correspondence; a lot of the letters are in the collection at Yale. Our relationship changed, of course. After all, I had read books, and all kinds of books, most of my life, and Wright was self-taught, without even any structured instruction.

Hersey: More than thirty years have passed since *Invisible Man.* You've grown and changed. America has changed. How will the big book you've been working on all this time differ in tone and purpose and method from *Invisible Man?*

Ellison: You see, John, *Invisible Man* took on its own life, and has more or less gone its own way. I am identified with it. I haven't read the book in years and years. I've read sections. It's out there, and I certainly appreciate the fact that it lives. But the main thing is to make a rounded form out of the material I'm dealing with *now.* The book uses comic effects; maybe ultimately what I write always turns out to be tragicomedy, which I think has proved to be the underlying mode of American experience. We don't remember enough; we don't allow ourselves to remember events, and I suppose this helps us to continue our belief in progress. But the undercurrents are always there. You and I were speaking the other

day about how we turn our eyes away from the role that religion
has continued to play in American life. It has re-emerged recently
as a very potent and, in some ways, dangerous force, and it has
taken on the danger because we were not paying attention to its
significance in all those earlier years. And this is not just to take
a negative view of it. Negro religion has been a counterbalance to
so much of the inequality and the imposed chaos which has been
the American Negro experience. When Martin Luther King [Jr.]
emerged as an important American figure, there was an instance
of the church making itself visible in the political and social life and
fulfilling its role in the realm of morality. So that the kinds of
things which are involved in this book seem to have grown out of
what has been happening all along.

Hersey: The religious element in these intervening years operates
in the book, then?

Ellison: Yes. I guess with all my work there is an undergrounding
of American history, as it comes to focus on the racial situation.
One of the characters is a Negro minister who was once a jazz
musician, a jazz trombonist; and he underwent an experience
which turned him from his wild life as a musician into a serious
minister, but one who also brought with him his experience as a
showman. He isn't always sure when he's using religious methods,
even though his motives are religious, or when he's allowing the
devices of his old past to intrude.

Hersey: Is this a metaphor for the tour of Ralph Ellison from jazz
musician to another kind of performer in the moral realm?

Ellison: No, I don't think of it that way. So much of American
life evolves around the dedication toward a religious outlook, but
religion always runs into the limitations of politics. Many of our
politicians were ministers. We had a recent instance of a Catholic
priest, Father Drinan, who had to be ordered out of Congress by
Rome. This book was conceived before Martin Luther King became
such a figure, but he, too, had to enter the realm of politics, while
trying to stay outside it. When he began to connect the struggle for
racial justice with Vietnam, he made himself quite vulnerable; that
might well have played a role in his being killed. This fellow
Hickman developed, as I worked on the book, from a musician who
adopted the more folkish ways of ministers into something fairly

sophisticated. He was always capable with words. He was the son of a preacher and thus inherited that kind of eloquence from his own family. The other part of it has to do with a little boy of indefinite race who looks white and who, through a series of circumstances, comes to be reared by the Negro minister. They used to go around, and the little boy preached; there have been plenty of examples of pairings like this, too, in actual life. One of the devices used was to bring the little boy into a service in a white coffin, and, at a certain point, when the minister would preach of Christ's agony on the cross, saying "Lord! Lord! Why hast thou forsaken me?" the little boy would rise up from the coffin!

Hersey: Can you recall a little of the history of the development of the book?

Ellison: I started working on it in 1958. Some of what I just told you appeared in the *Noble Savage,* for which Saul Bellow was one of the editors. It was the same period when, at Saul's urging, I started teaching at Bard College. That was an unsettled period for us. We had spent two years in Rome, and Fanny was working, having gone back to the job she had had before we went to Rome— where incidentally she had worked, too. The Catholic Church had set up something called La Lampada della Fraternita, which was a veterans organization, and they needed someone to set up a clerical system, and she went in there with her Berlitz Italian . . . it was quite admirable the way she went about it. When I came back, I didn't have a job. I was trying to stay out of activities in New York, so Bellow suggested that I live in his house in Tivoli, as he and his wife and baby were spending most of the year in Minnesota, at the university. I got started on the book and wrote quite a lot of it, but was never satisfied with how the parts connected. The sections I have published have gotten good responses, and I've given public readings of other sections, always with satisfaction. I'm finding myself having to try first-person narration, and then try it again as third-person, in an effort to stay out of it as narrator myself. It's exasperating, but at the same time I've come to feel that one of the challenges for a writer who handles the kind of material I'm working with is to let the people speak for themselves, in whatever way you can. Then you draw upon more of the resources of American vernacular speech. One of the narra-

tors is a newspaperman, a white, who had had some radical
experiences during the thirties and had had an affair, which didn't
end well, with a Negro girl.

Hersey: What sort of time span do you cover?

Ellison: Roughly from 1954 to 1956 or 1957. That is time present
in the novel, but the story goes back into earlier experiences, too,
even to some of the childhood experiences of Hickman, who is an
elderly man in time present. It's just a matter of the past being active
in the present—or of the characters becoming aware of the manner
in which the past operates on their present lives. Of course, this
gets into the general history, because one of the characters is a
senator—he, too, is a trickster!

Hersey: In our earlier talk you said: "I believe that fiction does
help create value, and I regard this as a very serious—I almost
said 'sacred'—function of the writer." I know you have very strong
views about the moral fabric of the country. To what extent does
fiction have a bearing on that fabric?

Ellison: At its best, fiction allows for a summing up. The fiction
writer abstracts from the flow of experience certain abiding patterns, and projects those patterns as they affect the lives and the
consciousnesses of the characters. So fiction allows for a summing up. It allows for contemplation of the moral significance of
human events. We don't always live up to the broader implications of
this aspect of fiction, I think, because sometimes, out of a sense of
frustration or disgust, we don't consider what a powerful effect vividly
projected images of symbolic actions can have upon readers. If you
think of the popularization of drugs and the let-it-all-hang-out syndrome—these are very suggestive; and I believe writers might think
a little bit about the implications of what they project, and of the
kinds of heroes or antiheroes they project. Of course I'm not
offering formulas. Everyone has to work out his writing for himself,
but the things he writes do have consequences. Sometimes you
touch upon forces which are implicit, and you establish moods
and give forms to attitudes. These are not always for the best.
Someone asked me about all the burnings of tenements which
occurred during the period after *Invisible Man* had been published,
and I had to point out that I had covered the Harlem Riot of 1943
for the *New York Post,* and I certainly wasn't recommending that

people burn buildings but was suggesting that that was a negative alternative to more democratic political action. When it was impossible to be heard within the democratic forum, people would inevitably go to other extremes. There was always somebody to suggest that we live in an era of revolutions. In any case, it is that aura of a summing up, that pause for contemplation of the moral significance of the history we've been through, that I have been reaching for, in my work on this new book.

Ralph Ellison's Territorial Vantage

Ron Welburn / 1976

From the *Grackle*, 1977–78, 5–15. Copyright 1978 by the *Grackle*. Reprinted by permission.

One cannot have even a casual interest in American cultural thought without knowing about Ralph Ellison. Best known as the author of *Invisible Man*, a novel that won the National Book Award in 1953, and in 1966 was the choice of 200 authors, editors, and critics as the single most distinguished American novel since the Second World War. Ellison has published several short stories, among them "Flying Home," whose musical impetus is the Lionel Hampton hit of 1940. Several of his essays are included in *Shadow & Act* (1964) where his two-pronged interests in literature and music are evident. Ralph Ellison has also proved to be a thought-provoking, though shy, interviewee, a man whose breadth of experience and reading have hewn his philosophy and judgments into some of the most crystalized assessments of culture and Americans for our time. There are excellent interviews with Ellison in *Harper's* (March, 1967), *Atlantic* (December, 1970), *The New Yorker* (November 22, 1976), and *Yardbird Reader*, No. 6. To these, *The Grackle* contributes another, conducted during 1976, in which Mr. Ellison recounted his boyhood in Oklahoma City and his experiences and insights with music. In keeping with *The Grackle's* intent to present a better understanding of music in America and its influence abroad, we found our encounter with Mr. Ellison most stimulating, and thank him for being willing to share his time and thoughts with us.

As a boy when did you become conscious of "improvised music"? What characterized it and what of it could you call "Jazz"?

There was so much of it around me that I suppose I was born with a consciousness of it. There were several bands sponsored by such lodges as the Elks. These were military and concert bands, but the musicians also played in jazz orchestras and gig combos.

Territorial orchestras were constantly in and out of Oklahoma City.
Moten, George E. Lee, T. Holder, Andy Kirk were among them.
And there were people who amused themselves by playing guitars,
Jews harps, kazoos, yukes, mandolins, C Melody saxophones, or
performed on combs by vibrating a piece of tissue paper placed
against the comb's teeth. Much of this was improvised music,
including blues and jazz riffs. The bandmen played standard
marches, such as those of Sousa, arrangements of the classics, and
novelty numbers, such as "Laughing Trombone," which contained
elements of ragtime and jazz. There were string orchestras which
played everything from the light classics to the blues. There was
not too definite a line drawn between the types of music, at least
not in my kid's consciousness. This happened later, after I began to
study music in school. Negro culture was music-centered, and in
grade school I became aware of the standard ways of playing
repertory, whether for single groups or for the school band and
orchestra. Those of us who tried to play jazz listened to whatever
was around, whether played by local or visiting jazzmen or on
records. Incidently, the first song taught me as a two-year-old was
"Dark Brown, Chocolate to the Bone." To this I was taught to
dance the Eagle Rock. I had older cousins who were in tune with
jazz and the blues while their mother was a great one for singing
hymns to the accompaniment of their player piano. I can still see
the image of Liszt on one of the boxes which held the piano rolls,
just as I can still hear one of my cousins picking out the early
version of "Sqeeze Me" on the piano keys. So, in such homes,
and it was more or less typical, you had a general openness to music
of various styles. King Oliver came and went regularly and was
very popular. But there was another side. In our AME church the
choir director was one of the local physicians who disdained the
spirituals. He preferred the more formal religious music. The church
had an organ, and orchestra, and a fair sized choir which performed the music of Handel. I have a vague memory of going to an
orchestral rehearsal with my father and seeing him play the drums.

*What kind of music education did the Oklahoma school system
provide?*
Thanks to Mrs. Zelia N. Breaux, who was a very influential

educator, it was quite extraordinary. The kids were taught music
from the early grades, including sight-reading. There was a music
appreciation course with phonographs and recordings taught city-
wide in the black schools, and rare for most schools even today, we
were taught four years of harmony and two of musical form.
There was a marching and concert band which I entered at the age
of eight, two glee clubs, an orchestra and chorus, and each year
Mrs. Breaux produced and directed an operetta. The leads and the
chorus were students. I participated in several, both as a musician
and as an actor. In my first I played one of the children in the
"Gypsy Rover." Later, when I was older, I was taught a tap
dance routine for a role in an operetta whose title I've forgotten.
Interestingly enough, Mrs. Breaux, who was an all-around musician, playing trumpet, violin and piano, did not encourage us to
play jazz. And yet as one of the owners of the local theater she
brought all kinds of jazz musicians before the public. King Oliver,
Ma Rainey, and Ida Cox were frequently on the bill, and Bessie
Smith and quite a number of T.O.B.A. circuit offerings came to her
Aldridge Theater. Before sound movies were common she employed a pit orchestra and such members of the original Blue Devils
orchestra as Walter Page, Icky Lawrence, and Willie Lewis were
employed there. A number of the local jazz musicians, such as
Page, were conservatory-trained and were capable of reading at sight
the scores that were issued with the motion pictures. Icky Lawrence
was a trumpeter who played with the Ideal Orchestra, the first
sustained group in our community. Icky Lawrence was their trumpeter, Crackshot McNeal was its elegant drummer—get hold of
musicians from the early Basie period and they'll tell you what an
excellent drummer he was. There was Willie Lewis, a jolly rotund
fellow who did the arranging and played the piano, and Gut Bucket
Coleman on trombone. These were versatile musicians and gifted
jazzmen. Later, the band that was to stay the longest and become
the most famous was the Blue Devils. Among its members were
Walter Page, Hot Lips Page, Icky Lawrence, Buster Smith, and
sometimes Edward Christian, Charlie Christian's gifted older
brother.

  Did bands like Sam Wooding's get out there?
  I don't recall Sam Wooding's, but it's quite possible. Alphonso

Trent was in and out of Oklahoma City; I think he was based
principally in Dallas. George E. Lee was a famous Kansas City
band; he called it a novelty singing orchestra and featured musicians who were versatile on several instruments. His sister, Julia,
performed with them and gave the group quite a bit of glamour
with her fine clothes and fine looks. Frequently, they played battles
of music against Bennie Moten, and often won.

Oklahoma City was home base for the Blue Devils while Bennie
Moten, Andy Kirk's Twelve Clouds of Joy, and George E. Lee were
Kansas City based. Of course, they sometimes spent months in
Oklahoma City, which like Kansas City was a good town for
dance bands. There were dressing towns and dancing towns; a good
dancing town was one in which bands could find employment
both among Negroes and whites.

*Who were some of the better-known local musicians, and which
of them went on to greater things?*

Edward Christian, Charlie's older brother, was an arranger and
band leader. He played violin, tuba, string bass and piano. Charlie
Christian and Jimmy Rushing were the most famous jazz musicians
produced by Oklahoma City, but there were also Harry Young-
blood, Harold Canon, and Frank Mead. During the forties Lem
Johnson was very active around New York. Oscar Pettiford, Al
Hibbler, Sammy Price, Ben Webster, and Lester Young were on the
scene from time to time. I remember Lester Young being there
in 1929.

So much of it is a matter of packaging a style for the white public.
A variety of art, music or dance, will have existed among Afro-
Americans for years, during which time it reaches a level of perfection, as did the style known as Stomp. By the time it was
introduced to white audiences it had been changed to "Swing." But
in those days there wasn't that kind of distinction made between
rhythm and blues; the Southwestern bands played both. During
public dances blues numbers were played as a matter of course.
When the band was swinging the dancers and the dancers were
swinging the musicians—usually around midnight—*that's* when the
blues were evoked. Earlier in the evening blues were played up-
tempo.

306 Conversations with Ralph Ellison

The term "Blue Devils" is English and referred to a state of psychic depression, but during the range wars in cattle country those who were given to cutting barbwire fences were called "Blue Devils." Perhaps Walter Page chose the name because of its outlaw connotations. Incidently, that orchestra merged with Bennie Moten's after Moten died, and later became Basie's. Moten was undergoing a tonsilectomy when a slip of the doctor's scalpel severed his jugular vein, Moten's fans wanted to lynch that Negro doctor.

Didn't James Reese Europe die similarly?—did you ever encounter him or Will Marion Cook?

No, Europe was knifed to death in 1919 by a drummer, so all I ever saw of him was a photograph of him directing a band. I knew of Cook because the boy's glee club sang several of his compositions. I did know Cook's wife, Abbie Mitchell, when she was on the faculty of the Tuskegee school of music. Cook's music was widely popular.

What of the Oklahoma City school music scene overall? And what others besides blacks were involved in the blues and jazz scene?

Oklahoma City had a number of school bands, most of them white. Our instruments were supplied by the Board of Education but our uniforms were bought with funds raised by the citizens, black and white, throughout the city. Usually our travel expenses were raised by public subscription. Our band accompanied the football team to such cities as Tulsa or Muskegee. I played varsity football, so on certain trips I traveled as a member of the team. We also traveled to Wichita and Topeka, and one year the Elks lodge took us out to Denver for a convention which featured an oratorical contest. Many whites supported our travels.

I don't recall members of other racial groups participating in jam sessions, although there might have been whites and others playing in the white dance halls that were unavailable to a kid like myself. But I don't remember any coming over to the East side, and this despite the relative friendliness between the races. Incidently, I'm told that a local white man copyrighted a blues as early as 1913. Yes, and there was an Indian looking guy who played

trombone in one of the Kansas City orchestras. He was called
Big Chief Moore.

In what shape was ragtime in Oklahoma in your youth?
The craze had given way to jazz, but people still played it. The
custodian of the Slaughter's building, where the most important
dance hall was located, would sit down at the piano and play a very
intricate rag; but he was such an evil bastard that I was afraid to
ask him what it was or where he'd learned to play. There were
musicians who worked as barbers or as packing plant workers
who played ragtime. And the spirit of ragtime was in many of the
military marches and you found it on piano rolls that had been
cut by Scott Joplin and James P. Johnson and others. I can't
remember a time when I wasn't familiar with the "Maple Leaf
Rag." It was played by small orchestras and you found it in band
books. There were also a number of comic numbers designed to
show off the trombone sections of concert bands, like "Laughing
Trombone" and "Papa Charlie Trombone." Ask any old military
or side show musician or look into old band books and you'll find
that the ragtime influence was widespread.

What was "Papa Charlie" style?
A lot of smears, imitations of preachers preaching, laughing.
These passages were written in. After a chorus there'd come a
break and the trombone would take over. Played by a good improvi-
sor it became real jazz.

What Ellington used with Tricky Sam and Bubber Miley?
Yes, the style was in the air. Listen to the trombone accompaniment on old blues recordings and you'll hear some of it.

What of your own musical experiences?
After I developed enough skill I played in pick-up groups—gig
bands—under Edward Christian. My first instrument in the school
band was the mellophone. I'd loan mine to Hot Lips Page and the
other Blue Devils trumpeters would borrow the mellophones from
the other members of the mellophone section in order to play
special choruses. In exchange I'd insist upon being allowed to sit
in on trumpet during a Blue Devils' rehearsal. I could read better
than some of the jazzmen so very often I'd be asked to arbitrate

when they got into arguments over interpretation. I also played
solos with the band and at weddings. I also held first chair in the
school orchestra. I wasn't able to do much about jazz gigs because
I was still an adolescent and my widowed mother kept a tight rein
on me.

At Tuskegee, where I majored in music, we were not encouraged
to play jazz. But the summer I arrived there I played in a band
under Shorty Hall. Shorty had been trained by Captain Drye, an
old 10th Calvary bandmaster who directed the Tuskegee band and
taught me trumpet. Shorty, by the way, taught Dizzy Gillespie in
North Carolina. That summer we played dances for teachers, for
students and for the physicians who staffed the Veterans Hospital.
We also played dances in nearby towns, such as Columbus,
Georgia and Montgomery, Alabama. During my time at Tuskegee I
played with one of the student orchestras. There were two, both
big bands. Jazz was discouraged because it was thought to degrade
the instrumental techniques which were being taught. Trumpeters
were taught the methods of Arban and St. Jacombe and it was felt
that jazz techniques would interfere. I went out for the football
team and was told to forget it. I was told: ''We're not spending all
this time and money training you to develop your embrouchure
and have you go out there and get your mouth stepped on or your
fingers mashed.''

*It's true that black colleges have historically discouraged blues
and jazz. Orrin Clayton Suthern, who taught at my alma mater,
Lincoln University in Pennsylvania, was no exception in the sixties.*
Suthern? He taught me at Tuskegee, in the thirties. But my
feelings about that matter are mixed. To an extent it was fortunate
that not everyone tried to teach the blues because they were not of
its spirit, and it was not part of their background. We have to
recognize that there are various cultural backgrounds and levels in
our group. Some people knew nothing of the blues or even of the
spirituals while others knew nothing of classical music. Others
knew both. Musicians like Walter Page had studied in conservatories but played jazz, blues and anything else. Other jazzmen were
more limited. At Tuskegee there were faculty members who had
studied in Europe: Andrew Fletcher Roseman, Hazel Harrison,

Portia Pittman and Abbie Mitchell. William L. Dawson, the director
of the music school, had played in everything from jazz orchestras
to the Chicago Civic Symphony, but he was the only faculty member
with that broad a range. Today I think it fortunate that jazz wasn't
taught because it has developed its own unique body of techniques
through its free-swinging, improvisational, irreverent attitude.
Teaching it formally might well have imposed too many thou-
shalt-nots and imposed stability upon a developing form. Dance
halls and jam sessions along with recording are the true academy
for jazz. However, one of the good things about the division of
musical culture in Afro-America is that there have always been
musicians trained in European styles and techniques, who pass it
on to youngsters who opt for jazz. Shorty Hall, who I mentioned
earlier, was hardly four feet tall, but he could blow the hell off of a
big-bore symphonic trumpet. And I mean that he played all the
difficult variations and triple tonguing. He had the facility of Al
Hirt. So there is a direct line leading from Captain Drye, the ex-
calvary bandmaster, through Shorty Hall to Dizzy. Mrs. Breaux
never played jazz herself but she taught the fundamentals to many
students who did.

*Did Alain Locke's "The Negro and His Music" of 1936 stir any
interest among black intellectuals then?*
I don't know to what extent. It was part of the *Bronze Booklet*
series and I read them all. I remember Sterling Brown's the best and
found them useful, but generally the series struck me as inadequate.
In Locke's there seemed to be so much which wasn't adequately
handled and I got more information from James Weldon Johnson's
Black Manhattan and *Along This Way*. He had been involved in
so much of our musical experience and some of the musicians he
mentioned had been out to Oklahoma City. The role of blacks on
Broadway was exciting and gave me a broader sense of possibility.
I really didn't need someone to tell me about the spirituals
because I grew up around them. In school we sang them and every
type of Afro-American music . . . except [chuckle] the blues.

I'm sure some of the newspapers in the area covered music.
Oklahoma had and still has one of our most famous papers, the
Black Dispatch. It was published and edited by Roscoe Dungee

and was widely read for its editorials. But I'm afraid that the music commentary we got usually came from the *Chicago Defender* or the *Pittsburgh Courier,* papers which emphasized entertainment and brought the excitement of the big cities to the provinces.

But were there no write-ups of a concert, or talk about the nuts and bolts of what bands like Basie and Hines were doing?

Not unless written elsewhere by columnists who covered entertainment. Local dances would be announced and reported, but there was little music criticism.

On more than one occasion you have stated that certain black jazzmen, like Coleman Hawkins and Pres, were influenced by white jazzmen such as Frankie Trumbauer: their biographies have verified that; but isn't the impetus for this "jazz" improvisory style something that sprang from the Afro-American imaginative genius?

This argument about who did what and who influenced whom imposes racial considerations which don't belong to discussions of culture. In those days when a musician was learning his instrument and trying to develop his own style he listened to any musician who had something to offer, who excited him; they weren't fighting the race problem but assimilating styles and techniques. The Ellington sidemen interviewed by Stanley Dance mention a number of white jazzmen who influenced their styles. It was the music, the style, the ability to execute that was important. If a white musician sounded good; if he had the facility with his instrument you took what you could use—just as they took what they could use from us. Jazz is Afro-American in origin, but it's more American than some folks want to admit. When I got to New York I was amazed to find white trumpeters working at developing what they called a "dirty" tone. These were men who could produce the brilliant tone associated with the classical trumpet style, and I came to realize that they were trying to develop the Negro blues voice as it sounds on the trumpet and trombone. In other words, they were studying the voicing and technique of jazz, techniques that were already well-rounded and complex but which hadn't been codified in textbooks. Having grown up around musi-

cians who couldn't produce anything *but* a "dirty tone" I found
this ironic. Especially in light of the fact that at Tuskegee we were
made to spend hours every day learning to make the trumpet
speak as a trumpet. That was a basic goal. You strove for a militant,
brilliant tone. If you played cornet your tone would be mellower,
but it had to be vibrant and you had to learn to control your vibrato
and make it speak in a number of voices, from the lyrical to the
militant. The blues timbre, the sound of the Negro voice, was
already in you, and if you didn't produce it instinctively you could
listen to those who used it; on the stage or on recordings, or from
hucksters selling watermelons and so on. I heard Louis Armstrong
in person for the first time in 1929, but I had been listening to his
recordings and admiring the sound of his trumpet for years. When
a black musician says he was influenced by white musicians I
believe him and see no reason to doubt him. It's most American.
This is a pluralistic society and culturally the melting pot really
melts. Trumbauer must have learned from black musicians. Here,
there's a long history of interchanging musical styles between
the races.

*You worked on the Works Progress Administration interviewing
people for the purpose of folklore research. Did the W.P.A. have
any disposition toward jazz? There were projects for collecting
memoirs; did any of that involve, in an official capacity, collecting
songs and recording blues musicians?*
Working with folklore was only a minor phase of my work on the
writers project. Most of my time there was spent doing research
for a history of Negroes in New York, but I had no contact with
what was happening on music projects. The music project was a
world within itself. I know that much attention was given to producing musicals and giving concerts, and that free musical instruction
was provided the public. I took a few trumpet lessons from a man
who held the first trumpet chair with the Metropolitan Opera
Orchestra. I seem to recall that the people who "discovered"
Leadbelly were employed by the W.P.A., and that collectors were
sent into the field with recording machines. I'm unfamiliar with
what their official attitude toward jazz and the blues might have
been.

*Minton's was becoming active in the late 30s–early 40s. How did
you respond to the nascent music there and were people dancing
to it, that you know of?*

Few people were capable of dancing to it; it was more a listener's
music. I did a piece for *Esquire* on Mintons (viz *Shadow & Act*).
You encountered the new style not only at Mintons but at the
Apollo as well. There you heard Earl Hines with Sarah Vaughn
and Eckstine, and you heard bebop flourishes at the Savoy Ballroom. I danced a lot and used to be there once or twice a week. I
went to the Apollo twice a week usually on Wednesdays and
Sundays, often with Langston Hughes. There was music all over
the district. The Renaissance Ballroom and Smalls Paradise, with
both local and nationally-known bands, Lucky Millinder's and
the Savoy Sultans, etc. I was very interested in Erskine Hawkins'
group because when I went to Tuskegee they were still at Alabama
State down in Montgomery. The state of Alabama didn't support
the college adequately so the orchestra would go out and raise
money. Erskine was the composer of "Tuxedo Junction" which
was popular with white bands at the time; but I always preferred the
way the Collegians played it—they put the real feeling into it. The
band was so successful in the North that they decided to go
professional—which led to real contention between them and the
President of Alabama State. He forced them to give up the name
"Alabama State Collegians" and they took the name of the leader,
Erskine Hawkins. Billy Daniels was their singer. I'm speaking of
a period which included part of the Depression, but there was quite
a ferment in entertainment. Perhaps all the more so because there
were so many good musicians out of work. Nevertheless there was
a great deal of dancing and experimentation. As a musician I
became discouraged. There was so much competition and having
no money I couldn't afford to join the union. However, I did hang
around the Rhythm Club so as to keep in touch with the pros. I
began trying to write in 1937 and finally gave up all hope of
becoming a professional musician. By 1940 I was living next door
to Teddy Wilson. He was playing at Cafe Society DownTown and
my wife and I often went there and frequently joined him and his
wife at various after hours hangouts where musicians met after
work to jam.

What was the reaction of New Yorkers to Gillespie and Parker?
It was mixed because most people couldn't dance to bop. Very
often Dizzy and Bird were so engrossed with their experiments
that they didn't provide enough music for the supportive rite of
dancing. That bothered me. And the political stance they took
was annoying because I thought it irrelevant. By political I mean
the idea they projected of inventing a music that whites couldn't
play—I touch on this in the article I did on Mintons—and their
studied ignoring of the audience I found a drag. I didn't need it. I
could write and express my political attitudes through other forms
of action. When I wanted to hear music I wanted to hear music,
not to be politicized. But the things they were doing with chords
and the melodic line were fascinating. But it didn't really develop; it
became much too quickly a series of clichés, and I was sorry for
that. With any new development there's that danger, especially
when younger musicians grab it as their thing. The lyrical phase of
bop was truly promising. Numbers like Tadd Dameron's "If You
Could See Me Now" sung by Sarah Vaughn fascinated me to no
end. Dameron and Fats Navarro were gifted musicians. There
were a number of brilliant trumpeters, one or two more brilliant
than Gillespie, who is part clown and part musician. As an ex-
trumpeter I wasn't nearly as excited by his work as I was by Clark
Terry. Just personal taste. Anyway, you didn't have to listen to
the boppers because there were always good bands playing somewhere in Harlem. And when you ran into the boppers at the
Savoy they usually played numbers that anyone could dance to.
Although I had given up music by the time bop began to flourish
I still went to jam sessions. There was a place on St. Nicholas
Avenue that was owned by Sidney Bechét, a shell-like place
somewhere in the 130s near Seventh Avenue where Art Tatum and
Teddy Wilson used to jam. And there was Clark Monroe's Uptown House, another bopper joint. At 136th Street and Lenox there
was a joint where the singing waiters sang dirty songs and improvised lyrics as they dashed back and forth serving drinks. Around
the corner on 137th there was the Red Rooster, and down on
116th Street Jimmy Daniels ran a club that was frequented by the
international set. A very sophisticated place.

When did you recognize the role that blues and jazz played in
shaping not only the national music consciousness but in having
an effect on the image that Americans had of themselves? You have
reiterated that idea several times in lectures and writings.

Here's a dramatic instance: In 1929 Louis Armstrong had been
playing in Kansas City and when he came down to Oklahoma
City the bandstand in our segregated dance hall was suddenly filled
with white women. They were wild for his music and nothing like that
had ever happened in our town before. His music was our music
but they saw it as theirs too, and were willing to break the law to
get to it. So you could see that Armstrong's music was affecting
attitudes and values that had no immediate relationship to it.
Then there was the popularity of Earl Hines' radio broadcasts and
that of the Mills Brothers. Back in '28 and '29, when they were
still in short pants we were pretending to be asleep and staying up
late just to hear them imitate instruments with their voices. White
kids were doing the same thing. Somehow music was transcending
the racial divisions. Listening to songs such as "I'm Just Wild
About Harry" and knowing that it was the work of Negroes didn't
change all our attitudes but it helped all kinds of people identify with
Americanness or American music. Among all the allusions to earlier
poetry that you find in Eliot's *The Waste Land* he still found a
place to quote from "Under the Bamboo Tree," a lyric from a song
by James Weldon Johnson, Bob Cole, and Rosamond Johnson.
During the '20s when *The Waste Land* was published many readers
made the connection. Johnson was secretary of the NAACP and
that was another connection which provided some sense of the
complexity of the American identity. A similar process was going
on in our segregated schools. We were being made aware in the
early grades that the poetry of Countee Cullen and Langston
Hughes had a connection with the larger body of American poetry.
Our teachers were excited over this and passed their excitement
to their students. Given the racial stereotypes Negroes must learn
to recognize the elements of their own cultural contribution as
they appear in elements of the larger American culture. If we saw a
new dance style we could recognize the black elements, the steps and
gestures, in it. If you watched Fred Astaire and admired his work

you knew nevertheless that you saw more exciting—and authentic—dancing on the stage of the Aldridge theater.

Henry Cowell's "American Composers on American Music"
(1933) reveals how unprepared its commentators were for blues
and jazz.

When you consider the facts that Irene and Vernon Castle learned
much from James Reese Europe and the influence of jazz in the work
of Copland and Gerschwin, I'm not so sure of that. I'm told that a
white man copyrighted a blues in Oklahoma City in 1913; and the
man who backed Scott Joplin was a Kansas publisher. Perhaps the
geographical location has a lot to do with it. Even back in slavery
times whites were fascinated by Afro-American music and certainly
the minstrel show, for many years our most popular musical
entertainment, owed its form, its content, and music to Afro-
American music and dance. I'd say that white American composers were mixed in their attitudes. The music was infectious, they
accepted its resources but when it came to identifying it as a
viable part of American music they were hindered by racial considerations. Nevertheless anyone writing music in the United States
was influenced by it; thus the spate of "Ethiopian Airs" written by
whites; Dvorak made use of Afro-American tonalities and
rhythms—as did Delius.

When I was growing up what is currently identified as Country
music was sold by 5&10 cent stores in the form of recordings and
we recognized Negro influences, just as we recognized Irish, French
and Spanish influences in Afro-American music. In Oklahoma
there were blacks who danced square-dances—not in imitation of
white people but because square-dancing was part of their culture.

Have you detected any so-called "Southwestern" styled elements
in later music at large, or in expressive culture at large, like the
"texas sax" projection of Louis Jordan that has been in part
incorporated into much media commercial playing.

Well, if you come up with anything musically new in this country
it gets watered down as it enters the mainstream. Singers and
instrumentalists imitate that which is original in other singers and
instrumentalists. The Southwestern rhythm and that great freedom within discipline that you first heard in Count Basie's band

was swiftly incorporated into Benny Goodman and most of the
white big bands. When a style is definitive, when it expresses the
time of day, that's what happens. But we know that "swing" was
generated in the southwest and quickly took over. Back when it was
called stomp or jump it created an effect quite different from what
you got on the East coast, say with Ellington; the orchestration and
the spirit was different. In it the presence of the blues was more
obvious, as were the kinds of improvisation. There was the percus-
sive of the brass section that you get in "Going To Chicago," and the
lyricism of the Basie band. Being definitive the feeling generated
was attractive to any number of musicians outside the Southwest.
If they're exciting, musical styles tend to be nationalized. They
enter the mainstream.

*Where do we go from the point of the dissemination of style in
the commercialized cultural forms?*

Cultural forms, especially forms of popular music, become trivialized through the efforts of promotors to package novelty. This
has a negative effect on art. The jazz of the 30s and 40s was not
exhausted artistically; they were supplanted by promotors who
were more interested in making money than in art. The big bands
were broken up by agents who convinced sidemen that they would
make more money by going on the road as members or leaders of
small combos. We can't overlook the economic conditions that made
it difficult to maintain a big band, nor the war, but the agents were
largely responsible. In this country the direction of culture is
always being tampered with by people who have little concern for
art, and yet their manipulations have consequences in other areas of
the society, often leading to chaos in our life styles and moral
disorientation. As with the Beatles, who with their Cockney
rebellion and Afro-American influenced music hit this country and
its young like a ton of bricks. I think that some of the attitudes
promoted by the boppers, their discouragement of the dancers, the
legend of Parker's drug habit—such things helped make the Beatles
phenomenon possible. The artistic quality of the Beatles' music was
masked by their irreverent behavior. It sounded easier than it actually
was and this was helped by the use of electrified instruments and
their costumes. Such details made many white kids believe that

they could create a do-it-yourself type of music. As I indicated in
the Minton's piece so many who didn't grasp the agony of Parker or
the music he created imitated his drug-taking and irresponsibility.
Suddenly you couldn't visit friends who had adolescent children
without having to listen to them bang on guitars and little electric
pianos. And yet for all its tastelessness, at a time when Johnny
Hodges was hardly making a living, such noise became the source
of great wealth and facile celebrity.

Willie 'the Lion' Smith mentioned in his autobiography that
music was more fun before the promotors got into it.
Jazz was part of a total culture, at least among Afro-Americans.
People saved their nickels and dimes in order to participate in it.
Hell, we used to work like the dickens to get the admission fee
when a dance was being played by someone we admired. Jazzmen
were heroes . . . I guess they still are.

Some of the musicians who've come along since 1960 have had
their music susceptible to its being qualitatively diminished.
It might be their artistic good luck. You always have an ambivalence toward this sort of thing because you feel that it is artistic
quality that should be promoted. It happens with classical music
but it isn't so susceptible to manipulation. But on the level of
vernacular music there's always this group of promotors who stand
between the audience and the musician. It suggests that today
jazz still demands sacrifice just as it did when I was growing up.
Dedicated musicians accepted the fact that it would often be
necessary to be out of work for weeks or even months. Such
difficulties went with the art. Duke Ellington never gave up his
one-night stands, perhaps because he realized that traveling around
the country involved a process that was musically fertilizing. It placed
him in contact with newer styles and undiscovered musicians of
talent. He was like a football scout, covering the fields and
listening to what was going on. It would seem to me that today's
musician might adopt such an attitude. Perhaps they'd do better
if they went back to playing for dances, go back to the communal
situation in which there's a closer identification between their
artistic goals and their prospective audience's desire to participate
in the creation of the jazz spell.

Dancers today seem programmed. For example, disco. But if you were to take a Gillespie or Moody or some of the younger acoustically inclined musicians, and have a music you could dance to without the disco sound, it might be beautiful.

I assume that audiences haven't been exposed to the kind of music you suggest. I suspect that the discoteque is itself the product of economic rather than artistic developments. It's just easier to get records and loudspeakers than to hire a good band and pay union wages.

Study and Experience: An Interview with Ralph Ellison

Robert B. Stepto and
Michael S. Harper / 1976

From the *Massachusetts Review* 18 (1977), 417–35. Copyright © 1977 by the Massachusetts Review, Inc. Reprinted by permission.

Stepto: Both you and Wright strove to read, and strove to write, but I think the situations were quite different. What we see sometimes is that people have the theory, an ancient one, of sons wanting to slay the fathers. . . .

Ellison: Well, Wright and I were of different backgrounds, different ages, and from different regions. What united us was our mutual interest in ideas and the craft of fiction, not some fanciful notion of father and son. I've heard the metaphor used in justification of actions taken after the disruption of friendships between younger and older writers, and inevitably it is the younger who uses it in his own defense. I don't buy it because it misnames a complicated relationship.

S: What do you mean?

E: For one thing, I mean that writers as artists are sons of many fathers, or at least the sons of many writers' *styles*. This was true even of Dostoyevsky and Henry James, and no matter what the personal relationship between two writers happens to be, unless the younger writer is a mere imitator his style will diverge from, and often negate in certain aspects, the style of his older friend. That's where the important conflict takes place and it's more or less inevitable and it only obscures matters when we drag in the father-son metaphor. Rather than a case of the son slaying the father, such rows are more like those instances wherein an unwedded mother gives her unwanted baby over for adoption. And

This interview took place at Mr. Ellison's home in New York City on March 8, 1976.

then, after the child has been brought through the precarious
period of infancy, toilet-training and whooping cough, she discovers
that she has safely weathered the terrors of shame and uncertainty
of her maternity and proceeds to demand the return of the child. In
doing so she makes noble noises about the sacredness of motherhood
and the imperiousness of the maternal instinct, and has nasty things
to say about the manners, morals, and low human quality of those
into whose hands she has thrust her squirming infant. Neither
metaphor is really adequate, but sometimes a young writer seeks
to place his infant talent in the care of an older writer whom he
hopes will nurture, instruct and protect it and himself against the
uncertainties that are a necessary phase of his development. But
then, after he has gained confidence and achieved a sense of his
own identity as a writer, he seeks to reclaim his psychological
independence. Thus it seems to me that instead of seeking for a father
principle, the writer, as *writer,* is seeking ways to give birth to
books. And what if during his formative period a male writer is
given support by a writer who is female? When he asserts values
that are in conflict with hers shall we say that the son must slay
the mother and thus brand him a "Mother"? Or if both writers are
women do we say that the younger mother of books is slaying
another mother? Seriously, a writer learns (and quite early, if he's
lucky) to depend upon the authority of his own experience and
intuition. He must learn to dominate them, but these are his capital
and his guide, his compass and crud-detector, his sword and his
cross; and he defers to the authority of others at the peril of his
artistic individuality. His drive is to achieve his own artistic possibilities by whatever artistic means necessary. Of course a young writer
may have feelings of dependency that have their source in areas
of his personality that are not necessarily linked to his drive toward
expression and would be present even if he were without artistic
talent. But in the writer, in the artist, such feelings of dependency
find relief in the action of creation.

    S: So how do you view the relationship between a younger and
older writer where one is established and the other just beginning.

    E: If we stick to the father-son metaphor I'd say that, given a
reasonable degree of psychological independence on the part of the
younger man, it would be difficult to decide who at any given

moment is in the position of "father," who of "son." Such relationships are dramatic; it is a matter of give and take. Insight is determined less by chronological age than by the density of one's felt experience and by one's consciousness of implication. A younger man whose adolescence was spent in a big city might well possess insights of which an older man whose formative period was spent in a small town may be innocent. I speak of possibilities, and of course the reverse is often true, with the small town providing experiences and insights difficult to come by in densely structured cities. Anyway, I would think that when a younger man designates an older writer as his symbolic father he would keep his projection subjective, miming it rather than giving it utterance.

Because to name his attitude would be to concede far more to another than most assertive young men (and writers are very assertive types, at least psychologically) would wish to admit. What Kenneth Burke terms "courtship" is implicit in friendship, which is a relationship between, shall we say, two consenting adults who "woo" one another. In such relationships there are risks for both participants. For awhile the older writer might consider it flattering to be elected the "father" of a gifted symbolic "son," there is also the possibility that he might be repelled by the responsibility of that role. Remember that both Hawthorne and Henry James regarded the imposition of one's will upon the freedom of another as a sin against democratic individuality and gave considerable attention to the theme in their fiction. The lessons of his own experience, his own apprenticeship, might lead the older writer to feel that his young friend should undergo the risks that are part of the task of achieving an artistic identity. These risks are a part of his extended initiation. And if he is in fact psychologically mature enough to act out the "father" role he will have learned that artists are self-creating types—or at least that they tend to *pretend* that they are—and thus in their efforts in this direction they're apt to savage those into whose hands they've delivered themselves. Then there is a wavery line between the pieties of friendship and the subjective compulsion which writers feel to project their individual visions. Each writer interprets life as he sees it, and in the conflict of passion and insight which occurs when writers strive to project their individual visions the son-slaying-the-father metaphor becomes a source of

needless confusion. Writers of different backgrounds and generations often disagree because they seek to make unique works of
art out of the subjectivity of diverse experiences which are connected objectively by duration and by issues arising from within
the social scene in which they find themselves. If friendships
between writers are not strong enough to overcome these built-in
sources of conflict and competition, they fail, but if the relationship
has been fruitful it finds continuity in the works of art that came into
being during the quiet moments of antagonistic cooperation which
marked the relationship.

S: Still the father/son metaphor persists . . .

E: Yes, but let's not forget that often it isn't the self-justifying
younger writer who drags it in, it is done by outsiders; this,
perhaps, because it seems to simplify the relationship between an
older and younger artist. It allows for a facile sense of continuity
between the generations of artists and does away with the mystery
surrounding the nature of artistic influence. This is especially true
of those who look at culture in strictly racial terms; people, let us
say, who don't know what to make of Richard Wright's early appren-
tice relationship with James T. Farrell. Here I'm reminded of an
incident that occurred back when I still thought of myself as
a musician.

Shortly after arriving in New York from Tuskegee I wrote one of
my teachers, that among other exciting developments, I had made
the acquaintance of a famous artist. In return I received an enthusiastic letter in which my teacher said in effect, "Isn't it wonderful
to be sitting at the feet of such an artist and to have the privilege of
breathing in the intellectual atmosphere which he exudes." Oh,
Lord! My reaction was to hit the ceiling. I wasn't particularly overt
in my youthful arrogance, but my teacher's well-meaning interpretation of that relationship outraged me. For awhile I realized that
the man had much to teach me about art (far more, in fact, than most
of the older writers whom I found incapable of discussing writing
techniques with any precision). I also realized that he was far from
being an intellectual. Not only was he innocent of a serious interest
in ideas, but he hadn't *begun* to read the books that I had read, even
before entering college.

And yet in the romantic imagination of my delighted teacher this man had been cast in the role of my intellectual "father"—simply because he had achieved a fairly broad reputation and was some years my senior. So given such misinterpretations the objective complexity of such relationships can get lost and can happen whether the younger individual is *looking* for a "father" or not.

But then again, most friendships have their vague areas of mystery and the older member of a relationship between writers might himself project the younger in a role which obscures the extent of his intellectual maturity or the extent and variety of his experience. One of my early experiences with Dick Wright involved such an underestimation, with him assuming that I hadn't read many books with which I was, in fact, quite familiar.

S: What sorts of things did he assume you hadn't read?

E: Well, among others, he assumed that I hadn't read any of Marx . . . Conrad . . . Dostoyevsky . . . Hemingway—and so on. I was somewhat chagrined by his apparent condescension, but instead of casting him in the role of misunderstanding "father," I swallowed my pride and told myself, "Forget it, you know what you know; so now learn what he thinks of in terms of his Marxism and the insights he's gained as a developed writer of fiction." And that was the way it went. At the time he was already working on *Native Son* and possessed a conscious world view, while I had only begun to write, had no consciously formulated philosophy or way of structuring what I had read and experienced. So I listened and learned even when I disagreed. Speaking of fathers: I lost my own at the age of three, lost a step-father when I was about ten, and had another at the time I met Wright. I was quite touchy about those who'd inherited my father's position as head of my family and I had no desire, or need, to cast Wright or anyone else, even symbolically, in such a role.

However, his underestimation did make for a certain irony in our relationship; because sometimes, thanks to my own reading and quite different experience, I was in a position to have made suggestions for solving problems from which he might have benefited. But since I recognized that his subjective image of me did not encourage the acceptance of certain levels of advice I usually kept my opinions to myself.

S: To what extent does Wright's essay, "Blueprint for Negro

Literature,'' represent his thinking when you were seeing him in
New York in the late thirties and early forties?

E: That essay was written rather early. Wright had come to New
York in June, 1937 and I met him the day after. He was preparing
it for the first issue of *New Challenge,* of which he was an editor.
Yes, I think it was a projection of his current thinking. It was
polemical in relationship to the current line of the Communist Party,
and his emphasis on nationalism, on how to deal with ''Negro
nationalism'' (or ''black chauvinism'' as it was termed) was influenced by Joseph Stalin's pamphlet on the *National Question.*
Wright was attempting to square the official communist ''line'' with
certain resentments entertained by black communists as a result
of their experience of American racism, some of which they found
within the party. And as a writer he was struggling to work out an
orientation for himself as one whose background lay in certain areas
of Afro-American culture.

S: One thing that has troubled me about that essay, and I wonder
if it troubled you, is the extent to which ''folk materials'' fall
under the rubric of nationalism for him. That seems to me to be a
rather limiting term for our various cultural traditions.

E: Actually, he was trying to work within the definitions of the
Communist Party, which viewed Afro-Americans officially as a
''nation'' with geographical roots in the Black Belt of the South; a
line which led some critics to hold that ultimately the white
communists planned to segregate the blacks by herding them into
the South and isolating them. I think that Wright was actually trying
to deal with the confusion between race and culture within the
limitations of communist theory. He held that ''nationalism'' was
not the ''black chauvinism'' for which it was taken by white
communists, and defined it as an ''emotional expression of group
feeling.'' However, I can't be too certain, since it's been years
since I was familiar with the essay. I do know that Wright's
attitude toward our Afro-American background was mixed. As a
communist intellectual he appeared to consider Afro-American
culture ''naive'' and ''humble.'' But then, in *Twelve Million Black
Voices,* he makes lyrical use of certain folk materials. It isn't an
easy question because at the time Wright was so embattled; fighting
the official line of the Communist Party, defending himself against

the anti-intellectual attacks of certain black communist leaders, attacking in turn those writers and intellectuals whom he considered "bourgeois Negroes." On a more objective level, however, his *Blueprint* was a projection of his own plan for action and, I would suggest, a manifesto through which he was announcing his authoritative assumption of literary and intellectual leadership. He was utterly serious in this independent assertion of leadership, but just as serious in his effort to maintain party discipline while remaining loyal to his racial experience.

Perhaps the last was why he was so embattled with those he considered bourgeois Negroes. He had little tact in dealing with them and I don't think that he was aware that his failure to communicate was often his own fault. He told me of an incident in which he went to a party at one of the colleges near Chicago where he was outraged to see that the black students were attired in tuxedos and evening dresses. As far as Wright was concerned, this alone marked them as "bourgeois" and I'm sure that his attitude made for the poor communication which resulted. His sartorial distrust of the group was reinforced by his communist ideology. However, Bill Attaway, the novelist, was present and although Attaway was not the intellectual that Wright was, he was certainly close to our Afro-American folk tradition—perhaps even closer than Wright— and a rather marvelous teller of folktales and a serious writer in his own right. I suppose it was a matter of Wright's having seen the clothing and missed the people, a matter of an ideology-grounded, "trained-incapacity" to respect or communicate with Negroes who were formally educated. Perhaps it is one of the purposes of ideology to render it unnecessary to deal with human complexity. At any rate, you've raised questions that require scholary investigation. In his essay on T. E. Lawrence, Malraux has stated that in revolutionary histories what runs counter to revolutionary convention (here let us say "ideology") is suppressed more imperiously than embarrassing episodes in private memoirs. I've always been struck by the fact that in the account which Wright gives in *Black Boy* of his running away from Mississippi he fails to reveal that the boys who helped him steal the canned goods and other articles with which he made his escape were, in fact, Zack and Wilson Hubert, the sons of the late President Hubert of Jackson College. This was

a rather interesting detail to omit, I thought, from the account of
one who was usually so sensitive to the class divisions within the
Afro-American group. I happened to have known Zack and Wilson at the time their father was president of Langston University
out in Oklahoma and found them rather lively and attractive
young men. But perhaps it was a matter of conscious selectivity, of
Wright's keeping his class views neat by filtering out certain
contradictions that might have embarrassed his ideologically structured projection of experience. Perhaps their having been, or
become, in his estimation "middle class" was inconvenient to the
larger point he was making.

S: I guess one reason I have been thinking more and more about
Wright is because we seem to be in a period of renewed interest
in him. Why do you think this is so? Is this merely something
cyclical, or is it something akin to the temper of the times?

E: Basically it's because he was a powerful writer and even
though many of the solutions he offered were obviously inadequate, the issues which he explored haven't gone away. But I think
much of it was stirred up by the Black Aesthetic people, who are
badly in need of a hero, and an answer to James Baldwin's criticism
of Wright. Now with Wright safely out of the way they can shape
him and his work to their own convenience. Some of them would
make him an outright cultural racist by way of giving authority to
their own biases and confusions. But I think there is another reason:
By now several generations of young people have been taught *Native
Son* and *Black Boy* in high schools and colleges. After all, given a
decade of emphasis upon "blackness" and "militancy" how
many writers of Wright's stature are there to conjure with? It
doesn't matter to the "Black Aesthetic" crowd that in tailoring
him to suit their own threadbare arguments they are forced to
overlook the fact that he was more concerned—at least during the
period when his most powerful books were written—with Marxist-
Leninist-Stalinist ideology than with even his own version of
"black nationalism." He wasn't, as they say, in their "bag" at all;
yet that's where they've sought to cram him, no matter that his
head and limbs refuse to accommodate their efforts.

It would seem that these black "Black Aestheticians" are so hung
up on race and color that they tend to imitate that species of

worm which maintains its ranks by following a scent laid down by
the leader. Introduce them to the rim of a swill barrel, let the
leader negotiate one circle of the rim and even though you remove
him the rest will continue to circle the swill indefinitely. It doesn't
matter that the leader might have been taken off and gone on to
become metamorphosed into a butterfly and flown away, they
keep on circling. Frequently it appears that somebody or some thing
has staked off a certain area of thought and endeavor and said, "Here,
this is yours; this is where you're to stay and we've marked it
'Black' so that you can be safe and comfortable. Therefore you
stay right there and everything will be O.K.—You hear?" And oh,
how so many Afro-American would-be intellectuals agree. They
can't seem to imagine that books or authors that fail to mention
"Black" explicitly might be of crucial importance in dealing with
their own racial, cultural, and individual dilemmas. Thus it's ironic
to see these people embracing Wright, because his was anything but
such an attitude. In his effort to make some sort of intellectual
Gestalt for himself, he read all kinds of books, entertained all
kinds of ideas. And during the days when I knew him well he
certainly didn't allow racial considerations to limit the free play of his
intellect. After all, most of his friends, like both of his wives,
were white.

S: Well, you mention the Black Aesthetic crowd: On the one
hand, we have their interest in Wright, yet on the other we have
very little fiction produced by these writers, these writer-critics.
Why, in your opinion, don't they write fiction? Is it because of
conventional notions of the novel being a bourgeois art form, or is
it because a novel is so damn hard to write (laughter)?

E: I can tell you this: they're damn hard for me! As for the
others, I have no idea. I don't know most of those people, even
though many seem to feel that we have a personal quarrel. But to
put it into the vernacular, I would think that there's a heap of
shucking going on and none of it stacks. They find it easier to issue
militant slogans while remaining safely in the straight-jacket of racist
ideology—the ideology that has been made of what they call
"Blackness"—than to deal with either the beautiful and confounding complexities of Afro-American culture or the difficulties
that must be faced by those who would convert experience into

the forms of the novel. If they can't grasp the meaning of what they live and read because their obsession with the mysticism of race and color has incapacitated their ability to see, then they certainly can't subject themselves to the discipline demanded by the novel. Which, after all, is a product of the *integrative* and *analytical* play of the imagination as it seeks to convert experience into forms of symbolic action. How can one abstract Afro-American experience from that of the larger culture of which it is so important a part without reducing it, in the name of "Blackness," to as vapid a collection of stereotypes as those created in the name of whiteness? As I say, imagination itself is *integrative,* a matter of making symbolic wholes out of parts. Afro-American culture is itself a product of that process carried on under the most difficult social and political conditions. Thus it would seem to me that any objective approach to its dynamics would lead to the basic conclusion that, here in the U.S. at least, culture has successfully confounded all concepts of race. American culture would not exist without its Afro-American component, or if it did, it would be quite different. Yet, certain people who are fixed on the concept of race at the expense of culture would claim Alexander Dumas as a true blue "Boot," "Race Man," or what not, but this is to ignore his achievement, the language in which he thought and wrote, and the image which he held of himself. All this by way of elevating a part of his blood line to a position of total (really totalitarian) importance.

But not only was Dumas culturally a Frenchman, he was a Frenchman who worked and achieved himself in the novel, a literary form which in itself was influenced by developments taking place in England, in Germany and in Russia. Such people also claim Pushkin as their own, and not because of the fact that he was the father of modern Russian literature, but because there was an African or Ethiopian in his background. The relationship between biology and culture is mysterious; perhaps General Hannibal's sperm was precisely what was needed to release the greatness of Russian literature. But although he was a distinguished military man and engineer in his own right, we know of him mainly because of his great-grandson's *literary* achievements, not for his influence upon the Russian racial mixture. I suppose what I'm saying is that an over-emphasis on our own racial origins in Africa (an origin which is only partial) at the expense of the way in which our cultural expression has transcended race, our present social status and our previous condition of servitude, is to ignore much of what is most intriguing and admirable in Afro-American experience. Worse, it is to miss the fact that American culture owes much of its distinctiveness to idioms which achieved their initial formulation through the cultural creativity of Afro-Americans. White Americans have put tremendous energy into keeping the black American below the threshold of social mobility but they still had to descend to see what Negroes were making of the new democratic experience, in order to know what to make of their own. This was especially true of the vernacular idiom in the arts, where lessons were to be learned in everything from power to elegance.

S: So what are we to make of people who say, in echo of a certain black poet, that the black masses are uninterested in elegance?

E: To accept that notion you've got to have a tin ear and absolutely no eye for style. Elegance turns up in every aspect of Afro-American culture, from sermons to struts, pimp-walks and dance steps. Listen to a sermon by Howard Thurman or the Reverend Franklin, father of the famous singer. Listen to Jimmy Rushing sing the *How Long Blues*. Listen to Basie, listen to Ellington; watch O. J. Simpson slice through an opposing line with a dancer's slithering grace. And doesn't all that Afro-American adoration of the Cadillac speak of elegance? Look at the elegance with which the dedicated worshiper of the Cadillac sits at the steering wheel of his chariot. If Bill Robinson and Honi Coles weren't elegant tap dancers, I don't know the meaning of the term. And if Louis Armstrong's meditations on the "Potato Head Blues" aren't marked by elegance, then the term is too inelegant to name the fastidious refinement, the mastery of nuance, the tasteful domination of melody, rhythm, sounding brass and tinkling cymbal which marked his style. Aesthetically speaking, when form is blended successfully with function, elegance results. Black Americans expect elegance even from prizefighters and basketball players and much of the appeal of Jack Johnson and Joe Louis sprang from the fact that each was as elegant as the finest of ballet dancers.

Such statements are products of ideological foolishness and are efforts to palm off sloganeering doggerel as poetry. Surprisingly, the verse of some of these people gives the lie to their assertions, for it reveals as much of the influence of e. e. cummings and Emily Dickinson as of Langston Hughes or Sterling Brown. Blacks alone didn't invent poetics any more than they invented the American language; and the necessary mixture of cultural influences that goes into creating an individual poetic style defies the neat over-simplifications of racist ideologies. Some of the "Black Aesthetic" people say that nothing written before 1967 is of any value, but I'm pretty sure that those who do would *not* say that nothing done in surgery or law before that date was valueless; but then such people don't chatter about law or surgery because they recognize that they are too difficult to be reduced to empty verbalizing. An unserious familiarity with literature breeds contempt, so they feel that they can get away with any kind of irresponsible statement. Perhaps they'd feel less secure if our people were as interested in literature as they are in music. The Kansas City physician who accidently severed the jugular of band leader Benny Moten while performing a tonsillectomy was almost lynched by his own people in their outrage over the discovery that inept medical technique could end the life of a musician whom they revered for his musical excellence. I quote an extreme instance, but sometimes Afro-Americans have been known to call their own irresponsibles to account.

S: What did you think of the *Black World* issue on your work?

E: Hell, man, what would you expect? It was obvious that I couldn't have a fair exchange of opinion with those who used the issue to tee off on me, so there was nothing to do but treat them as I had bad dogs and bigoted whites down South: Mentally, I walked away from it. Long before that issue was published they had been banging away at a hateful straw man whom they'd labeled "Ellison" and were using it as a scapegoat for their discontents and disappoint-ments, and it appeared that the more I refused to be provoked the more strident they became. I was amused by the time they wasted attacking me when it was really a couple of *books* that were making them mad, and the only way to win a fight with a book is to write a better book. I could have respected them had they done that, but

I saw little evidence that this was going to happen. However, I did appreciate the essays by those who used the issue to express serious disagreement with my work and my position on social issues. I hoped that younger writers would read them as antidotes to the rantings of those who tried to reduce literary discussion to the level of the dirty dozens. I was also amused by the extent of the bad-mouthing because the editor of *Black World* was so persistent in his attempt at scapegoating, while I continued to function very much as I had always done. Even having a bit of influence. His conception of the cultural reality of the U.S. was puzzling because he appeared to have no idea of how books can reach beyond the boundaries of the black community. He seemed to think that he could kill the influence of a novel by attacking its author. That struck me as strange, since his organ reached but a few thousand readers while my books were being read by *many* thousands.

Then there was the other contributor to the issue who gave the impression of being as eager to burn books as any Nazi *gauliter*—which was rather obscene, considering that the man is an old communist and has spent a good part of his life working in a library. His example and that of a like-minded fellow contributor demonstrated that they could be just as vehement, provincial, and totalitarian in the name of "Black Militancy" and "Black Aesthetics" as they had been in the name of "Soviet Communism" and "Socialist Realism." I guess it's a case of Reds infiltrating Blacks, running into a stubborn Negro and turning blue in the face. But I can say this for them: Safe behind the fence provided by a black capitalist, they had one big "barking-at-the-big-gate" go at me. They even managed to convince a few students that I was the worst disaster that had ever hit Afro-American writing. But for all their attacks I'm still here trying—while if I'm asked where is *Black World* today my answer is: Gone with the snows of yester-year/ down the pissoir—Da-daa, Da-daaa—and good riddance!

S: Our talk about groups reminds me of something Leon Forrest once said. He was asked if he belonged to a group or crowd, and I believe his response was, "I guess you might say that McPherson, Toni Morrison, Albert Murray, Ralph Ellison and I might constitute a crowd." Now what is your response to that?

E: It's an interesting grouping of writers whom I respect; still I

am by instinct (and experience) a loner. There is no question,
however, but that we share what Malraux has termed a "collectivity
of sensibilities" and a high regard for the artistic potential of
Afro-American experience. And certainly we're all more concerned
with art than with ideology or propaganda. But as to our constituting a school, that kind of thing—no. I don't think it desirable even
though it offers some relief from the loneliness of the trade. For
when writers associate too closely there is a tendency to control
one another's ideas. I'm not implying that association is itself
necessarily a negative matter, but I suspect that the loneliness of
writing causes us to seek for a kind of certainty among our peers—
when very often it's the *uncertainty* of the creative process which
leads to new insights and to unanticipated formulation. Nevertheless,
I share ideas and certain goals with such people as Forrest and
McPherson, just as I do with a number of white writers, and certainly
with Al Murray, whom I've known since our days at Tuskegee; but
they do their own thinking and I do mine. (I don't know Miss
Morrison personally.) Perhaps Forrest was really describing a collectivity of outsiders who are united by a common attitude toward
the craft.

S: He is also describing a group of *fiction* writers, and I can't
help but continue to link this issue to genre . . .

E: I agree, because a writer's point of view is determined to a
large extent by the form in which he works. The form shapes his
sensibility, it structures his emotions, and guides his imagination
and vision. That's most important: The novel is a complex agency for
the symbolic depiction of experience, and it demands that the writer
be willing to look at both sides of characters and issues—at least
while he's working. You might say that the form of the novel
imposes its morality upon the novelist by demanding a complexity
of vision and an openness to the variety and depth of experience.

Kenneth Burke says that language "moralizes" both mankind
and nature, thus the novel "moralizes" the novelist. Dostoyevsky
could be pretty rabid in some of his ideological concerns, pretty
bigoted in his attitudes toward the members of certain groups, but
when he chose to depict characters identified with such groups he
gave them all the human complexity that the form and action of the

novel demanded. I don't think that you can do this if your mind is made up beforehand. You end up creating stereotypes, writing propaganda.

Harper: Is there any sort of organization that you now see in the fiction you've published over the years since *Invisible Man?* I've put together the fiction I've seen in various places and it seems to me that it is all of one piece—that is, I see certain kinds of relationships. For example, could one go out and collect "Song of Innocence" and "Juneteenth" and make a case for works-in-progress being sections of the same novel?

E: Yes, they *are* parts of the same novel, but whether they will remain in that relationship I don't know, because, you know, I lost a good part of the novel in a fire. It's a long manuscript, and it just might be two books.

H: I remember talking with some students at Harvard and two of them were offended by "Juneteenth" where Hickman says that Africans were heathens who didn't have any souls. They said this is a terrible thing! You got to get him up here!

E: They went on to say other things, didn't they? Did they read what was *there?*

H: Yes, but they were bothered by "heathen." Again, this is the old question of ideology. I think the source of their agitation was that they thought you were making a statement to the effect that when Americans came to this country they were soulless.

E: Oh, for God's sake! I didn't make that statement, *Hickman* did. He was preaching about transcendence; about the recovery from fragmentation; about the slave's refusal, with the help of God, to be decimated by slavery. He was speaking as a Christian minister of the role his religion had played in providing a sense of unity and hope to a people that had been deliberately deprived of a functional continuity with their religions and traditions. Hickman didn't attend college but, hell, he knew that all of our African ancestors didn't belong to the same tribe, speak the same tongue, or worship the same gods. . . .

H: If they had proposed the argument that either Bliss or Hickman was the persona of Ralph Ellison *that* might have been debatable—it probably wasn't *right,* but it might have been debatable. The one-dimensional character, the way they view literary creation, is what bothered me. We got in a similar row over "Song of Innocence." In the mind of some students who are not familiar with literary convention and the whole business of creation, anything you write is autobiographical, it's about you.

S: This reminds me of students who write papers for me about *The Autobiography of an Ex-Coloured Man,* and begin, "When *Johnson* gets off the train in Atlanta. . . . [Laughter]

H: Do you get many inquiries about the chapter deleted from *Invisible Man* that appears in *Soon, One Morning?* Did you willingly cut it out?

E: Well, the book was long and they wanted cuts, and I found a better way than just cutting was to restructure. So, instead of that particular handling of the narrative sequence I just took it out. I think it would have probably worked better in.

H: Why isn't "Society, Morality and the Novel" in *Shadow and Act?* It came before.

E: I wanted to put it in but my editor said no. I think it was because we already had enough material.

S: Can you tell us about your teaching experiences? I'm especially interested in experiences resulting from attempts to teach certain texts side by side. For example, in 1970, I once began a course on the Harlem Renaissance by assigning *The Great Gatsby.* I still think it was a great idea, but the students couldn't get with it—even on the level of establishing a milieu, or "countermilieu."

E: I have had the same trouble getting that across with *Gatsby.* For instance, I find it significant that the character who saw who was driving the "death car" was a Negro; and yet, some students resist when I tie that in with Tom Buchanan's concern over the rise of the colored races, the scene in which blacks are being driven by a white chauffeur, and the characterization of the Jewish gangster. They miss the broader context of the novel that is revealed in the understated themes of race, class, and social mobility. The novel is set in what was called the Jazz Age, but what is the difference between Fitzgerald's Jazz Age and that of Duke Ellington and Louis Armstrong? I point out that Fitzgerald was familiar with Brick Top's nightclub and was often at the Harlem Cotton Club, and I suggest that after reading what Fitzgerald made of the

experience the student should take a look at what Langston
Hughes and other writers of the Harlem Renaissance made of it.
It's ironic that some of the white writers were more open to
knowledge relating to the Harlem of that period than are the black
kids who refuse to study it seriously because they feel that they
know it through their genes. They think affirmations of "Blackness"
resolves all mysteries of time and place, circumstance and personality. But for a writer like Fitzgerald, Harlem was one of the places
where the action was, so, being a good novelist, with an interest
in people and an eye for exciting new developments in the culture,
he went where the action was unfolding. Now we don't have to
like what white writers, musicians, and dancers made of what went
on, but I do think we should recognize that across the division of race
they were attempting to absorb and project some of the cultural
complexity of the total American scene. They were responding in
their individual ways to the vitality of the Afro-American cultural
idiom. The "Black Aesthetic" crowd buys the idea of total cultural
separation between blacks and whites, suggesting that we've been
left out of the mainstream. But when we examine American music
and literature in terms of its themes, symbolism, rhythms, tonalities,
idioms and images it is obvious that those rejected "Neegroes"
have been a vital part of the mainstream and were from the beginning. Thus, if a student is to grasp the complex sources of
American cultural tradition he should assume that a major part of
that tradition springs from Afro-America; because one of the few
ways the slaves and their descendants had of expressing their inner
sense of identity was by imposing their own aesthetic will upon
those who assumed that they would have nothing to do with defining
American experience. Today sociologists, many of them the first
members of immigrant families to attend college, and who now
teach at universities and advise politicians, are telling us that the
American melting-pot didn't melt. But despite discrimination and
other inequities in the society, its various cultural idioms did,
indeed, melt and are continuing to do so.

H: Don't you teach a course in the vernacular?

E: Yes, from a base in American lit. I teach a course which
allows me to touch many areas of American culture. American
literature grew out of the development of American vernacular

speech as it asserted its modes against European tradition and
proper English usage. As the young nation achieved coherence the
very pressures of Nature, of the New World "scene," forced
Americans to create a flood of new terminologies: for naming the
newly created social forms, the nuances of the individualism that
was spreading throughout the young society, and the relationships
between diverse groups. Out of the democratic principles set
down on paper in the Constitution and the Bill of Rights they were
improvising themselves into a nation, scraping together a conscious culture out of the various dialects, idioms, lingos, and meth-
odologies of America's diverse peoples and regions. In this effort
the English language and traditional cultural forms served both as
guides and as restraints, anchoring Americans in the wisdom and
processes of the past, while making it difficult for them to perceive
with any clarity the nuances of their new identity. Given the
reality of slavery and the denial of social mobility to blacks, it is
ironic that they were placed by that very circumstance in the
position of having the greatest freedom to create specifically *American* cultural idioms. Thus the slaves had the unnoticed opportunity to be culturally daring and innovative because the strictures of
"good taste" and "thou shall-not" of tradition were not imposed
upon them. And so, having no past in the art of Europe, they could
use its elements and their inherited sense of style to improvise
forms through which they could express their own unique sense of
American experience. They did so in dance, in music, in cuisine
and so on, and white American artists often found the slaves'
improvisations a clue for their *own* improvisations. From the very
beginnings of the nation Afro-Americans were contributing to the
evolution of a specifically *American* culture.

   H: Are you happy with your students at N.Y.U.?

   E: With some of them; you know, the quality varies from class
to class. I am unhappy with the numbers who can't write. I
consider myself as having had a fairly incomplete education, but as
I look back I realize that even in high school there were a number
of us who could write rings around some of my graduate students.
Most of my students are white. I haven't had many black students, but when I work with those who are having difficulty I say to
them, "All right, you are here now, so recognize that you have

certain disabilities which I can't ignore. So let's not kid ourselves
but face the fact that there's some catching up to be done. There's
nothing wrong with your mind but there *is* a lot wrong with the kind
of training you've had, if not then with the kind of attention
you've given to learning. Face that fact and allow your experience
to feed your study and you'll be surprised at how fast you can
come up to par." Fortunately, a few understand that this isn't a
put-down, but the truth.

The other day I had to tell a black student who wants to substitute
militancy for study and who came up with an easy criticism of
George Washington Carver that I didn't like Dr. Carver either, but
for a specific and personal reason: At Tuskegee he was always chasing
me out of Rockefeller Hall where I'd go to work out my harmonic
exercises on the piano. My investigations into the mysteries of
harmony interfered with his investigations of the peanut, and to me
harmony was more important. But today I realize that not only
did a large industry draw upon his experiments but by manipulating
strains of peanuts he was growing himself an American President!
Dr. Carver has been called an "Uncle Tom," but I keep looking at
the announcement of prizes given in such fields as science and
architecture, in biology and electronics and I'm chagrined over the
fact that few of our students are getting them. Sheer militancy isn't
enough, and when used as an excuse to avoid study it is disastrous.
Today we're in a better way to learn and participate in the intellectual
life of this country than ever before, but apparently we're taking
fewer advantages of our opportunities than when we were limited
to carrying bags and waiting tables. The availability of ideas and
culture means little if we don't take advantage, participate, and
compete with the best in our elected fields.

H: Bob and I know a folklorist who thinks you are one of the few
people who really understand what folklore is and how it ought to
be used. Would you care to comment on that?

E: Folklore has been such a vital part of American literature that
it is amazing that more people (and especially writers) aren't
aware of it. Constance Rourke points out that there are folk motives
even in the work of Henry James. I guess one of the difficulties
here is that people think of folklore as "quaint," as something that
is projected in dialect, when in fact it is its style and wisdom that

count. The same problem arises when you speak of *American folklore* in the general sense and overlook the complex influence of vernacular idioms, the mixture of vernacular styles, that operate in American culture. Considering the social condition of the slaves, what is to be made of their singing a comic song which refers to a black girl's dancing "Taglioni" in the street? Or what are you going to do with fairly illiterate jazz musicians who interpolate phrases from the likes of Bach, Verdi, or Puccini in their improvisations on the Blues or popular melodies? In this country it is necessary to redefine what we mean by folklore, because, culturally, Americans are heirs to the culture of all the ages, and it is through the vernacular process that we blend folk and classical modes into an art that is uniquely American. Thus I believe it a mistake to think of the slaves as having been separate from the eclectic processes, the general culture, when in fact they were participating in it in many unexamined ways. Art was an inseparable part of their African forebearers' lives, and they did, after all, do most of the building of Monticello! They made the bricks and did the carpentry and cabinetry. Recently *The Crisis* published an article calling attention to the manner in which historians tend to omit the slave craftsmen when describing the "cultural activities" of Thomas Jefferson, but my God, somebody was there doing the work and receiving the instructions necessary for carrying it to completion. If there are doubts as to this, all one has to do is observe the demonstrations down at Colonial Williamsburg. Slaves were craftsmen and artists as well as field hands and as such they absorbed and mastered the styles and techniques around them. That's how I see it and I can't imagine a human situation that would *not* be like that.

Perhaps we have too damn much of a wound-worshiping investment in the notion that the slaves were brutalized beyond the point of exercising their human will to survive. Which reminds me of an aspect of the uproar centering around *Time on the Cross*. Whatever the viability of their methods, the authors were saying that slavery wasn't as brutalizing as the usual view would have it. They held that the slaves were *not* reduced to a gas-oven state of docility, a view that would see each and every slave master as a Hitler and American slavery as a preview of the Holocaust. I'm no historian, but their view seems to offer a more adequate account-

ing for the character of the ex-slaves whom I knew in Oklahoma
and Alabama. After all, I did see my grandaddy and he was no
beaten-down "Sambo." Rather he was a courageous, ingenious old
guy who owned property, engaged in the Reconstruction politics
of South Carolina, and who stood up to a mob after they had
lynched his best friend. When ordered to leave town, he told the
lynchers, "If you're gonna kill me, you're gonna kill me here where
I've got my family, and my property and my friends." He died
there years later, in his own bed, and at the age of 76. I also knew
one of his friends who, after years of operating a printing business
for a white man, came north and set up his own printing shop
in Harlem.

The other argument that I find interesting in *Time on the Cross* is
the authors's statement that, while the slaves in the Caribbean
and Brazil died off every ten years and had to be replaced from
Africa, those in the United States managed to reproduce themselves. And of course they did! There were times when native-born
blacks outnumbered native-born whites. Unlike the slaves of the
other Americas, they had a good injection of white European
chromosomes which made them immune to many European diseases.
(Laughter!) They also became "Indianized," and certainly these
biological facts show in our faces. Still, many historians and
sociologists act as though these factors are irrelevant, and by
ignoring them they contribute to the divisive mystification of race.

S: I pointed that out to an historian the other day, and I could
tell by the look on his face that I was embarrassing him!
(Laughter)

E: Then Fern Brodie published a biographical account of Jefferson's long affair with his black mistress. Why don't the historians
allow these people their human complexity?

H: Well, we did!

E: That's right! (Laughter) It's amusing the way this thing works.
In my class I get raised eyebrows by pointing out that race is
always at the center of our uneasy preoccupation with American
identity. It is as abiding as our concern with the principles of
freedom and equality. Thus, when you read American literature and
fail to see the words "Black" or "Negro" or "Afro-American"
in a given work, it doesn't mean that they are not operating there

symbolically. The old phrase "There's a nigger in the woodpile" was more fact than fantasy. Just examine the logic of a work's symbolism and you'll discover that there are surrogates for Blacks and the hierarchal motives they symbolize; just as Negroes are often surrogates for the American Indian. Once we were discussing the tragedy of the Indian, and someone said, "Yeah, the Indian, he stood up to the white man; he didn't take that crap." This went on until someone got serious and said, "Yeah, but look here man, what *happened* to them damn Indians?" And I said, "Well, don't you know? *You* became the damn Indians!" They laughed but I don't think that it really got across. As a child watching cowboy and Indian movies I frequently pulled for the Indians to win, but as you know, they seldom did.

H: What would you like to see people researching and writing that would begin to correct things?

E: Well, I would really like to see more studies that deal with the actual pre-Emancipation scene; works that would place people. Who was doing what jobs? And what happened to them after Emancipation, and later after the betrayal of Reconstruction? Where did people go? I'd like to see more done on the role of geography in American Negro history. Many black cowboys were slaves who, after their owners moved west, were taken out of the cotton patch and put on horses. Many Afro-American characteristics that are assumed to spring from the brutality of slavery are partially the results of geography, of the localities in which they were enslaved. Some of this is suggested by the phrase "sold down the river." The Mississippi was as tremendous a force in Afro-American history as it was in the vision of Mark Twain. The geographical division of the country into political districts and regions with complementary agricultural and economic systems underlies much of Afro-Amerian poetic symbolism. That the star points north is not important because of some abstract, mystical or religious conception, but because it brought into conjunction Biblical references, concrete social conditions and the human will to survive—including the fact that if you got safely across certain socio-geographical boundaries you were in freedom. Writers have made much of the North Star but they forget that a hell of a lot of slaves were running away to the West, "going to the nation, going

to the territory,'' because as Mark Twain knew, that too was an
area of Negro freedom. When people get to telling stories based on
their cooperate experience, quite naturally such patterns turn up.
Because as significant scenes in which human will is asserted, they
help organize and focus narrative. They become more poetic the
further we are removed from the actual experience, and their
symbolic force is extended through repetition.

I'd also like to see someone write about jazz in such a way that
they cover those people who are the intermediaries, the mentors,
the teachers, the transmitters of classical tradition. All around the
country there were musicians, bandmasters, etc. who disapproved of
the jazz life but who, nevertheless, were training people to read
music and to perform on instruments. People who taught voice
and staged operettas, and so on. You still have them in the colleges,
you have them in the towns, giving piano lessons, teaching
harmony. These are the links between the classical and folk traditions and jazz.

H: Thanks for letting us visit with you this afternoon.

E: It's been my pleasure. I enjoyed it.

The Essential Ellison

Ishmael Reed, Quincy Troupe, and Steve
Cannon / 1977

From *Y'Bird Magazine* 1 (Autumn 1977), 126–59. Copyright
1977 by *Y'Bird Magazine*. Reprinted by permission.

IR: You once wrote for *Black World,* is that correct?

RE: No, for the old *Negro Digest;* or more precisely, they
reprinted a short story which appeared first in the *New Masses.*
The *Negro Digest* was founded by Alan Morrison and George
Norford, then with the coming of World War II, it was taken over
by the founder of Johnson Publications. *Black World* is actually a
metamorphosis of the *Negro Digest.*

IR: What would you say was the source of the conflict between
you and the present editor of *Black World?*

RE: That's a mystery to me, but the conflict is one-sided. I don't
know the man, and you can look high and low, but you won't find
an attack nor even an ironic comment coming from me. I suppose
his motive is ideological.

IR: But, at the same time he's lashed out at you, hasn't he?

RE: Oh, yes, over and over again. He's made me a sort of
scapegoat. I don't know why, but perhaps it's simply because
I've been around longer. And yet, there are older writers than
myself who are still active. It could have something to do with my
reputation; if so, I guess it's a matter of negative flattery.

IR: George Schuyler has been around, but they don't even mention him. As you say, the conflict is ideological. What would you
consider Fuller's ideology to be?

RE: I suppose it's some sort of Black nationalism—I almost said
"Black racism"—but, whatever it is, it seems to have given him
an Ellison phobia. All I know is that I've never replied to his
attacks. My attitude toward this complex Negro American situation
leads me to feel that there's so little to be gained from our fighting
with one another that I can afford to ignore such attacks. I learned
long before I became a writer that there were Blacks who preferred

342

to put you down rather than try to understand your point of view. Either you agreed with them, or you were the enemy. Black ideologists complain that white people are always giving us hell, but, in truth, we get our first hell from one another. We suffer chronically from Booker T. Washington's "crabs-in-a-basket" syndrome: let one crab try to climb out, and others try to yank him back. But, perhaps this is inevitable. After all, we grow up in our own segregated communities and have our initial contacts and contentions with our own people. So our initial conflicts are with those near at hand. But then there is the factor of race as it operates in the broader society. Following the Reconstruction, Southern Blacks in many localities were allowed to kill one another without too much fear of punishment, so people who didn't dare lift a hand against a white man would give other Blacks hell. I guess we're observing that tendency being acted out by today's Black ideologists. They seem to hate Negroes worse than white racists. But as I see it, we are part of the larger American society and thus subject to the same pressures and responsibilities and that must be confronted by other writers. Sure, we can cling intellectually to the relative safety of what is now termed the "ghetto," where it appears that there are no consequences to flow from our attacks upon one another, but I see this as but another form of the obscentiy we have in the vicious crimes Blacks commit against other Blacks. There are bigger and more important targets for intellectual assault out there in the broader society. Given the complexity of American society and the difficulties of art, I have always felt that it was more important for me to learn how to write than to be a H.N.I.C.*—which seems to be the goal of certain Black critics. Instead, you keep trying to master those ideas, those perspectives—wherever they arise—that will make the most sense out of your experience. Black ignorance has little to contribute to the achievement of freedom.

IR: I made a remark about your blurb for James Alan McPherson's book of short stories.

RE: I know. You said . . .

IR: Just a minute. I'm interested in craftsmanship at this point,

---

*Head Nigger In Charge.

and you are, and I think you said something about other writers
being "publicity-sustained" . . .

RE: OK.

IR: And you made other remarks about the younger Black writers lacking craftsmanship . . .

RE: Not really—I hope I didn't generalize to that extent. But,
there are those who have no respect for craftsmanship. If they
were posing as jazz musicians, dedicated jazzmen would chase them
off the bandstand—and *keep* them off until they'd come up to
standard. They'd be told to go pay their dues. For instance, Eddie
"Lockjaw" Davis was thrown off the bandstand at Minton's a
number of times before he was accepted by the jazzmen, whose
company he wished to join. They knew that the major responsibility for the quality of art doesn't belong to the critic or to the public,
but to the artist.

IR: Of course, but some jazz musicians can't read music.

RE: True, but literature is a different medium. Such jazz musicians know their instrument well enough to release their creative
ideas, and they've steeped themselves in the traditional jazz idioms,
much of which they can learn simply by listening to other musicians and to recordings. Once they've achieved a certain compe-
tence on their instruments, and being gifted musically, they can
bypass the formal knowledge which is indispensable for the writer.
Music is a more natural art form, by which I mean that unlike the
art of literature, wherein literacy, syntax, grammar and a knowledge
of literary form must be acquired before emotions and ideas can
be communicated successfully, musical skill can be acquired and
expressed by ear. In improvised jazz, performance and creation can
consist of a single complex act. Incidentally, as a small child I heard
Blind Boone perform an intricate repertory of piano classics.
Many fine jazzmen have been illiterate, but for comparable figures
in the field of literature you don't go to the ignorant writer, but to the
gifted oral storyteller. Anyway, if you want me to say explicitly that
I didn't include you. . . .

IR: Oh, no, no! (Laughter.) The criticism you receive is mild in
comparison to the kind I receive.

RE: Certain critics give you hell.

IR: Somebody said I should be flushed down the toilet and my books with me. I was saying, however, that McPherson used that blurb like the witch in *Snow White* used the mirror. The witch asks who's the fairest of them all, and you have that blurb on this book which answers, "Why you are, Jim."

RE: Well, Jim *is* a gifted writer—which doesn't exclude other serious writers. Why can't writers be as concerned with quality as jazz musicians?

QT: I notice that in the interview that you did with Steve quite a while back, you commented on the writers of the Forties and Fifties. Now I would like for you to talk about some of the specific differences in regard to vision and influence that you see between the writers of the Forties and Fifties and those who emerged during the Sixties and Seventies. Would you address yourself to the novelists first, and then to the poets?

RE: Well, I don't care to talk about specific works because so much has been published and so many writers have appeared that I wouldn't pretend to know what all of them are doing. That's no longer possible. Now, let's go back a bit. One could say that during the Forties we were still being influenced by the attitudes and values of the Twenties and Thirties, and by perspectives introduced to our specific community of writers by Stalinists and the Trotskyist Left. There was also the influence of the WPA, which provided a number of us with our first opportunity for becoming writers. It also provided others who were already working at the craft with an opportunity to earn a living. And there was also present a current of intellectual influence derived from existentialism. I became aware of Kierkegaard and Unamuno a good while before existentialism became a literary "movement." I picked it up through the writings of André Malraux, who was depicting existential concepts long before Sartre and Camus made them fashionable. I became interested after reading *Man's Hope,* in which Unamuno appears as a character. In 1937, I was present at a party where Malraux was raising funds for the Spanish Loyalists, and shortly afterwards, Richard Wright and I were reading and discussing Unamuno's *The Tragic Sense of Life.* Such ideas were new to me and very exciting in that they made me aware of existential elements in the spirituals and the blues. At the time, I was trying to make connections between my own background and the world of ideas, connections that I hadn't been taught in college but which I felt to exist. As a musician, I had no problem in seeing connections between European and Afro-American music, so why not between my segregated condition and the world of ideas? So, I was groping. Marx and Freud were the dominant intellectual forces during that period, and I had become aware of Freud even before finishing high school. Marx, I encountered at Tuskegee—but how did you put the two together? I didn't know, so I read, I talked, I asked questions and I listened. Such ideas concerned me as I turned from music to literature.

Now for the main ideological and intellectual forces operating within the small group in which I found myself: There was the psychological in the form of Freudianism, the political in the form of Marxism, and in Malraux's fiction and criticism, which questioned the assertions of both, there were the concepts of existentialism. With these there was the living presence of Langston Hughes, Claude McKay, Countee Cullen, Sterling Brown and Alain Locke. Now I don't mean that these figures were "influences" in any simple-minded way, but that their examples were part of the glamour of Harlem and thus important to your sense of opportunity. And, although you had a vague but different set of tunes tinkling in your head and sought other solutions and perhaps a more complex form in which to work, you respected them and their achievements. You respected them even after you discovered that some of them like, say, McKay, were inarticulate when it came to discussing technique. In fact, Wright was far more articulate in that area than either Hughes or McKay.

But, there was another factor which I found most important. The writers I've just mentioned related to Harlem and to the waning influence of the Negro Renaissance, but there was a wider world of culture to be found in New York, and I made my closest contacts with it on the Writers Project. There you were thrown in contact not only with black and white writers of your own age grouping, but with a number who had already achieved broad reputations. McKay was one of these, but most were white. Then there was the old League of American Writers whose programs made it possible for me to meet important writers who had nothing to do with the WPA. My friendship with Wright gave me entree to a number of such people, and they came to form, for me at least, a scattered but most meaningful intellectual community. Within it, the craft of fiction was passionately discussed. The philosophical and political implications of artistic styles were given endless attention. Myth, ritual and revolution got slammed around. On the Project, I hung out with a few fellows of my own general age and the same subjects were discussed. Incidentally, most of them were Jewish, but this was before we realized what Hitler was really up to, so little time was spent discussing race or religion. Instead, we discussed craft, form, and ideas relating more immediately to writing. And even in Harlem, there was no such concentration upon what is now termed the "Black experience" as one encounters it today, not even between Wright and myself. I was concerned, but I felt it to be something one worked out for oneself. I was *living* that experience, so what I wanted was to be able to make my own intellectual sense of it. Nor was there any question in my own mind about who I was or where I came from. It's in my face, it's in the neighborhoods where I grew up, it's in the Afro-Methodist Episcopal Church into which I was baptized, it was in the ex-slaves I knew as a child. I'm out of slaves on both sides of my family. That was history, and I couldn't undo it; my question was how did one bridge the gap intellectually (or at least *imaginatively*), between what one felt about Negro life, between what one felt about our people, and what was said about us—that is, the stereotyped identity imposed upon us by society. Yes, and what was there being written in areas lying beyond the confines of our own neighborhoods that could be used in the task of adequately defining our humanity? How did one get American Negro life, that great, bursting, expressive capacity for life, into writing? Where did one discover ideas and techniques with which one could free one's mind and achieve something of one's possibilities?

In those days, interestingly enough, I knew a couple of the writers who've attacked me from time to time in *Black World*. They had little talent as writers but were then part of the communist apparatus and given to preaching internationalism, really meaning Russianism. Today they're preaching "Blackness" in the same inept accents. Around the Communists they acted like whipping dogs that were so glad to be associated with whites that they accepted

anything they were told and parroted any absurd interpretation of
Negro experience that was handed down from above. Today, barking behind what they consider to be the protective "big gate" of
Black World, they perform like Supercargo in *Invisible Man,* barking
and snarling at me in order to keep other possible dissenters in line.
Years ago, after hearing me state some unorthodox opinions, one of
them shook his head and said, "Ellison, you say you want to be
a novelist, but you'll never make it, thinking like that." No, I won't
give his name; I'm interested in the pattern, not the individual.
These two have lived in New York for years, but they still retain
their Calvinist compulsion to control the acts and imagination of
others that you find in certain Black, down-home communities.
They consider themselves the Black man's white man and will do
almost anything to prevent other Afro-Americans from testing their
individual possibilities. Perhaps it's because they sense that the
assertion of the independent imagination is a gesture toward freedom, and freedom is dangerous; freedom frightens them, so wanting
to have it both ways, they growl like tigers in their blessedly
segregated journals and then move among whites flinching as
though expecting a blow. Every once in a while, I bump into one of
these gents on the streets of Harlem, and after bad-mouthing me
in *Black World*—which he knows I disdain to read—he approaches
me with his tail wagging and grinning like a jackass eating briars.
It's so obscene that it's damn near charming.

And yet, such people have been around for a long time. Years
ago, the playwright Carlton Moss told me of attending a party
during which my ambition to become a writer was discussed. At the
time, I had been writing for two or three years, nevertheless, they
decided right then and there that I was wasting my time. Since they
couldn't imagine themselves being successful writers, I had to be a
fool for trying.

IR: Well, that's a current problem . . . a problem of discipline.
You get it in Chester Himes, you get it in your work, you get it in
Richard Wright—the attempt to control the Afro-American imagination. Now there was a strident attack on all Afro-American writers in
the *Saturday Review.* I don't know if you saw that.

RE: I missed it.

IR: We're going to do a whole book on it, Steve and I. Someone

calling himself Moss, who's taught a Black Literature program at
Camden, New Jersey, wrote it, and the word "discipline" kept
coming up again and again. And, in the last paragraph, he quoted
Du Bois, which tells you which ideological ballpark he's in. He said
nothing has happened in Afro-American writing since 1959. He
also had a chronology of Black achievements in which some of the
dates were wrong. For example, he said that Wheatley's first
book was published in 1775, and there were other errors. He was
inaccurate. So, I'm sure he didn't mean discipline in the sense of
scholarship, because he would have applied it to himself. [Laughter]
So, he concluded by saying that Black writers should, instead of
"furtively pilfering" from white authors, from white artists, they
should just copy the stuff altogether. Just imitate the white man—he
used the term "masters," "white masters." They should be more
exposed to white culture than they are instead of "polemicizing,"
polemicizing American literature usually means you don't agree
with the point-of-view of the narrative and you don't agree with
the point of view of the characters, and so that's polemic.

I want to ask you what you thought about that, the idea that he
could say nothing's happened since 1959, and that we should stop
"furtively pilfering scraps." And that we have not produced a
Hindemith or a Schoenberg—I don't know why he gives us this
schmaltzy, whiney Schoenberg [laughter]—but our musicians have
not produced that, our writers haven't done anything worthwhile, and
the dancers haven't done anything worthwhile. They're polemicizing, and what else . . . that was the gist of it.

RE: It seems to be a very provincial view of how art bridges the
gaps of race, class, and individual background. What if the subject
was shoes? What the hell are you to do then? Even though you
could point to historical fact and say that a Black man invented
the machine technique now used for attaching the upper to the sole
of a shoe, it would do nothing to alter the fact that *whoever*
contributed that technique to shoe production, everybody has to
wear them. And, if you must wear shoes, you wear the shoes that are
available. And, if you're going to *design* shoes, you still have to
work with the basic elements and examples of shoe design. Form,
design, and technique are the basic elements, not race. A student
of surgery has to master the techniques that were handed down from

the past, no matter who developed them. He can't start out by saying, "I can't use this surgical technique because some peckerwood developed it." Surgery, like literature, has been around for a long time. If you wish to become a surgeon, you have to line up with its techniques and traditions. You master its disciplines and adapt them to your own task of saving lives. Hopefully, you'll improve them and devise new ones. I think the same applies to the arts. Beyond all questions of race, class, nation, and geography, the arts are the possession of all humanity—and especially of the artists. They are a common heritage. Once a work of creative art has been placed before the public, it becomes the possession of anyone who has the sensibility and interest to grasp its method and message. Whatever elements of the new it embodies, whether in content, technique, form or vision, will be taken over by any artist who finds it a meaningful aid in getting his own work done.

Where on earth did the notion come from that the world and all its art has to be re-invented, recreated, every time a Black individual seeks to express himself? The world is here and art is here, and they've been here for a long, long time. After all, a few of the contributions to culture, to civilization, were made by people who possessed African genes—if that means a damn thing, which I doubt . . .

IR: The point is that this was a Jewish intellectual. I'm leaving New York in a minute, so I don't have to fear any demonstration. But, it seems to me, objectively, and you don't have to be an anti-Semite, you know [he mentioned "Levy's" and Yiddish theater], Jewish intellectuals seem to give Afro-American writers the hardest time. How do you account for his saying that we haven't produced a Hindemith, when Hindemith wrote in Ragtime, an Afro-American form. He said we hadn't produced any kind of theater, but, of course, Al Jolson made his reputation "blacking up," and the Marx Brothers performed minstrel crossfires and conundrums. Why do you think this came about? You teach and you know this, and you see that the most flagrant attacks on Afro-American artists seem to come from Jewish intellectuals. For example, in *Partisan Review,* Morris Dickstein says that we ought to be imitative of Philip Roth, that we ought to imitate Jewish intellectuals. Why is that?

RE: I don't know; but perhaps the answer to the last part of your question has something to do with the fact that so many intellectuals happen to be Jews; who like the rest of us can't help trying to shape other groups to their own image. Looked at historically, however, there is no question but that this society started out with a divided mind—if not with a divided conscience. Its founders asserted the noble idea of creating a free, open society while retaining slavery, a system in direct contradiction to their rhetorically inclusive concept of freedom. Thus, from the beginning, racism has mocked the futuristic dream of democracy. The people who won their revolution by throwing the British off their backs and who declared that they were rejecting the hierarchical division of the past in the name of democracy began their experiment loaded down with hypocrisy and wrapped up to their wigs in facial self-righteousness. They declared themselves the new national identity, "American," but, as social beings, they were still locked in the continuum of history, and as language-users they were still given to the ceaseless classifying and grading of everything from stars and doodlebugs to tints of skin and crinks of hair (given, that is, to what Kenneth Burke has termed the "moralizing" of nature, of themselves, and of society through language), they had to have a standard by which they could gauge the extent to which their theories of democracy were being made manifest, both in the structure of the new society and in the lives of its citizens. Theoretically, theirs was a "classless" society, so what better (or easier) way of establishing such a standard than to say, "Well, now, here we have all these easily identifiable Blacks who're already below the threshold of social mobility—why not use them? They're not even human by our standards, so why not exploit them as the zero point on our scale of social possibility? Why not designate to *them* the negative ground upon which our society shall realize its goals? By looking at their permanent, Bible-sanctioned condition, *any* white man can easily measure his individual progress toward achieving the promises of democracy." This is to telescope a hell of a lot of history and sociology, but you can see what I'm driving at. The poorest, least gifted of white men could say, "No matter how poor or miserable I am, I'm still better than a nigger." Or, if he saw himself slipping downward on the social scale, he could say, "Hey, I'm being forced down to the level of a nigger." "Nigger" took on

social, economic and moral connotations which operate in areas far
beyond that of race. It became a powerful principle of American
social order. The quality of justice and equality in this country is
still gauged by our condition.

IR: That's what women are saying as of now.

RE: And when the student protest was going full blast there was
a widely disseminated essay titled "The Student as Nigger."
Such racially grounded attempts at orientation continue because it
is a basic pattern of American society. Even Afro-Americans
do it.

IR: It was the Irish in the nineteenth century.

RE: Yes, because the Irish were rated close to zero. Want ads
frequently warned that no Irish need apply. But, being white, the Irish
were above the threshold of social hierarchy, therefore they had a
possibility of moving upward and many of them did. But for us it
was otherwise. Even the Emancipation didn't break the pattern,
and race is still a most important principle in the drama of
American social hierarchy. The fact gets lost in discussions of
culture, but it reveals itself when works of art are discussed not
in terms of culture, but in terms of race. Certain white intellectuals
can be terribly oxymoronical when it comes to works or perform-
ances by Afro-American artists. Just as they give us "benign
neglect" and "affirmative discrimination," they give us cultural
criticism in which the assumption of racial superiority takes over
the role of broad knowledge and informed taste.

IR: Let me ask another question related to this article. It seems
to me that some of the immigrants brought along a disdain for
things American. You talk to people in New York, they talk about
America being plastic, homogenized—and these are first- and
second-generation people.

RE: I suppose it's to be expected when you consider that it's
possible for those who choose to do so to get an intensified sense
of self simply by learning the epithet, "nigger." But that's being
unfair—although it's true. Some simply feel nostalgic for the
certainties of the societies they left behind. I don't think that most
of them bring their disdain with them. They develop it after
discovering the difference between the American dream and our

day-to-day American reality; a complex reality which is consistently questioned by our condition and our protests.

On the other hand, that kind of disdain is a put-down which an immigrant might well find irresistible. They didn't create the negative aspect of our society; they weren't here, and most would deny that they even benefited from the injustices we've had to live with—although they damn well have, and do. So, in this instance, they have the easy satisfaction of feeling morally superior. Anyway, it's a tradition for Americans to put down things American; it's part of our idealism and our uncertainty regarding our identity.

IR: But, I mean, it seems to me that the Jews would be the last ones promoting a master-race theory of art.

RE: Well, Ishmael, I don't think that that's what happens. What you're observing, in many instances, is the effort of Jewish intellectuals to deal critically with aspects of American culture that haven't been given adequate study. In doing this, they identify themselves with the values native to older, more stable cultures in which race plays no immediate role (many know more about Europe than they know about the U.S.), and since they're moving upward in social status, many tend to identify with the values of older, more established Americans. In an essay, I've termed this a form of "passing for white." That was naughty of me, but the pervasive operation of the principle of race (or racism) in American society leads many non-Blacks to confuse culture with race and thresholds with steeples, and prevents them from recognizing to what extent the American culture is Afro-American. This can be denied, but it can't be undone because the culture has had our input since before nationhood. It's up to us to contribute to the broader recognition of this pluralistic fact. While others worry about racial superiority, let us be concerned with the quality of culture.

QT: There were a couple of questions that I wanted to tie into that. One concerns an interview with Marlon Brando, the actor, which came out in *Crawdaddy,* a national magazine. Marlon Brando suggested that, indeed, it was a fact, as far as he could see, that in the modern day and age, the Jewish people in the arts, in the movie industry, in television, in publishing, and the record industry had forgotten what had happened to them in Germany. And that, in fact, today Negroes were the people who were being oppressed. Especially Third World people, Native Americans, Black Americans, Puerto Ricans, and some other white Americans. What would you say?

RE: I would say that the statement is too general, much too general. It doesn't allow for the human ambiguity which arises when people try to express themselves across the divisions of race, culture and religion, or the dilemma we're all up against as we try to make it in a world in which every gesture toward the ideal conflicts with the necessity of looking out for Number One. Sure, the statements of certain Jews can be very annoying. They can be critical of works by Blacks in the name of the highest standards, but then they'll promote some of the worst writing by Blacks that was ever published.

IR: Would you give specific instances?

RE: No, I wouldn't.

IR: Don't you think that's rhetoric?

RE: Not rhetoric, truth. And the truth doesn't have to be spelled out. This isn't the place to go after either the authors or the promoters of the bad writing or the terrible movies that I have in mind. Nor is this the place to list those contributions to civil rights and cultural improvement through which Jews play an important and liberating role. So, I'll leave it at that. Besides, the goal of publishing houses is to make money; the quality of his published work should be the concern of the writers.

QT: Later, I want to ask you something about your new novel.

RE: I'm not going to talk about it.

QT: I'll ask you anyway. Aren't you a member of the American Academy of Arts and Letters?

RE: I was recently elected to the Academy.

QT: First of all, I'd like to ask you about the criterion that they've maintained over the years in regard to the selection of artists who are granted their annual awards. Would you talk a little about that criterion?

RE: Well, the criterion is the promise of or the achievement of artistic excellence as judged by a group of artists who are appointed to serve on the several awards committees for a limited period. The standards of the various departments which make up the organization are not imposed abstractly, but reflect the knowledge and taste of those who comprise the membership of the various departments. These are art, literature, and music.

QT: Encompassing the world?

RE: No, nationally. Except for honorary members the Institute-Academy operates within a national American perspective. It tries to fulfill the national goal of maintaining and encouraging artistic quality. Remember, however, that its members are artists who have an investment in certain styles and standards arising within their chosen fields. Such an investment can lead to their being blind to the excellence, say, of new styles or techniques, but, it is human despite the possibility of its being irritating to the exponents of such new styles and techniques. The members of the awards committees are not robots but highly individualistic artists who are unified by a common regard for excellence. And, actually, their concern with excellence goads them to a continual effort in seeing to it that new talent is encouraged and new styles and values are identified and recognized. Reed here wasn't given his recent award as a gesture of tokenism. Indeed, a number of awardees have later been made members of the Institute. In carrying out their obligation, the members consult with one another and keep an eye on developments in their various fields. This is a ceaseless process that's aimed at insuring the continuity of excellence. No candidate is picked uncritically and the admission of new members is determined by the entire body through voting. I've seen well-enough names brought forward and fail to make it (incidentally, members of the Academy proper are elevated from the ranks of the Institute). So, the process is neither abstract nor loaded as complaints from the outside would have it. You might say that it involves a process of elimination through which a few are called and even fewer chosen.

Now I'll speak about my personal experience on award juries, both in the Institute and elsewhere. It is true that sometimes award juries are manipulated by cliques who manage to enforce their will upon the other members. This is a human possibility that must be faced and controlled. Artists are involved, and artists just happen to have a lot of ego—if you don't believe me, take a look at our friend. [*Points to Ishmael Reed, followed by general laughter.*] An awards jury is a collectivity of individuals, each fighting

for a point of view; initially his own, individual point of view and
for his *own* standard of excellence. I've participated in some
knock-down-drag-out fights myself, and there was no money or
prestige involved, only an ideal. You don't get paid for acting on
Institute juries, and being elected to serve implies in itself a certain
prestige. And, if you suspect that race plays a dominant role in
the selection of awardees, I'd call that incorrect. The only person
who's going to get any money or other benefits out of such delibera-
tion is the awardee, and whether he's black or white, he's selected
through a process which involves a thrashing-out of tastes through
the combat between strong-willed artists acting in the interest of
some ideal of art. A jury session is a contest through which
mutually acceptable candidates are arrived at. If a clique takes over,
it is because the jury has been poorly selected, or because the
other members fail to assert their wills and their responsibility.

QT: OK, I'd like to ask you the second part to this. I don't know
how many Black writers or painters or musicians and composers
are members. Could you say how many Black American or Native
American, or even some of the popular traditional kinds of
American composers, or popular composers, for example, blues
composers . . .

RE: We have several composers of electronic music, but that is
not a category, per se, and there is no category for blues composers. Just as there's no category for dancers. . . .

SC: It's kind of strange, isn't it?

RE: Well, in the chartering of the organization no such categories
were assigned.

IR: Doesn't that reflect an American puritanical hang-up related
to dancers, a puritanical hang-up on the body?

RE: Oh, no, I don't think so. Let's look at this historically—

IR: What I mean, Mr. Ellison, is that that's not only the case in
the Institute or the Academy, but in schools, universities. You
know, dance departments are discouraged.

QT: Well, how do you account for it?

RE: Well, I would say this: that when the Academy was char-
tered, certain categories of art were selected by using the French
Academy, I suppose, as a model. [Laughter] You want to look for
the historical models for such institutions. Most European na-

tional academies followed the French example, so Americans, who arrived late, were far from having invented the concept. When Americans set up their own institutions they got locked into the frame projected by those institutions which preceded them, and as you know, it takes a lot of time and consciousness to break the historical precedent and democratize it. For how long and in how many Black schools do you find jazz being taught? It wasn't taught at Tuskegee, although we had two to three jazz orchestras and a fine music school; because jazz was not recognized as a legitimate body or style of music. Jazz was ours and a seminal force in the mainstream of American culture, but no one at the top had given it a "Good Housekeeping" seal of cultural approval. So, we're dealing with a kind of cultural lag that I would trace back, not to the manipulation of white folks per se, but to the American's difficulty with cultural self-acceptance; to our inability to deal with the Americanness of American culture.

IR: I think they gave Aaron Copland awards, and Aaron Copland borrows from jazz techniques. And Leonard Bernstein, too.

RE: Perhaps, but neither is a jazz composer. Let's put it this way, they've tried to span the gap between American vernacular styles and European classical styles. For better or worse, Madame Boulanger has had more influence on our symphonic composers than any of our native vernacular styles.

IR: Yeah, see, we'd say vernacular . . .

RE: . . . Vernacular, by the way, is a positive term for me.

IR: Well, I know it is, I used to think vernacular as something that only appeals to a select group . . .

RE: No, that's not what I mean.

IR: What do you mean by that?

RE: By "vernacular," in the context of American culture, I mean that blending of traditional European forms and styles with native folk and popular idioms. I see this as part of a general, eclectic process of culture through which, having started out by imitating British and European models we've improvised our own unique idioms and styles. American vernacular is an amalgamation of prior cultures, including a strong component of the African.

IR: But, European tradition is only one tradition; there are many other traditions.

RE: I agree, but we're still speaking within the frame of history; and, unless you just want to fight about something, I think it's better to understand what's going on. Rather than fighting blindly, we should consider such factors.

IR: Could we just say that . . .

RE: No, no; I'll *tell* you what I'll say. [Laugher]

IR: Yeah, but there are mostly white males sitting on those awards committees.

RE: Not when I'm there. [Laughter] You see, I'm willing to admit both the historical background and the present-day fact that there are only a few Afro-Americans in the Academy-Institute, but I'm unwilling to say that the deliberations which take place there are determined on a racial basis. It just doesn't account for the membership of Du Bois, Langston Hughes, Jake Lawrence, Romare Bearden or Gwendolyn Brooks. I can remember an instance when I was chairman of the literary awards committee, and there were two poets tied for an award. One of the two was Black, and I happened to vote against him, and . . .

IR: Was that John A. Williams?

RE: No, no, no, no! [Laughter] I was not even a member at the time. He believed that I was and held me responsible for years. He was up for the Rome prize, but when his name came up, I wasn't a member of the Institute.

IR: I think he wrote a letter where he said he didn't hold you responsible.

RE: Later he did. We talked about it, and I believe he was convinced; but, for years, people were telling me that he held me responsible.

IR: Do you know what happened there?

RE: No, I don't. I heard some vague rumors but nothing definite. I *do* know that I wasn't in the position to do such a thing—and I wouldn't have; I'm not that kind of guy. Let's put it this way, I've seen writers receive grants who don't write as well as Williams, but that happens. And here's where the factor of chance comes into the picture: Your name comes up, it is proposed and seconded by members who admire your work. But, this only gives you a chance to be considered along with other candidates. There's nothing certain about it because you've actually been placed in competition.

Some candidates make it and some don't, and part of one's luck
depends upon who is sitting on the awards committee and who, all
unknowingly, happens to be competing with you. I've proposed
good people who lost out, so I think that the element of chance
should be kept in mind—even while we put pressure on people to
broaden our institutions and become more conscious of uniquely
American cultural achievements.

QT: Well, do you think that what you're hinting at or suggesting,
that the traditional kinds of rejection of things American by Americans
has been or had led to, perhaps, the exclusion from the Academy of
people like Miles Davis and Count Basie?

RE: Miles Davis! Hell, there's no category for Louis Armstrong,
Duke Ellington, or Benny Goodman—which doesn't mean that
their work isn't appreciated. I say that it's a mistake, all right? But
there are no categories for the performing arts either, and it
wasn't done on the basis of color. It was the result of tradition. The
French set the pattern and we've followed it. This makes for a
certain irony, because it was the French, after all, who first recognized jazz as being a viable art form and worthy of serious
criticism. We still haven't accepted it to that extent.

IR: What about Ortiz Walton, have you read Ortiz Walton?

RE: No, I don't know him.

IR: He was the first Black performer with the Boston Symphony.
He wrote a book titled *Music Black, White and Blue in America*.
He is also a sociologist and has attempted to give categories to
other outlaw music. For example, he refers to jazz as Afro-
American classical music. These terms are winning acceptance
among the intellectual avant-garde of the Afro-Americans.

RE: Well, classical or not, it sounds like an interesting direction.
But, what I'm saying is that so much of native American culture
was not (and is not) recognized or accepted. Even Mark Twain and
Stephen Crane were rejected by people who identified with the genteel
tradition, and, at the time Faulkner was doing some of his best
work, a critic of Lionel Trilling's stature considered him a provincial.

QT: I wasn't sounding any type of racial overtones. I was trying
to get you to direct some answers to the American situation. I
agree with you one hundred percent in regards to the traditional

way of looking down upon native culture, because I feel that jazz
or Black American music, especially jazz, is the American classical
form. You know, I really feel that way. And, I feel that its non-
recognition by such institutions as the National Institute of Arts and
the American Academy is a slap in the face. . . .

RE: I wouldn't call it a slap in the face; rather, it's a matter of
cultural lag. Nevertheless, jazz *has* influenced the music of William
Schuman, Aaron Copland and a number of our other members,
including Bearden and Stuart Davis. That's one of the ways jazz
gets into the sensibility of the larger areas of society. I feel that
Duke Ellington should have been a member of the Academy, but what
you're asking for can only happen in time. After all, who was it who
resuscitated the reputation of Scott Joplin? The Black Aestheticians? No, it was people in conservatories—like Gunther Schuller, a
member of the Institute. Others were involved, but most weren't
Black.

IR: But, there is kind of racism implied. For example, Samuel
Eliot Morrison says, in his three-volume *Oxford History of
America,* that jazz became an art form when Aaron Copland and
Roy Harris—

RE: But, he was speaking for himself, not for the Academy-
Institute—and he revealed his ignorance of jazz.

IR: That was based on the idea of inferiority, in other words. In
plantation days, they used to say that the Blacks were too inferior to
have invented the spirituals, so it must have been the work of their
mistresses. We received the same kind of treatment in the *Saturday
Review* article in which they gave everybody a master, saying that
certain people were influenced by so-and-so. At least, I got a
WASP. You know, everybody's got a slavemaster.

RE: Who did you get?

IR: William Burroughs, he's my "master."

RE: Well, the first time I met you, you and Burroughs were
together. [Laughter]

IR: I guess you call that guilt by association. It's said that you
were influenced by Richard Wright and Chester Himes. Were they
influenced by you?

RE: [Laughter] I tried my damnedest to influence Chester Himes,
but I got nowhere with him. After all, Chester preceded me as a

writer, you know. He goes way back. Chester and I used to argue
over technique and ideas, but I don't know to what extent I
influenced him; but, certainly Wright influenced me, although it was
not in the simplistic way that certain pseudocritics would insist.
I've recorded in writing that I sought out Wright the day after he
arrived in New York. I was still a musician, and it was at his
suggestion that I wrote my first review and attempted my first short
story. Obviously, he influenced me to begin writing. What gets
overlooked is the fact that I was a rather well-read young trumpeter
from Oklahoma who had studied music for most of my life, including
four years of harmony in junior high and high school I had tried
composing marches and popular songs and had arranged spirituals, and I had majored in music theory and trumpet at Tuskegee.
My point is that I had been concerned with art and its creation
long before I met Wright. I was also a bookworm who became
interested in Wright because I had discovered Eliot, Pound and
Edwin Arlington Robinson at Tuskegee. It's interesting that no one
says that I was influenced by Langston Hughes, whose work was
taught in my grade school and whom I knew longer than I did
Wright. I don't think that Wright appreciated the background that I
brought to his discussion of creative writing because frequently he
seemed to assume that I was totally ignorant of the works under
discussion. But, I didn't argue with him. He possessed the certainty
that came from having an organized body of ideas, and he could
write—so having confidence in my own ability to think, I listened
to him and kept my disagreements to myself. . . .

IR: I'm just saying that in essays and interviews you always
mention Hemingway as an influence.

RE: Well, he was.

IR: But, you don't mention Wright. I may be wrong—

RE: You're wrong as hell [Laughter].

IR: All right.

RE: Damn right, you're wrong as hell.

IR: OK.

RE: People are still arguing over what I've said or haven't said
about Wright as though I have no right to disagree with him. But,
they forget that I wrote some of the most appreciative criticism of
him that's ever been published. Wright and I were friends, but I quit

showing him any of my fiction in 1940 after I was unable to get his reaction to a novelette. Finally, I pressed him for an opinion and he became very emotional about it and said, "Well, this is *my* stuff." You might say that with that he influenced me *not* to be influenced by his style of writing.

SC: Was this when he was living over in Brooklyn?

RE: No, he was living on 140th Street, across from City College; I was living on Hamilton Terrace. Chester Himes mentioned the incident during a television interview . . .

SC: With John A. Williams?

RE: No, with Nikki Giovanni . . . I find the assumption that no Negro can do anything unless another *Negro* has done so before him rather simple-minded, and as far as I'm concerned, it's an inverted form of racism. An artist can't do a damn thing about his relatives, but he can sure as hell choose his artistic ancestors. I had read Mark Twain and Hemingway, among others, long before I even heard of Wright.

IR: I wanted to mention that because I read about the incident in a book on the WPA which just came out. There's a new thing going around called "super fiction," which is a term invented by Jerome Klinkowitz and others. They claim that the modern writer is influenced by more than writing. When I read your work and when I read Wright's work, I do see influences of the movies. Would you say there are popular influences in your work and Wright's?

RE: Oh, sure, I use anything from movies to comic strips.

IR: Radio?

RE: Anything; radio, sermons, practical jokes. In fact, anything that suggests ideas for handling narrative; even jazz riffs. I've never been squeamish about using whatever there is to use.

IR: It's not a new thing then, like they're saying?

RE: Far from it. Mark Twain drew on the minstrel show. Fitzgerald and Faulkner did time in Hollywood. Henry James was a fan of P. T. Barnum's museum and Dos Passos adapted devices from the newsreel.

SC: Chester Himes said he saw the first draft of *Invisible Man,* did he?

RE: He might have seen parts of it, but I doubt if I showed him

the whole thing. I rewrote so continuously that one draft blended
into the other. But, Chester and I were freinds. My wife and I knew
him and his first wife, Jean, rather well, but I didn't show my
manuscript around; the 1940 incident with Wright had made me
leery. I was close to Wright, but I quit showing him my fiction
because I had no desire to offend him. I accepted the fact that our
sensibilities were different, as were our feelings for style. But, I
held no antagonism toward him. Questions of style and influence
aside, we still had a broad basis for a relationship. I admired and
respected him, and we remained friendly. During the Fifties whenever I was in Paris, I visited him, and whenever he returned to
New York, he got in touch with me.

IR: I call you a Hoodooist.

RE: Do you know who he is? That's the master. You see, he's
looking at you from both the front and back of his head [points to
a sculpture of Eshu, the trickster god].

IR: No, you said in *The Invisible Man* that New Orleans was the
home of mystery, that's the reason I called you a Hoodooist.

SC: You mentioned over the years (you were addressing yourself
to the National Academy), do you find that Kenneth Burke was
only one of the few critics that you could learn anything from who
was around at the time? Or were there other people? The second
part of the question is who do you see, as far as criticism is
concerned, who's qualified on the scene right now, for the type
of stuff that you're doing?

RE: Critics?

SC: Yeah. The first part of the question was—do you feel you
learned a lot from Kenneth Burke in terms of dealing with the
type of writing that you were doing at that time? In other words,
going back to *Invisible Man,* in terms of vocabulary, in terms of
speaking—of kinds of things that were going on in the novel. Second
part of question: Who do you see as good interpretive critics who're
around nowadays?

RE: What I learned from Burke was not so much the technique
of fiction but the nature of literature and the way ideas and
language operate in literary form. I first became interested in Burke
after hearing him read his essay, "The Rhetoric of Hitler's
Battle." It was a critique of *Mein Kampf,* and the time was 1937. I

was absolutely delighted because in the essay, he made a meaningful fusion of Marx and Freud, and I had been asking myself how
the insights of the two could be put together. On that occasion,
Burke was hooted at by some of the left-wing intellectuals, but not
too many years later, the discovery of the gas ovens revealed that
Burke knew what he was doing. I was just starting out as a writer,
and as I went on struggling to understand his criticism, I began to
learn something of the nature of literature, society, social class, and
psychology as they related to literary form. I began to grasp how
language operates, both in literature and as an agency of oral
communication. In college and on my own, I had studied a little
psychology, a little sociology, you know, dribs and drabs, but
Burke provided a *Gestalt* through which I could apply intellectual
insights back into my own materials and into my own life.

Critics are all over the place, and there's always been something
that I could learn from a few of them. Sometimes, you get a man
who is very good with comparative literature, so you go to him. Joe
Frank, for instance, who's over at Princeton, is a very good
Dostoyevsky man, but, in order to be a good Dostoyevsky man, he
has to know a hell of a lot about literature generally. John McCormick,
who teaches at Rutgers, is very good on American literature, in the
comparative context. And R. W. B. Lewis, the expert on Edith
Wharton, is very good on American literature generally. But, I
don't go to any of these people expecting the whole thing. I learn
what I can and use what I'm prepared to use. During the late 1940s
when I was walking around with holes in my shoes, I was
spending twenty-five dollars a volume for Malraux's *The Psychology
of Art*. Why? Because trying to grasp his blending of art history,
philosophy, and politics was more important than having dry feet.
So that's the way it continues to go: anywhere I find a critic who
has an idea or concept that seems useful, I grab it. Eclecticism is
the word. Like a jazz musician who creates his own style out of
the styles around him, I play it by ear.

QT: I want to ask you another question. You said here in this
interview with Steve, quote:

> What is missing today is a corps of artists and intellectuals who evaluate
> Negro American experience from the inside, and out of a broad
> knowledge of how people of other cultures live, deal with experience and

> give significance to that experience. We do too little of this. Rather,
> we depend on outsiders, mainly sociologists, to interpret our lives for us.

I'd like to ask if you still think that is true?

RE: No—or at least it isn't as true as it once was. Perhaps I
shouldn't have made the statement at that time since Steve and
the others were making such an attempt. Still, such groups are still
quite small while the sociologists with their "benign neglect" and
"affirmative discrimination," their "pathology of the Black family"
and their "psychological castration of the Black male," so forth
and so on, are legion.

SC: We want to get out of that world anyway.

RE: Well, you're still badly needed. Returning to your question,
I'll say something which is apt to outrage certain people—present
company not included. During the Sixties, I observed the attention
paid to the intellectual pronouncement of an intellectually, not
too sophisticated ex-pimp who had sprung to prominence. Now I
don't mean to imply that pimps can't be intellectuals or intellectuals
pimps, or that they can't become politically responsible and even
become capable of heroic action. Obviously, this man had undergone
a profound transformation and had learned how to exploit the media
for his own purposes. I myself took him seriously as a political
activist, or at least as a political force, but not as an intellectual. As
an exhorter, yes. As a rabble rouser who had transformed Afro-
American barbershop and poolhall rhetoric into a force for scaring
the hell out of white folks over television, yes. But, as an
intellectual leader capable of making insightful analyses of American culture and politics, no! So, given his effectiveness among so
many of us, I concluded that many of us hadn't overcome our Afro-
American vulnerability to easy formulations and slick slogans.
Just give the most banal statement a rhyme and a rhythm, put a
little strut into it, and we'll grab it like a catfish gulping down a
piece of dough-bait. Toss us a slick, emotional phrase and we
victimize ourselves, even go up against Sherman tanks with shotguns.

QT: I think that's very good, because I had a question to ask you
along that line. It's about the glorification of people who have been in
prison. They come out, and all of a sudden, you know . . .

RE: Sure, they're treated as though serving time has endowed
them with a mysterious, god-granted knowledge. And, especially

if they say that they've been to the depths of hell and have been reborn into a new vision. Well, I've known a few guys who spent time in prison and none of them underwent any such mystical transformation. Nevertheless, for Americans—and especially Christians—the confession of sin and the assertion of rebirth and redemption has tremendous appeal. This is especially true of our own people, who understandably are hungry for heroes and redeemers. I used to collect the handbills distributed by fly-by-night faith-healers in Harlem, and most of them stated that after being up to their eyeballs in crime, they'd had the scales struck from their eyes while in prison, and this had prepared them to lead their people. During the Sixties, this myth of the redeemed criminal had a tremendous influence on our young people, when criminals guilty of every crime from con games, to rape, to murder exploited it by declaring themselves political activists and Black leaders. As a result, many sincere, dedicated leaders of an older generation were swept aside. I'm speaking now of courageous individuals who made sacrifices in order to master the disciplines of leadership and who created a continuity between themselves and earlier leaders of our struggle. The kids treated such people as if they were Uncle Toms, and I found it outrageous. Because not only did it distort the concrete historical differences between one period of struggle and another, it made heroes out of thugs and self-servers out of dedicated leaders. Worse, it gave many kids the notion that there was no point in developing their minds; that all they had to do was to strike a militant stance, assert their unity with the group and stress their "Blackness." If you didn't accept their slogans, you were dismissed as a "Neegro" Uncle Tom. Years ago, Du Bois stressed a leadership based upon an elite of the intellect. During the Sixties, it appeared that for many Afro-Americans all that was required for such a role was a history of criminality (the sleazier the better), a capacity for irresponsible rhetoric, and the passionate assertion of the mystique of "Blackness." At least, that's how it appeared to me.

QT: There are some great writers who suffered tremendously at the hands of a certain clique of people out in Chicago. For example, my favorite poet, Robert Hayden.

IR: He is a bit high-strung, though; I like his work very much, and I like him as a person.

QT: But, I think that he suffered . . .

IR: Well, everybody suffered . . .

QT: But, they stomped on him, I thought, because of the fact that he is a great poet.

RE: He's a fine poet.

QT: And he did his homework.

IR: I was thinking of *Kaleidoscope,* in which Hayden seemed to make condescending remarks about other Afro-American poets.

QT: I thought that too, and I told him to his face that it wasn't the job of an editor to make those kinds of remarks in terms of biography. I think he should have said this man is from so-and-so, and this man has been published and so forth. He didn't have to say that this man didn't rewrite and things like that. That was ridiculous. Why should he say something like that? Why even include it?

IR: . . . Around the country we have this feminist movement, which always reminds me that the Amazons came out of Dahomey, and we have a situation which people murmur about but don't bring out in the open. And, I think, I'm all for the oppressed getting their share of everything—whatever they want—but when today's oppressed become tomorrow's jailers and start picking up habits of people they're trying to get rid of—which always happens, we have a situation where homo-erotics, both in the closet and out of the closet, are commenting on the behavior of hetero-erotics. [Laughter] We have people going around talking about conflict between Third World men and Third World women when the birth rate is soaring, so somebody must be getting along, you know. And I'm saying it's possible that some of these homo-erotics are using their literary power to create some kind of conflict between hetero-erotics to get defections. [Laughter] I know it's a pretty delicate question, but the people have a lot of influence. They're writing novels that have overtones of lesbianism, which is okay and all that. I could name you some novels and poetry in which you don't know the gender of the person who's getting laid. And these people get currency, they get into newspapers, they have influence—what do you think about that?

RE: I would answer that by saying that when old Black Moses starts blowing *his* top the whole country goes nuts [Laugher]. Seriously, though, I'd add that the abstract Black Man is so deeply associated in the American mind with the concept of freedom and the denial of freedom that when we roil up the American conscience and consciousness, all other repressed groups get out and start doing their thing—and in public. And just as some of the Blacks are using the opportunity of freely expressing themselves to put the damper on other Afro-Americans, other hitherto quiescent, repressed groups are attempting to repress people *they* don't like.

IR: Yes, and some of these people are high yellows.

RE: With black declared beautiful the lighter the skin the blacker the rhetoric.

IR: At least it looks that way.

SC: They talk the loudest.

RE: They give me more hell than the whites did down in Alabama.

QT: I want to ask a couple of different questions. I see that you have a wonderful art collection. Wonderful . . .

RE: Thank you.

QT: I love African art, and as many times as I've been over there, I still find it beautiful. But, in this regard, I want to get back to the question of influences. I know there's obviously the influence of music on your work, but what about the influence of certain artists like Romare Bearden? What about the technique of collage and such? And beyond that, what other American artists, painters, and sculptors are you interested in today?

RE: First, I should tell you that although I've been collecting African art for a long time, I am not a Pan-Africanist. I love the art itself. Nor am I anti-Africa. [Laughter] No, as far as writing goes, I've not been influenced by Bearden, although I met him during what I believe was his first period. He was doing the heroic, mural type of painting which was developed by such artists as Diego Rivera. Later, I was to have many talks with him, and over the years, I always found him stimulating and conscious of where he was going. As a serious artist in his own field, Bearden still affirms and strengthens me in my own work.

SC: You've written a piece on him, too.

RE: Yes, it was the catalogue copy for one of his shows.

QT: Yes, I've got the catalogue.

RE: Getting back to your question concerning the influence of one artist upon another, I'd say that it frequently takes other forms than that of copying or trying to do what another artist or writer does in his precise manner. That is mere imitation. But, sometimes, by working in his chosen form, a fellow artist can affirm one's own efforts and give you the courage to struggle with the problems of your medium. So, in that light, you might say that Bearden influenced me. Just by knowing him at a time when we were both working hard and without much recognition, I found strength for my own efforts. He had faith in the importance of artistic creation, and I learned something about the nature of painting from listening to his discussions of his craft. Look around, and you'll see that I own a number of his works. So, as I see it, it's not the imitation of an artist's work, or even his endorsement of your talent, that's of basic importance, but his assertion of artistic ideals and the example of his drive to achieve excellence. But, then I've found a similar affirmation in the examples of football players, jazz musicians—who for me are the most important—tap dancers, and even a few bootleggers [Laughter]. Such people attract me with a certain elegance and flair for style, as have certain preachers and teachers. I never attended anything but segregated schools, from first grade through graduation, and yet certain fine teachers inspired me to do the best I had in me. Being angry over segregation, it took me a while to realize that despite a handful of indifferent teachers, I also had a few that were excellent, people who still inspire me.

QT: Did you know Melvin Tolson?

RE: Yes, I knew Tolson.

QT: Could you give us something about him?

RE: I knew Tolson first when I was in high school and he was teaching in Texas at Wiley College. He was the coach of the Wiley debating team, and I became aware of him when they came to Oklahoma City to debate the team from Langston University. This serves to highlight one of the crazy aspects of segregation in the United States: Tolson's team wasn't allowed to debate the teams of white colleges in Oklahoma, but the English team from Oxford

University used to come out to Oklahoma on tour and were known to
be defeated by the debaters of Tolson's segregated college. This
gave us a tremendous sense of affirmation. Ishmael Reed here has
taken a few potshots at the art of rhetoric, but, man, rhetorical skill
is a vital part of Afro-American cultural heritage. Tolson was a
skilled rhetorician, as was true of Frederick Douglass and many
other 19th century leaders.

I got to know Tolson personally during the Forties, when he was
in New York for an extended period. We had many long discussions and one of the subjects we fought over was my admiration for
the work of Pound and Eliot. At the time, being dedicated to earlier
poetic styles, Tolson saw nothing in Eliot, who had inspired my
half-conscious attempts to write poetry at Tuskegee. But, later,
in '53, when I was given a reception at the old Paul Laurence
Dunbar Library in Oklahoma City, Tolson gave a talk in which he
castigated the teachers for not encouraging our kids to go into
creative writing. After pointing to me as an example of what could
happen, he shocked the hell out of me by complaining that segregation was preventing [mimicking Tolson's voice] "our young Black
boys and girls from becoming acquainted with the works of Teee
Ssssssss Ellllliot and Ezzzzzzra Pound!" (He was very precise in
his diction.) This was so different from his position back in New
York that it both shocked and pleased me. But then, Tolson was
a very complex man. I don't quite understand the combination of
forces that led to his later poetry, but, perhaps our arguments had
something to do with it—but for god's sake don't interpret this as
meaning that I "influenced" him! He was very knowledgeable,
and I know that he was shaped in his earlier life by those eddying
currents of New England education which were brought into
Negro schools with Emancipation—

SC: Oh, you're talking about the "Mississippi school marm";
they came down when the abolitionists came down.

RE: Right! They introduced the Freedmen to the New England
educational tradition. I myself had a few teachers who were just
old enough to have been taught in such schools; people who knew
Greek, Hebrew and Latin. There weren't a lot of them, but they were
dedicated products of New England classical education.

SC: That was almost a black-face minstrel show in reverse, huh?

RE: Perhaps. It appeared impractical, but knowledge is colorless, and I wish that *I* knew those languages.

IR: Trollope's mother set up schools for Blacks around Nashville and wanted to make it the Athens of the South. [Laughter]

SC: That's what I mean.

IR: They all ran away. [Laughter]

QT: I'd like to ask you who, if any, of the younger poets do you know?

IR: Did you mention names?

QT: Yes, I've got some names . . .

IR: Good, I've got some names too.

QT: OK. But, I mean poets that you might admire, or if you know anything about their work. I've got some names.

RE: You'd better give them to me because I don't know many of them.

SC: I've got some novelists, but you know them.

QT: OK, here are the poets: Jayne Cortez, Calvin Hernton, Al Young, Kay Curtis Lyle, Elois Lofton, Stanley Crouch, Lorenzo Thomas, Sonya Sanchez, Don L. Lee, Baraka, Nikki Giovanni—

RE: When did Baraka become *young?* I know Stanley Crouch as a correspondent; he's a very intelligent guy, but I don't know him as a poet.

QT: We went to school together, he and I.

RE: Is that right?

QT: Jayne Cortez and myself.

SC: He's writing jazz criticism for the *Village Voice* now.

RE: I know that he can write prose, but I don't know his poetry. As with Hernton, I've only read a few of the poems by people you've mentioned, so I wouldn't be able to judge their work. I don't think very much of what Miss Giovanni does, but that doesn't mean anything; it's a matter of taste.

IR: And Don L. Lee?

RE: Once, I met Lee on a plane, leaving Buffalo, I think, and flew beside him to Chicago. He sent me some of his work. He was very amiable, but his ideological emphasis got in the way of my really getting to his poetry. Maybe it's a case of generation gap.

QT: My last question: Can you tell us the difference in terms of

form and structure and language and character between your
works in progress and *Invisible Man?*

SC: Quincy, I had a question in mind before you get to that. I
was looking at *Invisible Man* while thinking about a few things
that happened in 19th Century American literature, and the whole
narrative sequence of events updated to the turn of the century.
It reads very much like a slave narrative, doesn't it? Would you say
you've borrowed the techniques?

RE: No, that's coincidental. And frankly, I think too much has
been made of the slave narrative as an influence on contemporary
writing. Experience tends to mold itself into certain repetitive
patterns, and one of the reasons we exchange experiences is in
order to discover the repetitions and coincidences which amount to
a common group experience. We tell ourselves our individual
stories so as to become aware of our *general* story. I wouldn't have
had to read a single slave narrative in order to create the narrative
pattern of *Invisible Man*. It emerges from experience and from my
own sense of literary form, out of my sense of experience as
shaped by history and my familiarity with literature. However,
one's sense of group experience comes first because one communicates with the reader in terms of what he identifies as a viable
description of experience. You project your vision of what *can*
happen in terms of what he accepts as the way things *have happened*
in the past, his sense of "the way things are." Historically, we
were trying to escape from slavery in a scene consisting of geographical space. First, to the North and then to the West, going
to the Nation (meaning the Indian Nation and later the Oklahoma
Territory), just as Huckleberry Finn decided to do, and as Bessie
Smith states in one of her blues. Of course, some of us escaped
south and joined the Seminoles and fought with them against the
U.S. Geography forms the scene in which we and our forefathers
acted and continue to act out the drama of Afro-American freedom.
This movement from region to region involved all of the motives,
political, sociological, and personal, that come to focus in the
struggle. So, the movement from the South to the North became a
basic pattern for my novel. The pattern of movement and the
obstacles encountered are so basic to Afro-American experience
(and to my own, since my mother took me North briefly during

the Twenties, and I came North again in '36), that I had no need of slave narratives to grasp either its significance or its potential for organizing a fictional narrative. I would have used the same device if I had been writing an autobiography.

Then, there is the imagery and the incidents of conflict. These come from all kinds of sources. From literature, from the spirituals and the blues, from other novels and from poetry, as well as from my observations of socio-psychological conflicts and processes. It comes from mythology, fool's errands, children's games, sermons, the dozens, and the Bible. All this is not to put down the slave narrative, but, to say that it did not influence my novel as a conscious functional form. And, don't forget, the main source of any novel is other *novels;* these constitute the culture of the form, and my loyalty to our group does nothing to change that; it's a cultural, literary reality.

SC: Well, I happened to notice a parallel, that's all, such as your putting Douglass's picture on the wall and the whole bit.

RE: Oh!—But, that's *allusion,* that's riffing. When you put a detail in its proper place in an action, it gathers up associations and meanings and starts speaking to the reader's sense of significance. Just as it spoke to *you* as you struggled to give order to your material. Placed in the right context, and at the optimum stage of an action, it vibrates and becomes symbolically eloquent. That's poetry, I mean, in the larger sense of the term. That's how we use the little marks on the page to communicate and evoke a symbolic reality. It's symbolic action. In *Mr. Sammler's Planet,* Saul Bellow has a Black pickpocket make the symbolic gesture of drawing his pecker out on the main character. The thing sets up all kinds of reverberation in the narrative. It becomes damn nigh metaphysical. It certainly caused a lot of comment, but if I had written the scene, I would have tried to make it even more eloquent by having the pickpocket snatch it out and hit the hero over the head with it. I would have further physicalized the metaphysic—soma to psyche! [Laughter] It reminds me of the story of the proud Negro who goes to the doctor to be examined for the clap—which he doesn't have, and knows it—simply because he wants an "expert" to admire what he believes to be an unusually fine member. "Hell, doc," he says, "I knew wasn't nothing *wrong* with it. I just wanted you to see what a fine one I have." Forgive me, Steve, for getting away from your question.

SC: Well, maybe what I meant by it was simply that the movement, the whole sweep through Georgia on the Greyhound bus suggested the slave narratives. The other question is, why since you hear the sounds we do, the sounds of technology, particularly the sounds of trains, why do you think they're absent from novels nowadays?

RE: Because the trains no longer have those whistles on them. [Laughter]

IR: What about Baldwin's *Tell Me How Long the Train's Been Gone?* That could be like a mournful train wail.

SC: OK. I remember what's his name—you knew a guy by the name of Bledsoe, didn't you? I was told last night that you did.

QT: Jules Bledsoe. He was an opera singer.

RE: I knew about him, but I never met him. My character is imaginary.

SC: I meant functionally . . .

IR: There was also a guy in the Civil War named Bledsoe . . .

RE: There are a number of Bledsoes, but I used the name for its sound and the associations it evoked. I did the same with Trueblood. I associate the names with the characters and their actions. I was trying to pun with them. Bledsoe "bled" his people.

SC: We were going to bring up a question about Rinehart . . .

IR: I want to ask you about novelists—Toni Morrison, Gayl Jones, John McClusky, Charles Johnson . . .

RE: Toni Morrison's work I know.

IR: You know her work?

RE: Yes, she's a good novelist.

IR: And Gayl Jones, you know her work?

RE: No. I have a book of hers that came during the summer, but I haven't read it.

IR: It's an excellent book, not like a lot of the feminist tracts and that sort of thing. Ah, (William Gardner Smith)?

RE: Smith's first book, *The Last of the Conquerors,* I liked; I didn't like the next one, I forget the title. He's dead, isn't he?

IR: Yeah, he died last year. And, Charles Johnson?

RE: I've never read him. I know the work of a writer named Boles, he has a certain skill.

SC: Robert Boles, an excellent novelist.

QT: Would you like to comment on Bill Demby and Al Murray? Did you look at Murray's first novel, the one he published, I mean. I don't know how many he's got at the house.

QT: *Train Whistle Guitar?*

RE: Sure, I think it's a fine book. The, ah, Demby, which title?

QT: *Beetle Creek.*

RE: It's a good book.

IR: What do you think of Joseph Okpaku, a Nigerian, representing Afro-American writers—

RE: What's his name?

IR: Joseph Okpaku, Third World Press. He received $250,000 from the Ford Foundation to begin a publishing company here. What do you think of the propriety of a Nigerian testifying before an American Senate committee concerning the plight of Afro-American writers? [Laughter]

RE: [Laughs] Well, ah, very seriously, I would ask how much does he know about it? If he knows about it—

QT: He's trained as an engineer. [Laughter]

RE: Come on now, there are writers who were trained in other disciplines. MacLeish was a lawyer and my discipline was music.

QT: No, I was just saying that in jest, but I don't think he knows that much about it after talking with him. . . .

RE: Well, strange things happen. I don't know how this could have come about. I just hope that he does well with it. Have you any idea why he was appointed, how he succeeded in . . .

IR: It just seems to be a general trend. Many timid Afro-American intellectuals, really, murmur about it. It seems to be something that the liberal establishment began when Afro-Americans stopped talking to them for a while. They brought over Africans to teach Afro-American literature.

RE: Now I see what you mean. Well, haven't the Blacks been telling the white liberals that we are all Africans? So, after taking a lot of criticisms from angry people with their hands out the whites say, "Hell, so we'll go and get us some *real* Africans." It's an ironic development. I've had nasty things said about me because I say

that I'm not an "African"—which is a geographical abstraction
anyway. I don't even know what tribes my great great great great
great grandaddies came from, so I'm certainly in no position to
identify myself as an African. Q.T.'s been to Africa, I haven't. I
wouldn't be able to tell you anything about it except what I've
read in books. And I certainly wouldn't be able to set up a press for
Africans except as a technician—if I *knew* the techniques of
running a publishing house. But often we help to confuse white
people, and sometimes this can be used to our disadvantage.

QT: Let me ask you, what do you think about the writing of
Garcia Marquez, Pynchon, and, say, Chinua Achebe?

RE: Well, I don't know Achebe's work too well. I've read a
couple of his books which I liked. However, Achebe raised the
question of what, precisely, is an "African" writer? He strikes me
as a Western writer—just as certain writers from former French
colonies, such as Cesaire, Senghor, and Ouologuem who are French
writer-intellectuals, no matter what they tell you about negritude.
I think that Amos Tutuola, who wrote *The Palm-wine Drunkard*, is
far more "African" than any of the others. Marquez? As far as
I'm concerned, his *One Hundred Years of Solitude* is the work of a
great novelist.

SC: Pynchon?

RE: Pynchon gets away from me. I find his work too diffused for
my own sense of things, which doesn't mean that I'm right about
him. Anyway, he doesn't need my OK. He's doing all right, despite
my lack of interest in his work.

SC: Would you like to comment on what Quincy was asking
before, as to why you got away from the "I" form, the first person
narrative, why you changed technique for your new book?

RE: There's no mystery about it, you change technique according to the demands of your material. In *Invisible Man,* I used the
first person just to see what I could do with it, and by way of arguing
across the centuries with Henry James, who considered the first
person as contributing to formal looseness. I'm not struggling to
wind up my current novel by using various points-of-view because the
material seems to call for it.

SC: Is it a big book?

RE: Well, it has a lot of pages, but whether it's going to be a big book in impact is something else. It's a crazy book, and I won't pretend to understand what it's about. I do think there are some funny passages in it.

QT: Could you say when you think you might finish it?

RE: No, I've done that too many times and been wrong.

Invisible Man, As Vivid Today as in 1952

Herbert Mitgang / 1982

From the *New York Times,* 1 March 1982, G1. Copyright © 1982 by The New York Times Company. Reprinted by permission.

Ralph Ellison is 68 years old today. Relaxing in his art-and-book lined apartment on Riverside Drive above the Hudson the other day, he took a little time away from his electric typewriter to talk about his working life.

"My approach is that I'm an American writer," he said. "I write out of the larger literary tradition—which, by the way, is part Negro—from Twain to Melville to Faulkner. Another element I'm aware of is American folklore. And then all of this is part of the great stream of literature.

"Americans didn't invent the novel. Negroes didn't invent poetry. Too much has been written about racial identity instead of what kind of literature is produced. Literature is color-blind, and it should be read and judged in a larger framework."

In March 1952, Mr. Ellison's first novel, *Invisible Man,* was published, and Random House is marking the occasion this month by bringing out a 30th-anniversary edition, which is also being distributed by the Book-of-the-Month Club. Since 1952, *Invisible Man* has gone through 20 hardcover and 17 Vintage Books paperback printings, and there has been a Modern Library edition.

The novel can also be read in Czech, Danish, Dutch, Finnish, French, German, Hebrew, Hungarian, Italian, Japanese, Norwegian, Portuguese, Slovak, Spanish and Swedish. The author's wife, Fanny, who magically finds just about everything he has written in their home files, says that a request came in for a Polish edition just before martial law was declared in Poland. He says that the Russians are aware of his writings, but that if a translation exists in Russian, he hasn't seen any edition.

What provides the greatest continuity for *Invisible Man* is that it

is recognized as an essential 20th-century American literary work
in just about every high school and college in the country. Anne
Freedgood, a Random House editor, enjoys telling the story of
the 17-year-old student she knows who recently learned that Mr.
Ellison had not written a second novel. "How could he?" the
young woman said. "This novel has *everything* in it."

It won the National Book Award in 1953 and, in 1965, some 200
authors, editors and critics, polled by *The New York Herald
Tribune,* picked *Invisible Man* as the most distinguished novel
written by an American during the previous 20 years.

The novel, which defies easy summary because of its subtleties
(a thumbnail description: It is about one nameless black man's
dilemma about his position in the white world), builds from one of
the most memorable opening paragraphs in modern American
fiction:

> I am an invisible man. No, I am not a spook like those who haunted
> Edgar Allan Poe; nor am I one of your Hollywood-movie ectoplasms.
> I am a man of substance, of flesh and bone, fiber and liquids—and I
> might even be said to possess a mind. I am invisible, understand, simply
> because people refuse to see me.

Mr. Ellison revealed that he had meant to write a different
novel—a war story rooted in some of his own experiences at sea
and observations ashore as a merchant seaman in Europe in the
1940's—when he was seized by the notion of invisibility.

"I had come back on sick leave from my service in the Merchant
Marine and, after a hospital stay, in the summer of 1945, my wife and
I went to a friend's farm in Waltsfield, Vt. Sitting in a lumberman's
cabin, looking at the hills, I wrote the first line of the book: 'I am
an invisible man.' "

The original interest in his book came from Frank Taylor, who
had read his short stories, and Albert Erskine, who were with the
publishing house of Reynal & Hitchcock after the war. When those
respected editors moved to Random House in 1947, the contract
for Mr. Ellison's book went with them. Mr. Taylor went to Hollywood, and Mr. Erskine remained as his editor.

Mr. Ellison said, "Once the book was gone, it was suggested that
the title would be confused with H. G. Wells's old novel, *The*

Invisible Man, but I fought to keep my title because that's what the book was about.'' Mr. Erskine recalled. ''His novel doesn't have the article in its title, although the mistake keeps cropping up, and I've been telling people to drop the word 'the' ever since the book came out.''

The author was born in Oklahoma City, educated at Tuskegee Institute, worked as a researcher on the New York Federal Writers' Project before World War II and hoped to enlist as a trumpeter (he still has a trumpet, but he says, no lip anymore) in the Navy—''but they were not taking any more musicians. So, instead, I became a second cook on a Liberty ship. I was in charge of making breakfast, and I also turned out cornbread, biscuits and fried pies.''

The war background—his own experiences in Europe and his father's as a soldier during the Spanish-American War—led to planning a novel that would show how Negroes (the word be usually uses rather than ''blacks'' in conversation, explaining that it has historical roots) fought not only for their country but for their own recognition and rights.

He had the unwritten novel's theme worked out. It was focused on the experience of a captured black American pilot who found himself in a Nazi prisoner-of-war camp. As the officer of highest rank, the pilot became the spokesman for his white fellow prisoners. The resulting racial tension was exploited by the German camp commander for his own amusement. ''My pilot was forced to find support for his morale in his sense of individual dignity and in his newly awakened awareness of human loneliness,'' Mr. Ellison notes in an introduction to the 30th anniversary edition of *Invisible Man.*

But then, creatively, ''the spokesman for invisibility intruded,'' and he was captured by a richer theme that grew more out of himself—''the voice of invisibility issued from deep within our complex American underground.'' Today, he says, he doesn't know where the manuscript about the captured black pilot is—''I probably tore it up.''

Inevitably, a talk with Mr. Ellison turns to his long-awaited work-in-progress. It will be his third book. *Shadow and Act,* a book of essays, came out in 1964. It can be reported that his second novel

is progressing, and apparently it is working—certainly, the author
is, steadily, every day. He has given the novel his full attention
since he retired in 1980 from his teaching duties as a Schweitzer
Professor of Humanities at New York University.

Author and novel suffered a setback in the summer of 1967, when
300 pages of manuscript were lost in a fire in Mr. Ellison's home
in the Berkshires. "It was quite a traumatic experience watching
the house burn and losing typewriters, cameras and other personal property," he said. "The only thing we saved was our
Labrador retriever. After that, I tried to put together as much as
I could, and I began to reconceive some of the characters; Now, we
have a photocopier at home and I keep at least two copies of what
I write."

Some Ellison fans, waiting so many years for his next novel, have
wondered if he had writer's block.

"If so, it's a strange kind of thing, since I write all the time," Mr.
Ellison replied. "The blockage is that I'm very careful about what
I submit for publication. I learned long ago that it's better not to
have something in print that you feel isn't ready. It's not a difficult
thing to turn out more books. I had a hell of a lot more material that
didn't get into *Invisible Man*. It may be a wasteful way of writing
but I'm careful about what is published. There is a lot of formula
writing today. I can't do certain things as a writer, but I enjoy the
act of writing even if it isn't published immediately."

There is a strong metal file cabinet containing much of the
manuscript of the untitled novel. He unlocked it for a visitor,
pulled out the drawer and measured the sections of manuscript with
a tape measure: it came to 19 inches.

"It looks long enough to be a trilogy," he said, smiling. "It all
takes place in the 20th century. I'm convinced that I'm working
with abiding patterns. The style is somewhat different from *Invisible
Man*. There are different riffs in it. Sections of it are publishable
and some parts have already appeared, in *American Review, Noble
Savage, Partisan Review, Iowa Review,* the *Quarterly Review
of Literature.*

"I'm dealing with a broader range of characters, playing with
various linguistic styles. Quite a bit of the book is comic. The
background is New York, the South, an imaginary Washington—not

quite the world I used to encounter on the board of the Kennedy
Center for the Performing Arts there.''

He has seen Washington from on high, in public service positions,
such as membership on the Carnegie Commission on Educational
Television. He was given the highest civilian honor, the Medal of
Freedom, from President Lyndon B. Johnson, and he is a member
of the American Academy-Institute of Arts and Letters, the ranking
cultural body in the country.

''The novel has to be more than segments, it has to be a whole
before it's ready for publication.'' He didn't say, nor was he
asked, when. ''But if I'm going to be remembered as a novelist, I'd
better produce it soon,'' he said cheerfully.

Book Essay: Invisible Man
Ralph Ellison
Walter Lowe / 1982

From *Playboy,* October 1982, 42. Copyright 1982 by *Playboy.*
Reprinted by special permission of *Playboy* magazine.

It's been 30 years since *Invisible Man,* Ralph Ellison's
National Book Award-winning novel, was published by Random House. To celebrate what was, in retrospect, perhaps
the most brilliant decision by a book publisher in the past 50
years, Random House has issued a special 30th-anniversary
edition of *Invisible Man,* Ellison's first and only (thus far)
novel. We thought a fitting way to mark the occasion would
be to check in with Ellison, so we sent Senior Staff Writer,
Walter Lowe, Jr., to do just that. Says Lowe, "When I
arrived, Ellison was editing his novel in progress with a
video terminal on a cluttered table in his den. Producing this
second novel has taken him the better part of three decades.
I asked him about the changes he's seen in that period.

Playboy: *Invisible Man* is about race relations in America as seen
through the eyes of a disenchanted young black man. Has your vision
of America changed in the past 30 years?
   Ellison: You mean, are black Americans still invisible? No.
There's no way, given the history of the past 30 or 40 years, for it
to be the same as it was then. Americans are much more aware now
that American culture is part African. American styles are heavily
influenced by Afro-American styles. I don't mean Americans think
about this consciously, but the awareness is there. It's an accepted thing. I was listening to Olivia Newton-John on the radio
this morning, and she sounded like a young Diana Ross.
   Playboy: Since you've been working on your second novel, you
must have been listening closely to the tune America is playing
now. What do you hear?
   Ellison: That's a hell of a question. First of all, I think I know
more about our society than I did then. One thing I know firsthand

is that *certain* barriers are down for any person who wants to take the risk of discovering what's out there. I remember some of the black students who went to big Eastern colleges in the Sixties and early Seventies immediately segregated themselves, mainly because the experience was strange to them, overlooking the fact that entering college is strange for *any* damn body, white or black. So they didn't take advantage of the opportunity to learn about the social processes, the inhibitions, the drives and hopes and dreams of their counterparts who had grown up in other areas of society. I remember going to some of those colleges and having black kids try to keep me from speaking to the white kids. I told them, "I didn't come here for that. I came to get my point of view across to as many people as possible. I've been segregated myself. I do not believe in segregation."

Playboy: Since you mentioned the inhibitions and drives of middle America, do you have any observations on where those drives are leading us?

Ellison: I think that one of the causes of the chaos in our society is the philosophy of "let it all hang out" that emerged in the early Seventies.

Playboy: Do you mean in terms of sex?

Ellison: Yes. We treat sex as if it were not one of the most creative and destructive forces in our culture. That attitude is always a sign of certain breakdown in society. That was true in the Twenties. It was, of course, one of the factors that contributed to the rise of Hitler in Germany. A lack of sexual discipline tends to have an effect that shows up in areas we don't link together.

Playboy: Such as?

Ellison: Well, for instance, we can't even discuss having a draft these days. We no longer remind the young that implied in citizenship is the obligation to serve in the Army, that ultimately, the right to vote rests upon one's own life. So we tend to act as if we had no obligations, as if we were totally free. But *there is no goddamned total freedom.* It's always relative. And the freedom of sexual expression rests ultimately upon holding the society in which you exercise that freedom together. This gets sticky, because I may sound like I don't want people to have a good time.

Playboy: What do you envision?

Ellison: It would help if kids today had to do some kind of voluntary service for their country—if not in the military, in some other area. Another corrective force historically, and one that humanity can't afford at this point, is war. If we get into a war, a lot of freedoms are going to be restricted. That is, if we have a conventional war. If it's nuclear, the question of sexual freedom is irrelevant.

Playboy: Are you saying that war is sort of a corrective force?

Ellison: I'm saying that if we had more sexual discipline, we might not need a corrective force. You're too young to remember the Depression, but back then, there was a complete breakdown of society. There was no money, very little housing. I slept in Central Park when I was at City College of New York, as late as 1936. There was no work to be had. Then came the war in Europe, and that gave a big assist to the Roosevelt Administration's efforts to bring us out of the Depression. By 1941, we were geared up as a war-industrialized nation, and that by itself imposed its discipline on people.

Playboy: You spoke of Roosevelt. What do you think of our current President?

Ellison: Reagan is dismantling many of the processes and structures that made it possible for me to go from sleeping on a park bench to becoming a writer. And he is assuring people, in the most cunning way, that this is good for us.

Playboy: So what's a young black man with the aspirations you had 30 years ago to do now that the Government is no longer a reliable source of assistance?

Ellison: One thing we Afro-Americans can do to resolve some of our problems—one of the keys to overcoming the conditions that hold us back—is to read. Use the libraries. We have to move into some of the important areas of today's culture. We need to get to the cutting edge of technology, of business, as we have been on the cutting edge of music.

Playboy: One more question: Why has it taken you so long to finish your second novel?

Ellison: Well, writing is a discipline. It's not important how much you write. Anyway, part of what's taken so long is that so many things have changed so fast in our culture that as soon as I thought

I had a draft that brought all of these things together, there would be another shift and I'd have to go back and revise all over again.

Playboy: And how does it look now?

Ellison: Coming along fine, thank you.

Television Makes Us See One Another

Roderick Townley / 1988

From *TV Guide*, 23 April 1988, 3–4, 6. Copyright 1988 by *TV Guide*. Reprinted by permission.

The cab speeds north through Harlem, past Spanish restaurants, bodegas, video stores, newsstands, the sunny streets crowded with black and Latino faces. Finally, we cut over to Riverside Drive and stop in front of a once-grand apartment building on the corner. It is here that the writer Ralph Ellison has lived for well over 30 years.

Ellison's powerful (and often very funny) 1952 novel, *Invisible Man,* explores the complexities of the black life in America. It won the National Book Award and very quickly was recognized as a classic. Since then, Ellison has taught, published volumes of essays and continued work on his yet-unpublished second novel. Despite his small output, he is among the most respected black writers in America.

Soon I am heading upward in a moaning old elevator. The door swings open. A black man with a gray mustache waves and calls hello from across the hall. It is Ellison, dressed for comfort in brown corduroys and an open-necked blue hunting shirt, looking a decade younger than his 74 years. In his eyes is that same hooded look of undeceivable amusement that had so impressed me many years earlier, when I'd taken a literature course of his at the University of Chicago.

He ushers me into the overfilled one-bedroom apartment that he shares with his wife. There, propped on a stand by his IBM computer, rests part of the manuscript of that long-awaited second novel. Through the study window, the Hudson glitters in the afternoon light.

The Ellison household is filled with paintings, African sculpture, plants and books without end. "The books are chasing us out of the

387

place," he says, laughing and gesturing with an extinct stogie that
he holds in his left hand. Actually it is a fine cigar, a Honduran
"finca," but right now it resembles a large wet, swatted cockroach.

Ellison's wife, Fanny, comes in and says hello but soon excuses
herself. She's been working on their tax returns and has papers
spread over the dining table.

Ellison and I settle into right-angled leather couches to talk about
television and its relation to American culture. He served for
years on the Carnegie Commission on Educational Television,
whose findings led to the formation of the Public Broadcasting Service; he cares passionately about the role of television in the
formation of the American culture. "The whole movement of the
society," he feels, "is toward discovering who we are." Television
is one of the primary forces in that process of discovery. It
mirrors our lives—although not without distortions—beaming back
at us images of our diversity.

That's one reason he found the nine-part PBS series *The Story of
English* so engrossing. It taught him something he already suspected about our language, "the connections between English as
spoken, say, in Wales or Scotland . . . and Afro-American speech."
Ellison remembers growing up across the street from two black kids
from North Carolina. One of them, a roughhouser named Buster,
was a good fighter who would inexplicably break into Scottish
phrases when he got angry. "People paid attention!" exclaims Ellison
with gut-rumbling laughter.

Ellison finds TV's coverage of sports another means by which
America is shown its own diversity and taught a degree of tolerance.
"Twenty years ago," he says, "you didn't see black athletes playing
on Southern teams. Now you see many of them. . . . The fellows
who play together on those teams are going to have different
reactions to the racial question than their parents had." And
television amplifies that lesson. It puts us all on the same team,
black and white.

Ellison also has a healthy and unsnobbish appreciation of television comedy and admits to relishing reruns of *Barney Miller*.
After all, comedy is a major ingredient in his own fiction. And

Barney Miller, he feels, deals in very funny yet realistic ways with "the struggles of social hierarchy within the police station."

The Cosby Show, he feels, "cuts across race and class" in its comic appeal and does the country a favor by showing that blacks can be cultured and well-off. "If you think of all Afro-Americans as being poor, then you have a distorted view of the society." Ellison cites an example of a family he frequently visited while growing up in Oklahoma who listened to classical music and had a set of the Harvard Classics on their bookshelf. He himself as a teenager, aspired to write symphonies. He didn't know that blacks weren't supposed to do that.

A lot of TV sitcoms, however, strike Ellison as foolish and unfunny because the writers don't realize that true comedy springs from painful realities. "If you forget the tragic underlayer of comedy," he says, "then the comedy becomes trivialized."

In fact, that's a danger of television programs generally: "I don't like the idea of censorship, but there should be some conscious concern [about] the ability of the medium to trivialize life, to trivialize the human body, to trivialize the relationships between men and women."

TV ads contribute to this trivialization, he feels, by frequently interrupting dramatic programs and thus destroying narrative tension, lessening the impact.

News programs do it by the repetitiousness of their coverage. The Challenger disaster, for instance, was "such a stunning, jolting thing" that Ellison says he wanted to turn it off the first time he saw it. But it was shown again and again, resulting in "a deadening of sensitivity, out of a need for self-protection." Ultimately, the images no longer seem tragic but trivial.

And of course dramatic series frequently trivialize life by relying on plot clichés, such as the inevitable car chases, explosions and implausible rescues. "But then I remind myself that much of television is now comic strip. How are you going to take a series like *Knight Rider,* about an automobile that can talk, analyze the structure of buildings, short-circuit powerful dynamos at a distance, and then give lectures to young boys on reasons they should

be interested in history?'' Ellison's rich baritone laughter fills the
living room.

The technology of television, he says, is like the Promethean gift
of fire. The challenge is to learn "how to tame it, how to allow its
positive features to operate with a minimum of the negative.''

Ellison examines his dead cigar a moment, then looks out the
window at the Hudson River. The more he thinks about it, the
more it seems that the negative and positive are intertwined. It's
sometimes hard to tell which is which. Ads, for instance, are
"among the best things on television"—ingenious, funny, touching,
often extremely creative. Yet the way they're used, they tend to
short-circuit concentration.

The imagery of TV news also has its positive and negative sides.
During Civil Rights demonstrations in the '50s and '60s, television
jolted awake the social conscience of a nation. "You see the con-
trasts," says Ellison. "If you produce the images, they teach,
very often when you don't say anything about them.''

On the other hand, the daily sleet of news images can blur and
blind us, contributing to what Ellison calls "a tradition of forgetfulness" in this country. "There are a lot of people now, even
blacks, who don't know what it was like during the '60s. And that's
fairly recent.''

Use television, he suggests; don't let television use you. Don't
buy the TV image of the sleek new car or the slick new political
candidate. Test drive everything you see. Television doesn't need
to be a blunt instrument of forgetting; it can be an effective
mechanism of recall, particularly as videotape makes images of the
past available at the push of a button. "Libraries have such tapes
now, I understand. . . . So this medium, which is very fleeting, has
its permanent side, too, which allows you to go back.''

Such a positive, conscious use of television to understand the past
is extremely important, contends Ellison, because America "is
still an undiscovered country," and Americans are still in the
process of defining who they are.

What will be the final definition of *genus americanus?* What sort
of person will the future American be?

Ellison laughs at the question, then takes a shot at answering it.
"He would be ingenious. He would certainly have a strong sense of
the comic. He would be one who hides himself as he [reveals]
himself—a bit of a trickster. He would be aggressive but not necessarily warlike. Aggressive as to ideas. He'd be a person who would
understand the past but who'd be determined not to be hampered
by the past. . . .

"I think," Ellison continues, "that there'll be an American who
will be at peace with the diversity of the country, racial and
otherwise." Television will help bring this about because it makes
us see one another—people we might never meet in person—and
eventually inures us to our differences. Familiarity breeds content.

"The worst scenario would be for television to get in the control
of a group of know-nothings who have fascist tendencies and who
try to make everyone embrace their values."

But there is an effective preventative for that nightmare future,
asserts Ellison, and an antidote for the negative aspects of television today: our own stubborn free will. In other words, if TV is
selling something that you don't want, don't buy it.

"The thing that Americans have to learn over and over again is
that they are *individuals* and they have the responsibility of individual vision."

Visible Man

David Remnick / 1994

From the *New Yorker*, 14 March 1994, 34–38. Copyright © 1994 by David Remnick. Reprinted by permission.

In a modest apartment overlooking the Hudson, at the weld of northern Harlem and southern Washington Heights, Ralph Ellison confronts his "work in progress." He has been at this for nearly forty years, and rare is the day that he does not doubt his progress. He wakes early, goes out to buy a paper on Broadway, returns, and, when he has exhausted the possibilities of the *Times* and the "Today" show, when the coffee and the toast are gone, he flicks on the computer in his study and reads the passage he finished the day before. "The hardest part of the morning is that first hour, just getting the rhythm," Ellison says. "So much depends on continuity. I'll go back to get a sense of its rhythm and see what it will suggest, and go on from there. But very often I'll start in the morning by looking back at the work from the day before and it ain't worth a damn." When that happens, as it does more frequently than he would like, Ellison will turn away and stare out the window, watching the river flow.

Ralph Ellison turned eighty on March 1st, and his peculiarly modern burden, the burden of a second act, grows heavier with age. The man is far too composed, too regal, to betray the weight of it, but the soul must weary of its persistence. So great was the celebration in 1952 for his first (and only) novel, *Invisible Man,* that the sound of critical applause, rattling medals, and whispered expectations took years to fade. Few novels have ever entered the canon so quickly. Ellison won the National Book Award, the Presidential Medal of Freedom, the Chevalier de l'Ordre des Artes et Lettres, a place in the American Academy of Arts and Letters, and a position at New York University as Albert Schweitzer Professor of Humanities. Here and there, critics' and readers' polls would declare *Invisible Man* the greatest American novel of the postwar period or of the century. Ellison's rite-of-passage novel absorbed everything from black folklore to Dostoyevsky's *Notes from the Underground,* creating something entirely new, lasting, and American. It was translated into seventeen languages, and the Modern Library produced an edition. But at the end of all this lingered the nervous, American question: What's next?

Ellison did not intend to distinguish his career with such an austerity of publication. By 1955, he had begun a novel set mainly in the South and in Washington, D.C. At the center of the story—as far as we know it from a few published extracts—are the community and the language of the black church and the relationship between a black preacher and a friend who eventually becomes a senator and a notorious racist. After a few years of writing, Ellison was not shy about showing excerpts to friends like Saul Bellow and the novelist and cultural historian Albert Murray. He was not reluctant to publish a piece here and there in literary quarterlies.

For a while, expectations for the book soared. "I shared a house with Ralph in the late fifties in Tivoli, New York, along the Hudson in Dutchess County," Bellow says. "At that time, he was hard at work on the book, and he let me read a considerable portion of it—a couple of hundred pages, at least, as I remember. We were running a magazine at the time called *The Noble Savage,* and we published an excerpt of Ralph's manuscript called 'Cadillac Flambé.' But all of it was marvellous stuff, easily on a level with *Invisible Man.*"

A couple of weeks before his birthday, I called on Ellison at his home: The apartment is lined and stacked with books. Here and there are African sculptures and piles of papers, mostly correspondence. As he and his wife, Fanny, showed me around, a small cloud of cigar smoke still hovered over his computer in the study. Slender and graceful, with the courtly elegance of his friend Duke Ellington, Ellison looks fifteen years younger than he is; a man of old-fashioned Southern grace, he is polite in the high style, careful in conversation almost to the point of deliberate, if ironic, dullness. I said that his friends have often remarked on the gap in style between the turbulence of *Invisible Man* and the reserve of its author.

"Well, one inherits a style from the people one grows up with," Ellison said, referring to his childhood in Oklahoma, which was segregated at the time but had never been a slave state. He studied

composition at Booker T. Washington's Tuskegee Institute, in
Macon County, Alabama—and was the intellectual star of his
class—before coming to New York, in 1937. "I am rather passionate about some of the inequities that are part of the country," he
went on. "But why should a writer be different? No one asks a
surgeon to be different. He has to be a surgeon first. He has to
know the techniques and traditions of surgery. That's how I
approach writing. I would do the same thing if I were an opera
singer. Black opera singers have to master the tradition. We all
have at least double identities."

For a while, Ellison skated amiably, and elliptically, around
various questions of the day, but when the subject turned to his
work in progress, the book that Bellow had remembered so vividly,
the one that Albert Murray used to hear Ellison read aloud from,
he seemed, at first, a little startled. Then, as he described a fire two
decades ago at his old summer house, in Plainfield, Massachusetts, he slumped back in his chair, resigned, his voice lowering into
a growly whisper. "There was, of course, a traumatic event
involved with the book," he began. "We lost a summer house and,
with it, a good part of the novel. It wasn't the entire manuscript,
but it was over three hundred and sixty pages. There was no copy.
We had stayed up in the country into November, in the Berkshires. We went to do some shopping and came back and the house
was burning. An electrical failure. And, being in the country with
a little volunteer fire department—well, they were off fighting another fire and didn't make it. They never got it put out. It all
burned down. They came and tried, but in the country it's difficult
to get water, especially there."

Ellison's friends say that it was years before he went back to
work on the novel; some say three or four, others five or six.
Albert Murray, who lives across town, off Lenox Avenue, and has
known Ellison since they were students together at Tuskegee,
had told me, "Ralph was just devastated. He just closed in on
himself for a long time. He didn't see anyone or go anywhere. At a
certain point, you knew not to say much about it. A wall, Ralph's
reserve, went up all around him." Ellison was reduced to trying
to summon up his novel from memory or from the memories of
those who had read it or heard him read it.

When I asked Ellison how much time he lost, he was quiet for a while, and then he said, in a tone that suggested we were talking about someone else and the question was merely *interesting,* "You know, I'm not sure. It's kind of blurred for me. But the novel has got my attention now. I work every day, so there will be something very soon. After the fire, I had certain notes here in the city and a pretty good idea of where I wanted to go. Snatches of it had been published. And I did a lot of teaching after that. Let's say I was disoriented, but I worked on it. I don't know how long the interruption was. Maybe four or five years. It wasn't as if I weren't working. I was trying to reimagine the situation. The characters are the same and the mixture of language is the same. But nuances are different. After all, when I write I am discovering things. One development suggests another, a phrase will reveal things. You just try to get through it.

"Letting go of the book is difficult, because I'm so uncertain. I want it to be of quality. With *Invisible Man,* I wasn't all that certain, but I had friends like Stanley Edgar Hyman, who worked on *The New Yorker,* and who was invaluable to me. There's a photograph of Stanley reading *Invisible Man* in Francis Steegmuller's office. I'll always remember: he looked up at me and said, 'Say, this thing is funny!' When you are younger, you are so eager to be published, I am eager to publish this book. That's why I stay here, and not in the country. I'm eager to finish it and see how it turns out."

Ellison's readers can be greedy and hope for more novels and essays—come to think of it, a memoir would be nice, too—but what's done is done and, in a sense, is more than enough. On the occasion of his eightieth birthday, it becomes clearer than ever that *Invisible Man* and his two collections of essays, *Shadow and Act* (1964) and *Going to the Territory* (1986), are the urtexts for a loose coalition of black American intellectuals who represent an integrationist vision of the country's history and culture. Ellison's books are a foundation for talents as various as the novelists Charles Johnson, John Edgar Wideman, Leon Forrest, and James Alan McPherson; the critics Shelby Steele, Henry Louis Gates, Jr., and Stanley Crouch; the poet Michael S. Harper. When Johnson, for

instance, received the National Book Award, in 1990, for his novel
Middle Passage, he devoted his entire acceptance speech to a celebration of Ellison. Johnson said he hoped that the nineteen-nineties
would see the emergence of a "black American fiction" that takes
Ellison as its inspiration, "one that enables us as a people—as a
culture—to move from narrow complaint to broad celebration."

The publication of *Invisible Man* predates the Civil-Rights movement of the nineteen-sixties, the drama of Malcolm X, and the
rise of Afrocentrism, and yet it anticipates, or answers, all of these.
The demagogic figure of Ras the Destroyer in the novel is based,
no doubt, on Marcus Garvey, but it turns out to be a prescient
depiction of the Farrakhans to come. The lancing portrait of the
Brotherhood was modelled on the Communist Party of the nineteen-
thirties, but it stands for all the doctrinaire utopianism and fakery
to come. The metaphor of the paint factory and the mixing of black
paint into white anticipates a sane multiculturalism, a vision of
American culture as an inextricable blend. Unlike so much fiction
labelled somehow as ethnic, *Invisible Man* is a universal novel. From
the first lines to the very last ("Who knows but that, on the lower
frequencies, I speak for you?"), it insists on the widest possible
audience.

In Ellison's view, America is not made up of separate, free-
floating cultures but, rather, of a constant interplay and exchange.
In the essays, he describes slaves on a Southern plantation watching
white people dance and then transforming those European steps
into something that is American; he speaks of what Ella Fitzgerald
has done with the songs of Rogers and Hart, what white rock
bands did with the blues; he watches the black kids in Harlem in
their baggy hig-hop gear walking down Broadway and on the
same day he sees white suburban kids on television affecting the
same style. What Ellison has called the "interchange, appropria-
tion, and integration" of American culture is evident in the music
we hear, the games we play, the books we read, the clothes we wear,
the food we eat. For him, integration is not merely an aspiration but
a given, a fact of cultural and political life. Without pity or
excessive pride, Ellison also sketches the facts of his own life—
especially his self-discovery, first through music, then literature—to describe the American phenomenon. *Invisible Man* itself

looks not only to the experience of Ralph Ellison at Tuskegee
Institute or in Harlem but to Ralph Ellison in the library, the young
reader that Albert Murray remembers as "always looking to the
top shelf." When Ellison finally came to New York, Richard Wright
and Langston Hughes became literary mentors and friends, but
their influence was secondary, following a youthful tear through
Eliot, Pound, Faulkner, Hemingway, Stein, and Dostoyevsky.
Out of many, one.

Ellison's vision of American life and culture has not always sat
well with critics, black or white. For the Black Arts Movement of
the nineteen-sixties and seventies, *Invisible Man* and its author
lacked the necessary rage. Amiri Baraka (LeRoi Jones) and other
nationalists denounced Ellison from platform after platform. And
that had its wounding effect, especially in the academy.

In 1969, Charles Johnson dropped by the library at Southern
Illinois University's new black-studies program. "Where can I
find a copy of *Invisible Man?*" he asked the librarian.

"We don't carry it," came the answer.

"Really? Why not?"

"Because Ralph Ellison is not a black writer," the librarian said.

An extreme example, no doubt, but it suggests the climate of the
time. "When Ellison got an award in 1965 for the best novel since
the Second World War, people were still under the sway of the
vision that came from Martin Luther King," Stanley Crouch, the
author of *Notes of a Hanging Judge,* told me. "Once the black-
power separatist agenda came along, and once white people
showed that they preferred some kind of sadomasochistic rhetorical
ritual to anything serious, Ellison's position began to lose ground.
That's been the central problem in Afro-American affairs since the
black-power-cum-Marxist vision took over the discussion. We
have had to deal with one or another intellectual fast-food version
of that these last twenty-five years or so. What it comes down to
is that Ellison perceives Afro-American history in terms of the
grand sweep of American life, not in terms of sheer victimhood.
And that has been very difficult in wake of the whole Malcolm X,
'You didn't land at Plymouth Rock, Plymouth Rock landed on
you' thing."

"Let's face it," Henry Louis Gates, Jr., the chairman of the

Afro-American studies program at Harvard, said. "Ellison was
shut out, and Richard Wright was elected godfather of the Black
Arts Movement of the nineteen-sixties because Wright's hero in
Native Son, Bigger Thomas, cuts off a white girl's head and stuffs
her in a furnace. For Ellison, the revolutionary political act was not
separation; it was the staking of a claim for the Negro in the
construction of an honestly public American culture. Wright's
real message was not that different, but no one wanted to see that."

The resistance to Ellison's vision was by no means limited to
black critics. In "Black Boys and Native Sons," an essay published in *Dissent,* Irving Howe adopted a strangely patronizing tone
to celebrate Richard Wright's authenticity and to reprimand
James Baldwin and Ellison for failing to possess a similar sense of
rage. Howe declared himself astonished by "the apparent freedom [*Invisible Man*] displays from the ideological and emotional
penalties suffered by Negroes in this country."

Ellison's passionate reply. "The World and the Jug," was published in *The New Leader,* and can be read as a manifesto, a
defense of his vision and art, and of the life that created them:

> Evidently Howe feels that unrelieved suffering is the only "real"
> Negro experience, and that the true Negro writer must be ferocious.
> But there is also an American Negro tradition which teaches one to
> deflect racial provocation and to master and contain pain. It is a
> tradition which abhors as obscene any trading on one's own anguish for
> gain and sympathy; which springs not from a desire to deny the
> harshness of existence but from a will to deal with it as men at their best
> have always done. . . . It would seem to me, therefore, that the question of
> how the "sociology of his existence" presses upon a Negro writer's
> work depends upon how much of his life the individual writer is able
> to transform into art. What moves a writer to eloquence is less meaning-
> ful than what he makes of it. . . . One unfamiliar with what Howe
> stands for would get the impression that when he looks at a Negro he
> sees not a human being but an abstract embodiment of living hell. He
> seems never to have considered that American Negro life (and here he is
> encouraged by certain Negro "spokesmen") is, for the Negro who
> must live it, not only a burden (and not always that) but also a discipline.

Ellison's answer to Howe was, in a sense, an elaboration of the
first paragraph of *Invisible Man,* with the hero's demand to be
seen as himself, as "flesh and bone, fiber and liquids—and I might

even be said to possess a mind." The mind of Ellison has been
deeply influential. Even if Leonard Jeffries and Molefi Kete Asante
have been successful in imposing dubious Afrocentric programs
on the City College of New York and Temple University, even if
such ideas have trickled into school systems as far-flung as
Portland's and Atlanta's, Ellison's godchildren have been at least
as influential in stating their case. His integrationist position has
shaped Black Studies programs at Harvard, Princeton, Yale, Stan-
ford, and many other leading universities.

"Ellison grants blacks their uniqueness without separating us
from the large culture," Shelby Steele, the author of *The Content of
Our Character,* said. "After reading Ellison, you realize that talk of
a 'white culture' or 'black culture' is simplification. In the academy, identity politics is often the thing, and people would prefer to
deal with finite categories: 'black culture,' 'white culture,' 'His-
panic culture,' and so on. Nationalist politics gets more attention,
because it's more flamboyant, more glamorous, more controversial. It's better press. But the vast majority of black people in this
country are not nationalist. My sense of the problem has to do
with the nature of black politics, an oppression-based politics since
the nineteen-sixties. People like me, who believe that there are some
difficulties of black life that are not the result of oppression, are just
branded conservatives, no matter what the range of opinion."

Stanley Crouch sees the ambivalence toward Ellison as a symp-
tom of the separatist drift represented by Ras the Destroyer. "Ellison
knew a long time ago what the dangers were," Crouch said. "All
the dangers are in *Invisible Man.* The dangers of demagoguery.
The dangers of trying to hold up a rational position in a country
that can become hysterical about race, from either side. You see, the
race hysteria that was dominated by white people for the bulk of
time Afro-Americans have been in America was overtaken by the
black-power, Malcolm X-derived, pro-Louis Farrakhan, anti-Amer-
ican, romantic Third World stuff that came up in the sixties. You
had thugs, like Huey Newton, who were celebrated as great revolu-
tionaries. You had West Indians, like Stokely Carmichael, who
were calling for the violent overthrow of the country. You had
LeRoi Jones ranting anti-Semitism from one coast to the other, and
black students on campus cheering and howling. And that's going

on now. If people had paid more attention to what Ellison had to say in 1952, we might have got beyond some of the stuff we're in."

Leon Forrest, a black novelist Ellison took time to praise in our meeting, told me, "Ralph goes back to a fundamental tradition in African-American life. He's what we used to call a race man. Areas that seem conservative, supporting businesses in the community, respecting the workingman, the family—that's part of it. A race man means you're in a barbershop conversation, and there might be a nationalist, an N.A.A.C.P. man, whatever, but they're all concerned with getting African-Americans ahead in the community. I know Ralph had a lot of respect for many of the things Adam Clayton Powell stood for at first, the way Powell broke the back of Tammany Hall, though not the shrill things he said at the end of his life. Ralph is for a robust onslaught against racism but, at the same time, for building within the race. What's happened is that there hasn't been enough building within the race: our families, our businesses, the inner strength of the people.

"What disappoints him today is that not enough black Americans are learning from the possibilities of the book. We don't read enough. His own literature is informed by a vast library, and yet we are cutting ourselves off from that. You've got a problem in Afro-American society these days: if a woman has a niece and a nephew, she'll give the niece a copy of a Toni Morrison book and take the nephew to the Bulls game. We don't do nearly enough to enrich our kids in the middle class in our body of literature—the body that fashioned Ralph Ellison's imagination and scholarship."

Sixteen friends and associates gathered on March 1st at Le Périgord, on the East Side, to celebrate Ralph Waldo Ellison's birth. Once the food and not a little wine had been consumed, Albert Murray, by way of toasting his friend, recalled his youthful admiration for Ellison as the smartest, and smartest-dressed, upper-classman at Tuskegee. It was, of course, impressive to Murray that Ellison always seemed to check out the best books in the library, but it was at least as daunting for him to set eyes on the nascent elegance of Ellison, a slender concertmaster in his two-tone shoes, bow tie, contrasting slacks, and whatever else the best haberdasher in Oklahoma had to offer. "I even remember the poetry Ralph wrote," Murray said. " 'Death is nothing, / Life is nothing, / How beautiful these two nothings!' "

"Thanks for remembering so much," Ellison said, smiling and rising to his feet. All evening long, he had been reminiscing at the table, about his friends in jazz, his ill-advised attempt to play the trumpet not long ago in the presence of Wynton Marsalis, his pleasure in everything from the poems of Robinson Jeffers to the liturgy of the black Episcopal church. And then, turning to Murray, he said, "Isn't it interesting and worth a bit of thought that from Booker T. Washington's school, which was supposed to instruct youngsters in a vocation, two reasonably literate writers emerged? Isn't that just part of the unexpectedness of the American experience? It behooves us to keep a close eye on this process of Americanness. My grandparents were slaves. See how short a time it's been? I grew up reading Twain and then, after all those Aunt Jemima roles, those Stepin Fetchit roles, roles with their own subtleties, here comes this voice from Mississippi, William Faulkner. It just goes to show that you can't be Southern without being black, and you can't be a black Southerner without being white. Think of L.B.J. Think of Hugo Black. There are a lot of subtleties based on race that we *will* ourselves not perceive, but at our peril. The truth is that the quality of Americanness, that thing the kids invariably give voice to, will always come out." And to that everyone raised a glass.

Index